Introduction to Research Methods in Psychology

Third Edition

Introduction to Research Methods in Psychology

Third Edition

Hugh Coolican

Hodder Arnold

A MEMBER OF THE HODDER HEADLINE GROUP

Dedication

With love to Rama, Kiran and Jeevan and with many thanks for your support.

Orders: please contact Bookpoint Ltd, 130 Milton Park, Abingdon, Oxon OX14 4SB. Telephone: +44 (0)1235 827720. Fax: +44 (0)1235 400454. Lines are open from 9.00–6.00, Monday to Saturday, with a 24-hour message answering service. You can also order through our website www.hoddereducation.co.uk

If you have any comments to make about this, or any of our other titles, please send them to educationenquiries@hodder.co.uk

British Library Cataloguing in Publication Data
A catalogue record for this title is available from the British Library

ISBN-10: 0 340 90757 6
ISBN-13: 978 0 340 907 573

First Edition Published 1995
Second Edition Published 1996
This Edition Published 2006
Impression number   10 9 8 7 6 5 4 3 2 1
Year   2009 2008 2007 2006

Hodder Headline's policy is to use papers that are natural, renewable and recyclable products and made from wood grown in sustainable forests. The logging and manufacturing processes are expected to conform to the environmental regulations of the country of origin.

Typeset by Tech-Set Ltd.
Printed in Great Britain for Hodder Arnold, an imprint of Hodder Education, a member of the Hodder Headline Group, 338 Euston Road, London NW1 3BH by **Martins the Printers, Berwick-upon-Tweed.**

Contents

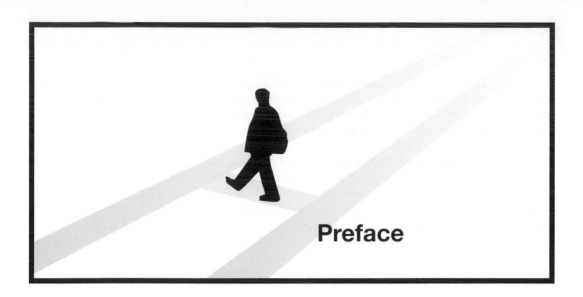

Preface

Hi! Let me make one first guess. You didn't pick this up because you were just looking for a good read, a can't-put-it-down book for the beach or something to keep you occupied on a barge holiday; an exciting, mind expanding… No, I don't suppose so. Students aren't renowned for rushing along to their research methods lectures with great enthusiasm. In fact they tend to view the prospect with about the same fervour as I reserve for custard with skin. Students are usually quite fascinated when they discover what psychologists have found out. However, finding out *how* they found these things out does not seem to pack quite the same punch.

I find this a shame, first because education can only be considered successful when students have learned to ask very confidently 'But how do they know that?', and second, because good research methods courses should deliver not just knowledge but also the *skills* of researching. Just in case you're quite young at the moment, I can assure you that these skills will almost certainly be of some use in later careers and life in general. Many of you will at some point be asked to 'go and find out what people think' and the way you do this will certainly be a psychological research method.

In fact, most of the issues and concepts of research methods, apart from the statistics, are about how people react in research situations: how can we get the best information?, how do people respond to being observed?, do people try to look good when tested? and so on. So, like the other perhaps seemingly more interesting areas of your psychology syllabus, studying methods still engages you in thinking about how people think and behave; you are still doing psychology.

Let's consider why you are looking at this book. I'll assume that most of you have started a course in AS/A Level Psychology, or a degree that includes psychology or perhaps you are on a course that deals with people and expects you to think about how we gather information about people. Your tutors have provided a reading list or you have already done some research and discovered that this is the kind of book you need for your studies. If so, welcome along for the ride! My guided tour through the world of methods and statistics will always attempt to be light hearted but even more so to be clear and to be based in real, concrete examples that you can get involved with yourself. After many years of teaching I still believe fervently that students arrive in psychology classes with many of the concepts they are expected to acquire in methods already in their heads. The concepts are there because students have had experience of life and interacting with people. Many 'scientific' notions are just common sense but applied a bit more strictly and carefully to the investigation of people and behaviour. Hence this book, I hope, helps you to uncover these concepts for yourself and to elaborate them so that you get a much fuller picture of what researching with people is all about.

A further strong assumption of this book is that statistics can be made accessible. Many students still think they are somehow 'non-mathematical' yet are pleasantly surprised when they find that they can follow, carry out and even understand the statistical procedures used in this book which require, for calculation, nothing more than a calculator that adds, subtracts, multiplies and divides – that's really all you need to be able to do!

In this third edition I have broken the chapters up so that you engage in a set of exercises after each bite-size chunk of information. Rather than digesting an entire chapter these *Progress review* boxes occur perhaps three or four times in a chapter and ask you to answer questions and note *Key terms*. The key terms are all defined later in a *Glossary* at the end of the book. This glossary tells you which of the key terms are actually stated on each of the four syllabuses for AS/A2 Level Psychology so that you know precisely which terms you should have a very good grasp of before you sit your AS or A2 level examination. Each chapter also starts with a *Summary of key points* to let you know where we are going or to remind you, once you've worked through the chapter, where you have been and the essential points made along the way.

Most students find the writing of a scientific report of a practical investigation one of the most daunting tasks they have ever had to face in their education so far. All the boards demand at least one report and most first-year degree courses demand several. To help and support you in this type of assessment there is an entire chapter on planning and writing a report which incorporates a lot of the knowledge I have acquired over the years of what mistakes students commonly make, the pitfalls they face, what to include and what *not* to include. However there is nothing like a good clear example and this book provides not just one but two – an 'average' report with full comments from an imaginary marker (well, me actually) and a 'good' report of the same practical work. Follow the directions given in this section and you cannot fail to get a decent mark so long as you use good English.

Finally, most A Level boards and degree courses include some form of written examination assessment in which you are asked to read a scenario of some practical research and then give short answers to several question about the research project. I have included seven of these along with full answers so that, if you seriously practice with these questions – that is, think carefully, write in full and do not check the answers until you've finished – then you will face your test or exam with the confidence of having learned just what to expect and hopefully with part of the wording for some of the more typical answers already prepared.

I very much hope then that your use of this book will help to make research methods accessible and human and to demystify statistics. I really hope it will support those who fancy psychology but who experience the fear barriers often associated with 'science'. I hope it will help you to roll up your sleeves and get your hands on the practice of finding out about people. And of course I hope it helps you do well in your Psychology course.

Hugh Coolican 2006

Acknowledgements

I would like to thank Cara Flanagan for asking me a lot of questions as she prepared her own book and thereby helping me to clarify some knotty problems, the answers to which have found their way into this third edition. Perhaps the late night e-mails themselves could one day be a book! I would also like to thank Emma Woolf, Joanna Lincoln, Susan Millership, Sue Thomas and Anna Thompson for all their support in the production of this book. Finally I would like to thank the many students on whom I have tried out much of this material for all their perhaps unwitting help in allowing me to fine tune and improve many of the ideas, tricks and demonstrations.

chapter
1

Psychology and research

BECOMING AN 'AH, BUT' THINKER

Do you trust all conclusions that scientists reach as a result of their research work? If you answered 'no' then that's a good start. Very often in the media, of course, dramatic conclusions (often unjustified) are actually drawn by the particular journalist, whereas the scientist, when interviewed, sounds far more cautious. For example, not long ago a newspaper article claimed that psychologists might have 'solved the Freudian riddle' (*Guardian*, 10 September 2004). The article was full of 'dramatic breakthrough' type language. It claimed that the researchers' work '… serves to prove part of' a theory that some processes suggested by Freud can be linked to specific activities of the brain. As we shall see later, neither psychologists nor any other good scientist would talk of 'proving a theory'. Only mathematicians prove a theory; scientists *support* theories with empirical findings and attempt to show where competing theories do not explain enough of the known facts. **EMPIRICAL** means based on observation of events in the world – in short, facts. What the psychologists in the newspaper story had in fact achieved was to identify an area at the back of the brain that appeared to be closely associated with dreaming, or at least with remembering the content of dreams. The finding was significant in itself, but it certainly does not prove Freud right nor show us that dreams are in fact a form of wish fulfilment. It shows us simply that this specific part of the brain is important in the experience of dreams. That's all!

Figure 1.1   The 'ah, but' thinker

Oh dear, is this book going to take the romance out of things, then? Well, in a way, yes – if by 'romance' we mean the need to believe in things just because they are attractive and would be nice if they were true. Our purpose here is to look much more closely at *evidence* than perhaps we would normally. We want to know what right anyone has to make claims about people and how they work. This is called 'doing science' and, in fact, you already do it because you cast a dubious look at outlandish claims, probably saying something like 'Well, how would they know that? What evidence did they have?'.

As you attempt to learn about research methods, and about psychology in general, the best thing you can do is to develop a somewhat annoying but ever so helpful 'Ah, but …' mentality, as I term it. This means that when you hear, for instance, that using the Internet a lot appears to *lead to* depression you say 'Ah, but couldn't it be that depressed people are more likely to use the Internet in the first place?'. In other words, always look for the *alternative explanation*; look for the flaws and limitations in the design of the research that led to the conclusion. Always *challenge*.

What drives research in any science is this process of challenge and then answering the challenge. Take a look at Box 1.1.

Box 1.1   Dear taxi-driver, I haven't got a tip but you do have a nice big brain

A research team led by Eleanor Maguire at University College London aroused media interest by showing that London taxi-cab drivers had more grey matter in a specific area of the brain (the rear hippocampus) than did other people (Maguire, Spiers and Good, 2003). It was strongly suggested that this area of the brain is concerned with navigation skills and that the cab drivers had developed the increased grey matter through their years of experience in driving round London's streets. The idea that the increased grey matter had been caused through taxi driving was supported by a strong relationship between number of years of taxi-driving experience and amount of grey matter – the more years driving, the more grey matter was present. However, the 'Ah, but' mentality kicks in at this point and asks:

But what if people who are naturally endowed with more grey matter in that area just find street navigation easier and are therefore drawn to taxi driving?

This is a typical cart before the horse manoeuvre. We can often reverse the apparently obvious direction of the cause. For instance, rather than spanking causing children to become aggressive, perhaps parents spank children who are particularly aggressive in the first place (I strongly believe that hitting children is not a good idea at all and teaches them aggression – 'You're little. I can hit you'. What a good model!).

In this case the researchers anticipated the objection that perhaps people with more grey matter are more likely to become taxi drivers. They looked at the relationship between amount of grey matter and navigational skills in a group of non-taxi drivers. If it is true that more grey matter is a cause of good navigational skills and therefore of becoming a taxi driver then we would expect a relationship between grey matter and navigational skills in this non-taxi-driver sample. There wasn't one. More grey matter was not associated with better navigational skills. Hence it appears that the years spent driving a taxi are the *cause* of the increased grey matter. It is not the case that more grey matter means better navigation skills and an urge to drive taxis!

We should note that this study earned the researchers an 'Ig nobel' prize. These prizes are awarded by the science humour magazine *Annals of Improbable Research* for published findings that 'first make you laugh, then think'. You can find out more about all sorts of weird and sometimes frankly ludicrous research, including the wonderful (and Australian) 'analysis of the forces required to drag sheep over various surfaces' on their web site: http://www.improb.com/

The important message from Box 1.1 is the way in which the researchers' *method* answers certain questions. Because their design is well structured, they do not just sit back and say 'We think taxi driving increases grey matter because taxi drivers have more of it'. They manage to show that *only* for taxi drivers does navigation experience relate to amount of grey matter.

Psychology has, over the 125+ years of research in the subject, reached some surprising and curious conclusions, just as in the 'discovery' of the seat of dreams and this study of the hippocampus and navigation. For instance, we know (or we think we know) that:

❑ many people will continue to obey a researcher's instructions to give electric shocks to a 'victim' to the point where it is obvious that the victim is either dead or seriously injured;
❑ in public, many people conform to the judgements of the majority, even when the judgements made are ludicrous;

- people tend to blame outside circumstances when they make a mistake ('Well, you didn't tell me!') yet attribute the causes of others' mistakes to that person's personality or internal weaknesses ('Well, what do you expect with Gordon's brain?');
- people who have undergone certain types of brain operation can recognize an object (e.g. an elephant) presented to one half of the visual system yet, when asked to name it, will give the name of an object that has been presented to the other half of their visual system (e.g. 'key');
- children do not copy language; they try out speech to see if it fits the 'rules' of language.

It is only because the researchers behind these findings used well-accepted methods and published their results in a way that other researchers could understand and challenge, that we have the body of knowledge that is psychology … and what a wealth of knowledge there is!

Let's begin to unravel the techniques of research methods. Of course, as I suggested in the Preface, many people would prefer to learn only about what psychologists have said, rather than about how they were able to say it. However, your syllabus writers have very wisely recognized the importance, for any psychology student, of learning *how* to do research, how to recognize good and faulty designs, and how to avoid being persuaded by dodgy results and flawed statistical methods. Studying research methods will give you skills, not just knowledge, and these skills should benefit you way beyond the boundaries of your psychology course. Immerse yourself in methods and statistics and you will be able to challenge the ideas of politicians who select their statistics in a very convenient manner, and to see through wily advertisements that make impressive claims. *Studying* methods helps you to *join in* with the psychologists in looking at the strengths and weaknesses of different kinds of research study and not just accept the results.

SCIENCE AT LEAST STARTS WITH COMMON SENSE – WE CAN ALL DO IT!

Everyone is a scientist if they want to be. The logic and reasoning of science are not skills exclusively available to only the extremely well educated (or perhaps extremely sad!). We all have them; you have been using them effectively since you were very small to understand and predict the erratic and capricious world around you.

To get us started on real research methods let's do an exercise that demonstrates what I mean. Whilst teaching research methods and even aspects of statistics I have always strongly believed that individuals will already have formed basic intuitive concepts for many of the notions that we will discuss in this book. You may not have realized it or dwelt in depth upon the implications, but you could say how many cats out of ten should choose Moggy Munch for you to be convinced that 'most cats prefer it to Poshpaws'. You could recognize a very biased sample for a survey and could think about how to make a sample more representative. You know, in other words, what generally counts as a 'fair test' in scientific terms, and here's a way to show that you do.

Suppose you overhear the following statement in conversation in your college canteen:

'I don't know. You hear about all these wars and they're nearly all in hot countries. I reckon heat makes people aggressive – you know, want to rush to fight instead of thinking about it beforehand.'

As you've started a course in psychology, and therefore presumably want to ask questions about people's behaviour and thinking, I hope you wouldn't be able to accept this gross assumption. Rather than accept this 'armchair' theory, I hope the first thing you'd want to do is to ask for evidence for this claim. So let me ask you to take on this problem yourself. How would you design and conduct a study to test the idea that heat makes people more aggressive? That is, what would you do to gather evidence to support or disprove this idea? Try to think of several alternative methods you might use.

When asked to carry out this task most people can have a fair stab at it and will come up with some of the ideas shown in Box 1.2. We are all potential scientists; we can all think of some kind of test, some way of gathering evidence. No doubt some of your ideas appear below or were pretty similar.

Box 1.2   Possible designs testing the idea that heat makes people more aggressive

1. We'd take a group of people and put them in a cool room, ask them to discuss a problem and observe whether they got aggressive or not; then we'd make the room hotter and observe them again.
2. We'd have one group in a hot room and show them a somewhat violent film and ask them to say how aggressive the people in the film were; then we'd do the same with another group of people in the same room when it's cool.
3. We'd take a group of schoolchildren and observe them in the playground playing and see which is the most aggressive pair, next most aggressive pair and so on. We'd split the pairs to form two equivalent groups for aggression. Then we'd get naive observers to watch one group playing in a cool room and the other in the same room when it's hotter and compare the pairs of children on their levels of aggression.
4. We'd have this guy and put him into a room and vary the temperature and each time ask him to do a frustrating task like threading a needle with thread that's too large for the eye. We'd measure his aggression with a questionnaire.
5. We'd observe and interview drivers in the rush hour in Iceland and in Mexico.
6. We'd take samples from different areas of the country on one day when the temperature varied across these different areas. We'd ask the people to do things like give prison sentences or say what they'd do if someone hit their little sister.
7. We'd follow a group of boys through the year, recording temperature and number of fights they've got into that week/month.

PSYCHOLOGY AND RESEARCH

Each of the suggestions in Box 1.2 is a **RESEARCH DESIGN**, a way of setting up conditions to gather **DATA** (information) with which to answer a **RESEARCH QUESTION**. The research question, originating from the rather sweeping generalization made by the person in the canteen, is 'Does heat make people more aggressive?'. All research studies ask some kind of research question concerning what the researcher wishes to find out.

HOW DO PSYCHOLOGISTS ANSWER RESEARCH QUESTIONS?

Basically, they do research. They decide upon an overall design, such as one of those in Box 1.2 (though with greater precision), and they then need to make several more decisions about their overall research study:

1. *what will be measured or observed* and how, exactly?
2. *who* will be studied?
3. *how* should we deal with the data we have gathered?

Decision 1 often concerns the *precise* measurement of **VARIABLES**. Variables are things that vary and need to be precisely defined in a research project. In order to measure aggression we must state exactly what will be taken as a measure of aggression. We might use a questionnaire or we might count the number of pre-defined aggressive acts per hour, for instance. Variables produce **QUANTITATIVE DATA**, that is, *data in the form of numbers.* Chapter 2 deals with the measurement of variables. Notice that only examples 4 and 7 in Box 1.2 give a specific means by which to measure 'aggression'.

Alternatively, decision 1 might involve setting up some method for recording **QUALITATIVE DATA** – *information that is not numerical.* This might consist of all dialogue in an interview. Qualitative data, and methods of recording them, are dealt with in Chapter 7.

Decision 2 concerns the **PARTICIPANTS** in the study. For instance, what is the advantage of testing the same participants in each condition, as in example 1 in Box 1.2, and what is the disadvantage? Conversely, what advantage does example 2 have in using different groups of participants … and what problems? A very large number of psychological studies are carried out on students, most of them reading psychology (see Banyard and Hunt, 2000). Does this mean it is fair to extrapolate the results of these studies to all other people? The questions concerning who to study, in what sort of groups, and how to ensure fair samples of people to study are covered in Chapter 2.

Decision 3 is probably the hardest, and the one that will tax you the most in learning to do psychological research. Let's approach the issue by looking at some types of research that generate different kinds of data and which therefore use different kinds of analysis. Take a look at the examples given in Box 1.3.

Box 1.3 What psychologists do in their research studies

❑ **Descriptive research:** sometimes we just want to know how the land lies: when do infants definitely recognize their mother?; how many children can count to ten by age three?; how extroverted are nurses? In this case we use numerical data to *describe* what we have found, hence we use the term **DESCRIPTIVE STATISTICS**.

❑ **Scale construction and testing:** very often psychologists invent a measurement scale (such as a measure of one's 'self-esteem') and then must try it out on various groups of the population in order to establish that it is indeed a worthy measure of something psychological. We talk of the scale's *reliability* and *validity* (see p. 80). They may also wish to demonstrate that an already existing scale requires adjustment or can be used effectively in a different culture from the one for which it was intended. In this case, again mostly descriptive statistics are used on the data from the research study.

❑ **Qualitative research:** a growing practice among researchers, especially over the last 15 years, has been the gathering of qualitative data through interviews or by observation. This means that no numerical data are presented but that the researcher tells us what participants actually said or what was seen. The data are qualitative because they are in text or even pictorial form and are not in the form of numbers. The issue of qualitative research is discussed more fully in Chapter 7.

❑ **Hypothesis testing:** we will look at hypothesis testing in more detail later in this chapter and more thoroughly still in Chapter 9. Most psychological research tests a **HYPOTHESIS**. This is basically what you do in everyday life when you check out a hunch. You might suspect that your brother is responsible for not shutting the freezer door properly, thus causing several sloppy ice cream incidents. After he has been in the kitchen, you check and, sure enough, the freezer door is open. You have already created a hypothesis, which is that your brother often leaves the fridge door open. You now have evidence (admittedly meagre) to support your hypothesis. However, we know that your hypothesis may not be correct. This might be a one-off lapse for your brother while your sister is, in fact, the real culprit. In psychological research the same logical procedure operates but, of course, the data gathered are more substantial and more scientifically analysed. Evidence is most often gathered in statistical form, for example, the number of words correctly recalled from a list under cold and warm conditions; a calculation is then made to help us decide whether the difference we obtained was 'significant' or not. Statistical significance will be explained in detail in Chapter 9 but, for now, let's just say that we need to know whether the data suggest a real effect of temperature on memory or whether the difference between conditions was too slight to take seriously. In the everyday example above, you generalized from the one incident with your brother to your general hypothesis. In psychological research we use **INFERENTIAL STATISTICS** to assess the likelihood that any statistical effect we find is just a one-off fluke or is likely to be evidence of a more general effect. From now on, when we talk of an 'effect' we mean either a difference between variables (e.g. people in hot rooms argue more than people in cold rooms) or a relationship between variables (e.g. the hotter it is, the more you drink).

PROGRESS REVIEW 1.1

EXERCISES

1. Could 'clouds' be a variable?
2. What is a research design?
3. How do qualitative data differ from quantitative data?

ANSWERS

1. Yes. Any physical or psychological characteristic could. We might, for instance, measure people's mood when there are a lot of clouds in the sky, a few or none. We would have to be careful, though, in defining the difference between 'a few' and 'a lot'.
2. The *way* in which a research study is carried out.
3. Qualitative data are not numerical; they are meaningful information such as text or pictures; quantitative data are records of measures taken.

> **KEY TERMS**
>
> Descriptive statistics   Qualitative data
> Empirical   Quantitative data
> Hypothesis   Research design
> Inferential statistics   Research question
> Participant   Variables

WHY MUST IT ALL BE 'SCIENTIFIC'?

There is a common misconception that science is all about discovering the facts. Actually, once science does uncover facts, those facts are not much use to scientists. They are certainly of more use to engineers, doctors, builders, child-care workers and the like – those who will *use* and *apply* knowledge in their daily work. Science is about *discovery* and *explanation*. We know that, generally, children express a crude grammar in their language from about 18 months of age; that they get upset from the age of 9 months if their main carer is suddenly absent, but not before; that they can believe that non-living things have some kind of life until they are at least six years old; and so on. What psychological scientists want to know, however, is *how* do they do this and, much more importantly, *why*? Psychological scientists, like all other scientists, develop theories and test them to see what those theories can and can't *explain*.

Figure 1.2   Just count them, Aristotle, COUNT them!

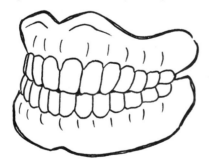

Science of this nature did not really happen before Francis Bacon and the empiricists came along in the 17th century; they introduced a completely new way of establishing knowledge. Until then, knowledge of the world had been rather limited by traditions of thinking that went back 2000 years to the world of Aristotle. To give you a flavour of just how different thinking had been in that age, consider that, according to Russell (1976), Aristotle's theory about teeth included the logical conclusion that women had fewer teeth than men. However, he didn't bother to check this out, even with the couple of wives that he could have used as research subjects. In his day, scientific 'truths' were assumed if they followed from logic and reason and if they fitted into a mainly religious view of the world and its maker. That is, the world view of Aristotle led to the logical conclusion that women *ought* to have fewer teeth. There was no real need to check this out *empirically*. This is why we need science: to stop people making all sorts of outlandish claims and other people believing them simply because they 'make sense' or 'fit in'. Think what scientific knowledge about men and women or immigrants we would have if it depended upon the forceful and clever-sounding arguments of the local bigot down the pub or the latest controversial politician.

THE SCIENTIFIC METHOD

Because philosophers in the 17th century became very dissatisfied with the Aristotelian way of thinking about the world, they moved quite rapidly towards a view of scientific investigation that most of us take completely for granted today. Even those who hated science at school would surely and instantly object to Aristotle's now ludicrous-seeming claim without any evidence. We would say simply, 'Well, have you counted them?'.

The generally accepted (but relatively recent – only a few hundred years old) model of how scientists think and investigate today, with examples, is shown in Table 1.1.

Table 1.1   The scientific method – more or less

Step Number	Method Example
1. Make observations (use measures categories etc.)	Note that individuals vary in amount of aggression
2. Detect and summarize general patterns among data	Observe that children who are physically punished are more aggressive
3. Propose explanation for patterns (theory or hypothesis)	Children copy the model of their aggressive parents
4. Test hypothesis by checking predictions with experiment or further observations	Observe results of banning punishment in Sweden from 1979 to 1999. Significant decline of youth involvement in crime, rape and suicide, among other effects (Durrant, 2000)
5. Support or challenge to theory	Supports punishment-causes-aggression theory
6. Find further support or challenge the challenge	Perhaps there were similar effects over same period in other countries (there weren't)

This method also goes by the gloriously complicated name *the hypothetico-deductive method*. We make theory and hypotheses, test them and deduce support for, or a challenge to, the theory.

Of course, most research does not follow these steps smoothly. There is rarely a straight line from making observations to testing hypotheses. Usually we already know plenty of 'facts' about the case but we want to investigate theories of why certain types of behaviour occur. We don't just wait for observations to mount up. Hence, the first two steps in the method are often taken for granted and we begin from step 3, trying to work out what might be responsible for certain kinds of human behaviour. We can intuitively suggest certain variables that might affect behaviour and set up studies to investigate these.

A classic example of beginning to gather data in the full knowledge of what needed explanation was the investigation into helping behaviour from the late 1960s onwards, triggered by the horrific Kitty Genovese murder incident in New York in 1964. Thirty-eight people were aware that a woman was in serious trouble outside their apartment block and, given the woman's cries, it would have been hard to miss the fact that she had been stabbed many times and then raped. However, only one person called the police and this was half an hour after the attack, when the woman was dead. Darley and Latané (1968) did not wait to gather many observations on helping behaviour. They set up a series of experiments which investigated several variables that could be responsible for such seemingly inhumane passivity, such as number of other people present, ambiguity of the situation, lack of action from others, personal safety, and several others. In this way they moved from a particular and distressing incident to launch a new and now long tradition of investigation into helping behaviour.

THE RULES OF A SCIENTIFIC APPROACH

The steps in the scientific method outlined above may not always be at the forefront of researchers' minds as they carry out their work. However, if research is to be done *scientifically* then it would at least have to be conducted according to the following principles.

❏ Measures are very carefully defined and are made as accurately as possible.
❏ All data are gathered in as objective a manner as possible.
❏ All measures, methods, equipment and data gathered are openly available for inspection, usually in the form of an article in an academic journal.
❏ Further details (such as the raw data – see p. 17 – or technical details) are available on request from the researcher(s).
❏ Findings (but not necessarily their implications) are accepted no matter how uncomfortable they may be.
❏ The personality of a researcher has no bearing on whether their findings are taken seriously or not. What matters is the content of their work. However, work by a researcher who makes grand claims based on minimal evidence or who is known to have 'massaged' their results would be viewed more critically.
❏ 'Common-sense' assumptions are always challenged and must be supported with empirical evidence.

Although I implied above that your everyday, common-sense thinking employs some scientific principles and will have provided you with the concepts required for doing science, I did not mean that everyday thinking will *always* do so. The trouble with everyday common sense is that it takes short cuts and it often assumes too much. Take the 'obvious' assumption that colds are common in winter because they are caused by cold and damp. They aren't. Colds are transmitted by viruses and, in winter, when we are all more closely huddled together indoors, it is far easier for a virus to travel from one person to another. So coldness and dampness are only *indirect* causes of the spread of colds – wrapping up snug and warm will not prevent them!

Also, common-sense thought doesn't often follow through carefully enough. Consider the following.

> 1. If I folded over a piece of paper several times, say four, you would of course see that the paper gets slightly thicker. What thickness would it be if I folded it over a further 50 times? Please think about this carefully now and give a rough estimate, e.g. the thickness would be greater than the height of a table, a wall, a house …
> 2. Which sex, male or female, is more physically aggressive towards their partner?

The answer to question 1 in the box is that the paper would reach to the sun and half way back again! That's about 135 million miles!

For question 2, according to research conducted by Archer (2000), females are more likely to be physically aggressive. However, before you howl me down as a sexist pig, note that males are *far* more likely to cause physical hurt or injury to their female partners. In Archer's research females simply used (probably very mild) physical aggression more often. Also, this research was conducted in the USA and is notable simply because it is so surprising. It tells us, though, that we must *always* check even the most 'obvious' assumptions before just assuming that they are true.

Psychologists have devised many tests to show that people just aren't logical beings most of the time. They do not follow the strict logic that most claim to use when making decisions. A knee-jerk, emotional or subjective conditioned response often dominates, and this applies equally to males and females. Ritov and Baron (1990) asked participants a hypothetical question. 'Imagine there is a flu epidemic during which your child has a 10 in 10,000 chance of dying. There is a vaccine which will certainly prevent the disease but it can produce fatalities.' They asked participants to decide the maximum level of risk of death from the vaccine that they would accept for their child. The average risk accepted was 5 in 10,000. In other words, participants were opting for twice the risk by rejecting the vaccine and chancing the epidemic. There is some 'magical thinking' going on here. Somehow the positive action of giving your child a vaccination that carries a slight risk of deadly effect seems more dangerous and perhaps more culpable than passively leaving your child at risk, even though the latter course carries double the chance of fatality! Something very similar happened for real in the UK in recent years when very flimsy, and in fact discredited, evidence that the MMR jab might be a cause of autism (Shimizu and Rutter, 2005) led parents to avoid it and probably contributed to a serious rise in the number of cases of measles, mumps and rubella measles (Jansen *et al.*, 2003).

WHY CAN'T WE SAY WE'VE PROVED THE THEORY TRUE?

I said earlier that scientists don't usually talk of *proving* theories. I will try to explain the reasons for this. Let's now look at hypothesis testing and how it proceeds to build up theories that stand the test of time. Try this exercise:

> I am thinking of a rule that generates valid sets of numbers. For instance, if my rule was descending odd numbers then 9, 7, 3 and 7, 3, 1 would fit but 9, 8, 5 would not. Imagine, then, that I have such a rule in my head and that the following sets of numbers fit the rule: 2, 4, 6 and 8, 10, 12.
>
> Suppose that I ask you now to generate more sets of numbers and I will tell you whether they fit the rule or not. Your task is to do this until you can identify the rule. What would be the next set of numbers you would try?

The chances are that you selected another set of equally spaced ascending numbers such as 14, 16, 18 or 3, 5, 7. Did you think of a set of numbers that *would* fit the rule you had in mind as a possible answer? I ask because really you can't get anywhere unless you find a set of numbers that *don't* fit. If you think the numbers go up in twos then what's the point of asking whether 3, 5 and 7 fit? If they do, I'll say 'yes', but you won't know if the rule is 'goes up in twos' or perhaps 'goes up in even amounts' or just 'goes up'. If you want to check out a hunch then try a set that would *not* fit your hunch. So why not try 1, 3, 7? If *that* fits then you can certainly *reject* 'goes up in twos' and also 'goes up in even amounts'. You then move on to another test that would lead you to reject *another* possibility. If we think the new rule might be 'goes up' then we might try 3, 2, 1 and so on. My rule was, in fact, 'goes up'. Try this one on your friends if you don't want to keep them!

Using this 'challenge the rule' system in science we can rule out many possible theories, leaving others more firmly established. Very many scientific and psychological studies are designed to *challenge* a hypothesis, a possible explanation, in order to rule it out. We don't prove true; we support by ruling out alternatives.

SO SCIENTISTS DON'T 'PROVE' THEORIES, THEY CHALLENGE THEM?

Using the system outlined in Table 1.1, researchers provide evidence that *supports* a theory rather than 'proves' it. What would be evidence for the theory that intelligence is passed down from parents through their genes? Identical twins have the same genes, so researchers have looked at the Intelligence Quotient (IQ) of pairs of identical twins. There is indeed a very close match. Does this 'prove' that intelligence is innate? Well, no, not at all. Identical twins are the same age and sex, live in the same environment and are generally reared by the same parents in the same family, economic and cultural environment. The close match between the IQs of identical twins is evidence both for the innate view *and* the environmental development, or 'nurture', view. When faced with this kind of ambiguous evidence, scientists search for a research design that would *rule out one of the views*, as we did with the number rule above. What would? Well, if intelligence levels are largely a result of nurturing, then identical twins who have been reared in *different* environments shouldn't have similar intelligence levels. However, so far as they have been studied, they do. But that is by no means the end of the story. We can't *experiment* with identical twins – see Chapter 2. We can only study those unfortunate twins who have sadly been separated from one another, reared in different homes and who have agreed to be tested. What we cannot easily do is find pairs of twins who have been brought up in *quite different* environments in terms of what counts – educational opportunity, family attitudes, economic circumstances etc. Most twins, if separated, are placed into fairly similar homes on these factors. We need go no further with this example for now but you might like to note that some of the fiercest and most ruthless academic battles in the history of psychological research have been conducted over this very issue.

> You might like to think now of other research designs that could provide evidence either way on the nature–nurture issue. Then look at Box 1.5 for some suggestions.

FINDINGS AND CONCLUSIONS

The point being made here is that no evidence 'proves' a theory or is unambiguously decisive. There is always another 'ah, but' question: another way to interpret the findings. What researchers present in a study are their **FINDINGS** – the data they actually gathered, summarized and analysed. They then *discuss* their findings and put forward a **CONCLUSION** that explains how the evidence supports (or not) the theory that the researchers set out to investigate – see Box 1.4. As you can see from the intelligence example, the motivation behind a lot of research is to attempt to *rule out* alternative explanations of previous findings. This is only, after all, an extension of normal everyday thinking.

Box 1.4   Findings and conclusions

> Take care always to distinguish between **findings** and **conclusions**. Findings are what actually occurred in a study – what the results were. Conclusions are what the researcher may deduce as a result of considering the findings in the light of background theory. For instance, that the

IQs of identical twins correlate quite highly is a *finding*. From this finding a researcher might conclude that heredity plays a big part in the development of intelligence. This is not the only possible conclusion, however, as we saw above. Perhaps twins are so similar because they share so many more common factors in their upbringing than normal siblings or even non-identical twins. We saw earlier that taxi drivers tend to have a larger hippocampus than non-taxi drivers. This is a *finding*. It represents facts as found by the researchers. A *conclusion* was that substantial experience of London's road system leads to physical growth in a specific area of the brain. Findings should always be clear, unambiguous and subject to little, if any, dispute. Conclusions, on the other hand, are very often contentious and disputed.

Box 1.5   Ways to investigate the nature–nurture issue

How about comparing adopted children with their parents? If genes are largely responsible for IQ then these children should not, in general, be particularly similar to their parents in intelligence; but if rearing is crucial, they will be. We can see what the relationship is between adopted children and their parents and then compare this with the relationship between children and their biological parents. The findings from this are that children are more similar to their biological parents. Support for the innate view? Yes, BUT there is another 'ah, but' problem here. Adoptive parents come from a much narrower band of society than do parents in general. The comparison is not a fair one. What we need is to use the same parents. Let's compare adoptive parents and their adopted children and then the *same* parents and their biological children. When this is done the difference between the two relationships is not a significant one. We could also try comparing an adopted child and their adopted parent with the same adopted child and their biological parent. Each design has its own problems and produces evidence that can be challenged.

LOOK FOR A TEST THAT CHALLENGES, NOT A TEST THAT CONFIRMS

Consider the following train of thought:

'I'm sure it's the margarine that's causing Henry's skin to blotch up like that.'
'I don't think so. How could it be? But OK, let's keep him off margarine completely for a while. If he still gets the blotches it just can't be the margarine.'

The test suggested is in line with the principle we outlined above: don't produce ever more evidence by continually giving Henry margarine. Try *stopping* margarine to see if the blotches continue. If you look back to the taxi-driver research described on p. 3 you'll see that here, too, the researchers needed to devise some kind of test to *rule out* the possibility that taxi drivers had a bigger hippocampus because they were born that way and were drawn to taxi driving as a result of the skills that it gave them. It was *not* the case among non-taxi drivers that better navigation skills were associated with a larger hippocampus, but this relationship *did* occur for taxi drivers. So we appear able to rule out the 'innately bigger brains draw you to taxi driving' hypothesis and provide further support for the 'taxi driving develops your brain' hypothesis.

PROGRESS REVIEW 1.2

EXERCISES

1. In what ways is the scientific method 'common sense' and in what ways is it not common sense?
2. What are the main stages in the scientific method?
3. What are findings and what are conclusions?

ANSWERS

1. The logical thinking involved is the same but we check things far more thoroughly and we do not accept 'obvious' theories at face value. We consider all possible alternative views and we try to eliminate these with further empirical findings.
2. See Table 1.1.
3. Findings are the clear results of a study – the summarized data analysed for significant difference or relationships. Conclusions are the means by which the researcher argues that the findings support or challenge a theory.

KEY TERMS

Conclusions   Scientific method
Findings   Theory
Hypothetico-deductive method

SO WHAT EXACTLY DO PSYCHOLOGICAL RESEARCHERS DO, THEN?

Conducting an experiment or other kind of research study is often only a small portion of the entire research process. In fact, we can think of the research process as a never-ending cycle. Take a look at Figure 1.3.

Figure 1.3   The research cycle – start at Box 1

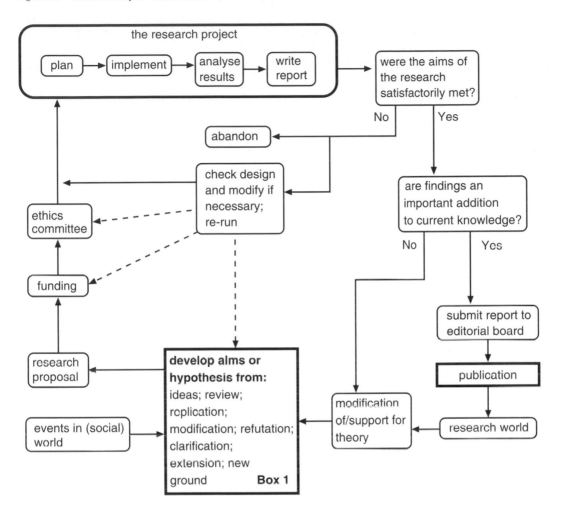

Some of the reasons why psychologists do research were listed in Box 1.3, p. 6. Usually, projects develop out of an analysis of recent research, from established theory or from new and important events in the world around us. The investigator might wish to replicate a study carried out by someone else in order to verify it. Typically, they will want to repeat the study but try to eliminate a possible explanation, for example the case of identical twins reared apart or studying only adoptive parents who also have a biological child. Researchers may also wish to extend the findings of a study to a wider population or to other contexts. For instance, many studies have shown that caffeine, taken as a controlled experimental substance, usually in tablet form, can counteract the effects of fatigue. But would normal energy drinks do the same thing? Reyner and Horne (2002) showed that a caffeinated commercial drink (Red Bull) had the same effect on healthy young adults undertaking a simulated and monotonous driving task after sleep deprivation the night before. This shows us that normal drinks can also reduce fatigue and driving errors, but we could extend the study still further. Would a caffeinated drink reduce fatigue in a real car-driving task (perhaps best performed on a track!)? How *much* sleep deprivation would Red Bull counteract? Research is, to some extent, about *finding the limits* of an effect.

REALLY NEW RESEARCH

Every once in a while researchers study a completely new phenomenon or break entirely new ground. Even the studies on taxi drivers and dreams, mentioned earlier and sensationalized by the press and presented as 'firsts', were in fact conducted as part of a general programme of research into how the brain organizes particular skills and experiences. However, in 1964 the brutal murder of Kitty Genovese in New York triggered the studies into bystander intervention by Darley and Latané (1968) mentioned earlier. Searching an electronic database of a very large number of published research articles in psychology (Psychinfo) reveals that from 11 September 2001 to late 2004 the number of studies mentioning 'terrorism' or 'terrorist' was more than double all articles containing the same terms published since 1872 when records began.

THE WHOLE RESEARCH PROCESS

There is much more involved in a research study than simply getting participants to do some test or other. Starting at Box 1 in Figure 1.3, the psychologist might have developed a new research proposal from any of the sources just discussed. The next step is to find some money to fund the project. Part of a university lecturer's job is usually to conduct research. However, in addition to the time devoted by the academics, many projects require equipment, questionnaires, research assistants employed to test participants, and so on. Sources of funding might include: university or hospital research funds; central or local government; European Union research organizations; private companies; charitable institutions; private benefactors (on rare occasions). These organizations/individuals, and the investigator's employers, will need to be satisfied that the research is worthwhile to them, to society or to the general pool of scientific knowledge. Seeking funding, by preparing project proposals, is a large but sometimes rather dull part of a researcher's working life.

Funding may be controversial where the researchers are at odds with the aims and activities of the organization offering funds (for instance, a large tobacco company). This is one of the issues on which the psychological researcher will have to make a decision, paying attention to their own personal moral principles but, more importantly, to the code of practice and ethical principles by which they are bound. In the UK the source of such principles would be the British Psychological Society, which also provides a set of guidelines for the ethical treatment of participants in research studies (British Psychological Society, 2000). University research work is usually reviewed for approval by an ethics committee, which will consider, amongst other things, the extent of stress or discomfort likely to be experienced by participants, whether deception or withholding of information are necessary, any degree of humiliation or embarrassment that might be caused to participants, and so on. In Chapter 13 we will discuss ethical problems and principles involved in psychological research.

Before the research design is fully implemented researchers may conduct **PILOT TRIALS** in order to see whether the materials and procedures are feasible and to iron out any unforeseen difficulties in the gathering of data. In pilot trials the experiment or testing is carried out on a few participants but the data are not used as final results; they might be used to adjust the measures. For instance, in a study on caffeine and memory, it might be found from a **PILOT STUDY** that the memory task is too difficult for any improvement resulting from caffeine to be shown, so the task might be made a little easier (or the dosage of caffeine might be increased).

The stages in the 'research project' box in Figure 1.3 are what most of this book is about. You will also experience these stages on your psychology course in the sessions on 'research methods'. As you can see, from the professional research psychologist's point of view this is a small part of the process. It involves thinking out the exact design, materials and procedures, obtaining equipment, finding participants and running the actual data-gathering sessions.

If the research achieves its aims and will in some way contribute to the sum of knowledge in a particular area, then it will be submitted by the researchers to a professional research **JOURNAL** (such as *The British Journal of Psychology*). The editorial board of the journal will have the report reviewed by 'referees' (learned peers) who should not be aware of the identity of the authors. If positively reviewed and subsequently accepted, the report will then be published.

Whether or not the research findings are published, they will probably have some small effect on the development of theory, if only as an indication that a promising line of investigation has proved fruitless or that an expected outcome has failed to be demonstrated. If findings challenge an existing theory or line of investigation then those academics responsible for the original theory may dispute the design or procedures of the study in order to try to defend their theory against the apparent challenge. They may ask the investigators for their **RAW DATA**. These are all the original, unprocessed results (e.g. completed questionnaires). Some academics will want to replicate the study, some to modify it ... and here we are, back where we started on the research cycle.

PROGRESS REVIEW 1.3

EXERCISES

1. Without consulting the text try to draw out all the stages of a research study, from its conception as an idea to its publication and effect on current theory.
2. Give the reasons for conducting a pilot trial. What might a researcher discover through conducting pilot trials?

ANSWERS

1. See Figure 1.3.
2. See p.16.

KEY TERMS

Ethics   Pilot trials
Journal   Raw data
Pilot study

chapter
2

Measuring people – variables and samples

What's in this chapter?

❑ We look at the idea of trying to measure people's behaviour and psychological characteristics.
❑ We ask 'What is a *variable* and what is a *psychological construct*?'.
❑ We look at how variables are strictly defined so that other researchers can work with the same concept and try to verify the same hypotheses.
❑ We see that the people tested in psychological research are considered a *sample* of a *population* and that therefore our *samples* must be representative of the population to which we want to generalize any findings.
❑ We describe several *sampling techniques*, some based on random selection and minimizing sampling bias, some that are haphazard in nature and still others that are purposefully-gathered small groups.

There are two important things we have to consider before discussing how psychologists investigate claims about people:

1. how psychologists construct measures of everyday (and some not-so-everyday) psychological concepts such as intelligence, dependence or memory;
2. how psychologists decide *whom* to measure.

To begin looking at this rather tricky area of measurement I'll resort to a rather silly but concrete and 'everyday' example that is not at all psychological, but which I hope will show that when psychologists investigate people they do not use methods that are really any more mysterious than the quite understandable and familiar ways in which we investigate our normal physical world.

Suppose you moved into a new house and wanted to investigate the healthiness of the lawn in the back garden. You might have been given a subtle clue by a neighbour who muttered, when nodding hello, 'Yeah, nice houses these but the lawns are rubbish!'.

First you need to decide on a measure of healthiness. Let's suppose you chose to measure this in terms of how fast the lawn grows. We call growth a *variable* and you will need to specify an exact measure of this. You might settle on *change in blade length in millimetres over two weeks* (not wanting to leave it longer than this between cuts for fear of being considered a slovenly gardener by your new neighbours). Of course, there is more to lawn health than this but, for the purposes of our comparison, this is what we shall call healthy. This is known as making an *operationalized* measure of the variable of grass growth – as we shall see in the first part of this chapter, which looks at how psychologists measure variables.

The next thing you'd need to do is to decide which blades of grass to measure. Clearly you're not going to measure the entire lawn! There are at least two ways you could go about making your assessment of growth. You could select one *sample* of blades and measure them at the start and end of a two-week period. Alternatively, you could select one sample at the start and then select *another* equivalent sample at the end. The problem here is, of course, how to select a representative sample of blades of grass. You won't select from the yellow patch that the neighbour's cat always pees on and you won't want the sparse, tiny blades underneath the conker tree. The problem of selecting equivalent and representative samples from a population (the entire lawn in this case) is the subject of the second part of this chapter.

VARIABLES – MEASURING THINGS IN PSYCHOLOGY

VARIABLES AND MEASUREMENT

The essence of studying anything, be it birds, geology or emotion, is the observation of *change*. If nothing changed there would be nothing to observe: if all birds had the same markings then there would be only one species and if birds did not move we could not describe their migration, mating habits and food preferences.

If something changes it is variable and in science we call it a **VARIABLE**. Here are some familiar variables:

Height	– varies as you grow older
Time	– e.g. to finish a jigsaw puzzle
Political party	– not a measure but a category
Feelings	– towards your parents, partner or sister/brother
Attitude	– towards bullies, fox hunting or alcohol abuse
Anxiety	– 'nervous' behaviour; internal feelings of fear etc.

Some of the variables in the box above are easy to measure. Funnily enough, it is the *psychological* ones that are the most difficult – feelings, attitude, anxiety.

Aggression is a variable very much studied by psychologists. Take a look back at Box 1.2 in Chapter 1. In which of the examples given would you say 'aggression' is most clearly defined?

Examples 1, 3 and 5 give no definition of aggression at all, so we don't know how it will be measured in those studies. Example 2 is slightly better but we don't know the means of asking nor exactly how participants should respond – open description or a questionnaire? Example 4 at least specifies a questionnaire but goes no further. Example 6 starts off with an easily-measurable suggestion – we could ask participants to state how many months in prison they would give a fictitious criminal found guilty. We assume that the more aggressive they are feeling, the longer sentences they would give. The second suggestion, though, is again tricky. How do we **QUANTIFY** (i.e. give a numerical value to) responses such as 'go and smack their heads' or 'sledgehammer their car'? Is one more aggressive than the other? Example 7 gives us the most exact measure, though we would have to establish first what counts as a genuine 'fight'.

PSYCHOLOGICAL CONSTRUCTS

The fact that there are several ways with which to measure aggression leads many people new to psychology to argue that those making the suggestions obviously don't know what aggression really *is* if there are so many ways to measure it. This statement assumes that somewhere there really is a *correct* way to measure aggression. There isn't. Worse than that, it seems to assume that somewhere there is a real *thing* called aggression. Think about it.

We are no better off with the concept of temperature. You won't find a temperature anywhere. Nor will you find a pressure, yet temperature and pressure are very sound and accurately-measured variables. This is because temperature and pressure are *states*. You can only tell that there's a high temperature because certain things happen – you feel hot, ice cream melts, the washing dries quickly compared with when it's colder. You can only tell there's a state of aggression because things happen – cars get smashed, people are hit, swearing happens. The analogy is not perfect but this way of thinking helps us along.

Aggression is what is known as a **PSYCHOLOGICAL CONSTRUCT**. How do we acquire these constructs? As children we are little psychologists: we observe behaviour and when it is systematic we learn to apply a known title. Hence we learn when Mummy is 'angry' (God help us if we don't!) and, later on, we learn what is a sign of 'anxiety'. Of course, this begs the question of whether, inside our psychological selves, there is something that could be identified as anxiety. Physiological psychologists would point to actions of the autonomic nervous system but cognitive psychologists would concentrate more on fearful thoughts.

Figure 2.1   Outward sings of an internal hypothetical construct

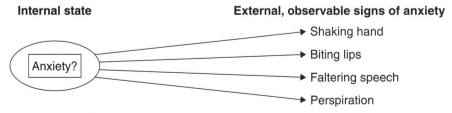

There is little space here to expand upon the huge philosophical debate we are almost entering into as to what kinds of things anxiety or aggression are and whether they 'really' exist or not. The point being made here is that, since we are made aware of aggression or anxiety in so many different ways, then it is hardly surprising that we can take measures of it in several different ways.

The black box approach to psychological constructs

Whether we are measuring something 'real' or not is not so much of a problem. To some extent, psychologists do what other scientists do: they use a 'black box approach'. They say 'We can't observe x (e.g. a quark) directly but if it exists then X should happen. Let's see if it does'. *If* it does then their theory about quarks is supported. In psychology we can treat the human mind as a black box. We can't see inside and we probably never will be able to do so. What we *can* do though, is to assume that psychological constructs are linked in a certain way, then test our theory using what we *can* measure. Figure 2.2 shows such a possible arrangement.

Figure 2.2   How a psychological researcher might propose a theoretical link between strict upbringing and discriminatory behaviour

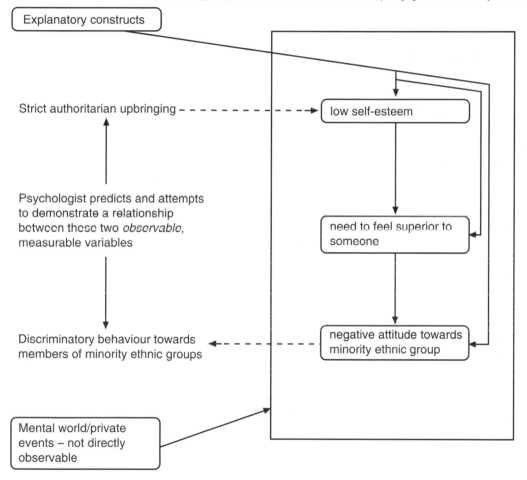

A researcher may propose that discriminatory behaviour towards minority ethnic group members (something we *can* observe) might be caused by an internal and strong attitude against such groups (something we cannot observe directly). In turn, this attitude might be a result of a need to feel superior, produced by low levels of self-esteem. Why might people have such low self-esteem? Well, an upbringing where one was bullied and always made to feel inadequate, that is, an authoritarian style of parenting, *might* be a cause of low self-esteem. We can observe people's upbringing; at least we can make objective measures of what styles are typically used by parents. The theory then can be tested by seeing whether people with a more authoritarian upbringing are more likely to produce discriminatory behaviour.

OPERATIONAL DEFINITIONS

To summarize so far. We may have doubts about the status of internal states and constructs, such as extroversion, as personality variables. However, what we *can* do is to measure the 'signs' of these states that we have learned through our experience to associate with a construct. That is, we may worry about what extroversion 'really' is but we can certainly measure things that are a sign of it, such as being more interested in things than ideas, or being eager to meet new people.

The point now is exactly how we measure these signs. In each of the studies in Box 1.2 there would need to be a strict definition of aggression. Remember that other researchers will want to replicate our study and they need to know *exactly* how we measured aggression. Psychologists like to use what are known as *operational definitions*. An **OPERATIONAL DEFINITION** of a variable such as aggression is *the set of actions required to measure the construct*. In a sense, the construct is defined by its measures *for that particular study*. For instance, in example 7 in Box 1.2 we are given a concise definition – number of fights in a month. Obviously this is not what aggression *is* in its entirety but it is being taken by the researchers as a sufficiently strong sign of aggression to be used as a measure in their study.

Definitions: being picky – but getting it right

I wish I had a pound, or a euro even, for the number of times I have written on a student's work *'Define your variable precisely'*, or something similar. Students initially find it very hard to define variables operationally. Here are some examples from student reports where the description of a variable is sloppy. What do I mean by 'sloppy'? Well, just imagine you wanted to repeat their study. What would you have to do to find out how to measure these variables? Basically you'd have to ask the researchers and this should *not* be necessary.

> '… *aggression* will be higher in the hot room condition.'
> '… the trained group will have better *memories*.'
> '… males will be more *sexist* in their attitudes.'
> '… participants will think they are more *intelligent* than their parents.'

The cause of the 'sloppy' definitions is probably the fact that in everyday life a rough definition will usually do. For instance, suppose you were describing the result of a demonstration performed by your tutor early on in a psychology course in which she showed you that it was easier to learn to put names to faces if you use an image that rhymes with the name (e.g. imagining a spanner unscrewing the teeth of a person called Hannah). You might say 'It really worked; the students given the image system did far better'. Well, that's good enough for chat but not for practical reports or answers to examination questions. What does 'they did far better' actually mean? How was this demonstrated or measured exactly? When we define variables in a psychological study we *must* be accurate, since other researchers may well want to check out what we did. The variable 'memory performance' in this case, then, might be *operationally defined* as:

> the number of names correctly matched to faces within 30 seconds of presentation.

We must have some limitation on time in order to run a standardized and fair experiment, and in any case to avoid participants coming back a week later saying 'I've just remembered it'!

As you will see from the results of exercise 6 in Progress review 2.1 below, researchers are picky about how variables are defined. This is because they want to be sure they are observing real changes in variables and not using 'sloppy' evidence. Your tutor will be picky about definitions too (or should be), because you are learning to communicate clearly to others. Psychologists must communicate this clearly because they want to be able to *replicate* each others' studies.

PROGRESS REVIEW 2.1

EXERCISES

1. How might you quantify love?
2. How do you know that someone is shy?
3. Why do psychological researchers always have to find a number for everything?
4. Try to think of a purely psychological construct. Hint: what do you say about people that implies they have some psychological quality that you cannot observe?
5. Why are psychological researchers (and teachers) so fussy about exact definitions?
6. In the exercise below, try to define one strict measure (or more) for the roughly-worded variables on the left. Cover up my attempts on the right until you've thought of an answer – don't cheat!

Physical punishment	❑ Number of times parent reports hitting child per week
	❑ Number of times child reports being hit per week
	❑ Scale to measure attitude to physical punishment
Stress (at work)	❑ Frequency of stress-related illnesses reported by employees
	❑ Number of times absent over 6-month period
	❑ Measured on 'perceived stress' scale
Sociability in 3-year-old	❑ Time (secs) spent talking to another child
	❑ Number of times toy/article is offered to another child
	❑ Number of times eye contact is made over period
Liking for Robbie Williams	❑ Position on a scale recorded by participants, from 1 = 'very much dislike' to 7 = 'very much like'
	❑ Number of times Robbie Williams is selected by participants from a set of ten famous stars
Compliance	❑ Whether or not participant agrees to give small change to person asking for it in the street
	❑ Percentage of people returning a questionnaire when asked to do so
Creativity	❑ Time (secs) to solve ten divergent-thinking problems
	❑ Number of uses for a brick thought of in two minutes

ANSWERS

1. A terrible task to request but, when you think about it, how do we know when we or anyone else is in love? It is easier to know about someone else, I suppose, so we could use a psychological scale with items such as 'I cannot stop thinking about XXX' (see p. 76); we could observe behaviour close up (not *that* close!); record the amount spent on gifts; how frequently gifts are bought; what *kinds* of thing are bought; and so on.
2. A little easier, this one. They say so; they hang back on introductions; they stutter when approached; they blush etc.

3. Because they want to know if psychological characteristics or behaviour are affected by or related to other events. In order to decide that X is caused by Y you need to observe whether X changes when Y changes. To do that you usually need to measure, no matter how crudely this is done. Most psychologists believe that in this way they can be involved in a true science of behaviour. However, qualitative researchers (see Chapter 7) would not agree.

4. We refer to people's intelligence, sensitivity, caring nature, conscientiousness, perseverance, attitude to Michael Jackson, prejudice, spirituality and so on. All of these can be assessed by observation of behaviour and by asking questions. That's all we *ever* have as evidence. But we also assume that there is an enduring something or other inside the person, or something that stays with the person, and that this is affected by events in the world. *How* it is affected and *what* it is related to is the essence of psychological research.

5. The answer is in the paragraph immediately above this Progress review box.

6. See the right-hand column of the exercise above.

KEY TERMS

Operational definition
Psychological construct

Quantify
Variable

PEOPLE – PARTICIPANTS IN PSYCHOLOGICAL RESEARCH

We have looked at what kinds of measures psychologists use and at the need to be strict in our definition of measures in research. Now it's time to take a look at *who* is studied in psychological research and the pitfalls involved in trying to make general statements about people. It is important to be aware, when 'doing' methods, that we are involved in *the* scientific method. The scientific method includes a set of procedures designed to test *general statements about the world*. Biologists, for instance, are not interested in individual flowers but in processes such as how plants hold water and why some of them prefer acidic soil. Likewise, psychologists are interested in trying to **GENERALIZE** the result they get from a sample to humans in general – just as in the attempt to generalize about lawn growth by sampling a few blades of grass.

Whenever a new group of students talks about human behaviour there are always some in the group who are a little resistant to making generalizations about human behaviour and who say things such as 'Well, we're all different so you just can't make scientific statements about people'. Trouble is, you can! If we put up a warning sign stating that there are now speed cameras installed along a certain section of road it is an absolute certainty that motorists will, *in general*, drive more slowly than before, at least for a while. Of course, *some* will maintain their old speed and it would be interesting to investigate further to see what these people may have in common. But we can often make quite definite predictions about, and observe quite definite changes in, human behaviour *in general*.

What this last statement means is that we can make predictions about the *population*, though we usually can't identify in advance specific individuals who will produce the expected changes in behaviour. We can conduct a conformity experiment knowing that *some* people will be affected in their judgement by the perceived judgements of others. We have not yet reached a stage where we can confidently predict precisely *which* individuals will be most affected. In much the same way, as a rough analogy, biologists cannot predict which individual plants in a field will most increase their growth after being given a new fertilizer; however, they can certainly predict increased growth overall.

SAMPLES AND POPULATIONS

What we have to recognize here is that psychological researchers are not specifically interested in the sample of people they test. What a heartless statement! What I mean is that, like the biologist, they are testing the *sample* in order to be able to make a more general statement about the *population* from which the sample has been drawn – see Figure 2.3. A **POPULATION** is not necessarily all the people in a country or a town but all the people to whom we think our theory (that we are testing) might apply. We *could* refer to a population of *magazines* if, for example, we were investigating the ways in which their articles represent older people. Whatever the target population (those we are interested in generalizing about), in psychological research we usually test a **SAMPLE** drawn *from* that population.

Figure 2.3   Psychologists research with small samples from populations

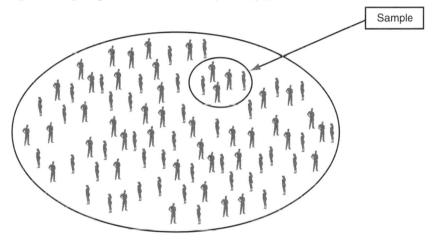

This is why we worry so much about whether the samples we test are only students, only sons and daughters of highly educated parents, whether the children tested were only from large cities. We worry just how far, in fact, we can generalize the findings of our research study at all. This issue of generalization is known as the issue of *population validity* and is at the heart of scientific research; we look at this in more detail when we consider *external validity* in Chapter 3. For now take a look at the idea of a biased sample in Figure 2.4.

Figure 2.4   A biased sample

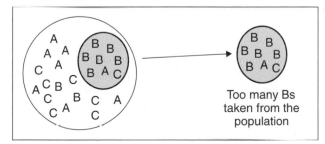

We need our sample to be as typical as possible of the population to which we want to generalize our results. Suppose we wanted to compare male and female driving behaviour for some reason. Suppose also that we chose to make sample observations at 8.45 a.m. and again at 3.15 p.m. Our sample would be likely to include a larger than usual number of women drivers with small children in the back of the car and this, of course, might have a direct effect on the ways in which these particular cars are being driven.

When a sample is overweighted with one particular category we refer to it as a **BIASED SAMPLE** and to the selection procedure as having **SAMPLING BIAS** or **SELECTION BIAS**. How might samples drawn for psychological research studies be biased?

BIAS IN PSYCHOLOGICAL RESEARCH SAMPLES

Very many psychological research studies are conducted on **VOLUNTEER SAMPLES**. People are not frog-marched into a psychology experiment but are asked very nicely whether they would like to take part, often via a public notice in a university psychology department, a medical centre, school, sports organization or similar – see Box 2.1.

Box 2.1   The nature of volunteers for psychological research

Back in 1965, Ora found that volunteers for psychological investigations scored more highly than non-volunteers on dependence, insecurity, aggressiveness, extroversion and susceptibility to social influence. Several studies have been conducted since then. Rosnow and Rosenthal (1997) reviewed many studies and came up with characteristics for which the evidence provided 'maximum', 'considerable' or 'some' confidence that volunteers were generally as described below, compared with non-volunteers.

Maximum confidence: better educated, higher intelligence, approval-motivated, sociable.
Considerable confidence: arousal-seeking, non-authoritarian, non-conforming, unconventional.
Some confidence: altruistic, self-disclosing, maladjusted, young.

Hence it is possible that some findings in psychological research are related to the characteristics of the biased sample (e.g. of volunteers) used in the study. However, do not jump to the conclusion that therefore all psychological research findings are somehow suspect. As we shall see later, if a study is designed well then it is likely that the effect of these participant variables (see p. 40) would be minimal unless the study itself focuses on these kinds of personality variables. However, we can't be too complacent and must always bear in mind that the selection method used to choose participants could have a bearing on our later interpretation of results.

THE UBIQUITOUS STUDENT IN PSYCHOLOGICAL RESEARCH

More important than volunteer bias is the predominance of *students* as participants in psychological research. Banyard and Hunt (2000) checked all volumes of two major British psychological research journals published in the years 1995 and 1996. They found that only 29% of the research projects had used a sample of non-student adults. In a few of these cases the adults were faculty staff within the university. Of the 18,635 people who made up the samples for the projects, 67% were students, and probably quite a large majority of these were psychology students.

This is not too surprising, as it is easiest for psychological researchers to ask those closest to them, in large numbers, to participate in their studies. These findings follow those of Sears (1986) who showed similar proportions of student participants in the USA some 14 years earlier. That was less surprising to those of us on this side of the Atlantic because in the USA it has long been the tradition that psychology students are required to participate in a number of research projects *or* face an extra written assignment; hence these participants were volunteers only in name. Similar systems are taking hold in UK universities now: for instance, students may have to participate in order to earn credits with which to obtain their own participants for their third-year project or to trade in for printing services or similar.

SAMPLING

REPRESENTATIVE SAMPLES

Ideally (though this rarely happens in practice) we need samples that are representative of the population in general or of the population that is the focus of the research (e.g. men, women, eight-year-old children, nurses and so on). In practice, what we try to do is to remove as much obvious sampling bias as possible; that is, we try to ensure that certain types of people in a population are not more likely to get into our sample than others. What the types are will vary with the nature of the project. If it is an experiment in visual perception, we don't really want too many members of the local camera club. If it is a study of children and logical thinking, we would like to avoid the latest child recruits to MENSA.

'Random' does *not* mean just 'haphazard'. Strictly speaking, a sequence of random choices implies that no one decision is predictable from any of the preceding sequence. When people think they are making haphazard selections there *may* yet be an underlying pattern of which they are blissfully unaware. This is not so for the butterfly. Nature has provided butterflies with the ability to make an endlessly random sequence of turns in flight in order to make prediction impossible for any predators.

A RANDOM SAMPLE

Which of the following procedures do you think would produce a study using a random sample of people? In each case assume the target population is the one identified (e.g. the 'general public' in item 1).

1. Selecting just anybody off the street.
2. Selecting every tenth person on the employment list of a company.
3. Sticking a pin in a list of names of all Wobbly College students.
4. Selecting slips from a hat containing all the names of Wobbly College students and giving those selected your sexual behaviour questionnaire.
5. Approaching people haphazardly in the refectory of Nollege College.

(Answers in a minute)

Part of the definition of a **SIMPLE RANDOM SAMPLE** is that *every member of the target population has an equal chance of being selected* and we shall concentrate on this criterion (the other part is that any *combination* is also possible). This is the principle underlying the selection of lottery balls. Students often write in their practical reports:

'We took a random sample of the population …'

Never be tempted to write this in your own report. It is almost certainly never going to be true, not just for you but for almost all psychological research projects. Just think what this would imply. However you gathered your participants (approaching the public, asking friends, asking in the canteen etc.) it would have to be that sick people, prisoners, shift workers, oil rig workers etc., *all* had an equal chance of falling into your sample. Of course they didn't!

The answer to the exercise above, then, is 'none'! In both items 1 and 5 it is likely that we will not ask those who do not look approachable and, anyway, we will only be sampling from those that use the street or the refectory. In item 2 we obviously don't satisfy the random sample criterion of equal likelihood of selection. The item 3 procedure would probably be biased towards the centre of the page and in item 4 we may initially *select* a fairly random sample but it is highly likely that the number of those who agree to *participate* will be much reduced by the nature of the questionnaire. In all examples like this some potential participants will be unobtainable or will refuse to participate, an interesting biasing factor in itself.

You *can* select a random sample of a limited population, such as all the students on your course or even all the students in your college, but you still won't be able to say that a random sample participated in your study because almost certainly many of those you select will be unable to participate.

RANDOM ALLOCATION TO CONDITIONS

You must be very careful to distinguish between selecting a random sample from a population (which is rare) and **RANDOM ALLOCATION** of participants to the conditions of an experiment (which is very common and quite simple). On p. 40, an experimental design is described in which we need to allocate, say, 20 participants to two conditions of the experiment on a random basis; that is, for every participant there should be an equal chance of being placed in one condition or the other. We want no **SELECTION BIAS**. To do this, simply select 10 participants from the 20 in the way described in Box 2.2 (and see Figure 2.6). You could also toss a coin and decide that tails will put the first person into condition 1 and the second into condition 2 and so on – a version of *systematic random sampling* that will be described in a moment. You could even toss a coin for each participant, but this may leave you with the necessity of allocating the last few to the same condition if there has been a run of tosses for the other condition – not a huge problem but not ideal. Random allocation will not divide participants into two *exactly* equivalent groups but, for most studies, we can assume that we have done our best to eliminate any effects from sampling bias.

Figure 2.5   Lottery balls are churned around to produce a random selection.

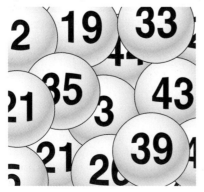

Box 2.2   How to sample randomly

If you need to select at random 20 people from 100 there are several ways in which to do it. First, you give everyone a number from 1 to 100. Then you need a way to select 20 of these on a random basis.

Generating random numbers: use a computer or Table 1, Appendix 2, to generate 20 random numbers. To use the table, just start anywhere and continue in the same direction noting down each number that occurs as you move. Select the 20 people with the numbers you have generated.

Lottery style: You will get as close to random as you can by writing each number on an equal-sized piece of paper, placing these in a box and shuffling like mad, then picking out 20 numbers. The shuffling is all-important, however. Just putting the numbers into a box will obviously create a bias in the way the numbers are arranged.

Figure 2.6   Random allocation to conditions should produce fairly equivalent groups (but it won't be perfect)

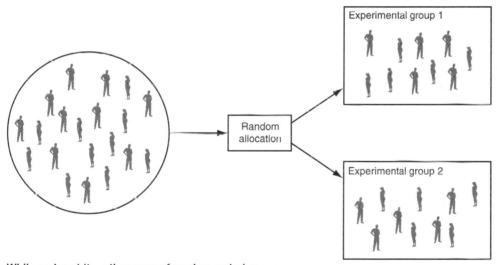

While we're at it – other uses of random ordering

It is sometimes necessary to order randomly a set of stimuli in an experiment. Stimuli might be a set of words to be learned and recalled or a set of anagrams to be solved. You might also want to present randomly a series of experimental trials – for instance, use of the left hand or right hand to balance a rod. Each participant would have, say, ten trials with each hand and we would want to order these left and right hand trials randomly. In either case you simply give every stimulus (e.g. word) or trial a random number as described above and then put the random numbers into numerical order. This will cause the words or trials associated with them to fall into a random order. This process is sometimes referred to as **RANDOMISATION** of stimuli/trials.

SYSTEMATIC SAMPLING

Another way to select people from a larger group is to use a **SYSTEMATIC SAMPLING** procedure. To select ten people from one hundred we simply select every tenth person on our list of one hundred people. If we want every person to have an equal chance of being selected (in the first place) we initially select a number between 1 and 10 at random and use this as our starting point. If our random number is 7 then we select the 7th, 17th, 27th person and so on.

STRATIFIED AND CLUSTER SAMPLING

Suppose you did not trust random sampling to extract from your college population a sample representative of all the courses or departments, in terms of a spread of subject areas. To be very simplistic, let's imagine that the four major departments in your college are Arts, Sciences, Social Sciences and Business Studies. Suppose the proportions of students in these departments are as shown at the top of Figure 2.7. We would sample randomly *within* each department and make sure that our final **STRATIFIED SAMPLE** contained the same proportions of students per department as the population. Notice that with this sample every individual has an equal chance of being selected *and* any final combination is also possible.

Choosing the relevant strata will depend on the nature of the research project. If we are investigating attitudes to unemployment then we might wish to represent the employed, the unemployed, self-employed, homemakers and pensioners proportionately. With small samples we cannot hope to represent several categories of people proportionately; for instance, we could not select just 50 people and make these representative of the local population in terms of *all* the following: gender, health status, educational level, religion, voting intention and ethnicity! We have to make choices as to which are the most relevant strata or else take very large samples indeed.

A version of the stratified sample is the **QUOTA SAMPLE** but this is just a less refined version used by street interviewers who are told, for example, what quota of women and men to question; the selection is not scientifically organized.

Figure 2.7 Proportions in college sections for a stratified sample

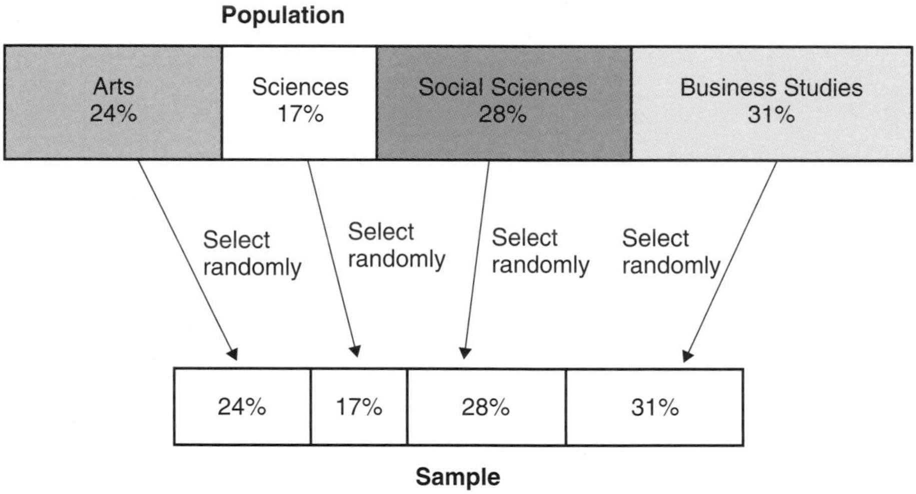

Population

Arts 24%	Sciences 17%	Social Sciences 28%	Business Studies 31%

Select randomly   Select randomly   Select randomly   Select randomly

24%	17%	28%	31%

Sample

NON-RANDOM SAMPLES

The opportunity or convenience sample

Very often, especially in student practical work, we recruit participants for a research study from among those we can simply get hold of – class colleagues, friends and relatives at home, another class that a tutor permits us to recruit into our study (with their permission of course!) or just those folk we approach in the college refectory.

Such samples are called, for obvious reasons, an **OPPORTUNITY SAMPLE** or **CONVENIENCE SAMPLE**. Calling a sample an 'opportunity sample', of course, tells us nothing at all about the way in which the participants were recruited, so never be tempted to use *just* this term in a practical report. I was discussing methods recently with Cara Flanagan, a long-serving moderator of A Level coursework. As we talked, I came up with the phrase 'homage to formal terms' to describe the strong anxious need that tutors and students often display at this level to find a name for everything and, having found one, to feel that all is now neatly 'explained'. It was this sort of term ('opportunity sample') that I had in mind. There is a feeling that all sampling methods *must* have a name and that if the name is used the reader will therefore understand everything about the sample. Well, whenever my students trot out the phrase 'Participants were an opportunity sample' they always receive the comment 'and how were they recruited?'. We want to know what inducements were made, how they were approached, what they were doing at the time and so on, because these factors might have a bearing on the findings. If they volunteered, for instance, we know from the work of Ora (1965) and Rosnow and Rosenthal (1997), previously mentioned, that they might form a sample of people different from the norm. Hence never say *only* that you took an 'opportunity sample'. *Always* go on to describe *how* the participants were selected.

The self-selecting sample

We saw earlier that volunteers tend to score higher or lower on some characteristics than the average for the population. Volunteers choose to be part of a study and so we can refer to them as a **SELF-SELECTING SAMPLE**. In other words, participants select themselves into a study, but this can be done knowingly or unknowingly. Suppose, for instance, we are interested in whether people give more to a street busker if the busker is wearing smarter clothes. We therefore have the busker perform in two sessions – one while wearing smart clothes and one while wearing scruffy clothes. Our sample is *only* the people who gave money, and these are self-selecting. We don't know whether the non-givers were also impressed by the clothes.

Panels, focus groups and snowball sampling

Panels, focus groups and snowball sampling are all methods of gathering data from people that are commonly used in qualitative research (see Chapter 9). **PANELS** are well-stratified and representative groups who may be asked to participate in several research activities over an extended period of time and are valuable simply because they are so well-balanced. **FOCUS GROUPS** tend to meet for a specific objective, which will often be a discussion of a particular issue, e.g. use of physical punishment on children or attitudes to healthy eating. **SNOWBALL SAMPLING** occurs, for example, where a researcher meets with a key person (for example, a community leader), conducts an interview and then asks who else might be in a good position to give an opinion. One contact leads to a few more and thus the sample 'snowballs' along.

LARGE OR SMALL SAMPLES?

Larger samples are usually better if you have the time and resources. Small samples are more likely to produce sampling bias. A simple example will demonstrate this. Suppose we select just five people from a group containing five Muslims, five Christians, five Sikhs and five Hindus; then it is *possible* to select only Hindus. With a sample of ten, however, this is not possible. So:

The larger the sample, the less the likely sampling bias.

However, this does *not* mean that very large samples are *always* required or even desirable. Large samples are not required because a small percentage of the population will give you a pretty good estimate. Check the newspapers at election time and you'll find that the polls they report produce an extremely good estimate of the eventual outcome by taking samples as small as 1500 from a voting population of more than 40 million.

An argument *against* large samples in experimental work is that if you need a *lot* of people just to demonstrate a small effect it may mean that you need to redesign your experiment. For instance, if you need a large sample for an experiment to demonstrate that caffeine speeds up reaction times, it may be that you are using doses of caffeine that are too small or that caffeine speeds up reaction only in certain types of people. You should redesign the experiment, based on these considerations, to try to demonstrate a more obvious effect, not just swamp your study with hundreds of people.

For studies carried out in the field, and especially surveys, it usually *is* better to go for larger samples because there could be so many uncontrolled extraneous variables in operation that a weak effect is all we can hope to show. Very often, scientifically-based newspaper articles refer to a 'small but significant trend'. Such trends can always be interpreted in many ways, but that they exist is valuable knowledge.

PROGRESS REVIEW 2.2

EXERCISES

1. A psychologist advertises in the university newspaper for students willing to participate in an experiment concerning the effects of alcohol consumption on appetite. For what reasons do you think the sample attracted to the study would not be a random one?
2. Which of the following methods would produce a truly random sample of psychology students in the County of Suffix?
    (a) Selecting a college at random and asking psychology students to volunteer.
    (b) Taking, at random, one student whose name begins with each letter of the alphabet from each college.
    (c) Putting the names of all psychology students of every college into a very large 'hat', shuffling and selecting the sample (without looking).
3. A psychology tutor carries out an experiment by allocating the front half of her class to an experimental condition. They are taught special techniques for problem solving. The rear half of the class serve as a control group (see p. 37). The experimental group do better. How might a fault in her procedure be to blame for the observed difference rather than the difference in instructions?
4. A student writes that she gathered an 'opportunity sample' for her research project. Is this all her tutor (or examiners) will want to know about her participants?
5. Why do we call the participants in a research project a 'sample'?

ANSWERS

1. The students taking part will be volunteers; no teetotallers will be included; the sample is biased towards the type of people reading the newspaper or being told about the study by those who do.
2. Only c. Method a includes (non-random) volunteers. Method b does not give each student an equal chance (you are much more likely to be selected if your name begins with 'z' than if with 't'). Even c will not produce a final random sample if not all students agree to take part.

3. She has not randomly allocated participants to conditions. Perhaps the front half of the class are more interested because they have had a better education and are therefore already better at this kind of problem-solving task.
4. No. She should explain exactly how the participants were recruited.
5. Because they are only a small group. We can't test the entire population. We *can* argue that an effect found in the sample is likely to occur generally among the *population* they came from. The sample needs to be representative therefore of that population so we can generalize our findings to it.

KEY TERMS

Biased sample	Randomisation
Convenience sample	Random sample
Focus groups	Sample
Generalization	Sampling bias
Opportunity sample	Selection bias
Panels	Self-selecting sample
Population	Snowball sample
Quota sample	Stratified sample
Random allocation	Systematic sample

chapter
3

Experimental methods

What's in this chapter?

❑ We outline the structure of *true experiments*, which involve control and manipulation of variables so that an *independent variable* can be seen to influence a *dependent variable*.

❑ We will see that uncontrolled or *extraneous variables* can become *confounding variables* that mask the true effect or lack of an effect in an experiment and produce spurious explanations.

❑ Several types of *experimental design* are discussed: *independent samples, repeated measures, matched pairs.*

❑ We look at the distinction between *laboratory* and *field experiments* or studies, and the advantages of each.

❑ We look at the more general topics of *internal* and *external validity* and the often-misunderstood concept of *ecological validity*.

❑ Finally we look at various sources of bias in experimental and other studies. Bias can emanate from the design of the study, the participants and the expectancies and influence of the investigator.

ALTERNATIVE EXPLANATIONS

In Chapter 1 we considered possible ways to gather evidence for the proposal that heat causes aggression. Psychologists usually gather data from people directly but they can also gather evidence *indirectly* by looking at various kinds of social statistics. For instance, if heat causes aggression to increase, what kind of statistics would we expect to see for records of violent crime in any particular area as the temperature rises? Well, presumably we would expect to see an *increase* in such crimes as it gets hotter; that is, in warmer weeks and months there would be more physical assaults, bodily harm and so on than in cooler weeks and months.

Anderson (1987) gathered data on these kinds of violent crimes in several large North American cities. Sure enough, the results showed that the hotter the year, the higher the incidence of violent crime. The results also demonstrated that the hotter the quarter of the year, the more violent crime; and even the hotter the city, the more violent crime.

Would you say that this evidence is impressive support for the hypothesis that heat causes aggression? Can you think of causes, other than heat, that might be responsible for the rise in aggression as evidenced by violent crimes?

Well, the difficulty here is that as the temperature rises, certain other factors also increase. For instance, the warmer the weather, the more people there are out in public places, the longer the queues for ice cream, the longer the traffic jams and so on. It may not be heat at all that causes the aggression but one of these other factors – see Figure 3.1. The problem with this kind of *non-experimental design* is that we can't remove those other factors because they operate in everyday life.

The point is that we can gather data that *support* a hypothesis but, very often in studies like these, we cannot rule out *competing explanations*; that is **we cannot confidently point to a clear cause and effect relationship between events and human behaviour.** We can't be at all sure that it is the heat that causes the observed increase in human aggression. It could be other variables, which we can't control in this type of design. As we shall soon see, in a true experiment we *can* control them.

Figure 3.1   Alternative explanations of the heat–aggression link

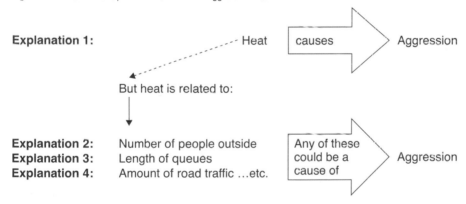

However, let's look first at another type of design where more control is involved.

Kenrick and MacFarlane (1986) observed the number of male and female drivers who honked their horn at a car parked at a green light in Phoenix, Arizona while temperatures fluctuated between 88°F and 116°F (approximately 31–47°C). There was a direct relationship – horn honking increased as temperature rose. In fact, this relationship was even stronger when only those drivers who had their windows rolled down were considered – the assumption here being that the discomfort was worse for these drivers since their cars presumably did not have working air conditioners.

There is more control in this design because the researchers could *observe directly* what the drivers did and their measure of 'aggression' was limited to one simple and unambiguous piece of behaviour

– horn honking. However, they could not control the temperature on any particular day and they had no control at all over the people they tested: these people had to be just those drivers who happened along on the day. Suppose, by chance, that drivers who are more aggressive tended to turn up on the hotter days; perhaps less aggressive drivers tend not to go out in the heat. Again we see there are alternative explanations to an apparent causal relationship between heat and aggression.

Again, the problem is that the researchers were not conducting a ***true experiment***. Let's move on now, through rather a silly example, to consider, what *is* a true experiment?

> Suppose you are dining with some particularly astral acquaintances and notice a resplendent flowering plant on the windowsill. Your mystical chums tell you that it got that way, compared with a dowdy-looking specimen above the TV, because they talk to it every day and encourage its personal development. You notice that the first plant receives more light, less heat and has a bigger pot. All these factors *could* be responsible for the differences observed between the flowers on the windowsill and the TV. A heated exchange now ensues as you attempt to debunk their theory of verbal vegetation enhancement.
>
> *How would you design a fair experiment to show that talking to plants does or does not have an effect on their development?*

As in Chapter 1, I hope that this exercise shows that people with no psychological training can easily work out what makes a fair experiment. I hope you devised something like this:

> Put two samples of plants, in identical containers with equal portions of the same soil and nutrients, in two places that receive the same amount of light and heat. Talk to one set of plants, but not the other, every day as they grow. After 12 weeks measure something about their development (e.g. height, width, colour depth etc.)

Of course, we have not yet defined what would count as '*better*' development, so, for the time being, let's take a rather limited measure – plant *height*.

1. In this design we have all the basic essentials of the **EXPERIMENT**.
2. The experimenter controls and manipulates an **INDEPENDENT VARIABLE**.
3. All other variables are eliminated or held constant, as far as is practical.
4. The experimenter measures any change in the **DEPENDENT VARIABLE**.

So in our experiment we have:

> Independent variable: Plant treatment
>
> Dependent variable: Height of plants after 12 weeks

LEVELS OF THE INDEPENDENT VARIABLE

Note that independent variables have **LEVELS**: we do *not* say that the independent variable here is 'talking or not talking'. It is useful to get into the habit of finding a *generic* title for the independent variable, e.g. 'plant treatment', and then defining levels of the independent variable – in this case 'talking' and 'not talking'. The reasons for this become more apparent when we deal with an independent variable of, say, caffeine where the levels might be 5 mg, 10 mg, 30 mg and so on. Note, then, that experiments do not always, or even usually, have only two conditions. We begin with a simple approach in this book but experiments can have as many as five or more conditions. A common design is three conditions – *experimental*, *control* (see below) and *placebo* (see p. 51).

In this case the 'not talking' condition would be called a **CONTROL CONDITION**, because we need to compare the plants in the **EXPERIMENTAL CONDITION** with some kind of **CONTROL GROUP** that receives no **TREATMENT** and provides us with a baseline measure. The dependent variable, we have decided, would be height after 12 weeks.

EXPERIMENTS INVOLVE CONTROL OF VARIABLES

In the examples above, of statistics on violent crime and of horn-honking behaviour, we noted that alternative explanations were possible and numerous. These were *not* examples of experiments. The researcher did not manipulate an independent variable. Several variables in each were not carefully controlled. However, in an experiment we *do* control variables. If all goes well we should be able to say that the only variable altered was the independent variable and, since we observed consequent change in the dependent variable, there is a cause-and-effect relationship between these two variables; we have isolated a cause of Y (the dependent variable) by manipulating X (the independent variable). An essential part of running an experiment is the attempt to control or eliminate all **EXTRANEOUS VARIABLES** – that is, variables that might interact with either our independent or dependent variables and therefore cloud the issue of whether the independent variable did directly affect the dependent variable. An important type of extraneous variable is the *confounding variable*, which we shall deal with next.

PROGRESS REVIEW 3.1

EXERCISES

1. What are the essential features of an experiment?
2. What are 'levels' of an independent variable?
3. Which produces the greater potential for alternative explanations of an apparent effect – experiment or non-experiment?

ANSWERS

1. An experiment involves the manipulation of an independent variable across two or more levels in order to observe and record any consequent change in a dependent variable. To eliminate alternative explanations of the effect observed, all other variables are either held constant or eliminated in some way.
2. The levels of the independent variable are usually the conditions of the experiment, for instance, 0 mg, 20 mg and 50 mg of caffeine, or hot and cold ambient conditions. Where the experimental task is performed under no change from normal, the experimental condition is known as a control condition – for instance, 0 mg of caffeine or normal temperature.
3. Alternative explanations for any apparent effect are always possible but in non-experiments there is usually a much wider range of possible alternative explanations because variables are less well controlled.

> **KEY TERMS**
>
> Control condition/group   Extraneous variable
> Dependent variable (DV)   Independent variable (IV)
> Experiment   Levels of the IV
> Experimental condition   Treatment

EXPERIMENTS AND CONFOUNDING VARIABLES

People new to studying psychology have a habit of calling any research study an 'experiment'. Make sure, from this point on, that you are not one of those. An experiment is a very specific type of research design that must have certain key features in order to deserve the title 'experiment'. Of course, none are perfect. In the example above, note that you have to breathe near the plants in order to talk to them. Perhaps it is the breath that causes the increased growth, rather than the talk. Variables that change *with* the independent variable, and could be an *alternative* explanation of changes in the dependent variable, are known as **CONFOUNDING VARIABLES** – see Figure 3.2.

Figure 3.2 Confounding variable in the plant experiment

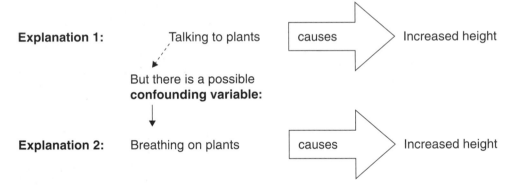

A major part of scientific activity is to look for possible confounding variables in a study that appears to support a researcher's theory. A further experiment is then devised that either rules out or experiments *with* that possible confounding variable. For instance, in the plant study, further research might involve either talking to the plants at a distance or by tape recorder (remove the confound), or simply breathing on the experimental plants *only* (experimenting *with* the confound).

Now have a look at how researchers used a true experiment to test the hypothesis that heat causes aggression.

> Rule, Taylor and Dobbs (1987) asked participants to complete stories under two different temperature conditions: 21°C or 33°C. Where stories finished ambiguously, with the possibility of an aggressive ending, the participants in the hot condition completed the stories with significantly more aggressive content and negative emotion than the 'cool' participants.

OK, this is not the same as real aggression in the real world. However, all scientific experiments have this so-called 'artificial' feature. They extract only the variables in question and try to exclude all others. They then try to show that there is an effect. In this case it looks as though only the change in temperature can be responsible for the differences in story-ending content. However, there is at least one other possibility (ah, but …!) and we shall look at it later; but make a note here if you can see an alternative explanation for the differences.

KEEPING CONTROL – STANDARDIZED PROCEDURES

We have seen that a key factor in the strength of experiments is their potential to show a cause-and-effect relationship *so long as all other variables are controlled.* For this reason experimenters use **STANDARDIZED PROCEDURES** when gathering their data. It is no use being as nice as pie with one participant, then a bit crotchety with another. It is silly to tell one participant more about how to perform a task because they're a little bit nervous. We need each participant to perform under *exactly* the same conditions so that everything stays the same, except the independent variable. Researchers give **STANDARDIZED INSTRUCTIONS**, which means that exactly the same instructions are given to each participant so that no one gets more or less information.

REPLICATION OF THE STUDY – THE NEED FOR CLEAR, FULL AND ACCURATE REPORTS

Suppose you read about a surprising effect. You hear that psychologists asked participants to hold a blanket on which someone had slept the previous night. These participants were asked to select, from a set of four pictures, a scene from the sleeper's dreams that night. They were able to do this well above chance level. This is a fictitious study but if you *did* read about it I'm sure you would want to know *exactly* how the study was conducted, with whom, under what instructions and with what equipment. You need a clear, accurate *report* of the study. This is the reason that your tutors will hound you for completeness and accuracy in a scientific report of a practical investigation. They are not being sadistic; they are trying to develop skills of communication that will serve you well, both on the course but also in later life whenever conditions demand that you give exact and precise information to a reader who needs to know what you did.

You might want to know exactly how the study was performed because you may want to **REPLICATE** it – that is, to *repeat* it in order to see whether you get the same effect. If an effect is replicated we can be more certain it is real; it has more **validity** – see p. 82. Not all 'replications' are exact repeats of the original study. For instance, we might suspect that the effect occurred because, foolishly, the correct picture was always presented to participants at the top left of the set of four. We probably favour top left since it is first in our reading sequence on a page. The 'replication' would involve all the main features of the original study but with one major modification – a randomised position for the correct picture each time. Here we would be attempting to *eliminate* a possible confounding variable.

TYPES OF EXPERIMENTAL DESIGN

THE INDEPENDENT-SAMPLES DESIGN

Look back at the Rule *et al.* (1987) study described on p. 38. These researchers used the following kind of experimental design:

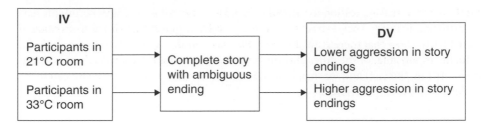

Why didn't they just ask the same participants to complete a story first in the cool room and then in the hot one? Well, just think what would happen. Participants would know exactly what the experiment was all about and they would be completing the same stories as they had in the first condition. It doesn't make much sense, does it? When we have this kind of manipulation in our experiment it makes sense to use two different groups of people for the two conditions or levels of the independent variable.

Unfortunately at this point we encounter, for the first time, a common feature of psychological research methods. Over the years, psychology has drawn scientists from many other disciplines, such as biology, physics, sociology and so on. Consequently, they have imported into their study different terms that mean much the same thing. For this design, which has the popular title **INDEPENDENT SAMPLES** (because the two samples of people are independent of one another) we also have the equivalent terms:

INDEPENDENT GROUPS
INDEPENDENT SUBJECTS
INDEPENDENT MEASURES
BETWEEN GROUPS

All these terms refer to a simple design where each level of the independent variable is tested on *different* people. They belong to a class known as **unrelated designs** because scores on one level of the independent variable are *unrelated* to scores on any other level of that variable.

Non-equivalent groups – the problem of participant variables

We have already encountered a common problem with this type of design. What did we say about Kenrick and MacFarlane's horn-honking study? Perhaps more aggressive drivers were on the roads on the hotter days than on the cooler ones. If more of one type of person gets into one of the conditions of an independent samples design experiment, we have a serious confounding variable. If the participants in the hotter condition of Rule *et al.*'s story-completion study were more aggressive then it would be this *participant variable* that might cause the story endings to be more aggressive, and not the temperature at all. A **PARTICIPANT VARIABLE** is one that differs among people and might be the real cause of any observed effect.

Random allocation to conditions

To deal with the possible problem of **NON-EQUIVALENT** groups we cannot ever, for certain, make each group have an identical level of aggression, as would be ideal. We can do our best, however, to get as close to the ideal as possible. The most common method of allocating participants to the conditions of an experiment is to use *random allocation*, as we saw on p. 29. This means that each participant has the same chance of being in one condition as in any other. Please don't, as students very often do, get random allocation to conditions mixed up with a *random sample* – see p. 27.

Other solutions to the non-equivalent groups problem

Instead of randomly allocating, we could make even more certain that our groups are equivalent by **PRE-TESTING** them. We might administer an aggressiveness scale (see Chapter 6), take the top two scorers and randomly allocate this pair one to each condition and so on down through all the scores. This way we should end up with two groups that are as equivalent as possible. However, we would be begging the question that the pre-testing scale is *valid* for our study (see p. 82). We could also allocate participants in a similar way to conditions balancing for sex, educational background, age and so on.

REPEATED-MEASURES DESIGN

One radical solution to the problem of non-equivalent groups is to make the groups identical. That is, we could have each participant tested in all the conditions of the experiment. We saw above that this is just not practical where taking part in one condition would seriously affect performance and knowledge in the other conditions. Rule *et al.*'s participants would have known exactly what was going on and might easily have adjusted their performance to suit what was required (see p. 38). They would also have to complete the same stories twice, which is unrealistic.

When participating in one condition does *not* seriously affect participating in another, we can use the **REPEATED-MEASURES** design. In this design each participant is tested in each condition of the experiment (i.e. each level of the independent variable). Figure 3.3 shows an experiment where participants were asked to perform a maze task (get a ball from one end to the other in a toy maze) both on their own and in front of an audience. This would test the hypothesis of social inhibition – that the presence of an audience would make performance worse in this type of task.

Figure 3.3   Repeated-measures experiment

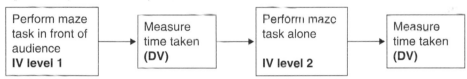

The independent variable in this experiment is audience (present or not) and the dependent variable is the time taken to complete the maze successfully.

Advantages of the repeated-measures design

An obvious advantage of this design is that we just do not have the problem of non-equivalent groups. Each participant takes part in both conditions. Hence we look only at the *difference* between performances for each participant. On some occasions, differences between participants might be relevant. For example, for some participants very well practised at a task, only small improvements might be possible, but for others new to the task, large differences could be possible. However, on most occasions a difference in the dependent variable between conditions is still likely to show up. Therefore it is important not to come up with a knee-jerk criticism of a study with a repeated-measures design, such as 'There could be differences between participants'. Differences between participants are largely irrelevant since we are *only* looking at the difference *within* each participant. This last point is made clear in one of the alternative names for this type of design – **WITHIN-GROUPS DESIGN**.

Another, though less important, advantage is that in a two-condition experiment with the same number of participants we get *twice* the number of results compared with an independent-samples design. Each participant provides a score in each condition, whereas participants in an independent-samples design provide just the one score for the single condition they are in. In a three-condition experiment we would get *three times* the number of scores or, put another way, we would need three times the number of participants in the equivalent independent-samples design, and so on.

Order effects – a serious problem with the repeated-measures design

In our social inhibition experiment we had a rather glaring problem. If all participants perform first in front of an audience, then alone, in the second condition they may improve simply because they have had more practice at the task. This **ORDER EFFECT** is a classic confounding variable but there are a number of simple ways around it.

1. *Counterbalancing*: if practice affects only the second condition we can make sure that only half of the participants take part in that condition second. So we test half our participants in the order condition A – condition B and the other half in the order B – A, in this fashion:

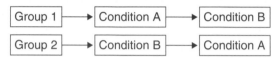

This is called **COUNTERBALANCING**.
   Important note 1: counterbalancing does not *get rid* of the order effect; it simply spreads it across both conditions so that it is neutralized.
   Important note 2: because there are two identified groups, don't be fooled into thinking a described design is an independent-samples design. The important question is 'does each participant contribute a score in each condition?'. The answer is 'yes'. There are two groups *only* because one group takes both conditions in the order A – B and the other group takes both in the order B – A.

2. *Pre-training*: we can train our participants on the maze until they are so good that a little extra practice makes no difference.

3. *Randomization of stimuli*: we can deliver the two levels of the independent variable simultaneously if each level consists of a test on several items. For instance, we might be testing the difference between memory recall of ten concrete and ten abstract words. Rather than deliver first the concrete words, then the abstract words, we can deliver all 20 words jumbled together. Later we can count separately the number of concrete and abstract words recalled and these constitute our two conditions.

MATCHED-PAIRS DESIGN

We saw earlier that a problem with the independent-samples design could be that the two groups of participants in the two conditions of an experiment might not be equivalent on some very relevant abilities or psychological characteristics. In many studies we just can't use a repeated-measures design that would eliminate this problem. If the study involves a comparison of males and females, extroverts and introverts or taxi- versus mini-cab drivers, then obviously we have to have different people in each 'condition' because the 'conditions' here are a difference between people.

Sometimes we want to give a group of people some kind of training programme, and then to compare these people with a control group who are equivalent but who have not experienced the training programme. Here, too, we can't use repeated measures. However, what we could do is to *match* people in the training condition with those in the control condition. Felmet (1998) gave a group of children with an attention and hyperactivity disorder eight weeks' training in karate whilst another group with the same disorder were put on a waiting list for karate lessons for the same period. The children were matched on age and the educational level of their parents. Results appeared to suggest that the karate-trained children performed better in some tasks requiring sustained attention. Here the independent variable was karate training and there were several dependent variables that were measures used with hyperactive children.

In this kind of **MATCHED-PAIRS** design children are first closely matched into pairs and then one child from each pair is randomly allocated to the experimental condition while the other goes into the control condition. The advantage is that we now have different people in each condition (and therefore no order effects or problems with participants guessing the experimental aim) but we know we have equivalent groups and can compare scores for matched pairs of participants as if they were one person in a repeated-measures design.

RELATED DESIGNS

The repeated-measures and matched-pairs designs are both termed **RELATED DESIGNS** because in both we end up with *pairs of scores* in our analysis. This is an important concept when we come to tests of statistical significance in Chapter 9. The differences between the sets of data provided by each design are shown in Table 3.1 where letters, or letters with numbers, are intended to symbolize different participants.

Table 3.1   Data arrangement for unrelated and related experimental designs

Unrelated		Related			
Independent samples		Repeated measures		Matched pairs	
Condition 1	Condition 2	Condition 1	Condition 2	Condition 1	Condition 2
A	H	A	A	A1	A2
B	I	B	B	B1	B2
C	J	C	C	C1	C2
D	K	D	D	D1	D2
E	L	E	E	E1	E2
F		F	F	F1	F2
G					

Table 3.2   Advantages and disadvantages of different experimental designs

Design	Advantages	Disadvantages
Independent samples	No order effects Participants unaware of other conditions and can't guess hypothesis	Non-equivalent groups because of participant differences on crucial variables Uneconomical – only one result from each participant
Repeated measures	Participant differences in ability etc. not so important Economical – a result from each participant for each condition	Order effects Problem of practice Participants can guess hypothesis and may act in accord with it Need different but equivalent stimuli in each condition (e.g. word lists or number problems)
Matched pairs	No order effects or problem of participants guessing hypothesis Participants in different conditions are equivalent	Perfect matching is rare, hence some participant differences could bias results Loss of one person means loss of whole pair

PROGRESS REVIEW 3.2

EXERCISES

1. Why are experimental procedures so strictly standardized?
2. Why would a researcher wish to replicate a study?
3. How many scores does a participant in an independent-samples design study provide on the dependent variable?
4. Remember the grass-growth exercise on p. 19? We looked at two possible ways of assessing growth. What kinds of experimental design are these two methods equivalent to?
5. What is a disadvantage of a repeated-measures design?
6. How is each participant in a matched-pairs design allocated to a condition?
7. Your tutor gives you a set of anagrams to solve, half of which are concrete words and the rest abstract words. The time taken to solve each one is recorded. In this classroom experiment what is the independent variable and what is the dependent variable? What experimental design was used with what special precaution?
8. Students are instructed to work in pairs, studying whether we learn a maze faster when using our left hand or our right. One student learns first with the left then with the right. The other student learns first with the right then the left. What design is this and what special precaution is taken? What are the IV and DV?
9. Caffeine is given to one group while plain water is given to another. Reaction times are measured. What kind of design is used, with what major weakness?
10. A busker plays in the same spot on a sunny day and on a rainy day. The number of people giving money is recorded, with the prediction that more will give on the sunny day. What kind of design is this? What are the IV and DV?

ANSWERS

1. In order to control any variables that might interfere with the causal effect between independent variable and dependent variable.
2. In order to check that the effect works or to eliminate a possible confounding variable.
3. Just one, because they only serve in one condition. In a repeated-measures design each participant provides a score in all the conditions of the study.
4. Measuring the same blades of grass twice is like a repeated-measures design. Measuring two separate samples on two different occasions is like an independent-samples design. Hopefully, 'within groups' and 'between groups' make sense to you here too. Note that these are not actually experiments in the true sense, since no one manipulates the independent variables of rain and sun – a neat introduction to the next chapter where all will be explained.
5. Order effects – often dealt with by counterbalancing.
6. On a random basis. For each participant in each pair there is an equal chance of being in one condition or the other.
7. IV: word type; DV: solution time; design: repeated measures with randomization of the stimuli.
8. Repeated measures; counterbalancing; IV: hand (L or R); DV: solution time.
9. Independent samples; possible non-equivalence of groups on participant variables.
10. Independent samples (one on each day); IV: type of day; DV: number of people.

KEY TERMS

Between groups   Participant variable
Confounding variable   Pre-testing
Counterbalancing   Related design
Independent groups/samples/   Repeated measures
    measures   Replication
Matched pairs   Standardized instructions/procedures
Non-equivalent groups   Unrelated design
Order effect   Within groups

THE LABORATORY VERSUS THE FIELD

Talk of the *laboratory* in psychology and people start to imagine victims wired to electronic contraptions that measure their thoughts. In fact, all we mean by the 'laboratory' in psychological science is the place where people are tested, i.e. the domain of the researcher, typically a room in a university psychology department. Some departments do use quite sophisticated equipment whereas others conduct interviews or administer paper-and-pencil tests.

By contrast, psychologists often work *in the field*. This means that they go out of their research department and conduct their research in the outside world, for instance, at a school, in a hospital, in an office or even simply in the street. This enables them to study people in their own natural habitat. Those people may or may not be aware that they are participating in research. They may be given a questionnaire to complete at a doctor's surgery; they could be interviewed in their workplace; or they might become a witness in the street to a fake robbery and then be asked what they saw.

The laboratory has the special feature that, once inside, participants are not on their own turf and are aware that they are being studied. People in a FIELD study experiment may also know they are being studied but they have usually not had to travel to a special and unknown place to be tested (there are always exceptions).

A colleague of mine, Cara Flanagan, likes to tease students with a devilish little problem. Suppose a participant is asked to attend a laboratory for an experiment. Whilst sitting in the waiting room an attractive man sits down and says complimentary things, then clearly steals £10 from a desk. The experiment is really about whether the participant will report the theft after compliments as against after no conversation (the condition for other unwitting participants). Here is the big question: is this a field study or a laboratory experiment?

This little problem brings out the essential point. From the participants' point of view they are still going about their normal life, albeit on a strange day when they attend for an experiment. However, as far as they are aware, that experiment has not started and the psychologist has not yet been seen. The situation is one akin to waiting in a doctor's surgery or having a mortgage interview – unusual but 'real life'.

You would not be asked in an assessment to answer a problem in a grey area such as this. I put it forward only to focus on the state of mind of the participant as a crucial factor in deciding whether the experiment is being conducted in a 'laboratory' or not and to emphasize the additional factors that cut in once a real laboratory experiment has started. Of course, as we shall see, participants in the field may *also* be aware that they are in an experiment. Awareness does not occur only inside the laboratory, but it is hard to see how a participant could be *unaware* that they are in a 'laboratory'.

ADVANTAGES OF THE LABORATORY

❑ In an experiment, the ideal is to control all irrelevant variables. This is most easily done in the psychologist's laboratory, when highly-accurate recordings of human performance (e.g. memory, vigilance) may be required. Some psychological testing equipment just could not be transported to a field setting.

❑ The independent variable can be carefully manipulated and the dependent variable carefully measured in a laboratory setting. Bandura (1965) was able to show carefully-selected and well-instructed children film of an adult being rewarded or punished for aggressive behaviour. Each child was then carefully observed in a play setting with the same Bobo doll that had featured in the film.

❑ To measure children's aggression in a less controlled field setting, observers might make recordings of school playground activity. The problem is, children are not constrained: they can move away, gang up, disappear behind others and so on. In the laboratory all such variation is controlled as far as is possible.

CRITICISM OF THE LABORATORY

Psychologists who prefer qualitative methods (see Chapter 7) criticize the laboratory for its study of fragments of unnatural behaviour taken out of the context of normal life. However, even hardened quantitative research psychologists also take issue with the artificial nature of studies in psychological laboratories. Neisser (1978) said of memory research to that date:

> We have established firm empirical generalisations but most of them are so obvious that every ten-year-old knows them anyway … If X is an interesting or socially-significant aspect of memory, then psychologists have hardly ever studied X. (pp. 4–5)

❑ **NARROWNESS OF MEASURES:** the problem is that the need to measure and control variables precisely leads to a very narrow measure of everyday concepts. Bandura's (1965) study, for instance, used the hitting of a doll as its dependent variable but this is a very narrow sample of all the aggressively destructive behaviour that a small child can produce! Although we do know from the study that children will copy exactly an adult's actions this is hardly news and a flimsy basis for the claim that aggression is learned from others in everyday life. Similarly narrow was Rule *et al.*'s (1987) measure of aggression described earlier – writing the end to a story.

❑ **LACK OF GENERALIZATION:** some effects seem to be a product only of the experimental set-up that produced them. 'Social loafing' was once thought to be a common psychological feature – that people worked less hard in a group than when alone. However, soon after the concept was accepted as a general psychological phenomenon, contradictions appeared cross-culturally. In several cultures people worked *harder* in groups than when alone (e.g. Earley, 1989). Then Holt (1987, in Brown, 1988) showed that, even in Western laboratories, if people were given just a little introduction to one another before being asked to work in groups, the social-loafing effect was not seen. The original experiment had been highly artificial in not permitting any interaction between participants before they had to work as a team. The study lacked *ecological validity* – it did not generalize to other situations, particularly from the laboratory to real life. Making tasks realistic is often a way to improve ecological validity – but not always (see p. 48).

❑ **ARTIFICIALITY:** The laboratory is a highly intimidating place for a participant, more so if the experimenter insists on a formal delivery of instructions without the usual smiles and gestures of normal human social interaction. However, the criticism of artificiality is usually aimed at the type of tasks that participants are asked to perform. In the early social-loafing studies, for instance, participants were asked to pull on a rope or make a lot of noise – rather narrow and unusual examples of 'work' – yet psychologists attempted to generalize the results to the world of employment. One needs to be careful with the criticism of artificiality. *Of course* a laboratory is artificial. Those who object to this are missing the point. In normal science we observe things roughly in real life, take things into the laboratory in order to conduct a rigorous test, then apply the finding outside the laboratory in real life – see Figure 3.5. This happens constantly in medical research, but consider the classic demonstration that all objects accelerate towards the earth at the same rate. We just can't see this in real life – to suggest that a feather and a piece of coal fall at the same rate seems nonsensical. However, pop into a laboratory, create a vacuum and drop in your feather and coal and you'll see that the uniform acceleration hypothesis is indeed valid.

Table 3.3   Advantages and disadvantages of the laboratory

Advantages	Disadvantages
Good control and accurate measurement of variables	Narrowness of measures
Can use complex equipment	Some effects may be created only in the laboratory and are not able to be generalized
Unpredictability of participants observed in the field is removed	Artificiality of tasks and measures of human behaviour

Figure 3.5   The reason for the artificial laboratory

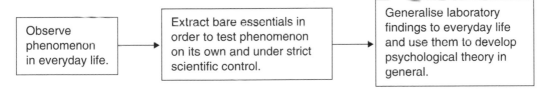

EXPERIMENTAL VALIDITY – INTERNAL AND EXTERNAL VALIDITY

Throughout this chapter we have looked at those factors in an experiment that, if not well-controlled, might to lead to incorrect conclusions from results. These factors have been termed **THREATS TO VALIDITY** by Cook and Campbell (1979). **INTERNAL VALIDITY** refers to factors such as confounding variables, statistical error, bias in data gathering and so on. These could lead to the impression that an effect exists when it doesn't, or to the conclusion that our independent variable made a difference when there was another variable that was responsible. **EXTERNAL VALIDITY** refers to the extent to which the result, if it *is* taken to be a genuine effect, can be *generalized* to other places (**ECOLOGICAL VALIDITY**), people (**POPULATION VALIDITY**) or times (**HISTORICAL VALIDITY**). Table 3.4 outlines the questions relevant to each type of validity.

Figure 3.6   Concepts of internal and external validity

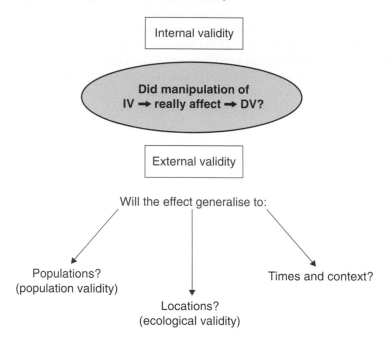

ECOLOGICAL VALIDITY

This term deserves a special mention since it is used very widely, and sometimes incorrectly, in several textbooks as well as in much teaching today. *Ecological validity* refers to *the extent to which a studied effect will generalize from the location or context in which it was demonstrated to other locations and contexts.* Typically, in the popular account, experiments are claimed to have low ecological validity because they are not carried out in the 'real world'. In fact, there is a good term for the issue of realism. Carlsmith, Ellsworth and Aronson (1976) used the term **MUNDANE REALISM** to refer to the extent to which a laboratory study mimics events and variables found in real life. They used the term **EXPERIMENTAL REALISM** to describe studies where, although the laboratory situation was quite unlike anything in real life, the context of the experiment was so gripping and engaging that any artificiality was compensated for by the fact that participants took the situation so seriously. An example would be the studies in obedience famously conducted by Milgram (1974).

Recently, there has been the tendency to say that *any* study carried out in natural surroundings has higher ecological validity than a laboratory study. This just isn't so. Many 'natural' studies produce results that cannot be generalized at all, because they were sloppy designs. On the other hand, many experimental laboratory effects *do* generalize from the laboratory to other settings: a prime example being Milgram's effects, which have been replicated in many different contexts. Another study on obedience among nurses in a real hospital setting (Hofling *et al.*, 1966) has never been fully replicated and a partial replication failed to produce obedience effects (Rank and Jacobson, 1977). So Hofling *et al.*'s 'naturalistic' study has low ecological validity whereas Milgram's is high.

Kvavilashvili and Ellis (2004) argue that an experiment may be quite unrealistic but if its effect generalizes then it *is ecologically valid.* As an example they cite Ebbinghaus's memory tasks with nonsense syllables. His materials and task were quite unlike real-life memory tasks but the effects Ebbinghaus demonstrated could be shown to operate in everyday life, though they were confounded by many other factors. The same is true of research in medicine or biology; we observe a phenomenon, conduct highly artificial experiments in the laboratory (e.g. by growing cultures on a dish) then re-interpret results in the everyday world by extending our overall knowledge of the operation of diseases and producing new treatments – see Figure 3.5. However, in psychology, it is felt that by making tasks and settings more realistic we have a good chance of increasing ecological validity. Nevertheless, ecological validity must always be *assessed* using research outcomes to show that an effect will generalize across situations. We may not *guess* that a study has high ecological validity simply because it is 'natural'.

PROGRESS REVIEW 3.3

EXERCISES

1. Without re-reading this chapter, think of two advantages and two disadvantages of using the laboratory for psychological research.
2. What kinds of validity are being referred to in each statement below?
   (a) Asch's effects wouldn't be found today.
   (b) That wouldn't work on many non-Western populations.
   (c) That might work in a hospital but not in a health centre.
   (d) I think you got those results because there were more drama students in the audience condition; either that or your measures are too narrow.

ANSWERS

1. See Table 3.3.
2. (a) historical validity.
   (b) population validity.
   (c) ecological validity.
   (d) both examples of internal validity threats.

KEY TERMS

Ecological validity	Internal validity
Experimental realism	Laboratory study
External validity	Mundane realism
Field study	Population validity
Historical validity	Threats to validity

POSSIBLE BIASES IN EXPERIMENTS AND OTHER RESEARCH

DEMAND CHARACTERISTICS – ISSUES OF REACTIVITY

Participants in experiments are **REACTIVE**. Unlike the bits of metal and stone tested in physics, human participants *react* to being studied. The experimental situation is one of human interaction – even though much of the old language of psychological research tried to create the impression that this was not so. Participants were known simply as 'subjects' and they were 'run' in an experiment, just like rats!

However, humans are curious by nature and, in a strange situation such as an experiment, are particularly likely to be searching for clues as to what is going on. Orne (1962) called these clues the **DEMAND CHARACTERISTICS** of the experimental situation. These clues may help the participant guess what is under investigation and what is expected; they may reveal the experimental hypothesis. Carlsmith *et al.* (1976) argued that experimental realism would lessen any effects of demand characteristics since participants were so engrossed in the experimental procedure.

REACTIONS OF PARTICIPANTS

If demand characteristics do operate then there is also the possibility of **PARTICIPANT EXPECTANCY** – various ways that participants might behave when they 'expect' a certain result to occur. They might simply want to **PLEASE THE EXPERIMENTER** by producing results they think are required. More subtly, they might wish to appear as normal as the next person, for instance when the questions are about personal habits. This is the effect of **SOCIAL DESIRABILITY**. Similarly, participants might be affected by **EVALUATION APPREHENSION** – a fear of doing badly or appearing *not* socially desirable, this anxiety affecting their performance in the experimental trials.

> **The Hawthorne effect**
>
> One of the first large-scale applied psychology projects was carried out by the Western Electrical Company at their Hawthorne works in Cicero, Illinois during the 1920s. This series of early studies in work psychology was reported by Roethlisberger and Dickson (1939). The investigations included the isolation of five female workers in a special room where various reactions to working and environmental conditions could be assessed. The peculiar and now famous finding was that whatever variable manipulations the researchers made (increased or decreased lighting, shorter or longer rest breaks) the effect on the workers' productivity appeared to be the same – it went up. The researchers concluded that behaviour is affected simply by the fact that the observed person knows their behaviour is being monitored and this entered the psychological terminology books as the Hawthorne effect. Hence we must always consider possible **HAWTHORNE EFFECTS** in any investigation where participants' behaviour might be affected simply by their knowing they are the subject of research scrutiny.

A further factor possibly linked to demand characteristics is that of **ENLIGHTENMENT**, where, it is claimed, psychology students become increasingly aware of psychological findings and of the tricks used by researchers to get genuine results by disguising their research intent. Since some 70% of research participants are students, mostly reading psychology (see p. 26), this concern about enlightenment is not trivial.

EXPERIMENTER EXPECTANCY

> Rosenthal (1966) gave students samples of rats, informing some that their animals were 'dull' and others that theirs were 'bright'. Surprisingly, the rats performed a task of maze learning in accordance with the label that had been given; the bright rats learned more quickly. I say 'surprisingly' because the rats had actually been randomly allocated to the two groups. The 'bright' ones were not particularly bright at all.

What do you think happened in this study? To say that the effect occurred because the student 'expected' bright behaviour from bright rats does not really tell us just *how* this happened. **EXPERIMENTER EXPECTANCY** refers to the possibility that experimenters who know the desired outcomes of a study may subtly alter the behaviour of their participants. However, expectancy is purely a state of mind. What we would look for is some actual behaviour of the experimenter that could possibly influence the rats' behaviour. Barber (1976) argued that the students probably deviated from the procedures they had been asked to follow – but why?

We must accept that in the pressured world of study and research it must often be tempting for young, aspiring and perhaps vulnerable experimenters to nudge effects in their favour. (An **EXPERIMENTER**, by the way, is someone who runs an experiment on behalf of a researcher or **INVESTIGATOR** who has overall responsibility for a research project). However, the issue of experimenter expectancy has not focused on *conscious* biasing of results but more on the suggestion that simply knowing an expected outcome makes the experimenter behave in ways that 'give the game away' or somehow influence behaviour in one particular way.

Rosenthal and Jacobson (1968) famously showed that teachers who were led to believe that some children would show significant increases in intellectual ability over a teaching year produced children who did just that, *even though the children's names had been selected at random*. However, between 1968 and 1976 when interest in this phenomenon was strongest, 40 experiments failed to demonstrate that experimenters *would* produce results in line with a direction that their investigators had suggested. Nevertheless, there are odd occurrences in the literature, such as this one:

> Wigal, Stout and Kotses (1997) asked naïve experimenters to collect data from participants who had been described as either likely or unlikely to respond to a suggestion of breathing difficulty. The participants' respiratory resistance was measured (a technical measure of breathing restriction). Sure enough, those described as likely to respond showed higher readings than the other group, yet the participants had been described as 'likely' or 'unlikely' on an entirely random basis.

In order to guard against unwanted variation because of experimenter expectancy, and to check on experimenters' data-gathering competence in general, researchers may employ a measure of **EXPERIMENTER RELIABILITY** – a statistical analysis of the extent to which experimenters' results agree.

INVESTIGATOR EFFECTS

Some people use the term **INVESTIGATOR EFFECT** to refer to *any* unwanted effect of the investigator on the research outcome. This would include expectancy effects, unconscious cues to the participant and so on, *but also* actions taken in *designing* the study such as selection of participants, materials, order of conditions, instructions, stimuli and so on. As such, this term is rather an umbrella concept and it is probably more useful to look individually at all the separate effects that can bias a study.

DEALING WITH EXPECTANCY PROBLEMS – BLINDS AND DOUBLE BLINDS

It seems we could avoid any expectancy effects if we simply didn't let people know what was expected in the results. Very often participants are not informed about the condition in which they are participating and in this case a **SINGLE BLIND** is said to be used. For instance, participants would not be told whether they had digested caffeine or a **PLACEBO** – a substance such as salt that has no effect on behaviour at all. When both participants *and* experimenters are kept ignorant of the expected outcomes, this is termed a **DOUBLE BLIND**.

PARTICIPANT AWARENESS – IT'S NOT JUST EXPERIMENTS

Some people seem to think that it is mainly experiments that suffer with all these problems of reaction, expectancy, demand characteristics and so on. A moment's thought, however, will help you realise that *any* study in which participants are aware of being studied, and possibly of the expected outcomes, might suffer from the same factors and faults. Children being observed in a playgroup setting may try to please; workers observed for increases in productivity as a consequence of changes in working conditions may well work according to theoretical expectations. If participants *know* they are being studied and could guess what researchers are predicting then all these factors apply no matter whether the study is an experiment or not and no matter where the study is conducted.

PROGRESS REVIEW 3.4

EXERCISES

1. In which of studies 7–10 in Progress review 3.2 could demand characteristics have an effect?
2. In which could blind procedures be used?
3. Why don't all experimenters get exactly the same results?

ANSWERS

1. Demand characteristics could operate in all except 10 where participants do not know there is an experiment.
2. All. Blind procedure is irrelevant to the participants in 10 since they don't know about the experiment. The recordings of numbers of people, however, could be made by 'blind' observers.
3. Very many reasons! Some may give away more to their participants; some may be more likely unwittingly to 'bend' their results in the direction of the hypothesis; some may be under real pressure to find something (but this is, I think, rare); some may engender more apprehension in their participants; some may be sloppy with their data gathering and/or statistical analysis; some may make participants more eager to please – I wonder why?!

KEY TERMS

Demand characteristics	Investigator
Double blind	Investigator effect
Enlightenment	Participant expectancy
Evaluation apprehension	Placebo
Experimenter	Pleasing the experimenter
Experimenter expectancy	Reactivity
Experimenter reliability	Single blind
Hawthorne effect	Social desirability

chapter
4

Beyond the experiment – other kinds of research approach

What's in this chapter?

❑ We look at the idea of *quasi-experiments*. These are structured studies, mostly in the field, that are not truly experiments because there is a lack of researcher control over certain aspects.
❑ We introduce various other kinds of non-experimental study, including those using *observations, interviews, surveys* and *case studies*, which are explained further in later chapters.
❑ We look at *cross-sectional, longitudinal* and *cross-cultural* designs.

QUASI-EXPERIMENTS

In the last chapter we said that the result in Rule *et al.*'s (1987) study on aggression and heat would be misinterpreted if too many already aggressive participants had been selected for the hot-room condition. The reason for more aggressive story endings in the experimental group might have been that the participants in that group were generally more aggressive. The extra heat in that condition might have had little or no effect on story endings. This is the problem of *non-equivalent groups.* Experimenters try to minimize this problem by randomly allocating participants to conditions. However, sometimes this is just not possible.

Experiments conducted in the *field* (see p. 45) are often limited to having a specific group of people allocated to the experimental condition and another group allocated as a control group. For instance, this would occur if a psychologist was working in a factory, looking at the effects of production-line speed on performance. Because it might not be possible to separate existing workgroup shifts, workers could not be allocated at random to one condition or the other. The best that might be possible would be to test one shift at low speed and another shift at higher speed – see Figure 4.1. The trouble here is that any resulting differences in stress level between conditions might be *pre-existing* – workers on the low-speed shift might *already* have lower stress levels.

Figure 4.1   True and quasi-experimental designs

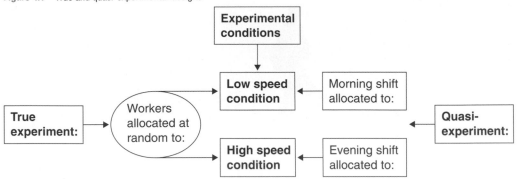

In a true experiment, as we saw earlier, a researcher manipulates an independent variable and holds all other variables constant, *including the random allocation of participants to conditions*. In a **QUASI-EXPERIMENT** there is still an identifiable independent variable, and change in the dependent variable is observed in a strictly operationalized way. However, the experiment does not *quite* meet the strict criteria for a true experiment (hence the title 'quasi-'). There are two typical situations where a study would be described as a quasi-experiment:

1. **Participants are not randomly allocated to conditions.** Sometimes the very *design* of an experiment makes it simply not possible to allocate participants to conditions at random, especially where the experiment is carried out on the general public. Cialdini, Reno and Kallgren (1990) left varying amounts of litter on a pathway and then observed whether unwitting participants who had been handed a publicity leaflet would drop the leaflet on the ground. More leaflets were dropped when there was already more litter on the ground, showing that people appear to follow the lead of others. In this case, more litter on the ground appeared to be a sign to others that dropping litter was OK. In this study the researchers had no control over who came along for either condition of the independent variable – more or less litter on the ground.
2. **The researcher does not have control of the independent variable.** A researcher does not always have to set up an experiment. Sometimes life has already created one. For instance, an education authority might decide to start an anti-bullying programme in selected schools. Although the researcher is not in control, and hence variables would not be controlled as a psychological researcher might wish, the situation can still be used by psychologists to investigate effects of the programme on children's bullying behaviour. The researcher would find an equivalent school with no anti-bullying programme, on the basis of catchment, average economic and educational level of parents etc., so that the two schools could be compared as fairly as possible.

THE NATURAL EXPERIMENT

Included in this category of study are **NATURAL EXPERIMENTS** – situations that life often throws up where no particular experiment has been arranged, not even by other professionals as in the above example, but where conditions can be sensibly compared. Ross, Campbell and Glass (1973) studied driver behaviour before and after the introduction of the breathalyser to the UK in 1967. They used traffic-accident statistics and established that people really were driving less whilst over the limit. They eliminated alternative hypotheses by using other data such as drink sales, accident rates and times, and so on. In an interesting recent study, Wardle and Watters (2004) provided evidence that exposure of younger girls to older girls in school is a factor that increases negative attitudes to weight and eating – see Table 4.1.

Table 4.1 Categories of girls, and results in the Wardle and Watters (2004) eating attitudes study

Category	Age	Type of school	Oldest pupils
'Exposed' girls	9 years	Middle school	13 years
	11 years	Secondary school	18 years
'Non-exposed' girls	9 years	Junior school	11 years
	11 years	Middle school	13 years

In general, 'exposed' girls had a thinner ideal, felt more overweight, had more friends who had dieted, scored higher on the Child Eating Attitudes Test, and had lower self-esteem.

This is an elegant design because the two samples of girls, 'exposed' and 'non-exposed', are exactly the same age yet are in different conditions. 'Exposed' girls have peer models at school who are four to seven years older than themselves whereas 'non-exposed' girls have models only up to two years older.

WHY THE FUSS ABOUT QUASI-EXPERIMENTS?

The point of concern about quasi-experiments is the 'threat to validity' (see p. 47) posed by the lack of control. The less control there is, the more we find possible alternative explanations of any observed result creeping in. Cook and Campbell (1979) are responsible for much of the debate about validity and quasi-experiments. The problem faced by them and others at the time was that the psychology research community trusted and respected true laboratory experiments far more than other research methods, most of which were seen as producing inferior results. Cook and Campbell worked in an applied field and, like many other psychologists such as those working in education, health or sport, found it difficult to conduct true experiments but ran very well-controlled studies on existing groups and under existing conditions. They argued that if other factors were well controlled and adjustments were made in the analysis of data, then such experiments should be accepted as making equally valuable contributions to the sum total of psychological knowledge. More about this issue can be found in Coolican (2004).

COMMON TYPES OF NON-EXPERIMENTAL STUDY

A large number of psychological research studies are neither true nor quasi-experiments, especially as one moves away from more scientifically controllable areas such as physiological or cognitive psychology. There is a limit to what can be called a quasi-experiment. In general there must be an experience, relatively short-term, to which groups of people have been exposed as levels of an independent variable. This is generally seen as a 'treatment'. For this reason we cannot include a study looking at differences between extroverts and introverts, or between people with high and low anxiety, as a quasi-experiment. In these cases there is simply no 'treatment'. Some people like to claim that a study of sex differences is a quasi-experiment but this is really stretching the concept too far. Being subject to one 'level' of the 'independent variable' (experiencing life as a female or male) cannot count as a 'treatment' in an experimental sense. There are far too many uncontrolled and confounding variables involved – thousands of them! Men and women score about the same on most variables, and that includes intelligence tests. Girls, in the UK until recently, the underdogs in maths and science, have overtaken boys in those subjects and generally do better. But to find some variable on which males and females differ – such as reverse parking – is not usually very useful in itself. The factor of 'sex' or gender is just too broad.

HOMAGE-TO-FORMAL-TERMS SYNDROME

I mentioned in Chapter 2 that students (and tutors) often show 'homage to formal terms' – the need to have a name for everything and a feeling of unease when the same concept crops up with a different name. The search for a 'correct' name for a research design was the kind of thing I had in mind. People go mad trying to find a name for any kind of research design. The simple truth is that many designs just do not have a single simple name and it's only examination boards that force us into trying to compartmentalize each study into a box with one name. Other than for experiments, you will find all sorts of names for the same kind of study in various kinds of textbook at different levels. DON'T WORRY! When writing a report you need not necessarily find a special term but just describe the variables and main procedures involved. When answering examination questions just learn from your tutor the quirks and preferences of your particular board. There are no absolutely correct answers in the world of non-experimental research. However, we will go through a few terms and explanations here to set the scene for the next few chapters.

POST-FACTO STUDIES

If two or more pre-formed groups (such as introvert and extrovert) are being compared then we can use the term **GROUP-DIFFERENCE** study or, more generally, for any situation in which the events and characteristics being measured *already exist* we can use the term **POST-FACTO** study. In examples such as the one in the paragraph below on anxiety and self-esteem, we simply measure variables that already exist in people or effects of events that have already occurred – there is no experiment.

CORRELATIONAL STUDIES

Some textbooks refer to *all* non-experimental studies as 'correlational'. The trouble here is that many such studies do not in fact use *correlation*. An example of a truly **CORRELATIONAL STUDY** (termed 'an investigation using correlational analysis', on the AQA Specification A syllabus) would be an attempt to see whether anxiety is related to self-esteem. One might hypothesize that people with high self-esteem would be unlikely to be anxious individuals, whereas those with low self-esteem might well have more anxiety (it might be that having an anxiety problem could lower one's self-esteem – correlation does not tell us which is the cause and which the effect – see Chapter 12). Here we might simply select some participants and ask them to complete two psychological scales, one measuring anxiety and the other measuring self-esteem. We are not manipulating an independent variable nor in any way conducting an experiment; we are simply measuring what is already there. We then use the statistical procedure of correlation (see p. 187) to measure the strength of relationship between these two variables.

OBSERVATIONAL STUDIES

Again, some textbooks even call all non-experimental studies 'observational', on the grounds that the researcher does not intervene in the situation but simply observes what is there in some way or another. However, generally speaking, a study would be called observational only when its main approach is to *observe*. We will say more about this in Chapter 5.

STUDIES USING QUESTIONS

Under this umbrella term I would list studies using mainly *interviews, questionnaires, survey studies* and possibly also some *case studies* where one or only a few individuals are subject to a lot of questioning. We will meet these in Chapters 6 and 7 so this is all we'll say for now, except to point out that these, along with correlational and observational studies, can suffer from the same weakness as any non-experimental study: the problem of determining *cause and effect*.

WEAKNESS OF NON-EXPERIMENTAL STUDIES – CAUSE OR EFFECT?

We saw in Chapter 1 that there is always an 'ah, but' question when a researcher reports findings that appear to support a theory. Suppose we run a study that observes the amount of time children spend watching violently-oriented television programmes *or* that asks them questions such as 'Do you enjoy Itchy and Scratchy in the Simpsons?'. In either case, our hypothesis is that watching violent television leads to higher levels of aggression in children's behaviour. We now observe the children's behaviour in the school playground or in other forms of free play. We then *correlate* our two measures and find that, sure enough, those watching more televised aggression show more aggression in play and *vice versa*. We present these findings as support for the conclusion that violent television leads to higher levels of aggression.

Figure 4.2   Problem of direction of cause and effect in non-experimental studies

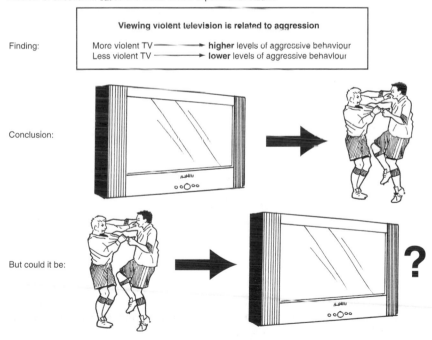

However, suppose the relationship is the other way around? How do we know that it is not the children's innate aggression that prompts them to opt for more violent television programmes than other children? This is the problem of determining the direction of cause and effect – see Figure 4.2. As we saw earlier, experiments are largely immune from this problem of interpretation since they *manipulate* an assumed cause and watch for consequent effects. Quasi-experiments are slightly weaker in that the differences between participants could be a cause of any effects found, as could uncontrolled differences in the situation where the researcher is not in control of the independent variable.

LONGITUDINAL STUDIES

One way to tackle the problem of causal direction is to conduct a **LONGITUDINAL STUDY**. In this kind of design, groups of participants are studied over a long period of time – often several years. Here, if we observe children's TV viewing well before they exhibit any signs of aggression then find that years later they have become more aggressive, we can be more confident that the television viewing had an effect on later aggression. Of course, it could be that innate factors prompt the initial choice of television viewing and are responsible later on for the emergence of aggressive behaviour. However, if two groups are studied, one where parents control viewing of violent television programmes and one where they don't, it becomes even more likely that the causal direction is from television to aggression, since it is not likely that innate aggression in the child caused the parental differences in viewing control.

Note that where a very large group of children are followed in this way the group is known collectively as a **COHORT**. There have been many national cohort studies, such as that by Ekéus, Christensson and Hjern (2004) which studied 800,192 Swedish children born between 1987 and 1993 and followed them up at age 7. The researchers found, among other things, that children of teenage mothers were at significantly greater risk of early injury, including intentional harming.

Telly really can make you aggressive

Eron, Huesmann and Lefkowitz (1972) followed up nine-year-old children whose preference for violent television viewing had already been correlated with aggression, as judged by peers. Ten years later the relationship was even stronger and, using several other statistical techniques, Eron *et al.* were able to establish a very probable causal link between violent television viewing and later aggression.

Some longitudinal studies use a control group in this way in a form of quasi-experiment. Kagan, Kearsley and Zelazo (1980) showed that children whose early years included a great deal of time spent in day care did not suffer in their development, compared with a control group of children who were always at home, providing the day care facilities were of good quality.

CROSS-SECTIONAL STUDIES

A longitudinal study has one big disadvantage: the researcher must wait all those years to get results. Surely there must be a quicker way? Well, suppose we are interested in when children develop a theory of mind – see Box 4.1. This concerns the ability to see how others think in specific situations.

Box 4.1   Testing theory of mind – the false-belief task (Perner, Leekam and Wimmer, 1987)

To test whether children have developed a 'theory of mind', researchers might use a tube of Smarties. The child is shown the tube and is asked what they think is inside. Not surprisingly (and perhaps with some vested interest), the child usually answers 'Smarties'. They are then shown that the tube actually contains pencils and are asked a key question. 'If James (a friend) came into the room, what would he think was inside the tube?'. Those without a theory of mind seem unable to see what James would see and tend to answer with the knowledge they have just obtained. Hence they answer 'pencils'. Those *with* a theory of mind answer more realistically 'Smarties'.

In order to assess the average age at which a theory of mind develops, researchers have typically tested a cross-section of children aged from 3 years upwards (e.g. Wimmer and Perner, 1985, who used children aged 3–9 years). Age is the most common cross-section used but a **CROSS-SECTIONAL STUDY** in general compares measures across different categories of people, such as occupations, types of education, minority ethnic groups and so on. The main advantage of the category age is that results that would take much longer to acquire in a longitudinal study are gained quickly. However, a longitudinal study follows the same people whereas a cross-sectional study, by definition, has the problem that different people are tested each time and so groups may not be equivalent.

CROSS-CULTURAL STUDIES

Example 5 in Box 1.2 (p. 5) is an interesting one. It is suggested here that we test the hypothesis that heat raises aggression by observing drivers in Mexico and Iceland. The problem with this study's proposal is that it seems to assume that driving behaviour is the same in principle anywhere, but if we find more aggression in Mexico then this will support our hypothesis. However, it depends what we take as a measure of aggressive driving. I'm pretty certain that if we took, as one measure, the amount of horn honking, then Mexicans would appear more aggressive. North European visitors to cities such as Rome or Bombay are often astounded by the apparent aggressiveness of drivers in these cities where horn honking is pretty well constant. It would be foolhardy, however, to assume that more horn honking implied more aggression. Very often in horn-honking countries the intention is simply to warn that you are there and, in the UK this is, in fact, the only legal reason you should use your horn. However, in the UK, horn honking is *perceived* as aggression since it is used in anger quite frequently. If it were taken as a sign of anger in Rome or Bombay then we would have to conclude that the entire driving population was super-angry all the time! This is obviously not so. Horn honking has a different function and purpose in the UK and in India, hence we do not have an equivalent measure of aggression in the two countries. To assume that horn-honking is aggressive in all societies is an example of Western *ethnocentrism*. This term means to assess the behaviour of others through the standards of one's *own* society only. In the past, people of some Eastern cultures have often been described as 'deferential' because they bow their heads on greeting. This is just a false Western interpretation of a traditional custom.

Cross-cultural studies attempt to make comparisons across cultures to see whether an effect found in the West also occurs elsewhere and is perhaps a psychological 'universal' – something that occurs in all cultures. Investigations are *also* made to test hypotheses in cultures where a variable existing in Western culture is absent. For instance, are people as affected by visual illusions if they have not been exposed to depictions of three-dimensional perspective in two-dimensional drawings? In the West such drawings are common but, in some societies, experience of them would be minimal. Likewise, does behaviour change in societies that have only recently experienced nationwide television?

Obviously, if comparisons such as these are made there will be a lot of potential for bias if measures devised only for Westerners are used, such as intelligence and personality tests. There is a famous story of Puerto Ricans gaining no marks on an IQ-test item that showed a boy holding an umbrella at the wrong angle to the rain. Why? Because in Puerto Rican society it was considered effeminate for a boy to carry an umbrella at all!

The methods used in early cross-cultural studies were inspired by anthropologists such as Ruth Benedict (1934) who believed that an individual's behaviour and thinking can *only* be understood thoroughly by viewing it through that individual's own cultural environment – a view known as *cultural relativity*. Other cross-cultural psychologists have taken a more *universalist* position in which they attempt to show that there are universal psychological dimensions but that Western studies have only looked at one end of each dimension. We can investigate how other cultures demonstrate the same psychological construct in very different ways, often at another extreme of the dimension. For instance, Stipek (1998) showed that Chinese students prefer to express pride in *other people's* achievements (e.g. a good friend) rather than their own, compared with US students' preference for expressing pride primarily in their *own* achievements. For many cultures in Asia this is just not the done thing.

You can read more about the methods and findings of cross-cultural psychological studies in the following publications:

Berry *et al.* (2002) *Cross-cultural Psychology: Research and Applications* (2nd edition)
Richards (1997) *'Race', Racism and Psychology*
Shirav and Levy (2004) *Cross-cultural Psychology: Critical Thinking and Contemporary Applications*
Smith and Bond (1998) *Understanding Social Psychology Across Cultures: Living and Working in a Changing World* (2005) and the *Journal of Cross-cultural Psychology*, published by Sage Publications.

PROGRESS REVIEW 4.1

EXERCISES

1. Which of the studies below are quasi-experiments, which are natural experiments and which are not experiments at all? Also point out which studies are in the field.
    (a) Smokers and non-smokers are tested in a laboratory on a reaction-time machine
    (b) A psychologist randomly allocates children to two different early-reading programmes in nursery school and their reading progress after 3 months is recorded
    (c) One of two very similar homes for the elderly passes from NHS to private control. Workers in each are assessed for job satisfaction before and after the change
    (d) Children are observed in a laboratory for aggression after one randomly-selected group has been subjected to mild frustration
    (e) Wallets bearing either a foreign or a local name are left in a telephone box to see whether more with local names are returned
    (f) Males and females are observed in a car park to see whether they reverse in or drive forwards into a parking place.
2. What two conditions would qualify a study as a quasi- rather than a true experiment?
3. State one advantage and one disadvantage of cross-sectional studies and longitudinal studies.

ANSWERS

1. (a) Not an experiment. A *post-facto* group-difference study on existing groups
    (b) A field experiment
    (c) A natural (and therefore quasi-) experiment (in the field)
    (d) A laboratory experiment
    (e) A quasi-experiment; the researcher cannot control who will become participants
    (f) Not an experiment. A *post-facto* group-difference study.
2. No random allocation of participants to conditions; researcher does not manipulate the independent variable.
3. Cross-sectional: advantage – quick results across different age groups; disadvantage – non-equivalent groups. Longitudinal: advantage – same group studied across time so no issue of non-equivalent groups; disadvantage – time taken to get results.

KEY TERMS

Cohort
Correlational study
Cross-cultural study
Cross-sectional study
Group-difference study

Longitudinal study
Natural experiment
Observational study
Post-facto study
Quasi–experiment

chapter 5

Observation

What's in this chapter?

❑ We look at the idea of observation as both a simple technique and as the main design of a research study.
❑ We look at the settings in which observation studies can be conducted, how the setting might influence behaviour and we look at the special design known as *naturalistic observation*.
❑ We look at the ways in which observations can be structured (or can lack structure) and at the methods for *coding* data.
❑ We look at *participant observation*, in which the observer can become a part of the group being observed.

EVERYTHING IS OBSERVATION

All scientific studies must use observation to gather data. In the most exact experiment observation is required to take measurements and read instruments. What is so special, then, about observation for psychological researchers? If you look back to the arguments on p. 46 you'll recall that a potential problem with the use of a laboratory or strict experiment is the artificial behaviour that such circumstances can produce. Instead of asking participants to memorize lists of nonsense syllables, a task rarely if ever performed in everyday life, a researcher might be interested in the strategies that people use to remember things in normal circumstances, such as shopping in a supermarket or what to say in an interview. Observation permits us to see what people *normally* do.

OBSERVATION AS TECHNIQUE

We may, however, not want 'normal' behaviour but to make careful note of what people do in a special situation. We may not want to measure responses but to count how many times they do certain things. One can therefore use observation as a *technique* within the constraints of an experiment. For instance, Bandura's famous studies (e.g. 1965), using observation of children's behaviour with a Bobo doll, were experiments. They took place within a laboratory setting and there was a manipulated independent variable – for instance, whether or not an adult model was rewarded for aggressive behaviour. The dependent variable was the observed copying of aggression by the child. Therefore, the dependent variable was recorded as how many times the children copied the adult model. The recording, however, was done via observation in a controlled environment.

OBSERVATION AS A RESEARCH DESIGN

If the *design* of a study is said to be observational then this contrasts with a more controlled experimental design. The emphasis is on the observation of *relatively free-flowing and unconstrained behaviour of an observed individual or group*, with or without their knowledge, as they perform (usually) in an everyday context.

VARIETIES OF OBSERVATIONAL STUDY

Observational studies can vary along at least three major dimensions:

1. The extent to which the setting in which people are observed is a natural environment or is structured.
2. The extent to which the observational data gathered are structured.
3. The extent to which the observer is engaged with those being observed.

Let's take each of these in turn.

1. THE SETTING

In Bandura's (e.g. 1965) experiments, children were observed playing with a limited number of available objects in a playroom and the children's responses were quite strictly *coded* – see below. This is really why Bandura's studies are usually referred to as *experiments*, with a manipulated IV and the dependent variable measured through observation (as a technique). This, then, is observation within a quite tightly structured experimental situation. By contrast, in Zimbardo's (1972) famous prison simulation study, events in the 'prison' were allowed to run their course whilst the unrestrained behaviour of the guards and prisoners was recorded extensively. There were initially few limits on what participants could do. In fact, as is well known, behaviour was so loosely controlled that events eventually got out of hand and the simulation exercise had to be stopped. The guards had become so aggressive that prisoners were in danger of severe mental suffering. It should be noted, however, that his study was run entirely within a psychology 'laboratory'.

Studies in the field, where people's naturally-occurring behaviour is observed and recorded, are generally known as **NATURALISTIC-OBSERVATION** studies. Here, the people observed are in their everyday setting. A typical example might be one in which trained observers rate aggressive behaviour shown by boys and girls in the school playground. Here the children would be going about their normal everyday behaviour at playtime whilst the observers use any of a number of techniques to record behaviour as accurately as possible and in an unbiased manner.

The main advantage of naturalistic observation is that we can observe naturally occurring unrestrained behaviour that is not distorted by what the researcher in some way *requires*. In Bandura's study behaviour was constrained by the laboratory setting and the limited items available for children to play with. In a laboratory experiment people behave because they are *asked* to by the researcher. In a naturalistic-observation study we observe behaviour as it would have occurred anyway, separate from the complications that occur if people *know* they are being observed. We shall discuss in a moment the problems of *disclosed observation*.

PROGRESS REVIEW 5.1

EXERCISES

1. Try to think of several reasons why a researcher might choose the method of observation as their research design.
2. Try to list some advantages and disadvantages of using *naturalistic observation* compared with controlled observation in a 'laboratory'.
3. Describe how Bandura's several hypotheses concerning the modelling of social behaviour could have been investigated using naturalistic observation.

ANSWERS

1. (a) The desire to observe and record unrestrained, natural behaviour, not behaviour that has been constrained by the instructions of an experimenter
    (b) The desire to record genuine behaviour rather than record what people report in an interview where *social desirability* might produce a distorted picture of the reality
    (c) Observation may be the only realistic option. If the subject of interest is babies' attachment behaviour towards their caregiver, or their spontaneous use of language, then direct observation seems the most useful and productive approach
    (d) Ethical principles might preclude an experiment and make observation the best alternative. For instance, we cannot create disability but we can observe the progress of people as they adapt to newly-acquired disabilities.
2. **Advantages**: the participant's natural behaviour should be unaffected by anxiety or a need to impress, though this depends on the obtrusiveness of the observer; includes the full context of the behaviour; useful where an experiment is unethical or where individuals could not cooperate (e.g. patients in a casualty ward, though permission would be needed here, too).
   Disadvantages: less control over extraneous variables; observer training may be lengthy and expensive; cannot use equipment that is difficult to transport; observer may have trouble remaining discreet or hidden; if a coding system is used and is too rigid, observer may not be able to record interesting and relevant behaviour.
3. Open answer. Hints: one could observe children in families watching television and record when imitation occurs.

KEY TERMS

Naturalistic observation
Observational design
Observational technique

2. STRUCTURE IN OBSERVATIONS

Structured observation designs are also sometimes known as **SYSTEMATIC OBSERVATION**. The idea is to record and categorize behaviour as accurately and with as much agreement as possible. A researcher using observation has the choice of several means of recording data. Researchers using observation but also following one of the *qualitative* approaches (described in Chapter 7) might argue that the simple act of categorizing behaviour in itself destroys the richness and the meaning of our actions in a social context. We will look more closely at these arguments in Chapter 7. For now, this chapter concentrates more closely on the conventional quantitative approaches to observational study. It should be noted, however, that *participant observation* (described below) is very often carried out from a qualitative perspective. In this case the emphasis is not on categorizing and counting instances of behaviour but on analysing the *meaning* of what is observed.

Observers often record data *as it occurs* (or *in situ*) using a check sheet such as that in Figure 5.1. They can make use of a one-way mirror so that the participants are not aware of being observed and therefore do not react as they otherwise might – see below. Of course, this introduces an ethical issue for the researcher. Usually, after the study, the people observed would be asked if they consented to the observations being retained as genuine data or if they would want the data destroyed. Similarly, behaviour can be recorded on some form of video system and, *before anyone at all has viewed the material*, participants can be asked the same question. Alternatively, participants may be made aware of the observation but a one-way mirror helps them to feel less of a target and hence more relaxed.

If statistical analysis is to be performed, then in all cases the data must be gathered using a **CODING SYSTEM**. This could be done on the spot if observers are trained in the use of the coding sheet. An example of such a sheet that could be used in the playground-aggressiveness observation study is shown in Figure 5.1.

Figure 5.1   Coding system for observations of aggressive behaviour

Child	Hits or shoves other with force – unprovoked	Hits or shoves other with force – following peer	Hits or shoves other with force – retaliation	Shouts at other – unprovoked	Shouts at other – following peer	Shouts at other – retaliation
A						
B						
C etc.						

In this coding system the *frequency* of events would be recorded – a tally would be made of the number of times the observed child shouts, either unprovoked or as retaliation, and so on. In other systems the *time* spent on a specific act might be recorded. Observers might also use a *scale* to rate, for instance, the degree of nervousness shown by an interviewee.

Whether the observers code behaviour as it occurs or whilst watching a video recording, the issue arises of *when* to observe behaviour. An hour's worth of video might take very many hours to code and therefore needs to be *sampled*. Observers in the playground cannot observe every child all the time. There are several standard sampling options. **TIME SAMPLING** involves observing a specific child or group for certain periods, e.g. for 15 seconds every five minutes. **POINT SAMPLING** involves observing what each individual is doing at a particular point in time (e.g. at the end of each 30-second interval). **EVENT SAMPLING** means concentrating on specific types of event each time they occur – for instance, how children attempt to answer a question asked suddenly by their teacher.

Reliability of observational data

We can get reliable data through observation, even if it may not always be valid. For instance, we can agree that Johnny raised his arm even if you think he was asking a question and I think he was just stretching. *Reliable* data are obtained if the same acts are recorded in the same way whoever is doing the observing (see also p. 80). To get close to this ideal (though we can never, in practice, reach perfection) we must:

❏ Use a clearly-defined and *operationalized* coding system; this is used in order to attempt to counteract any **OBSERVER BIAS** that might occur. That is, one observer might rate a particular action as aggressive but another would not. The more unambiguous and clear the coding scheme, the less the potential for bias.
❏ *Train* our observers in the use of the system using practice observations.
❏ Check that observers are indeed producing data consistent with our observational coding system by checking for **INTER-OBSERVER RELIABILITY** (sometimes called **INTER-RATER RELIABILITY**). We do this by *correlating* (see Chapter 12) one observer's data with those of another. Table 5.1 shows a very good correlation between observer 1's and observer 2's recording of aggressive acts in participants. Where one is high, the other is high and *vice versa*, except for participant F. The agreement overall is very good, but we might want to see what could have caused this one larger discrepancy.

Table 5.1   Number of aggressive acts recorded in one hour for nine observed participants

	Participant identification								
	A	B	C	D	E	F	G	H	I
Observer 1	3	4	2	7	6	3	7	2	8
Observer 2	3	3	3	8	6	6	6	1	8

Disclosed and undisclosed observation

We have hinted already that there are major differences between studies where participants are aware of being observed and where they are not. Nothing new is really introduced here. Chapter 3 introduced the concept of *demand characteristics* and we should expect that participants, aware of being observed, might try to obtain cues from the research context as to what hypothesis is under investigation, even if this is an everyday setting for them. *Hawthorne effects* were mentioned on p. 50, as were other aspects of participant expectancy. If participants are aware of being observed then any one of these factors might have a significant effect upon our findings. Such effects are often referred to as features of participant *reactivity* – that is, participants react to being studied and this reaction can cloud later interpretations of what really happened. For instance, Brody, Stoneman and Wheatley (1984) found that, under observation, siblings tended to tease each other less, not quarrel so much and to use less threatening behaviour. Gittelsohn *et al.* (1997) studied behaviour in Nepalese households and found that positive health behaviour increased while negative social behaviour decreased in the early days of their investigation. A lesson (now rather dated) in how to avoid these reactive effects was given by Charlesworth and Hartup (1967), who made several visits to a nursery school, played with the children and learned their names. In this way they could become a familiar part of the environment of the children who might then react less to having their behaviour scrutinized by the researchers.

   Where observation is undisclosed, obvious new ethical issues arise, beyond those of seeking informed consent (which obviously is ruled out) and informing participants that they can withdraw their data from the study. As already mentioned above, one way to deal with this issue is to record the behaviour but to ask later for the participant's permission to use the recordings before anyone has looked at them.

3. OBSERVER PARTICIPATION – IN OR OUT?

We have so far given examples where observers watch others from *outside* the social setting. Charlesworth and Hartup (1967), for instance, were visiting researchers; they were not part of the school organization in any way. Some researchers have felt that observing in this way runs the risk that the observers will not appreciate the *context* in which behaviour is produced; they will not know what it is *like* to work under pressure, deal with clients and so on. A strong argument for participant observation is contained in the second quotation from Whyte (1943) in Box 5.2 below about his Chicago study. Some researchers have borrowed the research method of **PARTICIPANT OBSERVATION** from sociology and anthropology. Here the observer in some way joins or works within the group of people being observed. This could be simply as a declared observer who accompanies people in the group about their daily business. It could mean that the observer takes on some role within the organization, for instance as a classroom assistant, so that children behave as normal. It could, however, mean complete and undisclosed participation, as in Rosenhan's (1973) famous study where research assistants presented themselves to several out-patients' departments complaining of hearing voices and noises in their heads. During their subsequent stays in psychiatric wards the other patients often spotted their 'normality' before the doctors. Some were hospitalized for up to 50 days and one 'patient's' discreet observational note-taking was recorded as 'excessive writing behaviour'.

Box 5.1   Give up smoking? – not while I'm in here

Lawn (2004) conducted a participant observation study in a psychiatric hospital with the aim of investigating suspected institutional barriers to patients giving up smoking. She conducted an intensive programme of observations in two separate Australian locations, the second serving as a follow-up in order to attempt to generalize findings from the first institution. Random visits to wards were made, lasting several hours, at which extensive notes were recorded on the spot or soon after. Discussions were held with staff and patients. Observers' own reflective notes were also recorded and several other sources of information added to the overall data collection.

The study was largely a qualitative grounded-theory approach (see p. 96) but quantitative observations were also made of those interactions between participants that involved smoking matters.

Lawn produced a set of fascinating findings, too detailed to outline fully here, but which highlight the central role of smoking to the lives of the patients and to the job roles of the psychiatric staff. Smoking breaks were seen as times for staff and patients to talk more closely and become better acquainted. Cigarettes were often used as instruments to help control difficult behaviour (for the staff) by taking patients for a smoke. Cigarettes were also used by patients as a central form of currency to exchange for food and even sex.

It is difficult to imagine how Lawn could have painted such a complete picture of the role of smoking on a psychiatric ward if she had simply used a preconceived questionnaire or even just interviews. Rather than a fixed interview, Lawn used her participation on the wards to engage in detailed discussions with staff and patients as part of being there, as things happened, rather than simply dropping in for a pre-arranged interview.

One other thing to note from this study is that contemporary investigations described as 'participant observation' are very often, as in this case, more than just observation but can include interviews, structured observations and (though not in this case) administration of questionnaires. Other participant-observation studies are often not much more than a series of semi-structured interviews in the field.

ETHICAL ISSUES IN PARTICIPANT OBSERVATION

The presence of the observer among the people being observed will obviously have an effect quite different from distant observation. The researcher must recognize that their presence may cause people to change their natural behaviour, as is exemplified in the third quotation in Box 5.2 about Whyte's Chicago studies. Where participation is undisclosed there is much the same problem as occurs in any study where people are deceived. In long-lasting participant-observation studies, however, this level of deception is very serious indeed, if only because it goes on for so long. Participants might say things to an imagined group member that they might never have said to an academic observer. In the best studies, researchers would go over all that they wish to publish with each participant before publication. They might also ask the participant for their views, having made them aware of the nature of the research project they unwittingly participated in, and include these in the report. Studies that do not seek final consent for publication run the risk of creating public distrust of the academic community.

Box 5.2   Whyte's (1943) Chicago gang study

White (1943) studied behaviour in a Chicago gang by saying he was writing a book about the area. Here are three quotations, the first two from Whyte after the study and the third from one of the gang members during the study:

I began as a non-participating observer. As I became accepted into the community, I found myself becoming a non-observing participant. *(1943: 321)*

I learned the answers to questions I would not have had the sense to ask if I had been getting my information solely on an interviewing basis. *(1943: 303)*

You've slowed me down plenty since you've been down here. Now, when I do something, I have to think what Bill Whyte would want to know about it and how I can explain it. Before I used to do things by instinct. *(1943: 301)*

SOME PROBLEMS WITH PARTICIPANT OBSERVATION

❑ Apart from the ethical issues involved, the third quotation in Box 5.2 demonstrates that the researcher may well alter the natural behaviour of the people they study. However, Whyte argued that the longer he spent in the group, the less his behaviour had any effect on what would have happened anyway.

❑ The first quotation above, however, shows just how much the objectivity and impartiality of a scientific observer can be compromised by being so close to and involved in people's lives.

❑ Participant observers, especially if undisclosed, might have problems taking notes. Some use subterfuge, as when Whyte took on the role of secretary to the Italian Community Club. However, very often researchers will rely on memory for an account of the day's happenings and your study of memory will have told you that recall of recent events is affected by many subtle factors. Besides, the researcher is the only witness to the event and so there is no possibility of a reliability check.

PROGRESS REVIEW 5.2

EXERCISES

1. Outline a research study using observation that could be used to investigate the following hypotheses:
   (a) During exploratory play, mothers permit their sons to venture further away from them than they do their daughters
   (b) In lifts, people try to stand as far as possible from other unfamiliar people
   (c) Women are safer drivers than men.
   In each case ensure that you operationalize variables and describe the exact method of data gathering, including sampling method, location, equipment and scoring system.
2. What are the advantages and disadvantages of structured observation?
3. A student decides to study her own student group using participant observation. She is interested in how her classmates cope with study demands, exam revision and social commitments. Discuss the ways in which she might organize the study, gather data and deal with any likely difficulties along the way.
4. A researcher obtains the results shown in the table below from two observers. Comment on the level of interobserver reliability that is shown.

Number of aggressive acts recorded for child X in *k*th 5-minute interval

	5-minute interval									
	1st	**2nd**	**3rd**	**4th**	**5th**	**6th**	**7th**	**8th**	**9th**	**10th**
Observer A	1	3	4	2	5	12	9	4	8	9
Observer B	2	10	8	7	1	3	5	5	6	13

ANSWERS

Questions 1 and 3 are open.

2. **Advantages**: can check observations for reliability; can replicate studies objectively. **Disadvantages**: coding forces narrow definition of some observed behaviours; reactivity if people know they are being observed.

4. This is not good interobserver reliability, as you can see from the wide variation for the two observers in several of the five-minute intervals. In each interval we would expect them each to record almost the same number of aggressive acts if they are well trained and using the coding system consistently. We can take a measure of their agreement using *correlation* – see Chapter 12.

KEY TERMS

Coding system	Participant observation
Event sampling	Point sampling
Inter-observer reliability	Systematic observation
Inter-rater reliability	Time sampling
Observer bias	

chapter
6

Asking questions – questionnaires, scales, interviews and surveys

What's in this chapter?

❑ This chapter is all about gathering data by asking questions. We will look first at questionnaires, and the main points will be:
- The variables psychologists try to measure with *questionnaires* and *scales*. 'Scale' is the preferred term for 'questionnaires' used to measure a variable.
- The types of *item* that are used in scales and how to create good, fair items.
- The general principles of questionnaire construction – how to get the best data from them without alienating the respondent.
- The various types of scale: *Likert, semantic differential* and *visual analogue*.
- The need for scales, like any measure, to be *reliable* and *valid*. We will investigate ways to establish *reliability* and *validity* and we will also look at the topic of scale *standardization.*

❑ Finally we will look at the processes and issues involved in *interviewing* and in running a *survey. Semi-structured* and more *formal* interviews are discussed.

PSYCHOLOGICAL SCALES AND QUESTIONNAIRES

We have looked at experimenting with people and we have looked at observing them. One obvious way to find out what people do and think is to approach them directly and ask them for information.

> Who do these psychologists think they are, trying to force people into categories and scales – we are all individuals!

Whenever I talk about psychological scales I sense people stiffening up and saying to themselves – 'This is the bit I hate …' and continuing as in the statement in the box above. Well, let's get one myth out of the way – taking measures of people does *not* stop anyone from treating other individuals as unique. Take height – everyone differs on that but some people will be the same height. Let's add weight – some people will have the same weight and height but there will be far fewer than those who simply share the same height. Now let's add in coursework marks for GCSE Maths … oh and perhaps number of close relatives called Heather, number of dogs owned and favourite colour. With just a few measures we can probably identify a very rare, if not unique, individual.

Everybody uses measures of people. Consider this comment:

> James is a big talker at home but he does become very inhibited in school with his friends.

This mother has done some rule of thumb measurement. She assesses James's talking against some standard at home (other siblings? outside the home? compared with his parents?) and then she uses a more general concept of 'inhibition'. If James is 'very inhibited' his mother *must* have some way of comparing him with others or with his behaviour at home. We could ask for her criteria and she might say 'Well, he talks less, his eye-contact is low and he does things very slowly'. Like it or not, notice it or not, we are constantly assessing people and this is hardly possible without comparing them with others.

There are two main approaches we can use to take measures of people's behaviour – we can observe them or we can ask them questions. We dealt with observation in Chapter 5; in this chapter we are dealing with ways to question. One of the most common ways to attempt to measure a psychological variable is to create a so-called **QUESTIONNAIRE**. This measure is defined in Box 6.1. Very often, what is used in psychological measurement is *not* a list of questions but a set of *statements*, comprising a **PSYCHOLOGICAL SCALE**, to which the participant responds using a level of agreement or disagreement. A **RESPONDENT** is a person who responds to a questionnaire or scale.

TYPES OF QUESTION OR SCALE ITEM – OPEN OR FIXED

❑ **OPEN-ENDED ITEMS**: an item such as 'Tell me what you think about cloning human beings' will produce an unpredictable amount of free human speech. This is an example of gathering *qualitative data* – see Chapter 7. This dataset could be left as it is or could be quantified using *content analysis* – also in Chapter 7. However, the value is in the richness of information produced and in the fact that the respondent does not feel constrained by having to give one of a set of fixed responses. We rarely have to only agree or disagree. However, open-ended answers from one individual are harder to compare with those from another individual than are closed or fixed-choice answers.

❑ **CLOSED ITEMS**: these are familiar items that ask us to give a specific answer. If this is within a range of choices we might call these *fixed-choice* or *multiple-choice* items. For example:

> I would describe myself as: (a) introverted
> (b) sometimes introverted/sometimes extroverted
> (c) extroverted

or

> Boxing is a barbaric sport
> Strongly disagree   Disagree   Undecided   Agree   Strongly agree

Other examples of closed items are:

On a scale of 1 (= strongly disapprove) to 10 (= strongly approve) please indicate your position on banning smoking in bars and pubs.

I am often nervous in public places   YES/NO

At what age did your baby start crawling: … months

From all these kinds of question it is possible to *quantify* data and therefore to produce summary statistics, make comparisons and test hypotheses in a numerical manner.

Box 6.1   Types of scale and questionnaire used in psychology

Questionnaire
Used correctly, a questionnaire asks questions, whereas most psychological scales do not. Usually used in *surveys* (see below) to gather information about people's lifestyles, habits, opinions on a current or specific issue, leisure activities, moral principles, child discipline techniques, voting behaviour and so on.

Attitude scale
This assesses relatively permanent and habitual responses of the individual rather than just an opinion. A typical example would be a measure of one's 'conservatism' in life. 'Conservatism' might comprise: the tendency to believe in strict adherence to dress codes, to favour punishment over rehabilitation for criminals, and not to take risks. Scales usually use *statements* (not questions) to which the respondent provides their level of agreement – as is explained below.

Psychometric tests
These are thought of as 'mental measures' and include the much-maligned IQ (intelligence quotient) test, along with measures of personality, creative thinking, linguistic ability, logical reasoning and so on. One can distinguish here between tests of:

Personality trait:	what you are normally like most of the time
Personality state:	what you are like right now, e.g. your current state of anxiety
Ability:	what you are generally able to do, for instance, your numeracy skill
Achievement	what you have achieved so far, e.g. your performance in a college test
Aptitude	your *potential* performance, for instance, a general logic test that is used to assess your likely success in computer programming.

QUESTIONNAIRES ARE DANGEROUS!

Questionnaires are ubiquitous; we meet them everywhere – on cereal packets, in the high street, posted through our doors, on television and even thrust into our hands by tutors at the end of a module or course! We seem to be asked constantly to evaluate the service we have just received or to be quizzed by one authority or another. When students create a questionnaire they often mimic what they have encountered, but without thinking ahead to the use that is to be made of the data collected. Hence I can think of at least two good reasons for my dramatic heading. Questionnaires are dangerous because:

1. They give the impression of being scientific in collecting data.
2. They can lead to trouble for students when completing practical assignments.

> Try now, with a student colleague or on your own, to jot down briefly what you would ask in a questionnaire designed to assess people's attitude to fox hunting.

The danger for students in using a questionnaire in an assignment is that it is so easy to create questions but very difficult to look ahead to what will be done with the data that is collected. A poor questionnaire collects poor data, which may be exceedingly difficult to analyse. Now let's see whether you have already fallen into any of the traps that await the unwary questionnaire designer.

ONLY ASK FOR WHAT YOU NEED

When creating a questionnaire, people often feel the need to ask several questions about, for instance, the respondent's age, sex, occupation, employment status, domicile etc. Why would you want this? You would need this information *only* if your research question concerned one or more of these aspects. For instance, you might want to know whether males differ from females or whether employed people differ from unemployed people. If you do *not* intend to analyse according to those features then you do not need the data. ***Always ask only for what you need.***

CATEGORY-ITIS

Some people feel a great need to categorize, so instead of asking people their age they present a series of boxes labelled '25–30', 31–35' etc. *Why?* Some argue that people don't like to give their exact age but, if your categories are shaped in 5-year blocks, the amount of shyness or embarrassment you can avoid by using them is probably minimal. Notice that if you *are* going to use categories *they must not overlap.* How is the 40-year-old to respond to the age scale shown in Figure 6.1, for instance?

Figure 6.1   Part of a typical questionnaire

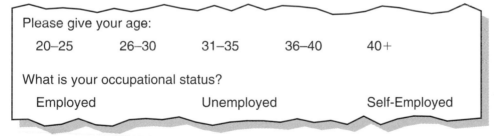

Please give your age:

  20–25   26–30   31–35   36–40   40+

What is your occupational status?

  Employed   Unemployed   Self-Employed

The reason for preferring age to be given as number of years and not as a category is to do with statistical analysis, and we haven't got to that point in the book yet – but you probably aren't reading it cover to cover anyway. On p. 105 we discuss *levels of measurement*. If we reduce age to categories we get what is called, surprise surprise, a *categorical variable*. Most of the time we would much prefer a *measured variable*. This is because we can usually perform more sophisticated and meaningful statistical analyses on measured variables. A measured variable is one for which you can obtain a *score* that locates your participant between other people, such as a maths mark or their height. When we use a categorical variable we end up with a *count* of people in the various categories. Examples of category variables are given in the box below.

Typical category variables

- ❏ Type of dwelling (house, bungalow, terrace etc.)
- ❏ Marital status (single, married etc.)
- ❏ Car owner (yes/no)
- ❏ Education level reached (A Level, Degree etc.)

As an example of the difficulty caused by categorical variables, imagine you had three respondents to the age question in the example in Figure 6.1. How would you find their average age? You have to assume that each is in the middle of the category they ticked, which is probably not the case. Otherwise you just can't compute the average at all.

INCOMPLETE CATEGORY SETS

A further problem with categories is leaving the set incomplete. Take a look at the second item in Figure 6.1. What do you tick if you are a mother at home, or a pensioner or even a full-time student? These categories have not been provided. The only way out in such cases is to provide another option 'Other' with 'Please specify …'. However, you then have the problem of what to do with the data given for this option. You can create new categories *post hoc* (after the event), but better to have thought through the categories in the first place. In some cases, your respondents could find omission of their own categories quite annoying.

DO NOT ASK WHAT IS IMPOSSIBLE TO ANSWER

I have often reviewed draft questionnaires for which I would do anything to avoid having to be a respondent. What do you respond to items such as:

In the past year how many times have you felt rather low?

How many hours do you relax per week?

How many times a month do you feel happy?

In the past two years how many times have you visited a doctor?

I have seen all these, and much worse, in draft questionnaires and even in questionnaires being used by students for an assignment project. For the very fit and healthy, of course, it is easy to recall number of visits to the doctor but who could seriously give a sensible estimate to the number of times they feel low in a year? Because they ask for a number, some of these questions can appear 'scientific' but the degree of precision in the numerical answers to at least the first three items above just has to be very questionable!

INVASION OF PRIVACY

Questions such as 'Do you have a criminal record?' or 'Have you ever suffered from a mental illness?' simply should not be asked by students, of course, and most examination boards make this very clear. If you are uncertain about this then have a look at Chapter 13 where we discuss ethical issues and procedures.

EXERCISES

1. Do questionnaires contain questions?
2. What are the advantages of closed questions or items?
3. What is wrong with the following questionnaire items?
   (a) How many cigarettes a day do you smoke?
       (i) 0–10, (ii) 10–20, (iii) 20–30, (iv) 30–40, (v) >40
   (b) What was your highest educational level reached?
       (i) GCSE, (ii) AS Level, (iii) A2 Level, (iv) Degree.
4. How many dreams do you have on average per month?

ANSWERS

1. Sounds a silly question if you weren't concentrating earlier on. Many so-called 'questionnaires' do not contain questions, they contain *items* that is, statements with which respondents are asked to show their level of agreement. This gives greater opportunity for scales to produce subtle distinctions along a measurement dimension and also means respondents do not have to be forced into a yes or no answer.
2. Mainly that answers can be counted or treated as numerical scores and hence we can analyse them statistically.
3. (a) Apart from the constant overlap (what do you answer if you smoke exactly 10 or 20 per day?), we have the problem of where to put all the many people who just don't smoke (it is odd to group non-smokers with those smoking 1 to 9 a day). There is also the slightly picky issue of whether or not respondents will all be able to interpret the '>' symbol.
    (b) There are levels higher than a first degree (e.g. Masters), and what happens if your respondent is from Scotland, let alone from abroad?
4. Can you seriously ask anyone to report accurately on this?

KEY TERMS

Open and closed questions/items   **Respondent**
Psychological scale   **Scale item**
Questionnaire

PSYCHOLOGICAL SCALES

The construction of psychological scales or 'tests' as measures of attitude, personality, intelligence and so on (see Box 6.1) is known as the practice of **PSYCHOMETRICS** or simply *psychometry*. The tests are called **PSYCHOMETRIC TESTS**. Those who like to think that psychology approaches the status of a true science refer to such scales as 'instruments'. For instance, if a scientist uses a technical measure of a metal's resistance to electrical current, it is assumed that all metals are tested under similar conditions and that the measure produced is a standard one understood by scientists worldwide. Attempts are made to treat psychological instruments in the same way. Hence all respondents should be tested in similar circumstances, under the same set of instructions and any score achieved should relate to a scale that all psychologists understand and agree with. However, for psychology, the ramifications of these requirements are far-reaching and just not as simple as they are for people testing inanimate objects such as metal. We shall discuss the problems later. First, we will look at several kinds of popular scale that you might use in a practical assignment.

WHY DO PSYCHOLOGICAL SCALES HAVE SEVERAL ITEMS?

It is assumed that a complex psychological construct, such as anxiety, has many aspects to it. It is also assumed that if we make several measures of it from slightly differing angles we will get a better picture of the construct as a whole. Hence each item in a *unitary* psychological scale is intended to measure the same construct, but perhaps only one aspect of it. By a *unitary* scale we mean that the scale is intended to measure *one* construct, e.g. *anxiety* or *stress* or *self-confidence*. Many scales have several *sub-scales* and each of these measures, theoretically, a single construct.

THE LIKERT-TYPE ATTITUDE SCALE

This kind of scale, originally produced by Likert (1932), is probably quite familiar and is certainly a favourite for student practicals. To produce a **LIKERT SCALE**:

1. Produce an equal number of favourable ('positive') and unfavourable ('negative') statements about the attitude object – see Box 6.2. The reason we have positives and negatives is to avoid **RESPONSE SET** — which is a possible source of bias for two reasons. People usually find it easier to say 'yes' than 'no'. In addition, if we are always answering in the same direction, whichever way we answer, then this can *strengthen* our tendency to do so again on the next item, *whatever* it might be. We may stop thinking very carefully and just answer automatically because all answers have been 'no' up to that point.
2. Ask respondents to indicate, for each item, their response to the statement according to the following scale:

1	2	3	4	5
Strongly disagree	Disagree	Undecided	Agree	Strongly agree

3. Whatever the scale, make sure that a high score means a *lot* of whatever the scale is intended to measure; I can't state this strongly enough in terms of avoiding confusingly low scores for high amounts. For instance, if the scale measures 'Attitude to physical punishment' then a high score means strongly in favour. However, and equally, if the score measures 'Caring' or 'Insecurity' make sure that a high score means high caring or insecurity. Even though you expect those who are high on approval of physical punishment to be low in caring do not be tempted to make a low score mean high caring. Just do it – you'll be grateful, I assure you!
4. In order to make a high score mean high we must reverse the scoring on half the items. This is where the instruction in step 3 first starts to make sense. We want people to get a high score if they agree with physical punishment. Hence they should get a high score on all items that are in favour, such as item 2 in Box 6.2. However, we *also* want them to get a high score on item 1 if they strongly *dis*agree with it. Hence we turn the '1' on that item into a '5'. In general, on this particular scale we would reverse the scoring on all items that are *not* in favour of physical punishment. Try this and see what would happen to someone who really *disagreed* with physical punishment.
5. Having reversed all appropriate scores, add up each person's final score on each item. The total is their attitude score.

Box 6.2   Sample items from a Likert-type scale

> 1. Children should never be hit for any reason.
> 2. Children need some physical punishment early on to keep them from danger.

If you had just invented a scale such as this, with perhaps 15 to 20 items, you would now want to test its *reliability* and *validity*. These concepts and ways to test them are discussed on pp. 80–5. To test internal reliability you would want to pick out those items where people's answers are not consistent with their scoring on all other items. For instance, an item such as 'Children are often hit when parents have lost control' might generate agreement by those both high *and* low overall on physical-punishment attitude. This might be because those who agree with hitting feel that they only do so when *in* control themselves. Such an item is not useful in the scale since it does not *discriminate* between believers and non-believers.

THE SEMANTIC DIFFERENTIAL

Osgood, Suci and Tannenbaum (1957) originally intended this scale to measure the *connotative* meaning of an object for each individual. This is the associations that the term has for us rather than its dictionary definition (its *denotative* meaning). For instance, whereas I can define a baby as a very young human infant, the *connotation* of 'baby' for me might be warm, cute, eager to learn; for someone else it might (also or only) be sleepless nights, expense, limitation of freedom.

The respondent given a semantic-differential scale is asked to mark a seven-point scale between several sets of two bipolar opposite terms. For baby I might mark:

Good	✓	—	—	—	—	—	—	Bad
Weak	—	—	—	✓	—	—	—	Strong
Active	—	✓	—	—	—	—	—	Passive

and so on. An analysis of responses to scales such as these caused Osgood *et al.* to propose that, no matter what the object, three overall factors of attitude emerged with which all bi-polar pairs could be associated. These were:

ACTIVITY   included opposites such as ACTIVE/PASSIVE, SLOW/FAST and HOT/COLD
POTENCY   included opposites such as RUGGED/DELICATE, THICK/THIN
EVALUATIVE   included opposites such as CLEAN/DIRTY, PLEASANT/UNPLEASANT

THE VISUAL ANALOGUE SCALE

Look back to page 73 and you'll see that I expressed a concern about the tendency to assess variables in *categories*. For instance, we might find a scale of categories such as:

> To what extent do you feel the victim was responsible for the crime inflicted upon her?
>
> Not at all responsible   Slightly responsible   Quite responsible   Very responsible

Here we find that we can group participants only according to the option they chose. One popular way to get around the need for a category measure is to use a **VISUAL ANALOGUE SCALE** (VIS). Here is an example:

> To what extent do you feel the victim was responsible for the crime inflicted upon her?
>
> Not at all responsible I_____I Very responsible

Instead of asking participants to check a box they are asked to mark a point along the scale to indicate their position. This is then measured and the variable is expressed as a distance. Some examples of VIS have wording at the mid-point or even at several points along the line. Of course, you're going to say 'Well, how do we know that *your* 2 cm. along the scale is the same as *my* 2 cm?', and you have a point – the scale is *subjective* – but at least we do have a measure that is not a category expressed in a form of words *forced* onto the respondent. We can at least use a VIS to indicate improvement or change within the same individual (e.g. before and after treatment or, in the example just given, after reading different types of crime scenario).

TYPES OF ITEMS IN PSYCHOLOGICAL SCALES

If you are going to construct a Likert or similar type of scale that uses statements, there are several common pitfalls to be avoided. Take a look a the potential items in the box below.

Problematical scale items

1. Where prisoners have shown the potential for rehabilitation they should be admitted to centres for social-skills training unless they have recently broken regulations or otherwise produced negative or aggressive behaviour and have not exhibited regret.
2. Objecting to children eating with their fingers is ethnocentric.
3. Immigrants should not be allowed to settle in areas of high unemployment.
4. Boxers earn a lot of money.
5. Benefit cheats should serve prison sentences and pay back what they have been given by the state.
6. It should not be possible to avoid taxation and not be punished for it.
7. The present Labour government is callously dismembering the National Health Service.
8. Don't you think student fees should be abolished?
9. When do you smack your children?

The problems

1. *Complexity:* this item is far too long and detailed, challenging the attention span and probably requiring a couple of reads in order to answer it sensibly. Simplify it and/or use several items instead of one.
2. *Technical terms and jargon:* always use terms that you *know* your respondents will understand. Will they know what *ethnocentrism* is? If the term must be used then provide an explanation in a preamble.
3. *Ambiguity:* this item was actually produced by students of mine some years ago. It was intended to be a statement that those with anti-immigrant attitudes would agree to. However, many pro-

immigrant or, rather, caring respondents agreed with it too. They had in mind the fact that immigrants might find it hard to get jobs in such areas.

4. **Factual items:** this is really another form of ambiguous item. Boxers *do* (or at least can) earn a lot of money. This is indisputable, and both pro-boxing and anti-boxing respondents will agree with it. Hence it is useless for measuring attitudes to boxing.

5. **Double-barrelled items:** suppose your respondent wants to agree with the return of money but not with the prison sentence? This item asks two questions in one and could be made into two separate items.

6. **Double negatives:** this item contains two negatives. Statements such as this can be very confusing, requiring unnecessary thought and checking on the part of the respondent. It could be reworded as: 'Tax avoidance should always be punished'. We saw above that it is a good idea to have half the statements in a scale positive and the other half negative on the issue or object in question. When students discover this in the middle of a scale-creation exercise they are sometimes tempted simply to insert the word 'not' into previously positive items. See how this can lose the intended meaning and end up sounding quite odd:

   Original: 'Children should be brought up lovingly, without being hit'.
   Reverse form: 'Children should not be brought up lovingly without being hit'.

7. **Emotive language:** a statement such as this may not get an attitude test off to a good start, particularly in 'New Labour' constituencies. If there are any emotive items, it might be best to leave these until the respondent is feeling more relaxed with the interviewer or with the test itself.

8 and 9. **Leading questions:** it is unlikely that question 8 would be asked but it is a leading question because it guides the respondent towards an obviously desired answer. Item 9 is also leading because it assumes that the respondent does indeed smack their children (unless a 'never' option is provided).

PROGRESS REVIEW 6.2

EXERCISES

1. What flaws can you see in the following scale items?
   (a) Do you feel that the monarchy should be abolished?
   (b) What do you think is the best way to punish children?
   (c) On how many days have you whistled in the last month?
   (d) People from other countries are the same as us and should be treated with respect.
   (e) There should not be laws stating that dogs should not be allowed off their leads.
   (f) Women are now getting top managerial jobs.
   (g) Tomorrow's sex-role models should be more androgynous.

2. Imagine the items below are a small part of a scale developed by some students to measure 'assertiveness'. What problem can you see?
   (a) ...
   (b) Do you take things straight back to the shop when you find a fault?
   (c) On a scale of 1 to 10, how loudly would you say you speak to shop assistants compared with how loudly other people speak?
   (d) ...

ANSWERS

1.   (a) Leading; invites agreement
     (b) Leading; assumes respondent agrees with punishing children
     (c) Probably difficult for many people to make an accurate estimate
     (d) Double-barrelled; respondent may agree that foreign people should be treated with respect but not that we are all the same
     (e) Double negative; difficult to follow
     (f) Fact; agreement with this fact does not necessarily indicate direction of attitude towards women and/or equal opportunity
     (g) Technical term; respondent may not understand the term 'androgynous'.
2. Items in a scale designed to measure one psychological construct must be of the same type; we cannot mix and match items like this because there would be no sensible way to add up the person's score on the scale.

KEY TERMS

Likert scale	Response set
Psychometric test	Semantic differential
Psychometrics	Visual analogue scale

RELIABILITY, VALIDITY AND STANDARDIZATION OF SCALES

Suppose you were in the unfortunate position of having to give a statement to the police accounting for your whereabouts one Saturday night. There are two ways in which your statement could be *unreliable*. You might contradict yourself *within* the statement or you might make a second statement some days later that conflicts with your first.

When we talk about the **RELIABILITY** of a psychological measure or scale we are talking about its *consistency* in a similar way. The two questions we can ask about consistency are:

1. **INTERNAL:** is the scale consistent within itself? Do the items relate to one another?
2. **EXTERNAL** (otherwise known as **STABILITY**): do scores on the test vary from one test occasion to another?

INTERNAL RELIABILITY

Internal reliability can be checked using several methods. Basically we are looking to see whether people tend to score the same on some items in the test as they do on the other items.

Split-half reliability

The items on the scale can be split into two halves, either by taking odd- and even-numbered items as two different sets or by creating two sets by random selection. If the test is reliable then people's scores on one half should *correlate* (see Chapter 12) with scores on the other half. That is, if a person scores high on one half they should also score high on the other and *vice versa* – see Figure 6.2a.

Figure 6.2   Split-half and test-retest reliability

Figure 6.2   Split-half and test-retest reliability

Internal reliability

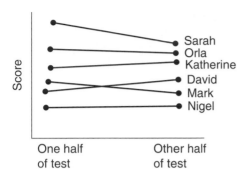

External reliability

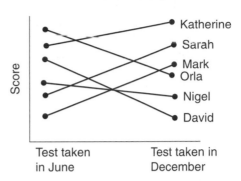

a. Good split-half reliability   b. Poor test-retest reliability

Item analysis

For a good psychological scale we want items that *discriminate* between people who are high and low on the measure. There are various methods of **ITEM ANALYSIS**, which generally compare scores on each individual item with scores on the scale overall. Poor discriminatory items are removed and thus the scale's reliability is improved. There are two problems with this. First, it is a *bootstrap operation*. We use scores on the original scale overall as a criterion for ditching poor items. But if the scale is quite unreliable to *start with* how can it be used as the comparison for poor items? The whole process is circular but is generally accepted. The second, strongly related, problem is that making a scale very reliable may well interfere with the scale's *validity* – a concept we consider in the next section. The validity of a scale is the extent to which it measures what it was supposed to measure. Tampering with reliability by taking out items may have a knock-on effect on what the scale eventually measures.

Most methods of item analysis require complex statistical programmes and are too sophisticated for this book. However, a simple and crude way to detect weak items is to do the following:

1. Select the respondents with the top 15% and the lowest 15% of scores overall.
2. For each *item* in the scale, add up what these two groups scored on that item.
3. If the two totals are close then the item does not discriminate well between the two extreme groups. Hence remove from your scale those items where you feel the two totals are too close (or simply remove a pre-determined number – say 10 out of 30 – keeping the better items).

When researchers construct formal scales they *pilot* a large number of items then perform an item analysis. They then go out again (and again …) to try the reduced set of items on another fair-sized sample of people. This is done until the scale produces highly consistent results and has also been checked for some form of *validity*, a concept that we will turn to next. Although student practicals cannot approach this level of development for attitude (or similar) scales, it is nevertheless a good idea to try out your items on at least a few people in order to spot troublesome or ambiguous items or those that are too similar to others and add nothing extra to the scale. It is also possible to conduct an item analysis after data gathering and to use *only* the items that were highest on discrimination; you would find participants' scores *only* on these items and refer to this as your overall scale score.

EXTERNAL RELIABILITY

This refers to the need for a scale to remain stable over time. We test for this using a measure of what is known as **TEST-RETEST RELIABILITY**. We simply take a group of people's scores on the test at time A and then test the *same* group some time later, perhaps after several weeks or months (see Figure 6.2b). Many students think that the second group tested should be a *different* group but this is mistaken; if we want to know if the *same* scores are obtained on *different* occasions this must be done with the *same* group of respondents.

VALIDITY

The **VALIDITY** of a scale refers simply to the issue of *whether that scale measures what it is meant to measure.* Remember in Chapter 3 we said that the validity of an experimental effect was whether or not it was the effect it appeared to be? This is similar. Suppose I had an impressive-looking instrument that I claimed was capable of measuring physical attraction. When you stand next to a particular person we switch on the machine and the dial needle passes several points from 'ughh!' through 'hmm, not bad' and 'fancy a little' to 'drop-dead gorgeous', indicating your degree of approval. In actual fact, being a charlatan, all I have is a simple blood-pressure monitoring device. If you had done hard physical exercise or if you were under sudden stress the dial would also rise through the same passion points. My measure would not be a valid one: it measures blood pressure, not level of attraction to another.

Figure 6.3   Perhaps not a very valid measure of attitude to textbook authors!

The blood pressure example may sound daft but it is questionable whether many measures that are used in psychology do 'what it says on the can'. A quickly-devised scale intended to measure 'extroversion' may in fact measure something more like 'sociability' (contrary to popular belief, these are not the same thing). There are many approaches to assessing the validity of a psychological scale or test and here are just a few.

Face validity

FACE VALIDITY concerns the superficial appearance of the test. A test of typing skills that comprises measurements of speed and accuracy clearly tests what it says it does, from both the researcher's and test-taker's points of view. Although this seems an obvious point, some measures, such as those known as **PROJECTIVE TESTS**, cannot have face validity. This is because they are based on the Freudian theory of projection, the idea being that faced with ambiguous stimuli (such as a blob of ink or an ambiguous picture) we will 'project' our poorly-guarded inner conflicts onto them and 'give away' feelings and anxieties that we are trying to keep hidden. Researchers using this type of test would *not* want participants (or their clients, if they are practising clinical psychology or therapy) to see exactly what the test was aiming at.

Figure 6.4   The type of item used in the Thematic Aperception Test – a type of projective test

Content validity

CONTENT VALIDITY is established by ensuring that a test includes a *representative sample* of the domain being tested. A test containing only addition and multiplication sums would be a poor test of general adult *mathematical ability* because this construct covers a lot more than just adding and multiplication. To establish content validity we need to ensure that all significant areas of mathematical skill are sampled by the test. For this kind of test, content validity might not be so hard to establish because an expert in mathematics should be able to tell us when skills and competences have been adequately sampled. For scales that are intended to measure more complex psychological constructs, such as *self-esteem*, *dependence* or *anxiety*, we would need to make a more thorough investigation of the concepts involved by consulting experts, researching literature, studying past attempts to measure the construct and so on. In the same way, a teacher would prepare an examination that covered all aspects and was not unduly weighted to any particular one.

Criterion validity

CRITERION VALIDITY refers to the extent to which a test of, say, anxiety can produce outcomes. If it produces the same kinds of outcome as do other related or similar tests then it is said to have **CONCURRENT VALIDITY**. For instance, a new test of anxiety should produce much the same scores among a group of people as did a previous test of anxiety. We would not expect scores to be *exactly* the same for each person on both tests because the researchers developing the scale might already have decided that the previous one was flawed. However, we would expect some degree of similarity and might also be able to show where and how the new test does a better job than the older one. **PREDICTIVE VALIDITY** is being able to make predictions on the basis of test scores. If predictions are confirmed then this adds to the test's validity. For instance, we might expect that children who score highly on a test of mathematical ability at age 10 years would be more likely to score well in maths exams at age 15, go on to study maths at a higher level, take up careers where mathematical competence is required and so on. In science a prediction does not necessarily mean an estimate of what will happen in the relatively distant future. Concurrent validity can therefore be seen as a form of predictive validity because all we really do is predict that the new scale will correlate quite closely with the old scale. The predictions made in scientific thinking are about what variable will be found to be associated with what other variables.

Construct validity

CONSTRUCT VALIDITY is an altogether different concept from those we have just covered. In its broadest sense this form of validation involves the whole process of putting forward a theoretical construct in psychology. Psychological research is littered with unseen variables such as 'locus of control', 'ego-strength' or 'dependency'. In order for other psychologists to take these seriously, each construct must be seen, preferably, to follow logically from developed theory, to predict relationships between other variables, to explain a network of findings already published and, finally, to be unique in the sense that no other variable or set of variables will suffice to explain all these phenomena. In physical science, 'gravitational force' or 'quark' are constructs that were validated by being thoroughly researched, are seen as pretty well necessary to explain all observed phenomena and are useful in predicting many more. Many psychologists (but not all – see Chapter 7) aspire to run the same kind of science and therefore to validate their constructs with the same kinds of scientific process.

Rotter's (1966) 'locus of control' (loc) construct was originally developed out of behaviourist reinforcement theory concerned with the ways in which people understand the reinforcements they receive. Loc is a measure of the extent to which we see our behaviour as largely the result of our own decisions and effort (internal loc) or as the result of external forces such as 'fate' and luck (external loc). The construct fits in very well with more cognitive theories of (self-) attribution, relates to many other variables and has been used constructively in probably thousands of research studies since it was developed. For construct validity to be established we look not only at what the construct *does* relate to but also at what it does not, and theoretically *should not*, relate to. Theoretically it makes sense that internal loc would relate positively to constructs such as self-esteem or ambition and *negatively* to constructs such as depression or helplessness. That is, the more internally a person views their locus of control, the less depressed or helpless they would feel. Findings such as these have been demonstrated many times over but it has *also* been found that loc usually relates little at all to constructs such as extroversion, e.g. Shriberg (1972). All these relationships, the replications of findings and the ability of loc theory to predict new findings lead to greater construct validity for the construct of locus of control.

STANDARDIZATION OF PSYCHOLOGICAL SCALES

STANDARDIZATION of a scale involves adjusting it, using reliability and validity tests to eliminate items, until it is useful as a measure of the population at which it is targeted, and will enable us to compare individuals fairly and with confidence. To make such comparisons, the test must be used on a large sample of the target population, from whom standard scores and means (see Chapter 8) are established. Tests and scales are usually adjusted until the scores from the large sample form a near-enough normal distribution – see p. 127 (a bell-shaped curve). From this it is possible to establish the overall average of various groups of interest, and the extent of variation around this average. From a large representative sample we can estimate the percentage of people who score between different points on the measurement scale.

Psychometric tests are used in research but also on an applied basis in decisions about people's life chances and opportunities with respect to education, job selection and so on. Therefore it is of the utmost importance that these tests do not discriminate, in a particular way, against some groups of people (a property that anyway would reduce their scientific value). Standardization has, therefore, both ethical and scientific importance.

One centrally important point about the standardization process is that scales can only be used with confidence on samples from the same or similar populations to that on which the test was originally standardized. For instance, we cannot assume that locus of control is a universal construct. That is, we cannot assume that the loc test, properly translated, will produce scores from people where the test was developed that will be comparable with scores from people in a completely different culture. This is the issue of *population validity* that we mentioned briefly in Chapter 3. Several researchers have found that for some cultures Rotter's scale produces two different dimensions (or even more), one dealing with *personal* control over everyday events and the other with control over wider social and political events (e.g. Smith, Trompenaars and Dugan, 1995).

PROGRESS REVIEW 6.3

EXERCISES

1. A student friend has devised a test of 'Attitude towards the British', which she wants to administer to a group of overseas students about to leave the country. (a) Could this test be tested for reliability? (b) How could the test be validated?
2. A friend says 'My dog loves Beethoven. Every time I play some he comes and curls up on my lap'. Is this a reliable test, a valid test or neither?
3. Another friend says 'I did a test while I was visiting that college in the States and I came out very low on "individualism" and "sociability". I wonder what that means?'. Comment on the friend's thoughts.

ANSWERS

1. (a) Yes but only internally. (b) Perhaps by comparing with scores on strength of desire to return; could also use separate interviews with the students and compare.
2. Reliable but not necessarily valid!
3. She is comparing herself with norms for an American student population. These two variables are ones for which we might well, given previous research, expect US students to have a higher mean. She is forgetting the issue of test standardization and cultural equivalence.

KEY TERMS

Projective tests	**Validity**
Reliability	Face
Internal	Content
Split-half	Criterion
Item analysis	Concurrent
External	Predictive
Standardization	Construct

INTERVIEWS

We looked above at the construction and content of questionnaires. A psychological research study might involve only the administration of scales or questionnaires and the psychologist need not necessarily come into contact with any of the respondents. The questionnaires could be distributed via health centres or by post, for example. However, when interviews are used to gather data there must be some *direct contact* between interviewer and interviewee; but again this need not necessarily occur face-to-face, though mostly it does. Interviews involve some kind of direct contact between research staff and participant and are designed to gather data through some form of questioning process.

Box 6.3   Comparison of interview methods with the use of questionnaires

One of the obvious differences between an interview-based study and one based on questionnaires is the effect of interpersonal variables in the interview situation that could affect the authenticity of the interviewee's behaviour. Participants might be tempted to 'look good' (be socially desirable) and may be affected in several other ways by the presence of a 'live' interviewer. Try to think of what some of these other factors might be.

❏ **Gender.** Research supports the suggestion that people respond more positively to interviewers of the opposite sex (Rosnow and Rosenthal, 1997). Interviewer sex interacts with interviewee sex. Wilson *et al*. (2002) found that Californian Latino men reported having fewer sexual encounters and partners to female rather than male interviewers.

❏ **Ethnicity.** Research suggests that interviewees who are members of an ethnic group different from that of the interviewer react more formally (Zanna and Cooper, 1974). It has also been found that interviewers rate interviewees more positively if they are from the same ethnic group (Awosunle and Doyle, 2001).

❏ **Formal roles.** No matter how relaxed the interviewer, he or she is an important figure to most interviewees, who may react accordingly and perhaps, for instance, search for more 'correct' language.

❏ **Personality.** The 'chemistry' between the two people may be constructive or detrimental to the production of authentic and complete research data.

❏ **Evaluative cues.** In a research setting, people will often want to know what kind of response is required (to be a 'good' participant). Interviewers therefore need to avoid reactions that sound critical or not quite satisfied with an answer.

On the other hand, there are some clear advantages in using most types of interview. However, the points made here should be reviewed in the light of the varying types of interview procedure described below. In general, a 'live' interviewer is able to correct any misconceptions that respondents might have of the questions asked; this is not the case for most settings where questionnaires are used. They can rephrase questions and give examples. They can make respondents more at ease and reassure them that they are doing a good job. On occasion they can include as data information which they had not expected to acquire, especially in qualitative research where this feature is often a built-in part of the data-gathering process – see Chapter 7.

STRUCTURE IN INTERVIEWS

In the last chapter we saw the dimension of structure involved in the method of gathering observations. We see it again here: interviews can range from being highly structured to very loosely organized. When studies are referred to as 'interview-based', however, they very often use a type known as the **SEMI-STRUCTURED INTERVIEW**. The range of interview types and their application is described in Box 6.4.

Box 6.4   The range of interview types used in psychological research

Non-directive/informal   Non-directive interviews are not usually used for information gathering but for helping a client in psychological practice through therapy or counselling. The idea is that the client is in no way constrained by pre-set questions and can talk as freely as they like with no direction from the interviewer, whose role is mainly to reflect and restructure the client's ideas.

However, this type of interview has been used in psychological research, for example, in the Hawthorne studies, as described in Coolican, 2004: 152. The idea is to obtain information, as far as possible, not only in the participant's own words but also in the ways they *construct* it rather than the way in which the interviewer might guide it. Qualitative researchers (see Chapter 7) often use this approach. Their aim is mostly not to gather data that can be statistically analysed and used to support a quantitative hypothesis but to gather rich, qualitative data as close to the participant's own meaning and perspective as possible.

Semi-structured   In a semi-structured approach an attempt is made to retain the advantages of an informal method (so that the interview feels as much as possible like 'a chat'). However, an attempt is also made to ensure that the same topics are covered in each interview and that information from the session can be compared with and/or added to information from other sessions in a relatively standardized way. Semi-structured interviews are often used in qualitative research but are also quite frequently used in quantitative studies where the aim is to obtain information that can be coded and compared as a sample of the population trend, and in turn used as evidence for a hypothesis.

The interview schedule covers pre-ordained topics and some specifically worded questions, but the interviewer may digress where the participant does not answer fully or is ambiguous in their response. The areas or questions on the interview schedule may be 'worked in' by the interviewer in as natural a manner as possible. Piaget (1936) used what has become known as the **CLINICAL METHOD** in his research. This was a semi-structured interview, as just described, where each child was asked a specific set of questions but which Piaget would ask in several ways in order to be sure that the child did or did not understand a particular concept.

Formal and fully structured   Here the interviewer asks questions in a fixed order and any digression is not recorded as a formal response from the interview. Items might still be open-ended. However, where they are not, the interview amounts to the administration of a questionnaire but in a face-to-face format.

Pros and cons

There are a number of advantages and disadvantages to either a loosely structured or quite heavily structured interview approach. Basically these amount to the same issues as for structured and unstructured observations (p. 64). With a lot of structure we get results that can be checked for reliability and a dataset that can be analysed in a conventional statistical manner. We might say that the approach was more 'objective' and scientific. However, a qualitative researcher (see Chapter 7) might argue that the rigidity and formality of a formal interview only introduces many of the problems associated with experimentation, in that participants might feel uncomfortable, might not respond in their normal, authentic manner, might try to guess what the point of the questions is and might be more susceptible to the factor of social desirability. So for these reasons there may be bias in the structured interview that is comparable with that caused by the interviewer being more relaxed and perhaps influential in the semi-structured situation. A summary of pros and cons is given in Table 6.1.

ROLE OF INTERVIEWS IN RESEARCH

Transcripts of an interview record the entire content of what a participant said, absolutely and strictly word for word, sometimes including coughs, stutterings and repetitions. The process of transcription – from, say, tape to word-processed script – can take a lot of time, perhaps as much as two hours for every ten minutes of recorded speech (so don't rush into using interviews for your project!). Interviews are much used by qualitative researchers and the use of the data will be discussed in the next chapter. Used as quantitative data, researchers might ask trained **RATERS** to assess the script for a category, for instance, 'warmth towards children' where mothers have been interviewed about their child-rearing practices. Content analysis (see p. 98) might be used to extract a set of categories or to count frequencies of qualities already decided upon – for instance, how many times the interviewee's family is mentioned as providing either support or problems. Therefore an interview study can provide either a *description* of what participants have reported as its findings or it can be used in regular hypothesis-testing research.

SURVEYS

A survey involves asking a relatively large number of people a set of questions. If an entire population is questioned the procedure is known as a **CENSUS**. Most surveys involve a team of interviewers, especially if face-to-face interviews are to be conducted with each respondent. However, one of the strengths of the survey is that large numbers of people can be included, providing that an efficient way of distributing questionnaires is selected. This puts a good deal of emphasis on the sampling method employed, because with larger samples we are usually more confident that the attitudes or behaviour recorded are representative of the whole population. For instance, we might want to know the proportions of working parents using different ways to manage the care of their under-5-year-olds during the working day. The final picture will be skewed if the sampling method picks out too high a proportion of parents with another relative living in their house, as would happen if we simply went knocking on doors during the working day. Surveys are more likely than other methods to use sophisticated versions of the stratified, quota and cluster-sampling procedures described in Chapter 2.

SURVEY SAMPLING

Problems with survey sampling depend upon the means used to communicate with respondents. Survey questioning can be conducted by selecting samples and following these up with face-to-face interviews, by post, by telephone or by email. Alternatively, samples can be completely self-selecting by leaving the questionnaire (to be voluntarily returned) in public places such as doctors' surgeries, schools or even on the Internet.

For each of the sampling methods listed below think about the problems each would have in producing a representative sample from a geographical area. What factors would bias the sample? Which would be likely to be least biased?

a. using the telephone directory
b. selecting samples of houses
c. posting the questionnaire on the Internet
d. using the electoral roll
e. questioning people stopped on the street.

Hopefully you selected the electoral roll as least biased. Even this will not include prisoners, the homeless, people in psychiatric care and so on. The telephone directory eliminates all those without a phone. Selecting houses eliminates all those not living in one, including those in residential institutions or in hospital etc. Access to the Internet still depends to some extent on being somewhat more affluent than average (Baker, Wagner and Singer, 2003). Selecting people on the street and considering them representative was a naïve concept discussed in Chapter 2.

USE OF SURVEYS FOR RESEARCH

Surveys can be used in a *descriptive* manner, simply to find out what's happening in the wider world, as did the now infamous Kinsey report (Kinsey *et al.*, 1953), which shocked Americans with its statistics on sexual activity (for instance, that about 15% of both men and women had sex outside their marriage, that 10% of men were gay and that 10% of women never experienced orgasm). The survey research reported in Box 6.5 shows that hypotheses can also be tested, in this case that early temperamental difficulties can be linked to later obesity.

Box 6.5   Example of a hypothesis testing survey study

Pulkki-Raback *et al.* (2005) reported on a longitudinal follow-up study of 619 men and women, first tested for temperament between the ages of 6 and 12 years and tested again for measures of body size including the Body Mass Index (BMI) at 24–30 years. It was found that temperamental difficulties exhibited in childhood, especially high negative emotionality, were linked with higher BMI 18 years later, even when other known risks of obesity had been controlled for in the analysis of the data. This study was part of a highly complex survey that involved the study of over 3500 Finnish schoolchildren for 24 years and which continues today.

PROGRESS REVIEW 6.4

EXERCISES

1. A researcher interviews participants and then goes through each interview transcript rating each respondent on scales of 'warmth' and 'openness'. What flaw is there in this procedure?
2. You are about to conduct an interview with the manager of a local supermarket. He is 43 years old, said to be fairly friendly and is active in a local campaign to bring back fox hunting. What factors, both positive and negative, might influence the production of rich and authentic data from the interview, considering your own personality and characteristics?
3. Make a list of advantages and disadvantages of structured interviews compared with semi-structured or informal interviews.

ANSWERS

1. The researcher might be biased through expectancy factors since she has already had an interview session with each participant. The solution is to employ a 'blind' rater to assess the transcripts.
2. Left open for you to decide, but consider your own attitudes, the possible age difference and sex difference involved. If you are similar in age and same sex, still consider how this would make the interview run differently from one with a very different interviewee.
3. See Table 6.1 (p. 90).

KEY TERMS

Census
Clinical method
Interview method
Rater

Semi-structured interview
Structured interview
Survey

Table 6.1   Comparison of structured and semi-structured interviews

Advantages	Disadvantages
Semi-structured/informal	
❏ Interviewee more relaxed and freer to respond as they wish; hence, able to produce more authentic and rich data	❏ Difficulties of comparison across different interviewers and with the same interviewer on different occasions; reliability is thus more of a problem if desired
❏ Possibly less subject to *evaluation apprehension*	❏ More scope for interviewer to influence data gathering by digressing from set questions or permitting interviewee to ramble on
❏ More scope for interviewer to be flexible and to follow up interviewee's own ideas as they appear and to permit interviewee to follow own train of thought	❏ Interviewers may need greater preparation in ways to avoid bias and allow interviewees to produce the fullest data
	❏ More difficulty in comparing the data quantitatively; if analysed qualitatively, the problems of subjectivity discussed in Chapter 7 are prominent
Structured	
❏ Easier for others to replicate	❏ Greater formality might encourage more evaluation apprehension and attempts by interviewee to be a 'good' participant, thus producing less authentic behaviour
❏ More likely that multiple interviewers will follow much the same procedure	❏ More rigid questioning format and order limit interviewee's freedom to express ideas fully and in a real context
❏ Interviewers need less training and expertise	
❏ Easier to analyse data quantitatively and to check on reliability	

chapter
7

Qualitative data and qualitative approaches to research

What's in this chapter?

❏ We look at the nature of *qualitative data* and what is meant by taking a *qualitative approach* to psychological research.
❏ We consider typical arguments against *positivism* and numerical measurement in psychological science.
❏ We look at the proposals of qualitative researchers.
❏ We look at the nature of qualitative analysis and safeguards to ensure research is credible and valid.
❏ We look at several contemporary qualitative methods including *content analysis*, which can be used to produce quantitative data from qualitative data. Other methods briefly described are *grounded theory, interpretive phenomenological analysis (IPA), discourse analysis* and *thematic (theory-led) analysis*.
❏ We look at the nature and use of *case studies*.

QUALITATIVE VERSUS QUANTITATIVE APPROACHES AND DATA

In the last chapter we talked about interview data. An interview is hardly worth the title if it does not include open-ended questions that the interviewee can answer at any length. Such answers appear finally as text – a faithful transcript of exactly what was said. The issue now is – what to do with the data? Traditionally, researchers used an approach known as *content analysis* (which will be described later) to count the number of times this or that theme or concept was mentioned by the speaker. An alternative approach, as we saw in the last chapter, would be to have independent raters code the transcripts, giving a numerical score to each participant on well-defined variables. In this way the interview data would be quantified, i.e. given a numerical value on some variables.

The trouble with quantifying qualitative data in this way is that all the other important information provided by the interviewee is lost. We no longer have a whole picture of what the participant said. It is a bit like keeping only the fins of a fish or telling someone only what colours were used in a painting and how much of each. This chapter deals with two intimately-linked issues:

1. QUALITATIVE DATA
2. QUALITATIVE RESEARCH APPROACHES.

QUALITATIVE DATA are any pieces of information that are not in numerical form. Very often they are text (for instance, an exact report of what someone said) but a list of all the possible types of qualitative data might include:

❑ text (e.g. transcript of an interview, diary entry, conversation in a focus group, comments in a visitors' feedback book)
❑ observations (e.g. observer's notes)
❑ pictorial data (e.g. graffiti, children's drawings, doodles)
❑ auditory data (e.g. music selections)

Where we take a piece of text produced by participants (e.g. a short description, an interview transcript) and count occurrences of items or ask a rater to give it a score on 'warmth', as has already been described, we are creating QUANTITATIVE DATA from the extracts of the qualitative *raw* data. Many traditional and quite well-known studies have, in fact, used qualitative information without necessarily quantifying it. Freud's data is almost entirely qualitative, though many would discount him as a 'scientist'. However, an example from very much within the scientific establishment is the work of Penfield and Rasmussen (1950). Although their work was highly scientific in a medical context, the major phenomenon that excited psychologists was the fact that their patients reported highly specific and vivid memories when their cortex was electrically stimulated. Rosenhan's (1973) reports on the experiences of several fake patients in US psychiatric departments would not be of much interest without the qualitative descriptions they provided. Much of Watson and Rayner's (1920) article on the conditioning of Little Albert is written up as laboratory diary extracts, with qualitative observation of Albert's reactions. Virtually no quantitative data are presented at all (see http://psychclassics.yorku.ca/Watson/emotion.htm).

Although psychologists have often published qualitative data as part of their research evidence, nevertheless the overwhelming nature of research in psychology has been quantitative. Over the past two decades there has been an ever-increasing reaction against the 'hard' scientific and quantitative nature of much psychological research. The reaction is largely against POSITIVISM. This is a philosophy associated with the advances in science made in the 19th century and is the assumption that what cannot be observed and numerically measured is not available to scientific investigation. Let's run through the central arguments *against* positivism advanced by qualitative researchers – however, I should stress now that there is no unified school of qualitative research but many approaches. Even so, the majority of qualitative researchers would probably agree with the following arguments:

1. Positivist research isolates people from their surrounding context. It even treats 'parts' of people as separable (e.g. their memory or their concept of self). Participants (who used to be known as 'subjects') are treated as identical units, apart from the variables under investigation. The researcher holds preconceived notions about those variables, which participants may not challenge. Participants are, in effect, variables to be manipulated and measured.
2. In the interests of scientific objectivity the researcher strives to remain separate and distant from the participant in order not to bias proceedings. However, the experimental situation is a social one and participants *will* respond in socially-constructed ways to the researcher, no matter that the researcher ignores it. When researchers want to say goodbye to the participants and rush off to score their psychological scale, participants will often want to discuss and debate certain of the items contained within it.

3. Constrained and artificial experimental procedures can only permit the gathering of superficial data. Participants lack the freedom to react normally, to plan and to consider the meaning of the whole situation. Nevertheless, data collected under these circumstances are treated as realistic and generalizable. The model of a person produced in this way is simplistic and mechanistic. As an example of this criticism, consider an experiment described by Harré (1981), which had the aim of showing that an increased sense of self would be likely to lead to an increase in helping behaviour. The means of increasing women participants' sense of self was to have them look at themselves in a video monitor for one minute. They then listened to a lecture on venereal disease and were asked, one or four minutes later, to contribute to a venereal disease remedial programme. Harré argued that this quantitative approach completely trivialized G.H. Mead's (1934) concept of self upon which the study was supposed to be based.

4. Tightly operationalized variables, as in the study above and in psychological scales, impose pre-ordained measures on participants. The most important and interesting information is therefore mostly missed by the research study.

5. Experimental research often involves deception and always involves an uneven power relationship between experimenter and participant. Where gross trickery is involved, the relationship is patronising, if not insulting.

WHAT, THEN, DO QUALITATIVE RESEARCHERS PROPOSE?

Although there is now a wide variety of qualitative approaches to doing research, most qualitative researchers would probably agree on the following advantages and superior principles of qualitative research:

1. Psychological research should concentrate on the meanings of actions in a social context, not on isolated, 'objective' units of behaviour – a 'holistic', not an 'atomistic', approach.

2. Research should, as far as possible, be naturalistic and gather qualitative data.

3. Research should be conducted as far as possible *with* the participant rather than *on* them. The researcher's own role in the research *relationship* is recognized and many approaches demand a **REFLEXIVE** account (or **REFLEXIVITY**), which means that the researcher takes into account, in the write-up, the possible influences they themselves had on the participants' reactions and on the interpretation of the data.

4. There is an emphasis on participants' own terms and interpretations of the world around them. There is not so much of an emphasis on hypothesis testing. Quite commonly, theory is expected to *emerge* from the data. Typically, researchers analyse their interview and observation data exhaustively, looking for themes and concepts in the transcripts that help to create a 'local' theory (i.e. not generalizable to an entire population) – but one which, for some approaches at least, might have the potential to develop into a more widely applicable theory.

SOURCES OF DATA FOR QUALITATIVE RESEARCH

Qualitative researchers tend to use the following major approaches or techniques, most of which we have discussed in earlier chapters:

- ❑ Open-ended questionnaires
- ❑ Semi-structured interviews
- ❑ Qualitative and participant observation
- ❑ Diary methods
- ❑ Role-play and simulation
- ❑ Case studies (see end of this chapter).

The procedure within an interview tends to vary depending on the principles of the particular qualitative approach used. Diary methods can involve the researcher maintaining a diary whilst, for instance, participating as an observer in a real context, such as a hospital or residential home. These methods can also involve the researcher asking *participants* to maintain a diary over an extended period. Jones and Fletcher (1992) asked couples to keep a daily diary of mood, stress and sleep variation over a period of three weeks, concluding as a result that occupational stress is transmitted from one partner to the other. Role-play and simulation are rather rare types of study but can involve the gathering of qualitative data concerning how participants felt whilst playing or observing a role. Case studies are described below.

DEALING WITH QUALITATIVE DATA – QUALITATIVE ANALYSIS

The data gathered from most 'qualitative approaches' is only ever analysed at a qualitative level. That is, meanings are not converted to numbers but left (mainly) as text. Should you find yourself tempted or even required to conduct a qualitative analysis you will need a book more advanced than this one. Box 7.1 shows you where to find detailed advice on how to proceed. In quantitative research you invent a design, pay attention to specific weaknesses, gather data and analyse them using the appropriate statistical technique – see Chapters 8 to 12. You do *not* have to decide which quantitative philosophy you agree with. There is one main positivist philosophy and the 'rules' of how to engage in it are pretty well universal. Qualitative approaches, however, come in many shapes and sizes and it is not a unified field that is in opposition to quantitative approaches. Most qualitative researchers are not *opposed* to statistical analysis (some are). Most use qualitative methods out of choice and because these are the most appropriate approaches for the kinds of work that they do and the aims that they try to meet. Developing out of related disciplines such as sociology and anthropology, there are several major approaches to choose from. These are *not* simply different methods within one agreed perspective on how to gain knowledge. They differ among themselves as to the actual nature of knowledge and the most appropriate means to gain it. Positivism takes a *realist* stance – the view that there is a single concrete reality in the world that scientists just have to discover; knowledge is about finding the best route. Most qualitative approaches take some form of *constructivist* stance – the view that knowledge is *relative*; one person sees reality differently from another and neither view is more valid. Knowledge is a *construction* out of the kinds of language and concepts with which we approach the world. For instance, one person's 'terrorist' is another's 'freedom fighter' or 'martyr'.

Having made this short introduction to the worlds of qualitative research we can now look at some general principles about the processes of gathering and analysing qualitative data upon which most, if not all, approaches are agreed.

❑ Overall, the analysis must be thorough and academic, answering questions about the data in a style that rises far above common journalism or personal speculation. Do not be tempted into doing qualitative research because it seems like an easier option than a quantitative approach. You must *not* write as if for a magazine article.

❑ The analysis must recognize that the researcher plays a central role in the interpretation of data. The principle of reflexivity should be recognized, with the author making clear in what ways their own position may have influenced the construction of an interpretation from the data.

❑ The analysis must stay close to the participants' original meanings with plenty of quotations directly from the transcript to support claims being made or concepts being developed.

❑ Reliability cannot be established in the statistical way that is possible with quantitative data gathered from psychological scales. In qualitative research there are several ways in which different researchers and authors have come to believe that their work can be evaluated for trustworthiness and authenticity (see the sources given for these in Box 7.1):

- TRIANGULATION – a term borrowed from surveying, refers to researchers' attempts to compare the same phenomenon from several different perspectives. For instance, interviews might be used to support interpretations already made from observations.
- FIT – the reader of a qualitative report should be able to see clearly the route back from researcher interpretations to the original data. Some talk here of 'coherence', and Smith (2003, see Box 7.1) takes up the idea of an 'audit' to be carried out by a colleague in which the chain of evidence is traced back and is verified as logical and credible.
- PARTICIPANT VERIFICATION – some researchers ensure that the final interpretations are seen by the original participants who can raise any serious objections to the ways in which their information has been used.
- SATURATION and NEGATIVE-CASE ANALYSIS – Saturation means that data gathering and analysis continue until no new significant concepts emerge. Where cases are found that do not fit the interpretation constructed so far then the analysis should continue until they *can* be interpreted by the theory. This is known as negative-case analysis. A crude example might be a study which looks at people's motivation for attending a self-help group for obesity. Data would be gathered and analysed for different themes such as reasons why people attend, notions of self and body image and so on until no new themes emerged. A description of all motivations would need to be changed if at least one participant described their only reason for attending as being for the social contact gained. Either they are hiding some real reasons or they are perfectly happy with their body and are genuinely just looking for social engagement.

Box 7.1   Some resources for further investigation of qualitative methods (see References section for full details)

For a fuller discussion of qualitative approaches within a general methods text:
Coolican (2004) *Research Methods and Statistics*.
Giles (2002) *Advanced Research Methods in Psychology*.
Robson (2002) *Real World Research*.

How-to-do-it qualitative research methods texts:
Willig (2001) *Introducing Qualitative Research in Psychology*.
Smith (2003) *Qualitative Psychology: a Practical Guide to Research Methods*.
Hayes (1997) *Doing Qualitative Analysis in Psychology*.

Guidelines on the evaluation of qualitative research:
Elliott, Fischer and Rennie (1999) Evolving guidelines for publication of qualitative research studies in psychology and related fields. *British Journal of Clinical Psychology,* 38, 215–29 (appropriate in the clinical psychology field).
Henwood and Pidgeon (1992) Qualitative research and psychological theorizing. *British Journal of Psychology,* 83, 97–111 (general guidelines).
Yardley (2000) Dilemmas in qualitative health research. *Psychology and Health,* 15, 215–28 (appropriate in the health psychology field).

Two easily-readable qualitative articles to try:
Abrahamsson *et al.* (2002) Ambivalence in coping with dental fear and avoidance: a qualitative study. *Journal of Health Psychology,* 7, 653–64.
Lawn (2004) Systemic barriers to quitting smoking among institutionalised public mental health service populations: a comparison of two Australian sites. *International Journal of Social Psychiatry,* 50, 204–15.

EXERCISES

1. Give some strengths and possible weaknesses involved in the use and analysis of qualitative data.
2. Think of some research studies you have learned about that have included the gathering of qualitative data.
3. Why exactly do qualitative researchers worry about reflexivity?

ANSWERS

1. See Table 7.1.
2. Though not commonly focused upon, both Milgram (1963) and Asch (1956) conducted interviews after their experiments and discussed the *reasons* participants gave for their apparently extreme degree of conformity or obedience ... or their reasons for disobeying or not conforming. In Ainsworth, Bell and Stayton's (1971) studies of attachment there were hidden observers who recorded by talking into a tape recorder all the infant's movements. There are many more examples – ask your tutor!
3. Have a look at this text and perhaps others. Typing the word into a search engine on the Internet turns up several useful discussions and descriptions. Basically, traditional science produces an image of neutrality and objectivity that is seen as false by qualitative researchers. The principle of reflexivity questions the ways in which the influence of the researcher is 'air-brushed' out of scientific reporting. A typical 'trick', to get you thinking, is the use of impersonal pronouns. Consider the difference in emphasis caused by saying 'One can see the strength of the evidence supporting heredity that has been presented' rather than 'You can see the strength of the evidence supporting heredity that I have presented'.

KEY TERMS

Fit
Negative-case analysis
Participant verification
Positivism
Qualitative data

Qualitative research approach
Quantitative data
Reflexivity
Saturation
Triangulation

ESTABLISHED QUALITATIVE APPROACHES

There is no space here to elaborate fully on the various kinds of qualitative approach now popular among researchers. However, I can give you a brief outline and then, should you be interested in any of these, you could follow them up in at least one of the dedicated qualitative texts listed in Box 7.1, of which I would recommend Smith (2003) as a good, recent, starting point.

GROUNDED THEORY (GT)

This is an import from sociology initiated by Glaser and Strauss (1967). In its original form it was argued that theory must emerge solely from the data gathered and must not be influenced by any

Table 7.1   Advantages and disadvantages of quantitative and qualitative data

Advantages	Disadvantages
Quantitative data	
❑ Can be analysed statistically	❑ Give no picture of complete individual or their connected thoughts
❑ Give clear view of typical scores and range	❑ Treat narrowly-defined variable as separate from rest of person and context
❑ Can be used to test well-defined hypotheses	❑ May give false impression of indisputable scientific findings
❑ Can generalize from sample to population	
Qualitative data	
❑ Retain all individual's original meanings	❑ Hard to generalize findings to other situations
❑ Rich and authentic if collected well	❑ Disagreements exist over appropriate way to gather and analyse data
❑ Give picture of individual's whole views and experience on specific topics	❑ Analysis and interpretation can be influenced more by researcher's own perspective and biases

preconceptions or prior theory. It is rarely used in this form and most researchers do relate their aims back to previous studies and findings. Data are analysed to saturation (until there are no pieces left unexplained). The first stages extract specific themes or 'categories' from the data. Further analysis involves developing higher-order categories and also, where necessary, going back out to gather more data from selected sources (*purposive sampling*) in order to check the emerging theory and remove any anomalies. The final framework that explains all the categories is in fact the *explanatory model*. Strauss and Corbin (1990) developed guidelines for conducting grounded theory but these were contested by Glaser (1992); so even within this approach there are several subdivisions of opinion on how research should be conducted. Both the easily-readable articles cited at the bottom of Box 7.1 use a version of GT.

INTERPRETIVE PHENOMENOLOGICAL ANALYSIS (IPA)

IPA is not a kind of UK beer but an acronym for a rather cumbersome title! This approach attempts to stay as close as possible to the experiences of the researched individual – their 'phenomenology'. This follows the path set by Carl Rogers (1961), who argued that no matter how bizarre the content of what a person reports it is *their* experience and we cannot invalidate it. IPA attempts to reflect that experience authentically whilst recognizing the principle of reflexivity – no one can reflect another's experience without colouring it with their own. The analysis is similar to that in GT and tries to extract central features of experience whilst allowing (unlike GT) some information to be dropped as irrelevant. Several people's experiences might be compared and themes can be integrated to form a wider picture of the phenomenon under investigation (e.g. experiences of being bullied). Good practical examples are provided in detail in Smith (2003) – see Box 7.1, p. 95.

DISCOURSE ANALYSIS (DA)

It is very difficult to give a full picture of the aims and procedures of DA, especially as there are several versions and some quite sharp divisions within the movement of those said to be using DA. A major principle is that discourse analysis is not seen as a way to discover what is in people's minds. This is viewed as a fruitless exercise in psychology. Rather like the behaviourists, DA theorists argue that all we know about so-called mental occurrences is the constructions people make of them when they talk. They do *not* argue that mental processes exist to be studied but that we just can't get at them. They argue (philosophically) that thinking of mental processes as 'things' is the wrong way to go about it. DA theorists and researchers concentrate on how people construct their experiences and motivations through talk. As a crude example, we know that politicians and representatives in the public eye word their speeches and interviews very carefully in order to give just the right message and not to give the wrong impression. In some ways we are back to the distinction between choosing to talk of 'terrorists' not 'freedom fighters'. A senior company manager making sweeping changes to the organization will talk of 'opportunities' rather than 'problems'. DA writers talk of people having a 'stake' in what they construct. We create a version each time we speak. If I ask you what you did at the weekend you will construct what you say, differently from the last time you were asked, and probably in keeping with the context of my perhaps being older, male, not a family member or close confidant and so on. A wild party might be described as 'interesting'. DA researchers typically analyse interview transcripts but have been known to take on famous politician's speeches (Edwards and Potter, 1992).

THEMATIC (OR THEORY-LED) ANALYSIS

With this approach it is possible to test hypotheses in the more traditional manner within a conventional scientific approach. Normally we are persuaded into accepting that scientific evidence must somehow be quantified, numerical in some form. However, courts of law often deal with qualitative evidence – witness accounts, statements of character, psychiatric assessments and so on – yet here, as in science, the aim is to support this or that theory. We can predict that young offenders will feel more alienated than other youths from middle-class society and can evidence this with qualitative differences in their accounts – *not* the number *of* aggressive terms that they use but the sheer animosity of the *types* of terms and statements produced.

A good example of theory-led thematic analysis is provided by Hayes (1991, available in Hayes, 1997) who made predictions from theory about differences in culture expected to be reflected in the interview data of workers in two different organizations.

ANALYSING QUALITATIVE DATA – EXTRACTING QUANTITATIVE DATA

We have just seen that qualitative data can be used to provide research evidence that tests hypotheses as in conventional quantitative studies. If, however, the researcher wishes to extract *quantitative* data from qualitative content, they can use an approach that has existed since at least the 1930s and that goes under the name of **CONTENT ANALYSIS**. Reasons for extracting numerical data from qualitative content would be the quite predictable ones of requiring precision, reliability and replicability in one's findings, for all the reasons outlined in the first few chapters of this book. This returns us to a hypothesis-testing and more positivist approach to research.

MATERIALS THAT CAN BE CONTENT ANALYSED

Content analysis can be carried out on either pre-existing materials (some examples of which, and what might be analysed, are given in Box 7.2) or on materials produced by participants in a study. For instance, we might ask participants to complete a story or even write an essay on a topic such as global warming, having presented some persuasive materials to see if this has an effect on their attitudes. Interview transcripts can also be content-analysed in a quantitative manner.

Box 7.2 Materials that could be content-analysed In a psychology project

Materials	Items to be identified in the analysis
Children's books	❑ Aggressive content
	❑ Sex or ethnic stereotypes
	❑ Messages of cultural morality – sharing, caring, helping
	❑ Dealing with emotional issues – death, love, jealousy
Children's drawings	❑ Size or inclusion of various family members
	❑ Parts of the body included (number increases with age)
	❑ Size of significant objects (e.g. Santa's sack before and after Christmas)
Television ads or soaps	❑ Sex roles
	❑ Violent themes
	❑ Healthy eating
	❑ Current moral or political issues
Newspapers	❑ Language used to describe famous people across different newspapers
	❑ Frequency of issues – murder, accident, robbery
Personal ads	❑ Mention of different features by different sexes
	❑ What is offered and what is sought
	❑ Differences across different cultures
Email and Internet chat sites	❑ As for personal ads where relevant
	❑ Presence of humour/ways to make demands (e.g. office emails)

CONDUCTING A CONTENT-ANALYSIS STUDY

Sampling

You must decide how to sample from all the material that exists in the medium you wish to study. If you study personal ads, for example, it is no use using *The Times* and then collecting a few more from the *Sun* and thinking these will be equivalent. As part of your study you might have a look at the difference between ads in two different types of paper. In this case you *do* need to choose two papers that represent the difference you're interested in. You will then have to sample with equivalence – using the same days of the week, periods of the year and so on. If you sample television advertising you would need to consider that advertising is usually linked to the content of the programmes either side of the slot.

Coding

This is the most crucial aspect of content analysis. You can decide, as in traditional studies, what you are looking for before the data are gathered. This is usually done by looking at previous studies, thinking about the hypothesis you want to test (e.g. males offer more financial incentives in personal ads) and creating the coding system that you will use. A good way to achieve this is to run a *pilot study* by sampling a few newspapers first to see what kind of language and concepts are used in regular ads.

You start your analysis with a set of rigorously defined **CODING UNITS**. These are the exact ways in which numbers will be generated from the material. Sometimes raters score material on a scale but very often the data are frequency counts (see Chapter 8). That is, you simply count up how many times each type of unit occurs. In a study of television commercials by Cumberbatch (1990), raters produced the following statistics by counting occurrences of each feature: 75% of men but 25% of women were judged to be over 30 years old. Men outnumbered women 2:1, and 89% of voice-overs, especially for expert/official information, were male. The ratio of women to men rated as 'attractive' was 3:2. Men were as likely to be engaged in housework for friends as for their family, whilst females predominantly worked for their family and never friends.

Coding units can then be defined, for instance, as:

Unit	Examples
Word	Analyse for sex-related words in different magazines
Theme	Analyse for occasions, in children's literature, on which boy/girl initiates and gets praised
Item	Look for whole stories, e.g. article on Iraq
Character	Analyse types of character occurring in TV cartoons
Time and space	Count space or time devoted to particular issue in media

Procedure

It is possible to decide on the coding units *after* gathering data. In this case, of course, the researcher is open to the criticism that they invented the coding units in order to 'get a result'. However, the coding units must be clearly related to the hypothesis to be tested and, providing no major portions of data are simply omitted from the analysis (because they do not fit), then there is no problem with this approach, so long as the researcher makes clear what the decisions were when writing up the report and is ready to produce all the raw data when asked.

The coding system, whether developed before data gathering or after, would normally be handed to trained raters, who might be given additional training on practice materials until they are consistent ('reliable') and who do the analysis whilst remaining ignorant of the research predictions. Correlations (see Chapter 12) between raters on the same materials should give a good idea of inter-rater, or inter-coder, reliability, as was explained in Chapter 5 for interobserver reliability (p. 66).

CASE STUDIES

Case studies are in-depth, detailed investigations of one person or group, such as a company or organization. People are usually selected for case studies because their character, abilities or experiences are outstanding in some special respect, or because they are representative of a special category of people about whom the researcher wishes to gather comprehensive information, often over a significant length of time. The person may have special abilities, such as Luria's (1969) journalist who could remember long word lists accurately for up to 15 years, or a special psychological condition, such as Thigpen and Cleckley's (1954) 'Eve', who exhibited three distinctly different personalities whilst undergoing psychotherapy. They may be studied because they are about to undergo a unique experience, such as Gregory and Wallace's 'SB' (1963), who underwent surgery at the age of 52 to restore his sight, lost just after birth. This last example shows us perhaps most directly how a single case, studied in depth and mostly qualitatively, can shed light on and provide insight into a general psychological phenomenon – in this case the development of perception and the rare opportunity actually to *ask* someone just beginning to see what the world looks like to them.

No two case studies are alike and they may involve a variety of methods. Very often, detailed interviews are conducted at regular intervals, probably semi-structured or just informal.

Observations might also be made, especially of children, and several psychological scales administered. There can be several reasons for conducting a case study:

❏ *Outstanding cases*: the examples given above are all in this category. The cases are studied because they are so rare and intrinsically interesting in themselves.
❏ *Contradicting a theory*: one single counter-example is a challenge to any theory. If a maternally deprived child is found to have developed quite normally in most important respects then we have to adjust the view that such deprivation is *always* damaging.
❏ *Data pool*: a mass of information from several case studies can be pooled and analysed for specific effects that might emerge. Once patterns emerge and are linked with others, more quantitative studies might be performed and this time not on special cases.
❏ *Insight*: the sheer richness of in-depth case studies can be their unique strength, whether or not they lead to further quantitative studies. Very often we could not possibly imagine the special circumstance of the individual nor their ways of coping with adversity. The findings can inspire researchers to formulate quite new ways of looking at a psychological phenomenon, can teach greater empathy and understanding, and can add to our overall psychological knowledge without necessarily testing a specific hypothesis.

PROGRESS REVIEW 7.2

EXERCISES

1. If you were going to conduct a qualitative study, which of the methods described here (the names of the different types appear in the Key terms box) would you use and why?
2. What is a coding unit?
3. How would raters in a content-analysis research project be checked for reliability?
4. Give one strength and one weakness of case studies.

ANSWERS

1. None is best. Just check that you have accurately reflected the main principles of the method chosen.
2. Type of category used in a content-analysis study; for instance, uses of racial stereotypes in newspaper stories, gender or sporting characters, number of times global warming is referred to in colour supplements.
3. By using *statistical correlation* (see Chapter 12).
4. A *strength* is the sheer richness or unique nature of information gathered. A *weakness* might be the subjectivity to which the researcher could be prone after immersion with just one very special and entertaining person over an extended period of time.

KEY TERMS

Case study
Coding unit
Content analysis
Discourse analysis
Grounded theory

Interpretive
phenomenological-
analysis (IPA)
Thematic analysis

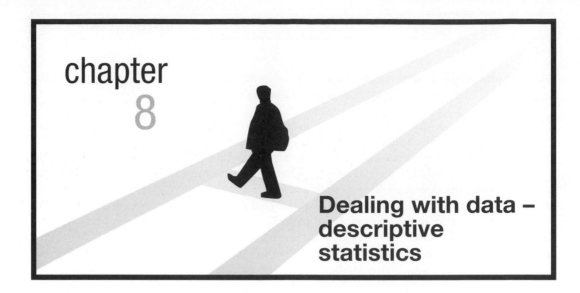

chapter
8

Dealing with data – descriptive statistics

What's in this chapter?

❏ We look at the general uses for *statistics*, especially in terms of presenting clear and unambiguous evidence (*descriptive statistics*) and for claiming a likely effect (*inferential statistics*).

❏ Levels of measurement are introduced – *nominal, ordinal, interval* and *ratio* with emphasis only on the first three as relevant to analysis in psychological research.

❏ Summaries of data in terms of *central tendency* (*mean, median, mode*) and *dispersion* (*range, interquartile range* and *standard deviation*) are introduced and explained.

❏ Summaries presented in *tables* and *charts* are introduced – including *bar chart, histogram, frequency table, cumulative frequency* – and appropriate presentation and scaling are discussed.

❏ *Distributions* of data are introduced, with special attention to the *normal distribution*, areas under it and *z values*; *skewed distributions* are also briefly described.

DO WE REALLY HAVE TO DO STATISTICS?

Right! This is the part that many of you will have been dreading. Yes we *do* have to deal with numbers here. Many people studying psychology at this level find the idea of statistics absolutely daunting and fear that they will be exposed as mathematical dunces. The reason for this might be that maths in general is seen by so many people as a distant, cold subject, in no way connected with real life, unlike English and Geography. However, when you try to work out whether you're getting a good bargain on four tins of beans on special offer at the supermarket, you will have to do some maths. As with the beans, the level of calculation you will need in order to cope with this section of your syllabus, let me assure you right now, is extremely simple and you'll need no more than a calculator (£2 from the local garage) that does $+ - \times \div$ and $\sqrt{}$. That really is it!

Let's try to demonstrate why statistics are useful. Let's see what you can gain, not only in psychology but in general, by having a built-in nonsense detector that challenges figures given out by politicians and advertisers, and that demands fuller explanations. In the following four boxes are some dodgy statistics actually published in the media at various times. Try to work out why I call them 'dodgy' – some are easy but others more subtle.

Box 8.1   Dodgy stats 1 – Want a baby? Pick your sex

A clinic was in the news because it advertised its services as helping couples to have a baby of the sex of their choice. In a radio interview a spokesperson for the clinic was asked how successful the treatments had been. He said that they had seen six couples so far and four had left happy with the outcome.

Box 8.2   The honest citizens of Glasgow

A newspaper published the results of a field experiment (quasi-experiment) in which ten wallets containing money had been dropped in each of several towns or cities. The wallets contained identification and the numbers that were returned are shown below.

	Returned	Kept		Returned	Kept
Glasgow	8	2	Pontefract	7	3
Leamington Spa/Warwick	8	2	Liverpool	6	4
Basildon	7	3	Exeter	5	5
London	7	3	Cardiff	4	6

Adapted from the Guardian, 17 June 1996

The journalist said, 'Residents of Glasgow and Leamington Spa/Warwick emerged as Britain's most honest citizens, each handing in eight out of ten wallets'. The author of the original article (Jack Crossley) claims: 'Medium-size towns were slightly more honest than cities', and shows that the respective totals returned were 27 and 25. What do you think?

Box 8.3   Great news! Twenty-five per cent of maths teachers to go!

A recent article, written in rather panicky terms, about the shortage of maths teachers in the country made the claim that 25% of them were due to retire in the next ten years. Is this an exceptional worry?

Box 8.4   Christian Dior's magic gel

Christian Dior ran an advert for Svelte fat-reducing gel in which it was claimed that 550 women had tried the gel for a month. At the end of this period the ad claimed 52% of women reported losing up to an inch from their hips and 56% up to an inch from their thighs. Would this make you rush out and buy some?

Box 8.5   Why these are dodgy stats

Box 8.1 – If the clinic's procedure was absolutely useless, a giant con, then how often would they get four correct-gender babies out of six? The answer is very often indeed. Three out of six should happen most often. If you think about it, for each baby they have a 50%, or one in two, chance of getting it right. For every six couples they deal with they should mostly get three right and three wrong. In fact, this would happen one-third of the time and four out of six should happen one time in four – not very long odds so not very remarkable.

Box 8.2 – The problem here, as in the baby gender clinic, is the size of the samples. Is there such a big difference between 4 in 10 and 8 in 10? Is a fair sample of the entire city of Glasgow or of Cardiff just 10 people? If only four more people returned the wallets Cardiff would be 'as honest' as Glasgow. This is far too gigantic a leap from small sample to whole population. Also, are all the non-returners dishonest? That's a big assumption. They might be too busy or just forgetful.

Box 8.3 – Well, in any profession the working span is around 40 years. Assuming people are fairly evenly spread across the age groups then in any profession there would always be around 25% in their 50s and 'coming up for retirement'.

Box 8.4 – This really is a little more subtle. The statistics sound quite convincing – at least in the way they were given in the original ad. But what we are not told is how Dior came by these statistics/what questions they asked the women involved. I suspect they asked women to take a measurement at the start of the month and then again at the end. What would happen? When we measure something twice we are bound to get a slightly different result the second time. The measures are variable because flesh is flexible and you can't measure exactly the same way each time. This is true even if you're measuring wood or steel. There will always be small, random differences in measurements. Hence, since the differences are random we'd expect overall about 50% of the women to appear to have gained a little and 50% to appear to have lost a little even if no gel at all were applied. Also, don't forget they could always take another group of 550 if the first group didn't turn up the right results. A commercial company is more likely to treat their advertising research as a trade secret than abide by the principles of objective science. I'm not saying they did, of course, just that we don't know.

DESCRIPTIVE AND INFERENTIAL STATISTICS

Statistics are used for two linked but distinguishable purposes. First, they are used to *describe* what happened. This means nothing more than what you tell me if I ask you how many accidents there were on your high street over the past few years and you give me back the data year by year. In the wallet-dropping study mentioned above, we have statistics that tell us what happened – frequencies of wallets returned, by town or city. Data such as these are called **DESCRIPTIVE STATISTICS** and the task in the current chapter is to learn how to manage groups of data so that we can give a fair and clear report on the data.

However, the implication in some of the boxes above is that the sample statistics tell us something *more* – about the *populations* the *samples* are taken from. The journalist infers from samples of ten people that the entire populations of cities differ from one another in honesty. The baby-gender clinic infers that it really is having an effect. The Svelte gel data is taken as evidence that the gel is working to reduce fat. When we infer from a sample that there is an effect in the population we are using **INFERENTIAL STATISTICS** and these are the subject of Chapters 9 to 12. There we will learn when it is fair to assume we have demonstrated a genuine effect using only a relatively small sample. An inferential statistical test is used to test a hypothesis – for instance that Svelte gel reduces fat. A psychological hypothesis might be that listening to music increases spelling errors in a word-processing task.

FINDINGS AND CONCLUSIONS

Descriptive statistics describe what happened in a study. They are the **FINDINGS** of the study. Mostly we are interested in generalizing our result to some sort of **CONCLUSION**. It is important that you distinguish between these two terms because they are often used in exam questions. If you are asked to say what you think researchers would *conclude* from a study you must be very careful not to simply repeat the *findings*. If researchers showed that a sample of 20 people produced more swearing and smiled less whilst carrying out a difficult task in a hot room, compared with a cold one, then the *findings* are the data gathered on these 20 people showing a difference. The *conclusion* might be that heat increases aggression (generally).

STARTING OUT – LEVELS OF MEASUREMENT

First, we must look at the types of numerical data we can gather. All such data are gathered at a **LEVEL OF MEASUREMENT**. The level of measurement is important because it limits the kind of inferential statistical test we can use on the data to test our hypotheses. To get us started on levels take a look at the following statements:

1. Gina is short	Nominal scale
2. Gina is shorter than Jane but taller than Samantha	Ordinal scale
3. Gina is 167 cm tall	Interval/Ratio scale

In the first statement we know Gina belongs to a *category*. The category 'short' can be compared only with other categories such as 'tall' and medium'. In the second case we know *where* Gina is relative to Jane and Samantha; we know she takes second place; we know the *order* that the three people are placed in height *and that's all*. We don't know how *much* taller than Samantha Gina is. In the third statement we know exactly how tall Gina is and we can compare her with anyone else in the world on a *standard* and *universal* scale. Measuring people psychologically on universal scales of measurement is the dream of the psychometrists mentioned in Chapter 6. Let's now look at an explanation of the scale names shown on the right of the examples above.

THE NOMINAL LEVEL OF MEASUREMENT – CATEGORICAL VARIABLES

The **NOMINAL LEVEL** of measurement is said to be used when we are dealing with values that are *qualitatively* different. In fact, it is not really measurement at all but simply counting how many in each category – these 'counts' are known as **FREQUENCIES**. If we make an assessment of toys in children's bedrooms we are hardly likely to go around measuring the lengths of their toy cars. A sensible approach would be to count how many cars they have, and how many board games, computer games, sports items, swords, dolls and so on. Table 8.1 contains typically nominal or *categorical* data.

Table 8.1 Frequencies of people using the college refectory

Category of person	Frequency
Students	650
Teaching staff	34
Non-teaching staff	15
Visitors	12
Other	3

In order to check whether or not you have category data ask this simple question:

What information have I recorded from each person observed?

If your answer is of the form 'whether they are X, Y or Z ...' then you have nominal-level data. If what you know about each person simply puts them in a category along with others, and you cannot in any way distinguish between these others on any kind of scale, then you have nominal-level data.

Very often a student project involves observing differences between the sexes on some other observable variable, such as whether they carry their books in front or at their sides. A common variable is whether car drivers reverse into a parking space or drive in forwards. In this case the variable of sex is categorical – you can (forgetting sexual deviations and quirks of physiology) only be male or female. The second variable is also categorical, since you either reverse in or drive straight in. The result is a table of data such as in Table 8.2. Such data are said to be at a '*nominal level of measurement*'.

Table 8.2   Frequencies of male and female drivers reversing or driving forward into a parking space (an example of categorical or nominal data)

	Male	Female
Drove in forward	85	72
Reversed in	45	43

THE ORDINAL LEVEL OF MEASUREMENT

Suppose your class tutor had asked your class of 20 students to organize itself so that you are in two equal groups, one 'tall' and the other 'short'. You would all shuffle about a bit and there would be some nipping across the room from one group to the other until finally you had the two groups. However, some students, depending on the strength of their egos, might feel quite irked to find themselves in the short group because they are, in fact, the tallest in that group and do not generally consider themselves as 'short'. The problem is (apart from their egos), of course, the crudity of using a categorical variable with just two values, as we did with Gina in the example above. It might make a lot more sense to have the students stand in *order* of height, and let's suppose that's what your tutor now asks you to organize.

When data are organized at an **ORDINAL LEVEL** the position of each member in their group is revealed. In this exercise the boy with the frail ego might end up with the value 10th and feel much better about it. We still do not know how *much* taller he is than the 9th shortest person – an ordinal scale does not tell us about distances *between* rank positions. It may be annoying to be beaten by 1/10th of a second in a cycle race when you and the winner were 10 km ahead of the bunch but 2nd is what you get, and the next person, who takes over 20 minutes to get to the line after you, is 3rd.

HOW TO RANK ORDER A SET OF DATA

Scores on a questionnaire may result in data such as in Table 8.3. The scores themselves are *not* ordinal-level data (though some tutors and textbooks say they are). Ordinal data always appear as a set of rank positions, as in the third column of the table. The decision to make them ordinal is *ours*; data do not usually *arrive* as ordinal and there are no types of score that *must* be treated as ordinal. We will discuss below and elsewhere when it is safer to treat data as ordinal.

Table 8.3   Changing scores to ranks

Person	Score	Rank	High (H) or Low (L)
Ann	18	5.5	H
Beth	25	7	H
Carol	14	1	L
Dawn	18	5.5	H
Emma	15	3	L
Fern	15	3	L
Gill	15	3	L
Heidi	29	8	H

In statistics we do not give rank 1 to the best score but always to the lowest value in the set. So in Table 8.3 the score of 14 is ranked 1. Emma, Fern and Gill *share* the next three places – in athletics they might be recorded as 'equal 2nd' but in statistics we simply share out between them the three rank positions that they occupy. They share 2nd, 3rd and 4th place, so their average rank is $(2 + 3 + 4) \div 3 = 9 \div 3 = 3$. The simple rule is: if there is an odd number of ranks shared (as there was here) then take the middle rank. If there is an even number of ranks to share out then take the position mid-way between the middle two. We can apply this for Ann and Carol who share ranks 5 and 6 for their equal scores of 18. The average of these two is 5.5, so this is what each gets. Finally, we have ranks 7 and 8 for scores 25 and 29. If four people shared ranks 6, 7, 8 and 9 then each would get 7.5.

THE INTERVAL AND RATIO LEVELS OF MEASUREMENT

The weakness of the ordinal level is that from the data we do not get an idea of how *far* one person's score is from another. At an **INTERVAL LEVEL** of measurement we *do* get that information. An interval scale uses equal units. Ideally there is the same amount on the scale between scores of 10 and 20 as between 40 and 50. This is true for time and for physical distances, whether measured in feet or metres. Weight is another example.

The ideal for psychometrists (Chapter 6) is that psychological scales would also produce this kind of data. If this is the case then it ought to be true that Jane, who has an IQ score of 100, is as far ahead of Peter in intelligence (IQ = 90) as Michael, with 125, is ahead of Sue (IQ = 115). Of course, we can't *see* intelligence like we can physical distance. In psychology, the best that test constructors can do is to make their scales mimic what would happen if they were *truly* interval level. If human measures are interval then they form a normal distribution, like height does. We will look at the normal distribution on p. 127 but, for now, if you look at Figure 8.13, p. 128, you will see what a normal distribution looks like. If psychological measures produce a distribution like this then they are treated as interval-level data. The comparison between the different levels of measurement and the information each provides is depicted in Figure 8.1. Note that some interval scales are **DISCRETE**. They cannot have values in between whole numbers. You cannot really have 2.4 children! You can have 2 and the next possible value is 3, no matter what parents might say about their child having half a brain!

Figure 8.1   The levels of measurement and the information they provide (based on data in Table 8.3)

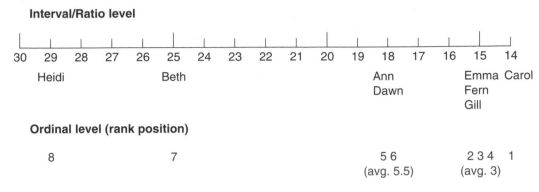

Your syllabus might ask you to understand the term **RATIO LEVEL** of measurement. Ratio data are on an interval scale that has a real zero, so the ratios on the scale make sense. Measures of temperature, for instance, do *not* start at a true zero. 30°C is not twice as hot as 15°C; the *number* is doubled but the quantity of heat is not. This is easily seen by converting to Fahrenheit, which would give 86°F and 59°F, respectively. Measures of temperature are interval measures but not ratio measures. Psychological measures are also mostly interval, not ratio. However, it doesn't matter anyway because psychologists never have to worry about whether their data are at ratio level. The statistics they use do not distinguish between interval and ratio. It is sufficient that data are interval for most statistical procedures. Hence, from now on, we will not mention ratio data but will refer to all data at this level as interval-level data and assume we mean interval or ratio.

WHEN TO TREAT 'INTERVAL' DATA AS ORDINAL

In psychology it is often not reasonable to claim that scores on a scale are truly equal intervals – even on a standardized attitude scale or intelligence test, though psychometrists aim for this. Quite often we have a scoring system that performs *well enough* as an interval scale and the data gathered on it are said to be on a **QUASI-INTERVAL SCALE**. This could even be true of scores gathered on a scale such as 'On a scale of 1 to 20 indicate how religious you consider yourself to be', so long as the data form a roughly normal-shaped distribution. However, *generally speaking*, if a scale is invented and unstandardized, like the one just mentioned or in any case where we simply ask humans to make a numerical judgement, it is usually safest to treat the resulting scores as *ordinal data* by ranking them. This would occur where, for instance, you asked people to rate pictures of people for 'attractiveness' on a scale of 1 to 10.

CHANGING DATA FROM ONE LEVEL TO ANOTHER – AND LOSING INFORMATION

Data are not fixed at the level at which they were first measured. We can always convert data from an interval scale downwards to another level *but we can't convert upwards.* This last point is the reason why you should consider very carefully what kind of analysis you want to perform, based on your hypothesis, before you start gathering data for a project. You need to make sure that your measuring instrument gathers the required level of data. A student of mine once had half her participants read a story that featured an attack on a 'modestly dressed' woman; the other half read 'scantily dressed'. Participants then had to answer the question 'Who was more to blame for the attack: the man or the woman?'. Of course, *all* the participants selected the male. The scale she had used had just two categories and it gave participants no room for manoeuvre. She needed to use instead a scale that gave at least ordinal-level data such as 'On a scale of 0 to 10 how much to blame for the attack was the man?' and then the same for the woman. *Then* she could have seen whether being 'scantily dressed' made participants slightly less sympathetic towards the victim. The measuring system she used was just too crude. This student actually went back and asked all her 120 participants to do the study over again!

Converting data downwards through the levels is always possible but we lose information on the way. Table 8.3, p. 107, shows our dataset converted from interval to ordinal level. The final column on the right has the data converted down to nominal level where we simply divide all the scores in the middle and call one set 'high' and the other set 'low'. Now, of course, we have no separation at all between participants in each category. At the ordinal level we have the separation but no idea of actual distance between two rank positions.

PROGRESS REVIEW 8.1

EXERCISES

1. A set of surgical records classifies patients as 'chronic', 'acute' or 'not yet classified'. What level of measurement is being used?
2. When judges in an ice-skating contest give their marks for style and presentation, at what level of measurement is it safest to treat their data?
3. Take a look at Table 8.4, p. 111. There is a measure in each of columns a, b, c and d. At what level of measurement is each of these sets of data?
4. Which of the columns a to d in Table 8.4 contains the most informative level of measurement?
5. Your sister argues that, since she came top in each of the three maths tests held in her class this year, she must be *far* better than all the other pupils. What might you point out to her? (Would you dare?)
6. Think of three ways to measure driving ability, one using nominal-level data, one ordinal and one interval.
7. Can you change the data in Table 8.5 first to ordinal level, then to nominal level? The blank tables are for you to fill in. **HINT:** For ordinal level, treat all the values as *one* group. For nominal, try splitting the scores into high/low categories.
8. Below are several methods for measuring dependent variables. For each measure decide what level of measurement is being used. Choose from: 1: NOMINAL, 2: ORDINAL, 3: INTERVAL.
    (a) People are asked which of three pictures, by Picasso, Matisse or Dali, they prefer.
    (b) Stress questionnaire for which various occupational norms have been established.
    (c) Photographs ordered by participants according to level of attractiveness, from 'most attractive' to 'least attractive'.
    (d) Participants' estimates of various line lengths.
    (e) Time taken to sort cards into categories.
    (f) People's choice of: the *Sun, The Times* or the *Guardian*.
    (g) Participants' sense of self-worth, self-estimated on a scale of 1–10.
    (h) Participants' scores on Cattell's 16PF questionnaire.
    (i) Distance two participants stand apart when asked to take part in an intimate conversation, measured from photos.
    (j) Critical life events given positions 1–10 according to their perceived importance to each participant.

ANSWERS

1. Nominal.
2. Ordinal (human judgements).
3.   (a) Ordinal.
      (b) Interval.
      (c) Nominal (or categorical).
      (d) Quasi-interval – safer treated as ordinal.
4. Column b.
5. 'Top' is a measure on an ordinal scale. We don't know how far ahead of the others she was.
6. Examples: Nominal – did/didn't hit kerb; Ordinal – positions after exercise on smoothness; Interval – measure speed in race.
7.

Ordinal level		Nominal level		
Consistent	Inconsistent	Consistent	Consistent	Inconsistent
6.5	11	Fastest nine	6	3
9	17	Slowest nine	3	6
1	11			
2.5	4.5			
16	18			
2.5	4.5			
6.5	8			
11	14			
13	15			

8.   (a) Nominal
      (b) Interval (because standardized)
      (c) Ordinal
      (d) Quasi-interval – best to convert to ordinal
      (e) Interval
      (f) Nominal
      (g) Quasi-interval – best to convert to ordinal
      (h) Interval (because standardized)
      (i) Interval
      (j) Ordinal.

KEY TERMS

Conclusion	Interval level
Descriptive statistics	Level of measurement
Discrete data	Nominal level
Findings	Ordinal level
Frequency	Quasi-interval scale
Inferential statistics	Ratio level

Table 8.4   Premiership table (top)

Premiership team	a Position	b Pts	c Area 1 = London; 2 = Northern; 3 = Southern	d Popularity rating (fictitious)
Chelsea	1	95	1	1
Arsenal	2	83	1	3
Manchester United	3	77	2	6
Everton	4	61	2	4
Liverpool	5	58	2	2
Bolton	6	58	2	5
Middlesbrough	7	55	3	8
Manchester City	8	52	1	7

Table 8.5   Reading times for exercise 7 in Progress review 8.1

a) Time taken to read (seconds)		b) Ordinal level		c) Nominal level
Consistent story	Inconsistent story	Consistent story	Inconsistent story	
127	138			
136	154			
104	138			
111	117			
152	167			
111	117			
127	135			
138	149			
145	151			
Mean of all times: $\bar{x} = 134.3$				

HOW TO SUMMARIZE DATA

The whole point of descriptive statistics is finding ways to present data efficiently and clearly, but fairly. We do not present all the raw data that we have gathered. **RAW DATA** are the untreated numbers that we take from each participant. Suppose we had measured the reaction times of 50 people under two differing conditions of illumination. It is of no use whatsoever presenting to our reader all 100 scores untreated. We have to *summarize* our data for the reader in order to give a clear picture of any trends or differences we have found. In this case, for instance, we would probably want to look at the average score in each condition.

BUT I CAN'T DO SUMS!

As with many of the ideas in this book, those we investigate here are based on everyday common-sense notions you have undoubtedly used before. Even if you hate maths, dread statistics and have never done any formal work in this area, you have undoubtedly made statistical descriptions many times in your life without necessarily being aware of it. You may believe that only clever, numerically minded people do this sort of thing, but consider this: imagine you have just come out of your first class at a new college and we meet in the refectory. Suppose I ask you what the other students were like and you decide to start with their ages. You would not proceed to tell me the exact age of each class member, this could take far too long. You'd be likely to say something such as 'Well, most people in the class are around 25 years old but there are a couple of teenagers and one or two are over 40'. You have, in fact, summarized the class ages statistically but of course a little loosely. First you gave me a rough *average*, the typical age in the group, then you gave me an idea of the *variation* from this typical age present in the group. These two concepts are absolutely *fundamental* to statistical description of measured data. This is an example of progressing from concepts that *naturally* occur to you in everyday life to a more formalized version of the same thing for statistical purposes. There are two general and formal terms for the two features of the class ages that you described. These are:

CENTRAL TENDENCY — this in some way refers to the most central or typical value of a dataset with different interpretations of the sense of 'central'. In the example above you gave me the value 25. In normal language, central tendency is better and more loosely known as 'the average'. In statistical description, however, we have to be more precise about just what *sort* of average we mean.

DISPERSION — this is a measure of the extent to which all the values in a set tend to *vary* around the central or typical value. This is an important concept and can be highlighted by looking at Table 8.6. Here, seven people from Dunton Parva, a rural community with a history of fox hunting, and seven from Slumditch, a deprived area of a large city, have been given an attitude scale concerning fox hunting where the top score possible is 40. The *average* for each group is identical but look at the *variation* within each group. It looks as if the people of Dunton Parva are quite divided on the issue whereas the people of Slumditch don't seem to have strong opinions either way – why should they; you don't get many fox hunts in Slumditch! Figure 8.2 shows the relative size of the two variations or dispersions.

Table 8.6   Attitude to fox hunting scores in Dunton Parva and Slumditch

Dunton Parva	Slumditch
38	19
12	27
36	23
8	24
25	21
34	22
9	26
23.1	23.1

Figure 8.2   Different sizes of dispersion for the fox hunting scores

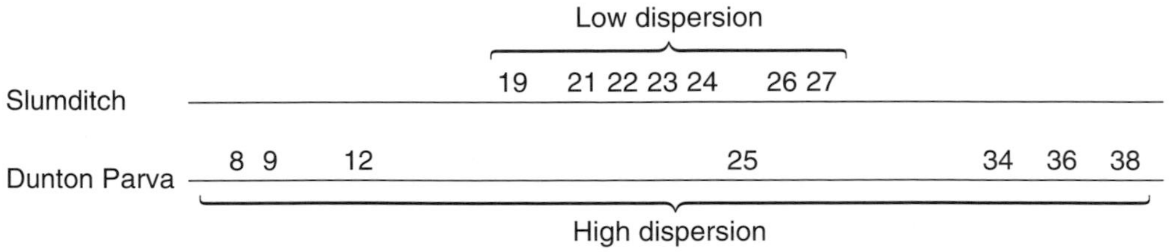

MEASURES OF CENTRAL TENDENCY

THE MEAN

The **MEAN** is what most people are thinking of when they talk about 'average' scores. To find the average amount you spend on telephone calls per month over one year you take all your bills for the 12 months, add them all up and divide by 12.

Box 8.6   Mean of five anagram solution times

> 17
> 10
> 23
> 12
> 13
> Total =   75 sec
>
> The mean is the total of all the scores divided by the *number* of scores. So if five people took 17, 10, 23, 12 and 13 seconds to solve an anagram, we have a total of 75 seconds and there are five values, so our mean is:
>
> $$\frac{75}{5} = 15 \text{ seconds}$$

THE FORMULA FOR THE MEAN

Let's not beat about the bush – we are going to use a *formula* for most statistical operations. A formula is simply a coded set of instructions – just like a food recipe – telling you what to do to find a certain statistic. In each case we will unpack the formula into the instructions, but don't worry, that's all formulae ever are – a tidy set of procedures.

The formula for the mean is:

$$\bar{x} = \frac{\sum x}{N}$$

The symbol $\bar{x}$ is used to denote the mean. The symbol $\sum$ is the Greek capital letter S and tells you to add up each of what follows. Each score is an 'x' so $\sum x$ simply means add up all the scores. N is the number of scores in the set. At the end of this chapter there is a summary of all kinds of notation such as this. When reporting results, 'M' is used for the mean.

Figure 8.3   Following a formula is just like following a recipe

PROCEDURE FOR FINDING THE MEAN

1. Add up all the values in the dataset – this is Σx.
2. Divide Σx by the number of values in the set – this is N – so we get $\dfrac{\Sigma x}{N}$.

ADVANTAGES AND DISADVANTAGES OF THE MEAN

ADVANTAGES

❑ The mean is a powerful statistic used in estimating *population parameters* (see p. 120) and this estimation is the basis for the more powerful *parametric* tests we can use to look for significant differences or correlations.

❑ It is the most *sensitive* and *accurate* of the three measures described here (because it works at an *interval* level of measurement and takes account of the *exact* distances between values in the dataset).

DISADVANTAGES

❑ Because the mean *is* so sensitive there is also a problem that it is easily distorted by one, or a few, 'rogue' and unrepresentative values. For instance, if six people did our anagram task (p. 113) and the sixth person took 225 seconds to find the solution, then the mean would become:

$$ x = \frac{17 + 10 + 23 + 12 + 13 + 225}{6} = \frac{300}{6} = 50 \text{ seconds} $$

225 is just not representative of the sample of scores in general. Five out of the six people were much quicker than this at solving the anagram. A score well outside the usual range, like this value of 225 in this group, is known as an 'outlier' and can seriously distort the mean value – see Figure 8.4.

A further small disadvantage of the mean is that with *discrete* variables we get 'silly' values for the mean and this is sometimes misleading, or at least distracting – for instance the notorious case of parents with 2.4 children.

Figure 8.4   A rogue value can distort the mean

A note on decimals and spurious accuracy, before we go any further – DON'T USE 5.42857!!!

Very often in a student report (and also sometimes because unformatted computer programs are used), the mean of 9, 8, 7, 5, 4, 3 and 2 might be reported as '5.42857'. The last four decimal figures add *nothing* to accuracy because the original numbers were *whole numbers* – the average just *cannot* be that accurate. A general rule of thumb is to round to *one decimal place below* the original values. Hence, here the appropriate mean value would be 5.4.

THE MEDIAN

The **MEDIAN**, unlike the mean, is not distorted by outliers. It is the *central value in a set*.

PROCEDURE FOR FINDING THE MEDIAN

1. Put all N scores into ascending order: 15, 7, 12, 20, 18 → 7, 12, 15, 18, 20
2. Find the median position $= \dfrac{N+1}{2}$. In the above example $\dfrac{5+1}{2} = 3$
3. If N is odd, the median position will be a number in the set and therefore this will be the median number. In the above example the median position is 3. The third value from the left is the median and this is 15. It is the *central* value of the set.
4. If N is even, the median position will fall between two values. Say there were six values. The median position would be $\dfrac{6+1}{2} = 3.5$. The value 3.5 tells us that the median is the mean of the third and fourth values in the set. For instance, with values of 3, 6, 9, 12, 20, 25 the median position is 3.5 and the median is the mean of the third value (9) and the fourth value (12): this is 10.5.

If the median falls among a set of values, as in 2, 3, 5, 5, 5, 5, 5, 8, 8, 9 where the median is among the 5s, there are precise but rather elaborate methods for finding the exact value of the median, depending upon how far into the set it falls. However, for most practical purposes 5 is a reasonable value for the median in the example just given.

ADVANTAGES AND DISADVANTAGES OF THE MEDIAN

ADVANTAGES

❏ Unaffected by extreme or 'rogue' values in one direction. Hence, better for use with '*skewed*' distributions – see later in this chapter.
❏ Easier to calculate than the mean (providing there are small groups and no ties, or the tied-values situation is overlooked).
❏ Can be obtained when the *value* of extreme data points is unknown. For example, if we add two values at the top end of a range of scores the median must simply move up by one position.

DISADVANTAGES

❏ Doesn't take into account the exact distances between values.
❏ Can't be used in estimates of population parameters – see later in this chapter.
❏ Can be unrepresentative in a small dataset; for instance, with values of 2, 3, 5, 98 and 112, the median would be 5.

THE MODE

The **MODE** is simply *the most frequently occurring value in a set*. For the set: 1, 2, 2, 4, 5, 6, 6, 6, 7, 8, 8, 9, the mode is 6, as there are more 6s than any other value. The set 2, 2, 3, 5, 6, 6, 7 is said to bi-modal since it contains two modes. The mode is the *value* or *data item* that occurs most often. It is *not* the number of times that item appears in the set, a mistake which is very easy to make. For instance, in Table 8.1 the mode is 'students' and not 650, which is the number of students that appeared in the set.

ADVANTAGES AND DISADVANTAGES OF THE MODE

ADVANTAGES

- ❑ Shows the most frequent or 'typical' value of a dataset.
- ❑ Unaffected by extreme values in one direction.
- ❑ Can be obtained when extreme values are unknown.
- ❑ Often more informative than the mean when scale is discrete.

DISADVANTAGES

- ❑ Doesn't take into account the exact distances between values.
- ❑ Can't be used in estimates of population parameters – see later in this chapter.
- ❑ Not at all useful for relatively small sets of data where several values occur equally frequently (1, 1, 2, 3, 4, 4).
- ❑ For bi-modal distributions two modal values need to be reported.
- ❑ Can't be estimated accurately when data have been grouped together into class intervals as in Figure 8.11. However, if people were originally asked only to choose an interval then we can have a modal interval.

CENTRAL TENDENCY MEASURES AND LEVELS OF MEASUREMENT

- ❑ **INTERVAL/RATIO:** the *mean* is the most sensitive measure but it should only be used if data are at least at the interval level of measurement. Otherwise, the mean is calculated with scores on a scale that does not have equal intervals. The resulting 'average' would then be misleading.
- ❑ **ORDINAL:** if data are not at interval level but can be ranked, then the *median* is the appropriate measure of central tendency.
- ❑ **NOMINAL:** if data are in discretely separate categories, then only the *mode* can be used.

The mode *may* also be used on ordinal- and interval-level data.
The median *may* also be used on interval-level data.

MEASURES OF DISPERSION

Take a look back to Table 8.6. We saw there that there was much more variation among the attitude scores of Dunton Parva residents than among Slumditch residents. This concept of variation is a feature of *all* sets of data and is of fundamental importance in statistical analysis. Even where a factory machine is programmed to produce components of *exactly* the same size there will always be some tiny variation among the components made. Cucumbers vary in length. Among people there is also obviously some variation in height and weight but also in psychologically important variables such as skills, attitudes and features of personality. Consequently, we need some measure of this variation within a group of values.

THE RANGE

The **RANGE** is simply the distance between the top and bottom values of a set.

PROCEDURE FOR FINDING THE RANGE

1. Find the top and bottom values of the set. In Box 8.6 these are 23 and 10.
2. Take the difference between the top and bottom values. In Box 8.6 we get 13.
3. Add 1 to the result of step 2. Here we get **14**.

Why add 1? Well, when we measure how long someone took to solve an anagram we cannot say they took *exactly* 23 seconds. For all interval measures like this we know only that they took somewhere between 22.5 and 23.5 seconds. The minimum could also be 9.5 so the range is $23.5 - 9.5 = 14$. When we measure on an interval scale we measure to the nearest *interval* not to exact points. We apply this approach even where scales are not truly interval, mainly because the idea is that they should be.

For the data in Table 8.6 we find that the range of Dunton Parva scores was 31 while the Slumditch range was 9. Same central tendency but very different dispersion!

ADVANTAGES AND DISADVANTAGES OF THE RANGE

ADVANTAGES
❑ Includes extreme values.
❑ Easy to calculate.

DISADVANTAGES
❑ Distorted by an extreme value at either end and can therefore be misleading.
❑ Unrepresentative of any features of the distribution of values between the extremes. For instance, the range doesn't tell us whether or not the values are closely grouped around the mean, with a few outliers, or generally spread out across the entire range.

THE INTERQUARTILE RANGE

A measure of dispersion that is a little more subtle than the range is the **INTERQUARTILE RANGE**. Here we simply have to find the score that is one-quarter of the way (the first **QUARTILE**) through the data and the score that is three-quarters (the third quartile) of the way through *when they are ordered* (don't forget this bit!). Remember that earlier we found the score that was half the way through and called it the median. The interquartile range is the distance between the two quartile values and the *semi-interquartile range* is, believe it or not, half this value! In the set of scores below:

7   7   9   12   14   16   16   17   19   20   22

9 is the first quartile and 19 is the third, so the interquartile range is **10** (and the semi-interquartile range is **5**).

ADVANTAGES AND DISADVANTAGES OF THE INTERQUARTILE RANGE

ADVANTAGES
❑ Tells us how the central data lie around the mean.
❑ Not affected by extreme scores at either end of the set.

DISADVANTAGES

❏ Makes no calculation on the lowest and highest quarters of the dataset.
   Cannot be used to check data for parametric tests (see Chapter 11).

WORKING WITH DEVIATIONS

Look back to Table 8.6. We saw there that the sample from Slumditch all had scores closely grouped around the mean of 23.1. The Dunton Parva sample had the same mean but their scores were very widely ranged around the mean. This was where we introduced the idea of variation within a group of scores. Now look at the scores as depicted in Figure 8.5. If we want to compare how much people vary from the mean of their group we need to look at their **DEVIATION SCORE**. *This is simply how far away their score is from the mean.* So how do we find that? Simply take the mean from their score. You should *always* take mean from the score and not the other way around otherwise things will go badly wrong. The formula for a deviation score is:

$$d = (x - \bar{x})$$

where *x is a score and* $\bar{x}$ is the mean.

If we take the mean away from the highest Dunton Parva score of 38 we get $d = 38 - 23.1 = 14.9$ and the size of this deviation is shown in Figure 8.5. You see that it is the largest deviation and far larger than any deviation in the Slumditch group. It is also positive, so it falls to the right-hand side of the mean in the diagram. The lowest Slumditch score was 19. Applying exactly the same approach (remember, take mean from score) we get $19 - 23.1 = -4.1$. The value is negative because it falls *below* the mean and is depicted to the *left* of the mean in the diagram.

Figure 8.5 Comparison of deviations of Slumditch and Dunton Parva attitude scores

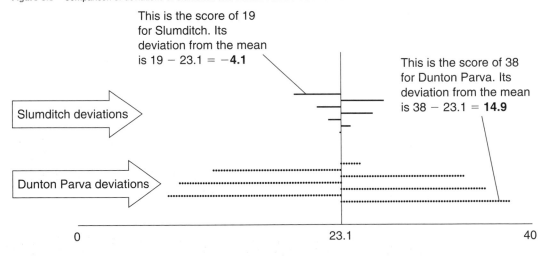

If we wanted to indicate how *much* variation there was within a group of values we could just take the mean of all these deviations. We would have to treat the negative ones as positive otherwise all the values would cancel each other out. We just take the actual *size* of the deviations without worrying which side of the mean they fall on. For the Dunton Parva crowd the average deviation would be quite high but for the Slumditch group it would be relatively small. The mean of all the absolute deviations in a group is known as the **MEAN DEVIATION**. It is little used in psychological research but the procedure for finding it is given in Coolican (2004). It is, however, just the mean of all the deviations in a group treating all the deviation values as positive.

STANDARD DEVIATION AND VARIANCE

As a measure of deviation within a group, statisticians much prefer something called the **STANDARD DEVIATION**, for some strange reason. Perhaps this is just because they like impressive-looking calculations. The mean deviation couldn't be easier to find and the standard deviation is a bit of a pig if you don't have a calculator – although Microsoft Excel will find it easily enough.

Actually I'm being a bit mean to statisticians here. There is a very *good* reason why the standard deviation is a very commonly used statistic in the social sciences. A little later in the book we will come across the issue of *parametric tests* and their reliance on the normal distribution. The standard deviation is intimately connected with this and is very useful indeed for *estimating* values in a population from values in a sample.

Hopefully you will have a calculator that will work out the standard deviation for you, or perhaps you may have some way of doing it on a computer. However, if you do have to work it out manually, here's how you do it. Let's first of all take a look at the formula for standard deviation. This is:

$$s = \sqrt{\frac{\Sigma(x - \bar{x})^2}{N - 1}}$$

Note that this looks easier as $s = \sqrt{\dfrac{\Sigma d^2}{N - 1}}$ when $d = (x - \bar{x})$ as explained above.

Note also that the **VARIANCE** is simply the square of the standard deviation and is therefore what is found in the above equation *without* the square-root sign.

PROCEDURE FOR FINDING THE STANDARD DEVIATION

What does that nasty little formula in fact tell us to do? Remember, a formula is just a set of instructions. It says take each d (which is the same as $x - \bar{x}$) and square it (multiply it by itself) and then add up all the results of this operation on each d in the set. Divide that result by $N - 1$, which is simply the number of scores in the sample minus one. Finally, take the square root of that result. The square root is the opposite of the square and any calculator will produce it (for instance the square root of 9 is 3 because $3 \times 3 = 9$). Let's work through it, step by step, on an example. Let's take the Dunton Parva scores from Table 8.6.

Procedure	Calculation on data in Table 8.7
1. Find the mean of the dataset	$x = 23.1$ see Table 8.6
2. Subtract the mean from each value in the dataset, obtaining the deviation values $(x - \bar{x})$ in each case but use d as shorthand)	See Table 8.7, column 2
3. Square each d	See Table 8.7, column 3
4. Find the sum of the squared deviations $(=\Sigma d^2)$	$\Sigma d^2 = 1060.87$ (total of Table 8.7, column 3)
5. Divide the result of step 4 by $N - 1$	$1060.87/6 = s^2 = 176.81$ **(this is the *Variance*)**
6. Find the square root of step 5	$\sqrt{176.81} = s = \mathbf{13.30}$

The standard deviation for the Dunton Parva scores is 13.30 (note that we have to put the zero at the end of the number to show that the decimals have been rounded – the calculator gave 13.296 etc.

If you use a calculator, make sure you use the version of the standard deviation formula that has $N - 1$ on the bottom of the equation. Most statistical calculators will show this with a symbol such as σ_{n-1}.

The symbol for standard deviation in a formula is:
    s if you have the standard deviation of a sample only
    σ if you have the standard deviation of a whole group or 'population'.

When reporting results, 'SD' is used.

ADVANTAGES

❑ Tells us how *all* the data lie around the mean.
❑ Used to make parametric estimates and checks (see Chapter 11).

DISADVANTAGES

❑ Affected by extreme scores at either end of the set.
❑ Harder to calculate than other measures of dispersion.

Table 8.7   Part of standard deviation calculations on the Dunton Parva attitude scores

Score (x)	$d = (x - 23.1)$	d^2
38	14.9	222.01
12	−11.1	123.21
36	12.9	166.41
8	−15.1	228.01
25	1.9	3.61
34	10.9	118.81
9	−14.1	198.81
		$\Sigma d^2 = 1060.87$

POPULATION PARAMETERS AND SAMPLE STATISTICS

Around election time you will often see the results of a survey of voting intentions claiming that the results are accurate 'to within + or − 3%'. These surveys are conducted by commercial organizations with a very strong vested interest in getting the outcome of the election right. Newspapers would not pay for their services if their outcomes were wrong. They take a sample, often as few as 1500 people, and from this they are able to predict pretty accurately how the entire voting population is thinking of voting *at that moment*. In psychology we are usually *not* interested in the features of the sample we have drawn for a research study specifically. We are, like the pollsters, interested in the *population* from which they have been drawn. Suppose a researcher reasons that having a pet helps to calm nerves and therefore that students with pets do better in exams than students who don't. It is impossible to test all students with and without pets. What we do is to take equivalent *samples* of students with and without pets and measure their exam performance. If we get a sizeable difference we assume, for the time being, that a pet has an effect on exam performance *in the population generally*.

Figure 8.6   Do pets improve exam performance?

Statistics that apply to samples are called, unsurprisingly, **STATISTICS** but those that apply to populations are called **PARAMETERS**. Tests that make inferences about the size of population parameters are known as *parametric tests* and we shall meet these in Chapters 11 and 12. In the formula for standard deviation we looked at above, the value $N - 1$ is used. If we were finding the *average* squared deviation we would use N, as we do in finding the mean of anything. However, the standard deviation used in parametric tests is an *estimate* of the *population* standard deviation. When we estimate we like to allow a bit of tolerance (what statisticians call *sampling error*) by making the estimate a little larger; this is done by using a smaller value ($N - 1$, not N) on the bottom of the equation. **SAMPLING ERROR** occurs when we take a sample and try to estimate the population mean or standard deviation from just the sample. We will always be a little bit out and that's the 'error'.

PROGRESS REVIEW 8.2

EXERCISES

1. The following times taken to solve an anagram were recorded (in seconds):
   12, 8, 23, 13, 17, 15, 18, 21, 18, 14, 18, 29, 55, 12.
   (a) Decide which would be the most appropriate measure of central tendency
   (b) Calculate the mean, median and mode for the data
   (c) Can you suggest why the mean is a little higher than the median?
   (d) Calculate the range, interquartile range and standard deviation (the last only if you feel like it and it's on your syllabus).
2. A set of scores includes a value of 3.2 and has a standard deviation of zero. Can you guess what is the mean and what the rest of the scores are?
3. What is a little odd about a politician's statement of outrage that 'as many as half the children were under the average reading age'?

ANSWERS

1. (a) The measure is at interval level, so the mean would be appropriate, but you might have noticed that the mean will be affected by the extreme score of 55, so perhaps the median is more fair
   (b) mean = 19.5; median = 17.5; mode = 18
   (c) as stated above, the mean will be affected by the score of 55; the median isn't.
   (d) range = 48; interquartile range = 21 − 13 = 8; standard deviation = 11.49.

2. If there are no deviations *at all* then all scores must be the same. Therefore all are 3.2 and so is the mean.
3. Unless there is a lot of skew (see p. 131) we would *always* expect just about half of any group to score under the group mean and half to score over it. It is a measure of *central* tendency!

KEY TERMS

Central tendency	Parameter
Deviation score	Quartile
Dispersion	Range
Interquartile range	Sampling error
Mean	Standard deviation
Mean deviation	Statistic
Median	Variance
Mode	

GROUPING DATASETS – DISTRIBUTIONS

The statistics we gather in a study are known as the **DATASET**. If you conduct a simple experiment on a sample of around 12 people you will obtain a dataset of 12 scores and there's really not a lot more you can do with the data other than summarize them with the mean and standard deviation. However, imagine you conducted a survey on the entire college or school population, asking them to rate the quality of the eating facilities. When we have a large dataset like this we can look at the overall *distribution* of the data.

Table 8.1, p. 105, shows results for a categorical or nominal variable – 'type of person' – and how many of that type of person were recorded. This number of how many there were is known as the '*frequency*' of occurrences. These frequencies are shown in the second column of the table. The table as a whole is known as a **FREQUENCY DISTRIBUTION**. Suppose we were recording the month in which parents fist notice their infant make a telegraphic utterance (e.g. 'Mummy sock'). If we record data from a lot of parents we can't present the data in a table but we can show the *distribution* of all data, recorded as in Table 8.8.

Table 8.8   Ages at which parents notice first telegraphic utterance.

Age (months)	13	14	15	16	17	18	19	20	21	22	23	24	25	26	27	Total
No. of children reported	1	0	5	12	37	64	59	83	17	41	12	0	4	5	0	340

A FREQUENCY DISTRIBUTION

FREQUENCY TABLES WITH CLASS INTERVALS

If we take a *measure* of some variable, such as time or weight, we have to work with *measurement intervals*. We met this point back on p. 117. If we measure how many seconds people take to solve an anagram we cannot measure to the exact second. If we are measuring in seconds and our stopwatch measures to tenths of a second then we might measure to the *nearest* second. Anything between 17.5 and 18.4 will count as 18 seconds. In Table 8.9 notice that the **CLASS INTERVALS** do *not* read '10–15', '15–20' and so on, as so often appears in poor tables. This is because we would have a problem entering a value of 20 – into which category would it fall? The interval 15–19 ends with anything that is not quite 19.5. Since our watch measures only to the nearest tenth of a second this effectively means anything at 19.4 or under. Timings of 19.5 or 19.6 seconds would go into the 20–24 interval. This is because we cannot measure *exactly* to 20 seconds: we measure the interval 19.5 to 20.4 seconds.

Table 8.9 Time (sec) to solve an anagram – frequencies in class intervals

Seconds	No. of participants (f)	Cumulative frequency	Number of participants less than:
5–9	2	2	9.5
10–14	0	2	14.5
15–19	8	10	19.5
20–24	18	28	24.5
25–29	13	41	29.5
30–34	5	46	34.5
34–39	4	50	39.5

A FREQUENCY TABLE WITH CLASS INTERVALS

Table 8.9 shows the frequency (f) of participants in each class interval. Hence we see that 8 participants took between 15 and 19 seconds to solve the anagram. The next column in the table is the **CUMULATIVE FREQUENCY** – that is, how many people have scored less than the top limit of this interval. The top limit of the interval is, in fact, 19.5 as was explained above. For the 15–19 interval, then, the cumulative frequency is the 8 in that interval plus the 2 below it, hence 10.

GRAPHICAL REPRESENTATION

It is very useful for readers to see a *summary* of the data in a chart. Note that all such charts are called 'figures', as are any other pictorial items, when you write your report. A table is different: it has columns and rows and is called a table! Here are a couple of other points to bear in mind before presenting any charts:

❑ **Don't waste time on prettiness and clutter**. Drawing a chart is not a contest in how pretty and impressive it can be. You need to present just the clear information required. Programs such as Excel will produce very elaborate three-dimensional charts in many colours but you will distract your reader with these if you are not careful. Stick to a simple conventional design and do not, under any circumstance, present the *same* data in lots of different charts – 'just for variety'!
❑ **Don't draw the raw data**. Charts are summaries of data *only*. The reader should get a good picture of the overall pattern in the data that you want them to see. A common error is to produce a chart such as that in Figure 8.7, with a bar or column representing each individual participant's score. What we see here gives no overall impression of a pattern in the data. It is *not* a summary of the data and it is quite unruly. The bars are arranged only by the arbitrary order in which participants were tested. We would not expect any pattern here and we have none. There is, in short, absolutely no point to the chart at all.

Figure 8.7   Inappropriate chart of individual participants' scores

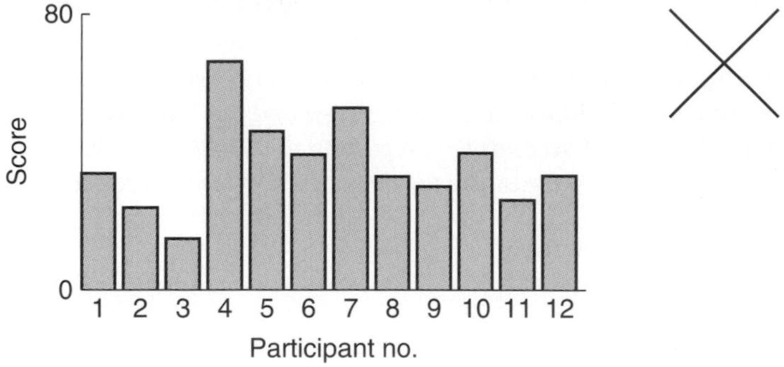

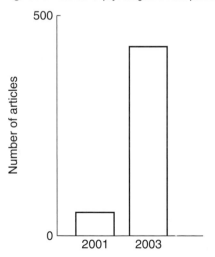

THE BAR CHART

A bar chart usually shows a statistic for groups or categories of people but the categories on the horizontal axis could also be newspapers, years, stores – in fact anything that is a set of categories where you have a statistical value for each category. The horizontal or *X* axis always depicts a nominal or categorical variable even if it is years as in Figure 8.8. Here a *selection* of years has been made in order to show an important contrast from the author's point of view. If *all* years were shown for which there were values then the chart would become a special bar chart known as a *histogram* – see below. Because the X axis represents discrete categories, the bars on a bar chart should always be *separated*.

Figure 8.8   Number of psychological articles published on terrorism

A bar chart

An example of a fair bar chart is given in Figure 8.9a. Here we can see that female A Level maths results in 2004 for grades A to C are slightly ahead of those for males – the percentages are in fact 79.1 for females and 73.6 for males. However, an unscrupulous newspaper journalist might exaggerate this difference as in Figure 8.9b, for an article perhaps entitled 'Girls streak ahead in Maths' or 'Big concern over male slippage in A Level Maths'. The chart is a cheat because it does not make obvious the fact that the Y axis (the left-hand vertical axis) does not start from zero. Hence the eye is drawn to an unrealistic 'big' difference between male and female results. There is a difference, of course, but not as big as Figure 8.9b makes out.

Figure 8.9 Percentage of female and male students obtaining grades A to C in A Level Maths, Summer 2004 (all boards)
Source: *Guardian* – http://education.guardian.co.uk/alevels2004/story/0,14505,1285751,00.html

(a) Fair bar chart

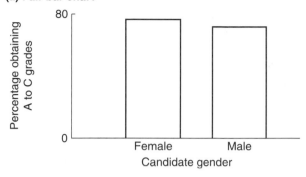

(b) Misleading bar chart

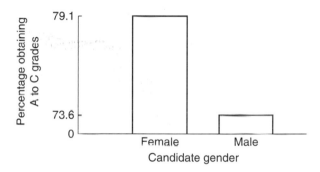

If the columns would be awkwardly tall were the Y axis to start from zero, the chart can show an obvious break in the Y axis to inform the reader that not all the Y axis is shown, as in Figure 8.10. This bar chart is also an example of a *combined* bar chart in which two measures have been displayed side by side, as denoted by the differently shaded adjacent bars.

Figure 8.10 Mean number of apparent movement detections made by four age groups in mid and extreme periphery (from David, Chapman, Foot and Sheehy, 1986), reproduced with permission from *The British Journal of Psychology* © The British Psychological Society

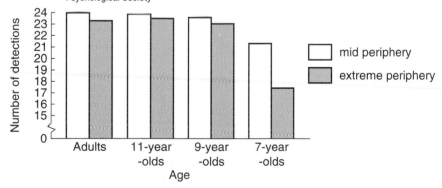

THE HISTOGRAM

A histogram of the data in Table 8.9 would look like the chart shown in Figure 8.11. The width of each column must be the same and represents the class interval size. The intervals are labelled according to their mid-point. The first interval (shown on the left) is the 5–9 interval. The limits of this are from 4.5 to 9.5, as explained earlier, so the exact mid-point of the interval is 7. The height of each column represents (*and can only ever represent*) the number of cases (frequency) falling into that interval. Hence the 15–19 interval (mid-point 17) has a column eight units tall because Table 8.9 tells us there were eight cases in this interval. Notice that all bars are joined together and we have to have a toothy gap if there are no cases in an interval, assuming there are cases either side. There is a reason for this, which might become clearer once we begin to look at the normal distribution in a short while. Basically, the area of any column or set of columns is proportional to the number of cases shown. Hence, because the columns are 1 unit wide and the 5–9 interval has a column two cases high, the area here is 2. The total area of the histogram is 50 because there were 50 cases altogether. The 5–9 column then takes up 2/50ths of the entire chart area. Because there are no cases from 10 to 14 we must show no area but must also show that there *was* no area (i.e. no cases). You could call the 5–9 column 4% of the total area because 2 is 4% of the total area of 50. However, it is conventional to think of the entire area of the chart as a unit, that is as 1, and then to express parts in decimals. This means that the 5–9 column would have an area of 0.04, which is the same as 4%. If you are a little hazy on decimals, fractions and percentages then Table 8.10 below might help.

We usually have the intervals or scores on the X axis (the horizontal one) and the frequency on the Y axis (the vertical one). Some programs (such as Excel) show a histogram on its side with categories to the left and bars running horizontally and increasing in size from left to right.

Table 8.10 Go on, admit it! You've forgotten how to convert fractions to decimals, or something like that

Percentage to fraction to decimal	Decimal to fraction to percentage
Start with 5%	Start with 0.01
Remove the % sign and put the number over 100 $(= \frac{5}{100})$	**Decimal to fraction** Any decimal number can be turned into a fraction as follows:
	❑ put the digits to the right of the decimal point over a number starting with 1 followed by as many zeros as there are digits in the decimal part.
Divide 5 by 100 by adding a decimal point* to the right of the 5 and moving it two places to the left:	❑ lose any zeros to the left of the first whole digit:
$\frac{5}{100} \rightarrow 5.0 \rightarrow 0.5 \rightarrow 0.05$	$0.01 \rightarrow$ 2 digits after decimal point so $\rightarrow \frac{1}{100}$
	$0.375 \rightarrow$ 3 digits after decimal point so $\rightarrow \frac{375}{1000}$
* if there already is a decimal point just move right on:	**Fraction to percentage** Percentages are just fractions of 100 so $\frac{1}{100} = 1\%$, $\frac{43}{100} = 43\%$
$2.5\% \rightarrow \frac{2.5}{100} \rightarrow 0.25 \rightarrow 0.025$	Hence 0.01 $\rightarrow \frac{1}{100} \rightarrow 1\%$
	For the fraction $\frac{375}{1000}$ we need the bottom part to be 100. Convert this by dividing top and bottom by 10.
	$\frac{375}{1000} \rightarrow \frac{37.5}{100}$
	(to divide by 10 just move the decimal point one to the left, so 375 becomes 37.5)
	Hence, 0.375 $\rightarrow \frac{375}{1000} \rightarrow 37.5\%$

Figure 8.11   Frequencies of times (in class intervals) to solve an anagram

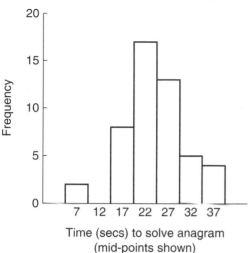

Time (secs) to solve anagram
(mid-points shown)

THE NORMAL DISTRIBUTION

Earlier in this chapter we learned that measurements on an interval scale should really be seen as intervals, rather than an exact point. Think of measuring someone's height. After all the squashing down of hair and arguments about sock thickness and tip-toeing, what you finally do is to look at the closest line on your tape measure – it is rarely the case that someone looks to be *on* the line. What you do, in effect, is to place them in an interval – nearer to 163 cm than 164 cm, and therefore between 162.5 and 163.5 cm tall. If we take a *very large* sample of people and measure their heights in this manner, then plot their heights on a histogram, we will obtain a chart looking pretty much like that in Figure 8.12. Because statisticians do a lot of things with the area under the curve formed by the bars, we must plot the columns adjacent to one another, without gaps, unlike a bar chart.

Figure 8.12   Frequency distribution of heights measured to the nearest centimetre

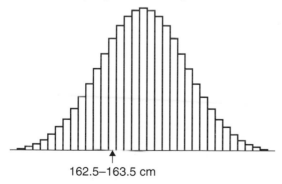

162.5–163.5 cm

The shape of the histogram approximates to a very important mathematical curve known as a *bell curve* – see Figure 8.13 – for what I hope are pretty obvious reasons! It is also more formally known as a **NORMAL DISTRIBUTION**. Remember, no set of data actually fits a normal distribution perfectly – that's the way with selecting things at random – but each very large random sample will *closely* approximate to it – you can count on that, too.

Figure 8.13   A normal distribution curve

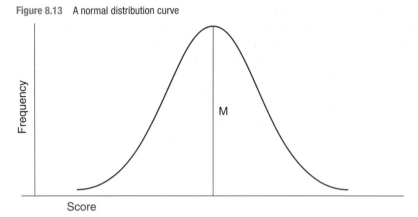

Approximations to the normal curve – and normal people

In what follows it's very important to remember that when psychological variables are said to be 'normally distributed', or 'standardized to fit a normal distribution', we are always talking about *approximations* to a pure normal curve. People *en masse* always differ a little from the ideal. This matters because, when we come to testing significance, the statistical theory often assumes a normal distribution *for the population from which samples were drawn*. If population values on the variable form nothing like a normal distribution, then the conclusions from the significance test may be seriously in error. It's also important not to be morally outraged by the term 'normal' when it seems to be used to describe people. The curve is called 'normal' for purely *mathematical* reasons (you may remember the use of the term 'normal' as meaning 'perpendicular' in geometry).

AREA UNDER THE NORMAL DISTRIBUTION CURVE

Suppose we devise a reading test for eight-year-olds, use it to test a large sample of children, and find the mean and standard deviation. No matter what the raw scores actually are we can convert them all so that the mean and standard deviation become figures that are easy to work with. This procedure is part of the process known as *standardization* that we mentioned in Chapter 6. The rest of the process involves fiddling with the test until it does indeed produce a normal distribution. Let's suppose that for our representative sample of eight-year-olds, the mean is 40 and the standard deviation is 10. I hope it is obvious, for starters, that 50% of eight-year-olds will therefore be above 40 and 50% below. The area for the top 50% is *all* the shaded area in Figure 8.14.

Figure 8.14   Distribution of reading scores for eight-year-old children

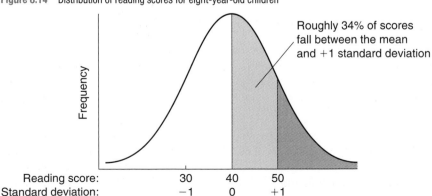

Remember earlier that we calculated a statistic known as the standard deviation. This is a kind of average deviation from the mean for all scores. In statistics we can say that *if a distribution is normal* then we know where the standard deviation will fall on that distribution; that is, we know the percentage of scores that will be above and below it. This is why researchers spend a lot of effort trying to make psychological measures fit a normal distribution.

On Figure 8.14 I hope you can see that about 34% of scores fall between the mean and one standard deviation above the mean. This isn't magic! It's because it *is* a normal distribution. So about 34% of eight-year-old children score between 40 and 50 because the mean is 40 and the standard deviation is 10 points. The same figure (34%) would apply to the number of children one standard deviation *below* the mean.

In more detail we know the following:

% of scores between mean and $\pm$ 1 standard deviation	34.13
% of scores between mean and $\pm$ 2 standard deviations	47.72
% of scores between mean and $\pm$ 3 standard deviations	49.87

These positions are shown on Figure 8.15 but here we have doubled the percentages to show the area of the curve and therefore the percentage of scores between 1, 2 or 3 standard deviations *above and below* the mean. For instance, 95.44% of scores should fall between -2 standard deviations and $+2$ standard deviations.

Figure 8.15 Positions of standard deviations and the areas they enclose on the normal distribution

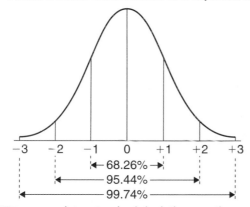

Area between $-n$ and $+n$ standard deviations on the normal curve

STANDARD SCORES (Z SCORES) AND THE NORMAL DISTRIBUTION

A person who has a score exactly one standard deviation above the mean is said to have a *z* score (also known as a **STANDARD SCORE**) of $+1$. Hence if the national average IQ score were 100 with a standard deviation of 15, and if you scored 115 on IQ, you would have a *z* score of $+1$. We can measure distances from the mean in units of one standard deviation. A person with an IQ of 130 has a *z* score of $+2$.

General definition: a *z* score is the number of standard deviations a score falls above or below the mean.

Let's take an easy example in order to introduce the formula for calculating z scores. Suppose the average shoe size in your class is 7, the standard deviation is 2 and big-footed Harry takes an 11. How many standard deviations above the mean is he? You probably worked that out easily enough but let's see formally what you did. You needed the following data:

$$x = 11 \qquad \bar{x} = 7 \qquad s = 2$$

You must have thought something like this: 'Harry is 4 sizes above the mean $(11 - 7)$; his deviation is therefore 4; each standard deviation is 2; so he's 2 standard deviations above the mean – his z score is 2'. Basically, you took Harry's *deviation* and *divided it by the standard deviation*. Here's how what you did looks as a formula:

$$z = \frac{x - \bar{x}}{s}$$

This is just the deviation divided by the standard deviation. z-score calculation is not usually as friendly as I've made out; means and standard deviations are rarely such simple numbers. However, all you have to remember to get a z score is *to divide the deviation by the standard deviation*. You get the deviation by taking the mean from any individual raw score.

If you now look back to Figure 8.15 you can see that there are not many people above Harry on a normal distribution. Assuming shoe size *is* normally distributed we would expect roughly 2.5% of the population to be above Harry. Why? Because roughly 95% of people (specifically 95.44%) lie between -2 and $+2$ standard deviations on Figure 8.15. There are 5% of people outside this range, half of them at the very low end and half at the very top end. Hence 2.5% lie above Harry.

That wasn't too hard to work out, I hope. However, how would we find out the percentage of people above a z value of 1.5? This is not shown on our figure. Fortunately, there have been people in the past who have worked out all the answers for us. If you turn to Table 2 on p. 254 you'll see that a z value of 1.5 appears near the bottom of the very left-hand column. The columns go in threes – first the z value, then the amount of the curve it cuts off above the mean; the third column is the amount that is left *above* this z value (i.e. to the right-hand side of the curve). The area referred to is the shaded portion in the diagram at the top of the second and third columns. In this case we find that 0.4332 of the curve (that's 43.32%) lies between the mean and a z score of 1.5. Above this lies 6.68% – look at the third column for this result.

Values for *negative* z scores are calculated using a mirror image. A z score of -2.2 traps 0.4861 of the area between it and the mean on the left-hand side – call it 0.486 and that's 48.6%. Since the *whole* of the left-hand side of the mean is 50% of the area, then by subtracting 48.6 from 50, we find that only 1.4% is left at the left-hand extreme *below* -2.2 standard deviations.

PSYCHOLOGICAL SCALES, STANDARDIZATION AND THE NORMAL DISTRIBUTION

The relationship between z scores and area under the normal curve is of crucial importance in the world of psychological testing. *If* (and it is a big 'if') a variable can be assumed to be normally distributed in the population, *and* we have a test standardized on large samples, then we can quickly assess the relative position of people by using their raw test score converted to a z score. This is valuable when assessing, for instance, children's reading ability, general intellectual or language development, adult stress, anxiety, aptitude for certain occupations (at interview) and so on. Educational psychologists can tell where a child is relative to the rest of the population of children their age. You should also note here that IQ tests do not measure a natural normal distribution of intelligence. IQ tests were *purposely* created to *fit* a normal distribution, basically for research purposes and practical convenience in test comparisons. Usually, an IQ test is *standardized* (raw scores are adjusted) to produce a mean of 100 and a standard deviation of around 15 points.

SKEWED DISTRIBUTIONS

If a distribution has more extreme scores in one direction than the other it is said to be skewed in that direction – see Figure 8.16. If the skew is large then the mean can be seriously distorted whereas the other measures remain relatively representative of the central tendency. Reaction times tend to be positively skewed because it is easy to be a lot *slower* than the average time but difficult to be very much *faster*.

Figure 8.16   Skewed distributions

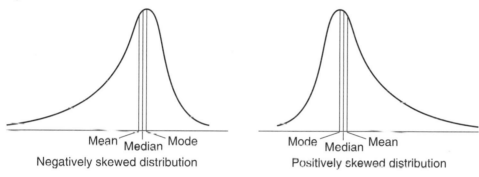

Negatively skewed distribution   Positively skewed distribution

PROGRESS REVIEW 8.3

EXERCISES

1. Find suitable class intervals for the data below and sketch a histogram:
      62 65 71 72 73 75 76 77 79 80 82 83 92 100 106 117 127
      65 70 72 72 74 75 76 77 79 80 82 88 93 102 110 121 128
      65 70 72 73 74 76 76 78 80 81 83 90 95 103 112 122 135
   (a) Inspect the histogram and decide what would be an appropriate measure of central tendency
   (b) Calculate this measure.
2. (a) Sketch two roughly normal distributions that have the same mean but different standard deviations
   (b) Also sketch two normal distributions with the same standard deviation but different means.
3. In a distribution of IQ scores where the mean is 100 and the standard deviation is 15:
   (a) What is the IQ value that 16% of people are above?
   (b) What percentage of people would score lower than 70?
   (c) What percentage of people would score lower than a person with a z score of -1.3?
   (d) What is the IQ score of a person with a z score of 2?

ANSWERS

1. a. data are skewed, hence use median which is → b. 79.
2. See Figure 8.17.
3. a. 115; b. about 2.3%; c. 9.68%; d. 130.

KEY TERMS

Bar chart	Negative skew
Class interval	Normal distribution
Cumulative frequency	Positive skew
Dataset	Skewed distribution
Frequency distribution	Standard score (z score)
Histogram	

Figure 8.17   Possible answers to question 2 in Progress review 8.3

a)

b)

STATISTICAL NOTATION AND SYMBOLS

N is the number in a sample
N_a is the number in sample A
x is a value from the sample, such as Jane's score
y is also a value where there are two measured variables
Σ Greek letter S ('sigma') – means 'add up each of what follows'. For instance: Σx means 'add up all the xs in the sample' (further examples below).

STATISTICAL SYMBOLS

SAMPLE			POPULATION		
Mean	Standard deviation	Variance	Mean	Standard deviation	Variance
$\bar{x}$	s	s^2	μ	σ	σ^2

Note: 'M' and 'SD' are used when reporting results. See p. 162, Box 11.1.

SOME RULES

1. In mathematical formulae it is confusing, especially in statistics, to use the multiplication sign ($\times$) because there are so many 'x's dotted around anyway. 'x' refers to a particular score or value. In formulae the multiplication sign is omitted, so when one value is immediately next to another we know we have to multiply them together. For instance, rN means 'multiply r by N'.
2. Always complete what is *inside* a bracket, or after a Σ or $\sqrt{}$ symbol, before going on to do the operation *outside*.

Here are some examples of the rules in action:

Σxy means 'multiply all the xs by their paired ys and add up all the results'. Notice that xy means 'multiply x by y' and we add up the results only after doing the multiplications on all xs and ys.

$\sum x^2$ means 'square all the xs, *then* add them all up'. *Be careful* to distinguish this from:

$(\sum x)^2$ means 'find the total of all the xs and square the result'.

$\sum x \sum y$ means multiply the sum of all the xs by the sum of all the ys.

$\sum(x - \bar{x})^2$ means subtract the mean from each score (x), square each result, then add up all these results.

$(N - 1)(N - 2)$ means find $N - 1$, find $N - 2$ and then multiply these two results.

$r\sqrt{\left(\dfrac{(N - 2)}{(1 - r^2)}\right)}$ means:

1. find r^2
2. find $1 - r^2$
3. find $N - 2$
4. divide step 3 by step 2
5. find the square root of step 4
6. multiply the result of step 5 by r.

chapter
9

Significance testing and probability

What's in this chapter?

❏ This chapter is all about making the decision that an effect shown in a study (difference or correlation) is probably a real effect and not just chance fluctuation in the data.
❏ We look at the logic of significance testing.
❏ We introduce the concepts of the *null hypothesis* and the *alternative* or *experimental hypothesis*.
❏ A brief introduction to *probability* is given. This is necessary to understand the basis on which the null hypothesis is rejected (when the probability of results occurring under it are too low).
❏ *Levels of significance* are described, the main one being 0.05 but the use of 0.01 and 0.1 is also discussed.
❏ Further concepts introduced are *Type I* and *Type II* errors and the link between *directional hypotheses* and *one-tailed tests*, and non-*directional hypotheses* and *two-tailed tests*.

Take a look back to Boxes 8.1 to 8.4 on p. 103 in the last chapter. Here we introduced a situation that is quite common in everyday life – that is, where you have to decide whether a difference is caused by some real effect or whether the difference can be written off as 'pure chance'. This chapter is all about making decisions like these but here we learn to do this in a formal and precise manner. In each inferential statistical test that we will look at in the following chapters the decision is always between:

      1. Do these data provide convincing evidence of an effect (that something is going on)?

and

      2. Do these data look as though only random factors are at work?

Let's look at a practical psychological example. It's best to remember that in carrying out a significance test we are *doing science*, checking out predictions from hypotheses to see if our evidence will support them. An argument for a research project might run like this:

Observation and argument	When a task is simple, people often 'do their best' when they are being watched and consequently their performance tends to improve. Triplett (1898) was the first to research this. He observed that cyclists trained harder when together than when alone. However, for more complex tasks, people often complain when they are being watched and say this puts them off. They also seem to do worse.
Hypothesis to be tested	People's performance on a complex task is worse when being observed than when alone.
Research and prediction	Participants will complete a 'wiggly wire' task like those seen at village fêtes. They have to pass a loop of wire on the end of a stick over an electrified wiggly wire without touching it. The number of times the wires touch will be recorded. They will do this alone and then again with an audience of six people. Conditions will be counterbalanced. It is predicted that the mean time for participants in the audience condition will be higher than the mean time for the alone condition.

Here we have a hypothesis and a proposed empirical test of it, along with an operationalized (see p. 22) **RESEARCH PREDICTION**. Note that the research prediction, if found valid, will *support* the research hypothesis. Let's suppose that two groups of students, one fastidiously correct and tidy in everything they do, and the other rather sloppy and careless, attempt to carry out the suggested experiment. Let's suppose their results are as shown in Table 9.1.

Table 9.1   Time (seconds) spent touching wire in wiggly-wire task while alone and when in front of an audience – for two student groups

(a) Results for sloppy student group		(b) Results for conscientious student group	
With audience	Alone	With audience	Alone
9.9	5.2	14.8	4.1
15.1	3.3	13.5	3.2
16.2	9.1	9.6	5.7
11.7	6.1	8.7	9.0
11.1	16.2	12.2	11.3
9.1	2.7	15.3	2.8
10.0	7.8	18.6	5.1
8.5	18.2	12.1	6.1
1.3	10.3	15.8	3.3
2.4	9.0	17.1	7.2
Mean = 9.53	Mean = 8.79	Mean = 13.77	Mean = 5.78

The sloppy student group might claim that the experiment 'worked' because the mean for the 'alone' condition is lower than the mean for the 'audience' condition. Is this convincing evidence that the audience caused people to perform worse? Well, the difference is rather small, especially when you look at the amount of *variation* there is in each condition (from 1.3 seconds to 16.2 seconds in the audience condition – a *range* of 15 seconds). A difference of just 0.74 seconds between the two means doesn't seem very convincing, does it?

However, when we look at the conscientious students' results we get a difference between the means of almost 8 seconds, yet the dispersion is similar to that for the sloppy group's results. That looks much more like it but we cannot, in psychological science, rely on a gut reaction that the results 'look good'. We need a convention that everyone involved with research agrees to and understands. This convention will tell us when to decide that results appear to indicate a real underlying difference (an 'effect') and when to decide that results are not sufficiently high above chance level. This system of *testing for significance* is what we are now going to look at.

AN EVERYDAY SIGNIFICANCE TEST INTRODUCING THE NULL AND ALTERNATIVE HYPOTHESES

People find the concept of significance difficult, yet everything that is in the logic of significance testing is contained in the thinking of Alfie in the scenario below:

Jake: 'I've learned how to toss a coin – see, that's one head, two heads, … eight heads in a row.'

Alfie: 'Let me see that coin. You don't get eight heads in a row with an unbiased coin very often. I bet it's a fix!'

It's as simple as that. We use significance-testing logic very often in everyday life – when we decide the milkman has overcharged us once too often, when we decide that the right-hand lane really does move faster.

The essence of Alfie's thinking was as follows:

❑ Assume the coin is unbiased or 'fair'.
❑ Estimate the probability of eight heads coming up in a row **if it is unbiased**.
❑ If the probability is very low then decide the coin is not 'fair'.

This initial assumption is known as the **NULL HYPOTHESIS**. Here it is that the coin is unbiased or, put more formally, that the frequencies of the coin landing on heads and tails are equal over large numbers of tosses. It is this latter form of the assumption that allows Alfie to estimate that the probability of getting eight heads in a row is very low – too low for coincidence. He therefore rejects coincidence as an explanation of the coin-toss sequence and assumes the coin is biased. This assumption is known as the alternative hypothesis. The **ALTERNATIVE HYPOTHESIS** is everything that the null hypothesis is not. The alternative hypothesis, also called the **EXPERIMENTAL HYPOTHESIS**, is usually what we have set out to support in conducting our research study. We have symbols for the null and alternative hypotheses as follows:

Null hypothesis H_0: The coin produces equal numbers of heads and tails.
Alternative hypothesis H_1: The coin produces unequal numbers of heads and tails.

WHY DO WE NEED A NULL HYPOTHESIS?

We need the null hypothesis because we simply can't go round saying 'Well, what's the probability of *that* happening *by chance*?'. What do we mean by 'by chance'? We mean something like 'if there's nothing going on' or 'if there is no other influence'. When learning about significance you should always try to substitute the words 'by chance' with 'if the null hypothesis is true'. Hence you get 'Find the probability of that happening if the null hypothesis is true' rather than the vague 'Find the probability of that happening by chance'.

The formality we have introduced is still reflected in everyday talk. We say things like 'If they're not seeing each other then how come he knew her number?', or 'If the milkman's not on the make then how come he's given us a pint short so often?'.

Here are some important points about a null hypothesis:

1. **The null hypothesis is always a claim about a state of affairs in the world.**
2. **It is a statistical claim about a *POPULATION*.**
3. **It is *not* a prediction about what will happen; it assumes what is the case.**
4. **The null hypothesis is an assumption that there is no effect *in general*.**

Let's use a rather stretched 'everyday' example in order to make the role of the null hypothesis a little clearer.

Working in the glove department – an ideal lesson on the null hypothesis

Imagine that you are working in the glove section of a department store. You have gone down to the stockroom in search of a particular pair of gloves. You know, or at least you think you know, that the drawer you are at contains many left- and right-hand gloves in equal numbers. Suddenly the lights fuse and you are left in the dark. 'No problem', you think, 'If I pull out several I'm bound to get a match.' You pull out five, assuming that should be enough to get a left- and a right-hand glove in your sample. However, on returning to the light, you find that they are all right-hand gloves. You could pass this off as remarkable coincidence, which it must be if no one has tampered with the drawer. On the other hand, if one of your colleagues tends to play practical jokes or is just awfully forgetful, you might suspect that they have indeed messed about with the glove drawer. Why would you suspect this?

Figure 9.1   What were the odds of selecting five right-hand gloves at random?

The answer: because five gloves of the same hand is a very unlikely outcome if only 50% of the gloves really are right-handed. Let's use Alfie's logic above:

1. **Assume the null hypothesis – H_0: there are equal numbers of left- and right-hand gloves** (note that this is a claim about the 'population' of gloves in the drawer).
2. **Calculate the probability of picking five right-hand gloves.**
3. **If this probability is very low remark 'blimey, that's too much for coincidence' and assume that the drawer does *not* contain equal numbers of right- and left-hand gloves – this is the alternative hypothesis (H_1).**

Now, put more formally, these are again the three steps involved in significance-test thinking.

THE LANGUAGE OF SIGNIFICANCE

If a result is too low for coincidence, we say we have a **SIGNIFICANT** result. We say we have picked a *significant* number of right-hand gloves. We say that 'the difference between error means for the "alone" and "audience" conditions is significant'.

PROBABILITY

Step 2 above needs a little expansion. How do we calculate the probability of selecting five right-hand gloves in a row if the null hypothesis is true? The null hypothesis assumes that there are equal numbers of left- and right-hand gloves. The probability of selecting a right-hand glove is therefore $\frac{1}{2}$. Why?

When we calculate probability for events of equal likelihood, such as a toss of a coin coming up heads or a roll of a die resulting in a '6', we use the formula:

$$p = \frac{\text{NUMBER OF WAYS SPECIFIED RESULT CAN OCCUR}}{\text{TOTAL NUMBER OF POSSIBLE OUTCOMES}}$$

With a coin we have two possible outcomes, heads or tails, so 2 is on the bottom. We are interested in a head and this can only occur in one way out of the two. Hence the probability of a head is $\frac{1}{2}$. You might like to think about why the probability of tossing two heads in succession is $\frac{1}{4}$ and then consult Box 9.1. You will see from looking at item 7 in Box 9.1 that the probability of tossing two heads is $\frac{1}{2} \times \frac{1}{2} = \frac{1}{4}$. The probability is the same for selecting two right-hand gloves from our drawer *if the null hypothesis is true.*[1]

Box 9.1 Putting a number on probability

> Have a look at the statements below. For most of them, you'll find you have some idea of how likely or not it is that these events will occur. Try to give a value between zero (not at all likely) and 100 (highly likely) to each statement, depending on how likely you think it is to occur:
>
> 1. It will rain on Wednesday of next week.
> 2. You will eat breakfast on the first day of next month.
> 3. Your psychology tutor will sneeze in the next lesson.
> 4. The sun will rise tomorrow morning.
> 5. You will think about elephants later today.
> 6. A die tossed fairly will show a 5 or 6.
> 7. Two coins tossed fairly will both come down tails.

Probability is always denoted by *p* and is measured in *decimal* values on this scale:

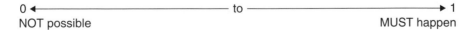

0 ◄─────────────── to ───────────────► 1
NOT possible   MUST happen

[1]Mathematical purists will say that this is not quite true since we are removing one glove and not replacing it, therefore the proportions in the drawer are no longer exactly 50–50 when we draw the second glove and so on. This is true, but I'm assuming that there are so many gloves that not replacing those selected will make only a trivial difference to the probability outcome –let's just keep things simple, eh?

If you now take the values between 1 and 100 that you have given to each event and divide each of them by 100, they should come out as decimal values on the scale above. For item 1, if you live in the UK, whatever the time of year you may have answered 50, which becomes 0.5 on the scale. However, if you live in Bombay, and the month is October, you'd perhaps answer 5, which becomes 0.05. For those who have forgotten their decimals note that 0.05 is ten times lower than 0.5 – something you'll need to be very careful with in significance testing. Item 4 in the list above cannot be given 1 as there is an infinitesimal chance that the sun will *not* rise tomorrow (in which case your work here on research methods in psychology will be rather wasted!). Item 5 has probably shot up in value now that you've read it! Item 2 depends on your own breakfast habits.

For items 6 and 7 we can use the formula that we introduced above. In item 6 there are six possible outcomes and we are interested in just two of these. Therefore the probability is $\frac{2}{6}$ or $\frac{1}{3}$ when simplified, or even 0.33. In item 7 there are four possible outcomes (head and head, head and tail, tail and head, tail and tail). We are interested in one of them, so p is $\frac{1}{4}$.

We can also get this result by saying that the probability of the first head is $\frac{1}{2}$ and so is the probability of the second. To get the probability of event 1 followed by event 2 we multiply probabilities and this gives us $\frac{1}{2} \times \frac{1}{2}$, which is $\frac{1}{4}$.

Box 9.2   Beware of subjective probability – the rain does NOT have it in for you!

> In studying probability we must put everyday subjective assessments to the back of our minds and rely on the actual data and calculations. During the summer I often swear and curse when, just as I get the mower out, having shifted the kids' bikes, footballs, pogo stick and the sun-loungers, it starts to rain. The same thing happens with supermarket check-out queues – someone always has five unpriced items and several redemption coupons or the spotty 16-year-old assistant takes a tea break or the sweetly smiling supervisor wants to exchange loose-change bags. My traffic lane suddenly slows up for someone wanting to turn right – or does it? I have to admit that the other day it started to rain just as I'd *finished* mowing the lawn! Perhaps I only remember the bad days?

BACK TO THE GLOVES

We can now return to the matter of the gloves and put a value on the probability of selecting *at random* five right-hand gloves in succession if the null hypothesis is true. Note that it is easier to say that we calculate the '**probability of our result under H_0**'. This is $\frac{1}{2} \times \frac{1}{2} \times \frac{1}{2} \times \frac{1}{2} \times \frac{1}{2} = \frac{1}{32} = 0.03$ (forgetting about the replacement issue). Now, we ask, is 0.03 sufficiently low for us to assume that the null hypothesis is *not* true? Put another way, is it low enough for us to assume that someone has messed with the drawer? Well, that decision depends upon what all other researchers agree is an appropriate level at which to reject coincidence and we shall move on to that level in a moment.

Remember, 0.03 is *not* the probability that the results 'occurred by chance'. It is *not* the 'probability that the null hypothesis is true'.[2]

IT IS *the probability that this result would occur IF the null hypothesis is true.*
This is our definition for p.

---

[2]These are mistakes made by several A Level textbooks on methods. If you are taught that either of these statements is correct then please produce this chapter for your tutor to read!

To summarize at this point:

❑ We have selected a sample of five gloves from a drawer that supposedly contains left- and right-hand gloves.
❑ We feel that selecting five right-hand gloves is an unusual occurrence, perhaps evidence that someone has messed with the glove drawer.
❑ We assume that there were equal numbers of left- and right-hand gloves originally – the assumption of equal populations.
❑ We have calculated the probability of getting five right-hand gloves, *if this assumption (i.e. the null hypothesis) is true.*

HOW LOW IS LOW?

We have found that the probability of getting this result under the null hypothesis is very low – actually 0.03. This *seems* low, but how low would p have to be to produce convincing evidence?

There is a value that all researchers use. If the p they calculate for the probability of their result under H_0 is below this value then they reject H_0 and assume that something is really going on – they have support for H_1, that there is an effect. So what is this value? Just to show that it isn't entirely arbitrary and that most people have a working value for p, let's try the following exercise:

Guessing the sex of babies

Suppose a friend said she could reliably forecast the sex of unborn babies by swinging a stone pendulum above the mother-to-be's womb. Let's assume she guesses your baby's sex correctly. Would you be impressed? Your personal involvement might well cause you to react with 'Amazing!' or, at least, 'Well, it is interesting; there might be something in it'. Stepping back coolly from the situation you realize she had a 50–50 chance of being correct if she was just guessing. Nevertheless, most people would begin to think she had something going if she managed to predict correctly the sex of two or three more friends' babies. Suppose we set up a scientifically-controlled test of her ability and give her a sample of ten babies' sexes to guess under strictly-controlled conditions. How many would you expect her to predict correctly in order for you to be impressed that she's not just guessing and being lucky? For instance, would 7 out of 10 convince you? Or would you want more, or would fewer do?

The decision of a vast majority of students to whom I have presented this scenario is that nine or ten correct out of ten would convince them, and this, as we shall see, pretty well coincides with the result that social scientists would want in order to record her result as 'significant'. If she gets only eight correct the audience starts to waver and perhaps only one-third of them are still convinced. A few romantic people tend to choose seven or even six as enough to satisfy them that her system works, but there is also always the odd cynic who claims that even ten out of ten is not strong enough evidence.

THE CONVENTIONAL 0.05 SIGNIFICANCE LEVEL

Social scientists, and most other people involved with statistical significance testing, accept that 0.05 is a reasonable limit at which to reject the null hypothesis. What this means is that:

IF THE PROBABILITY OF GETTING THEIR RESULT, WHEN THE NULL HYPOTHESIS IS TRUE, IS EQUAL TO OR LESS THAN 0.05 THEY WILL REJECT THE NULL HYPOTHESIS.

Now you can see that ordinary individuals have an intuitive grasp of this sensible level. Most of my audiences of students are fairly convinced of the friend's success with nine correct guesses out of ten. The probability of this happening is 0.011. You can see this value in Figure 9.2, where each column represents the probability of getting the number of correct guesses out of ten, shown at the foot of the column. This probability, of course, is under H_0, where we are assuming that each sex prediction is entirely random. Less than half the audience usually accepts that she can authentically guess babies' sexes if she only gets eight correct guesses out of ten and there is a lot of hesitation. This is interesting because here the probability is *just* over the accepted 0.05 significance level at 0.055.[3]

Figure 9.2   Probabilities of (n) correct baby-sex guesses out of 10

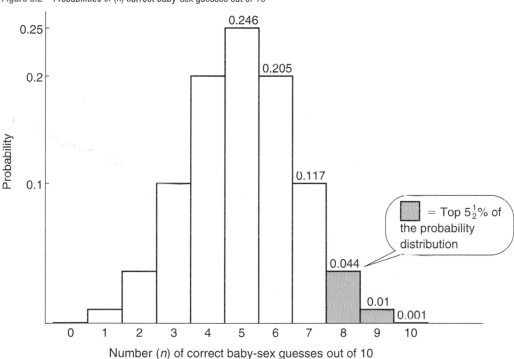

Number (*n*) of correct baby-sex guesses out of 10

CRITICAL VALUES

We have seen that if we get eight correct choices out of ten we do not reject the null hypothesis. If we get nine out of ten the probability is down to 0.011 and well under the accepted level of 0.05. The value of nine is therefore known as a **CRITICAL VALUE** because it is the number of choices that must be correct (or better) in order for us to reject the null hypothesis.

---

[3]The probability is 0.044 + 0.011 + 0.001 and not just 0.044 because we have to *add* the probabilities for getting eight, nine *and* ten correct. We do not predict that she'll get exactly eight right but that she'll do *well*. We have to take the probability of her getting eight right *or better*. For nine correct the values are 0.01 + 0.001 = 0.011

PROGRESS REVIEW 9.1

EXERCISES

1. A researcher reports that a difference is significant with $p = 0.049$. What might her rivals say and do about this?
2. Another researcher decides to publish results whenever the probability of them occurring under the null hypothesis is less than 0.1. What might his colleagues and rivals say about his work?
3. A researcher tests samples of Scottish and English 8-year-old children on a reading test. She is looking for any difference between the two groups. In the statistical test what would be the null hypothesis?
4. You are handed two boxes each containing thousands of pencils of differing lengths. You are told that the null hypothesis is true – the mean length of pencils in one box is equal to the mean length of the pencils in the other box. If you took a sample of 30 pencils from one box and 30 from the other, what would you expect to find if you compared one sample mean with another? What would you expect to happen if you did this operation 40 times over?

ANSWERS

1. They might say 'That only just made it' and they might very well be tempted to *replicate* her study. If they get a non-significant result they might suggest that her result was 'just a fluke' – see *Type I error* in the next section.
2. He would gain no credibility. 0.05 is the conventional level. Using 0.1 gives too much opportunity for 'fluke' results to be taken seriously. He would be likely to make more Type I errors – see the next section.
3. That the population mean for 8-year-old Scottish children on this test is equal to the population mean for 8-year-old English children.
4. You would expect (and predict) that the two sample means would be very close. There would be very little difference between them. There would be *some* difference because of *sampling error*. If you did this many times you would expect the differences between means all to be rather small. Extra Brownie points if you noticed and said that one time in every twenty you would get a 'significant' difference.

KEY TERMS

Alternative hypothesis (H_1)   Research prediction
Critical value   Significance
Experimental hypothesis   Significance level
Null hypothesis (H_0)

MOVING TOWARDS REAL PSYCHOLOGY RESULTS

So far I have introduced the idea of significance testing using only coins, gloves and baby-gender guessing! The conscientious reader might wonder when this is going to be made relevant to the typical psychology experiment. Well, the answer is 'in a moment' and I want to move us there through one more stretched, but at least concrete, example.

THE CASE OF THE DODGY SCREWS

Suppose you work in a screw-manufacturing company and are looking after the production line, churning out screws into large barrels each containing around 500,000 screws. Your supervisor approaches you one day and says 'We think the machine cutters went out of line and that barrel there, with the big yellow cross, is suspect. The screws might not be cut accurately. Can you check it for us?'. At first you think 'Bang goes my weekend', because you imagine sitting and measuring every last screw in the barrel. However, an old hand tells you what to do – take a decent *sample* from the suspect barrel, take a similar-sized sample from a normal barrel and compare the difference using a significance test.

The situation is depicted in Figure 9.3. What do we mean by a 'decent' sample? Well, this takes us back to the issues of sampling discussed in Chapter 2. In order to be an unbiased representation of the whole barrel of screws we should *randomly* select our samples, not simply take some off the top where perhaps the shorter screws have congregated. We also mean a sample of a decent size – perhaps 20 or 30 and not just one or two. When we have these samples we can take the mean of each one and compare them to see if one is larger than the other.

Figure 9.3   Populations of standard and suspect screws

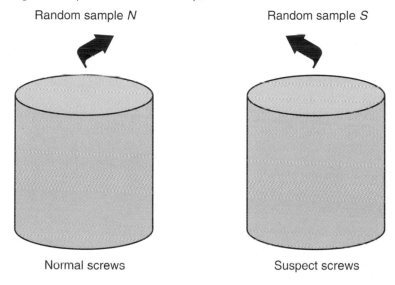

Random sample *N*   Random sample *S*

Normal screws   Suspect screws

Now one mean *will* be larger, if only because of regular *sampling error* – there's always going to be some tiny difference. However, what we are looking for is a difference appreciably larger than that which we might expect for any two samples drawn at random from the same population.

What is the null hypothesis in this example? If the two barrels contain identically-manufactured screws then the means of the two barrels should be identical. The barrels are 'populations' from which we are selecting samples. We are testing the *null hypothesis* that **the mean of the normal screw population is equal to the mean of the suspect screw population**. Our *alternative hypothesis* is that the two population means are *different*.

GETTING BACK TO PSYCHOLOGY RESULTS, THEN

I said we would get to real psychology results via the example of the screws. Let's revisit the sets of scores we looked at in Table 9.1 at the start of the chapter. Take the set of scores produced by the conscientious students – part b of the table. Here you need to see the two samples of scores as being just the same as the two samples of screws in the last example. The only difference here is that the populations of screws were finite. We knew there were rather a lot but there was a definite number in each barrel. In testing social and psychological statistics it is rarely the case that we can refer to a real and finite population of scores. What we mean when we say 'population', statistically speaking, is 'all the scores that could be taken in this way'.

To summarize using the psychology results

The *null hypothesis* is H_0: mean of 'audience' times = mean of 'alone' times.
The *alternative hypothesis* is H_1: mean of 'audience' times $\neq$ mean of 'alone' times.

These two hypotheses refer to the *populations* of scores in each case

From H_0 we can predict in our research that there will be only a small difference between the two *sample means*.

We can calculate the probability, under the null hypothesis, of getting a difference between *sample* means of the size that we did. We'll learn how to do this in Chapter 11. For now, assume we can.

If this probability (p value) is less than or equal to 0.05 we will reject the null hypothesis and state that we have a **SIGNIFICANT DIFFERENCE**, hence support for the alternative hypothesis – presence of an audience increases error times.

NOTE: we can only state a null hypothesis when we know exactly what kind of statistical analysis is to be performed on our data. Typical null hypotheses are:

❏ The means of the two populations are equal.
❏ The medians of the two populations are equal.
❏ The correlation in the population between variable A and variable B is zero.

WHAT IS THE POINT OF 0.05?

There are two important points about the significance level of 0.05, and the first is practical. If a result is significant with $p \leq 0.05$ (sometimes referred to as the **5% LEVEL**) then this usually means that other researchers will accept it and we can publish our result in an academic journal – we 'go public'. This is true where we are supposed to be showing an effect – for instance, a difference between groups or a correlation (see Chapter 12). What happens if we don't reach 0.05? Well, we are not in a macho game to 'get results'. The 0.05 level is only a convention and, as we shall see in a moment, it does not guarantee that an effect was 'really' there. If a piece of research narrowly failed to reach significance it might be repeated with a tighter design or with more participants until significance *was* achieved and *then* submitted for publication. However, in some research articles the aim is *not* to show a difference. We might want to show that two groups do *not* differ where myth or social expectation might expect them to (e.g. the ever-present attempts to demonstrate sex differences). We might want to show that an effect apparently demonstrated by someone else really does not work. For example, our theory might demand that extroverts do not differ from introverts on a certain variable whereas they do differ on others.

This brings us to the second point. The 0.05 limit is not a guarantee of an effect being present. The result could be just a fluke. How do we guard against flukes?

INTRODUCING TYPE I ERROR AND TYPE II ERROR

Because we set our significance level at 0.05 it should be that every time we do 20 random tests, 1 in 20 of these should be significant, on average. If we were to take random samples of 30 raffle tickets from two equal boxes and keep determining whether the number total for one is higher than the other, about one time in 20 we should get a 'significant' difference. This is just another way of defining the significance level. This is what it *does*. Mostly researchers don't do random tests. They usually fully expect there *will* be a difference between their samples because they have argued for it from their theory. However, it is always possible that there is no real effect but a researcher gets a 'significant' result by chance. If this happens we call it a **TYPE I ERROR**. Of course we can't *know* when it happens. We can only find out by *replication* of studies. If I get an effect but ten follow-up studies, doing exactly what I did, do not, then we might assume that my result was just a Type 1 error.

What about our sloppy students whose results appear in Table 9.1a? There might really be an effect from an audience (there usually is, in fact) but their design might be so sloppy that they didn't show it. If this is the case then they have produced what is called a **TYPE II ERROR** – there *is* an effect but this result did not reach significance. The outcomes that produce Type I and II errors are displayed in Table 9.2.

Table 9.2   Type I and Type II errors

		Null hypothesis is:	
		Retained	Rejected
Null hypothesis is actually:	True	Correct decision	Type I error
	False	Type II error	Correct decision

So achieving significance is not a 'proof' of anything. I'm sure I've already said that you should delete the word 'proof' from anything you write in psychology. A significant result provides *evidence* to support our theory; it will need other evidence, and a failure of other studies to contradict our findings, to bolster the theory further. On the other hand, failure to reach significance is not 'proof' that an effect does not exist. It simply means that we have not added any further evidence or that we have contradicted the findings of other researchers. In all these outcomes the job of researchers is to try to *explain* why findings do or do not support theories.

OTHER LEVELS OF SIGNIFICANCE

I think I'll repeat the meaning of the p that is calculated in a significance test. It is the probability of getting the result you saw (e.g. a difference so large) if there's really nothing going on. Think of it as the probability of getting three flat tyres in a week if there really is no one puncturing your tyres at night. If we use the 0.05 level of significance, then about 5 times in 100, even if the null hypothesis is true and there is no effect, you will obtain a 'significant' result. For instance, about 5 times in 100 you will deal five or more of the same colour card off the top of a shuffled deck; just over 5 times in 100 you will get exactly eight heads when you toss ten coins.

USING p ≤ 0.01 (THE 1% LEVEL)

Sometimes researchers are not happy with the fact that their result would occur about 5% of the time even if there were no effect. Sometimes they want less risk of making a Type I error. Hence what they do is to say that they'll only reject the null hypothesis if the probability of their result under it falls less than 0.01. This means that they have *more* chance of making a Type II error. In other words, it may be that, for instance, temperature in a room really does affect memory. However, if the significance level is set low at 0.01, even though heat really did affect memory, the result would be considered not sufficiently strong enough to reject the null hypothesis. $p \leq 0.01$ is a 'strict' level. It might be used where a researcher is making a groundbreaking claim, typically overturning the work of several previous researchers. If you are challenging what others have typically found then you need really strong grounds on which to make your claim. A further circumstance for the choice of a low significance level would be when there is only one opportunity to obtain the data. In a field study on the effects of an anti-bullying programme in schools there may be only one possible occasion on which a fair comparison of schools can be made, with and without the programme. In this case we would want to be fairly sure of any claimed effects since other researchers will not be able to replicate our study. We might also want a strict level where the results of our study might lead to the treatment being applied to people in a real setting (e.g. drug therapy).

USING p ≤ 0.1 (THE 10% LEVEL)

Few if any journals would accept a study for publication if its results were significant only with $p \leq 0.1$ However, in preparatory work, where perhaps a team of researchers is trying various ways to test a certain hypothesis, it may well be that designs where p comes lower than 0.1 might be retained and then modified, sample increased etc., in order to prepare for a full set of trials and hope that a result significant at 0.05 is eventually achieved. Table 9.3 summarizes the properties associated with difference levels of significance.

Table 9.3   Use of different levels of significance

Level of significance	Comment	If null hypothesis is true, chances of making a Type I error are
$p \leq 0.05$	The conventional level for research	5%
$p \leq 0.01$	A 'strict' level; harder to get significant results. Use when there is a greater need for certainty about reality of effect	1%
$p \leq 0.1$	Too high for academic acceptance of a genuine effect; may be used as guide in pilot work	10%

USING THE TERM 'SIGNIFICANT'

If a result turns out *not* to be significant, please do not describe this as an 'insignificant result'. This is to mix the technical and statistical language of hypothesis testing with the ordinary-language use of 'significant'. Many things are 'significant' in life without being *statistically* significant. Many results in psychology studies are significant yet do not amount to much in the great scheme of things. The term to use is 'non-significant', as in 'a non-significant result'. Researchers often say 'The difference between control and experimental means *failed to reach significance*'. A non-significant result can very often indeed be significant in the non-statistical sense. Failing to show what another researcher claimed to show is a significant event but the 'failure to show' is evidence with a non-significant *statistical* result.

MORE TERMINOLOGY

'The null hypothesis was rejected.'
'The null hypothesis was retained.'
'The alternative hypothesis was provisionally accepted that ...'
'Support was found for the alternative hypothesis.'

Never say that the alternative hypothesis was 'proven'. We simply don't 'prove' things in psychology. In fact, 'proof' is mainly the preserve of mathematicians. In psychology, as in all other science, we find *support* for hypotheses or we *challenge* previous support or we might simply *find no support*.

ONE- AND TWO-TAILED TESTS

From Figure 9.2 you'll see that we only calculated the probability that our baby-gender guesser would get eight or more guesses *right*. The probability is the shaded area in the figure to the right-hand side of the distribution. This is known as a **ONE-TAILED TEST** because, as you can see from the figure, we used only one tail of the probability distribution shown. We *could* have found the probability that she would get eight or more right or eight or more *wrong*. To do this I hope you'll see that we would have to *add* the probability area on the left-hand side to that on the right. Our overall probability would double from 0.055 to 0.11. However, that would be an odd thing to do on this occasion since we were only interested in her doing well in guessing *correctly*.

However, when we test other psychological research questions, such as 'Does the presence of an audience help or hinder performance?', we would use a **TWO-TAILED TEST**. The type of test is directly related to the type of hypothesis – directional or non-directional. In a **DIRECTIONAL** hypothesis we predict the direction in which results will go – e.g. 'An audience *improves* performance'. In a **NON-DIRECTIONAL** hypothesis we don't make the commitment of direction – 'Caffeine will affect reaction times'. Tests and hypotheses are related like this:

Hypothesis	Test	Significance level
Directional	One-tailed permitted	Half that of two-tailed test
Non-directional	Two-tailed obligatory	Double that of one-tailed test

When you conduct the inferential tests described in the following chapters you will always need to decide if you are using a one- or two-tailed test when you go to find your probability value in the tables in the Appendices. Basically, using a two-tailed test is rather conservative. As you have just seen, the probability doubles for a two-tailed test. That means that if your results gave you significance with a one-tailed test they might not with a two-tailed test. Say the one-tailed test gave significance with $p \leq 0.05$. The two-tailed equivalent says that p is ≤ 0.1 and this would *not* be a significant result.

ANSWERING EXAM QUESTIONS ON ONE- AND TWO-TAILED TESTS

We have, however, stepped into an area of bitter dispute between statistical purists and other psychological researchers. As a general rule in psychology, **_researchers almost always use two-tailed tests_**. The reasons why are rather complex but an account can be found in Coolican, 2004: chapter 11.

During preparation of this book at least two of the four A Level boards still required students to answer questions about one- and two-tailed tests; they were expecting students to state that a one-tailed test _should_ be used when a hypothesis is directional.

In an examination, suppose you are told that a researcher predicted that dogs, after training, would bark _more_ at a horizontally-striped pullover than at a plain one. A question might then be: 'Would the researcher use a one- or two-tailed test?'. I am afraid that you'll need to answer 'one-tailed' to this question 'because the researcher made a prediction about which way the results would go'. You could always add, if you're feeling confident, 'but, _in fact_, almost all research uses two-tailed tests'. This is just one of those areas where exam question writers are often not really in contact with the actual world of research. The fact is that a researcher _might_ use a one-tailed test on special occasions but there would need to be a good argument as to why a result in the opposite direction to that predicted would be completely ignored. The more realistic situation is one where we might predict, for instance, that music would interfere with memory and then we would be surprised to find that performance is actually increased. We would want to know more, and significance with a two-tailed test would allow us to say that there was an effect, albeit not the one we expected.

PROGRESS REVIEW 9.2

EXERCISES

1. State whether the following hypothesis tests would _permit_ a one-tailed test or would _require_ a two-tailed test.
   (a) Diabetics are more health-conscious than non-diabetics.
   (b) Extroverts and introverts differ in rating their self-esteem.
   (c) Anxiety correlates negatively with popularity.
   (d) More blame is attributed to a driver when the consequences of an accident they caused are serious than when the consequences are mild.
   (e) Generosity correlates with temperature.
2. A researcher sets out to show that people who are paid more to speak contrary to their views will change their attitude more than those paid less to do the same thing. This prediction runs counter to most previous findings on cognitive dissonance.
   (a) What would be an appropriate level of significance for her to use?
   (b) With this level are Type I errors more or less likely than with the usual 0.05 level?
3. I just have to give you these questions (they will appear in exams):
   (a) What is p a measure of in a significance test?
   (b) What is meant by 'The difference was significant with $p \leq 0.01$'.

ANSWERS

1. (a) One-tailed test is possible (directional hypothesis)
    (b) Must be two-tailed (non-directional hypothesis)
    (c) One-tailed test is possible (directional hypothesis)
    (d) One-tailed test is possible (directional hypothesis)
    (e) Must be two-tailed (non-directional hypothesis).
2. (a) $p \leq 0.01$
    (b) Less likely.
3. (a) p is the probability of this result occurring if the null hypothesis is true
    (b) The probability of the result occurring under H_0 was less than 0.01.

KEY TERMS

5% level	Significant difference
Directional hypothesis	Two-tailed test
Non-directional hypothesis	Type I error
One-tailed test	Type II error

Choosing a significance test for your data

What's in this chapter?

❏ This chapter has just one central theme – *helping you to find the appropriate significance test for your data*.
❏ All the significance tests in this book are introduced here but for fuller explanations please turn to the appropriate section of Chapter 11 or 12.
❏ Each test is chosen on the basis of three decisions – type of data relationship that is tested, level of measurement of DV and type of design; these are explained but also illustrated in Figure 10.1.
❏ The difference between *parametric tests* (or *distribution-free*) and *non-parametric tests* is explained.
❏ Practice in the decisions is provided as an exercise.

TESTING YOUR DATA

So – you have gathered data and now want to know if you have supported your hypothesis. To be able to say that you have you must show that the result you obtained, a difference or a correlation, was unlikely to occur if there really is no effect. You want to achieve significance with $p \leqslant 0.05$, as explained in the last chapter. The test you need to use depends on just three decisions, which concern:

1. the type of comparison you are making – difference or correlation
2. the level of your data – see p. 105
3. whether the design of your study is related or unrelated – see p. 43.

All the tests that we will cover in Chapters 11 and 12 are depicted in Figure 10.1 and, by making the three decisions above, in order, you should arrive at the appropriate test for your data. The three decision stages are shown in Figure 10.1. You can also consult Figure 10.2, which shows how data are arranged for different types of test. Please note also that Table 11.2 gives you the general procedure for conducting *any* significance test, once you have chosen here the one that you need.

Figure 10.1   Three decisions to find the appropriate significance test

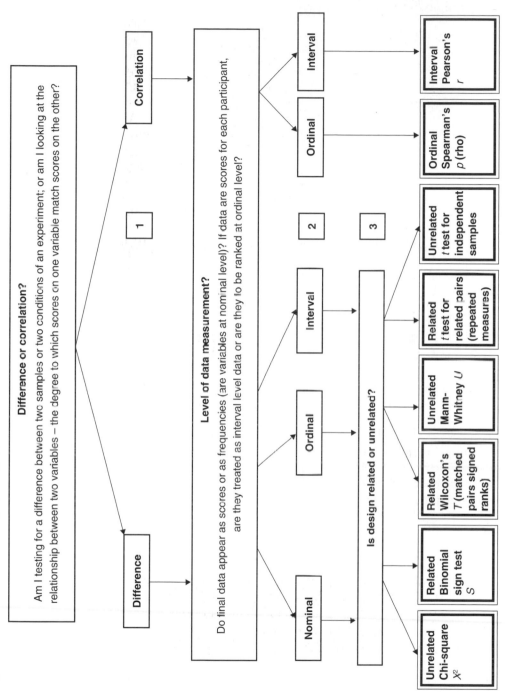

Difference or correlation?

Am I testing for a difference between two samples or two conditions of an experiment; or am I looking at the relationship between two variables – the degree to which scores on one variable match scores on the other?

1

Correlation

Difference

Level of data measurement?

Do final data appear as scores or as frequencies (are variables at nominal level)? If data are scores for each participant, are they treated as interval level data or are they to be ranked at ordinal level?

2

Interval

Ordinal

Ordinal

Interval

Nominal

3

Is design related or unrelated?

Interval
Pearson's
r

Ordinal
Spearman's
p (rho)

Unrelated
t test for
independent
samples

Related
t test for
related pairs
(repeated
measures)

Unrelated
Mann–
Whitney U

Related
Wilcoxon's
T (matched
pairs signed
ranks)

Related
Binomial
sign test
S

Unrelated
Chi-square
χ^2

1. DIFFERENCE OR CORRELATION?

If you are testing for *difference* you will have two sets of scores and you will want to show that scores in one set are higher than scores in the other set. There is a special case where your data are in *categories* and you'll want to see whether one group differs from another across two or more categories. For instance, you might have observed males and females and taken a tally of whether they carry their books in one of two positions. Alternatively, you might have observed cars inappropriately using a disabled parking space and taken a tally of which category each car belonged to (e.g. luxury, mid-range, cheap) – see bottom right Figure 10.2. Whenever you use a tally like this you are observing frequencies and you probably want to use a Chi-square test. You are testing the difference between frequencies for each category. Rather than explain more now, if you think this is the test you need then please turn to p. 170.

If you are testing for *correlation* you will be asking a question such as 'Is there a relationship between height and confidence – are taller people more confident?' or 'Do people with higher extroversion scores tend to go to bed later – is there a relationship between extroversion–introversion and bedtimes?'. Correlation looks at the *relationship* between two variables. Where each person has a score on two variables, correlation assesses the extent to which these scores tend to rise or fall together. Correlation is an important topic in its own right and is dealt with separately in Chapter 12.

2. LEVEL OF DATA MEASUREMENT

To decide the level at which your data have been gathered you need to return to p. 105. If you have scores for each individual then your data are at interval level. Interval-level tests (*parametric* as explained below) involve making certain assumptions about your data and *t* tests are rather tricky to calculate if you do not use a computer program. Therefore if you have scores for each individual you can always conduct an ordinal-level test ('non-parametric') in preference to an interval-level one. You can do a **Mann-Whitney *U*** or **Wilcoxon's *T*** in preference to a *t* test for differences, or a **Spearman** rather than a **Pearson** correlation. The non-parametric tests are not quite so powerful as the parametric ones, so it is possible that the Mann-Whitney, for instance, will not give significance when the unrelated *t* test does. However, if you have conducted a well-designed study you should still be able to trust your results and, in 96% of cases, the two tests will give the same result. You can always struggle a little harder with the *t* test if you are close to significance with the non-parametric test.

If you have a pair of scores for each participant and you want to test for difference you *can* reduce the data down to categorical (nominal) level by recording for each participant simply whether they improved, worsened or stayed the same from condition one to condition two. You can then conduct a **sign test**. This is rarely wise, however, since so much information is lost in the process and you have a much weaker test than the Wilcoxon or related *t* test. The test can be used, however, where *all you know* for each participant is whether they can be given a plus, a minus or a zero – for instance if you had asked them whether they agreed with hunting, disagreed or had no opinion.

A few tips:

❏ If each participant is part of a tally – that is, they go into a 'box' because they have done or chosen X rather than Y – then data are nominal and a chi-square test is appropriate.
❏ If your dependent variable (the thing on which people were measured) is a standardized test (see p. 84) then data may be treated as interval-level.

❑ If participants have been asked to rate using subjective judgement (e.g. 'On a scale of 1 to 10 how strongly would you support fox hunting?' or '... how attractive is this man?') then it is always safer to treat data as not truly interval and to use an ordinal-level ranked data test.

3. RELATED OR UNRELATED DESIGN

This decision applies only if you are not doing a correlation since *all* correlations use a related design. Related and unrelated designs were dealt with back on p. 43. If each of your participants performed in *both* conditions of the independent variable then you have a related design. If you *paired* your participants so that one of each pair performed in one condition while the paired partner performed in the other then you also have a related design. Otherwise your design is unrelated – this usually means you had one group of participants do one level of the independent variable and a different group do the other. The design is also unrelated if you tested two different categories of people, typically males and females, on a dependent variable (e.g. motor skill or reading ability). Each male in one group is obviously unrelated to each female in the other group in terms of the testing (though you might *accidentally* test brother and sister!).

Figure 10.2   Arrangement of data for different kinds of inferential test

Testing **difference** between two conditions				
Separate groups			Same people (or pairs)	
Sample A Condition 1	Sample B Condition 2		Condition 1	Condition 2
3	6		12	23
5	7		13	12
6	5		15	24
.	.		.	.
.	.		.	.
Unrelated *t* test **Mann-Whitney**			**Related *t* test** **Wilcoxon Matched-Pairs** **Sign test**	

Correlation			*Association or difference*			
Same people (or pairs)				Type of car		
Measure 1	Measure 2			Luxury	Mid-range	Cheap
12	23		Parked	23	19	12
13	12					
15	24		Did not park	10	24	21
.	.					
Pearson's *r* **Spearman's rho**			**Chi-square**			

PARAMETRIC TESTS – WHAT ARE THEY?

I have mentioned **PARAMETRIC TESTS** a few times and now is the time to explain, a little, just what they are and why they are preferred over other similar tests. Parametric tests are those that make estimates of *population parameters* from *sample statistics*. I explained these terms on p. 120. Because they depend on making estimates about the underlying distribution of scores, they are probably better known as **DISTRIBUTION-DEPENDENT TESTS**. Generally we would prefer to use a parametric test because these are usually more powerful than their non-parametric equivalents (but only to the degree that the non-parametric tests are around 96% as powerful). What this means is the parametric test is that little bit more likely to come up with a significant difference on the same data. It is a little bit more sensitive to the data; it uses more of the available information. In the long run we are that little bit more likely to be able to publish support for effects that will be accepted by other researchers. A **NON-PARAMETRIC TEST** does *not* depend on assumptions about underlying distributions.

This greater sensitivity of parametric tests and power to show significance, however, comes at a price. Because the tests make estimates of population parameters we are warned against using such a test if the data are likely to make those estimates unreliable. Hence, for the tests used in this book the following assumptions are required about our dataset:

1. The level of measurement must be at least **interval**.
2. The sample data should have been drawn from an underlying **normal distribution**.
3. The variance of the two samples should not be significantly different – this assumption is known as that of **HOMOGENEITY OF VARIANCE**. 'Homogeneity' means 'of the same type', so this just means that we assume variances are the same.

❏ **ASSUMPTION 1 — Interval-level data**: note that we said earlier that data are not usually gathered as ordinal. We rank data if we think they are not truly interval. This is advisable where the data gathered are human estimates, as explained on p. 108.

❏ **ASSUMPTION 2 — Normal distribution**: it is the underlying population from which samples have been drawn that must be assumed to be normal. However, we don't have the population and we rarely know that it is normal. We *do* know this if we're using a standardized psychological scale since these are *constructed* to produce a normal distribution. Usually normality is tested for by looking mainly at skew – see p. 131. At the level you are working you won't be asked to calculate this but you can simply inspect the data in a histogram by eye and spot where data are definitely skewed.

❏ **ASSUMPTION 3 — Homogeneity of variance**: this limitation can be ignored in all cases except where you have independent samples (two separate groups of participant scores) and very unequal numbers in the two groups. The easy way to avoid this problem is simply to ensure that you have roughly the same number of participants in each condition – they don't have to be exactly the same. If you do want to check whether variances are similar or not, a rule of thumb is that you have a problem where one variance is more than four times the other. Remember that the variance is the square of the standard deviation.

It is likely that on your course you will be required to justify the selection of the test you have used, and for parametric tests this includes checking the data for these assumptions just listed. A way to avoid this in a practical project, if permitted, is simply to elect to use a non-parametric test, which as we said earlier will usually also be easier to calculate. Unless your syllabus stipulates a parametric test there is no good reason why you should not simply use a non-parametric test.

EXERCISES

To help with your understanding of the procedure for selecting tests, and to see if you can do this already, here are a few very common hypotheses tested in psychological practical work at this level. See if you can decide which test is appropriate then consult the answers in Table 10.1.

1. One group of participants is asked to rehearse each item in a set of words that are to be memorized. A second group is asked to form a vivid mental image of each word. Both groups are asked to recall the words after two minutes. Does imagery increase the number of words correctly recalled?
2. Participants are given a test for extroversion and asked to rate on a scale from 1 to 10 how confident they tend to feel when asked to speak in public. It is expected that more extroverted people will feel more confident.
3. Students collect lonely-hearts advertisements from a local newspaper and test the hypothesis that females are more likely than males to mention long-term relationships and security concepts. They note the sex of the advertiser and whether or not they mention security etc.
4. A researcher suggests that larger class sizes are a cause of lower A Level results in Maths. She uses national A Level results and, for each sufficiently large school or college, she notes their average Maths class size and average A Level Maths points.
5. Participants are asked to perform a sorting task in front of an audience and also when alone. It is predicted that the audience condition will produce lower performance, which is measured in seconds.
6. Students record whether or not cars stop at an amber traffic light. They also record the price range of each car: cheap, mid-range or expensive. They predict that the more expensive the car, the more likely the driver is to stop.
7. Students observe whether males and females do or do not walk under a ladder. They are testing the hypothesis that one sex is more superstitious than the other.
8. Males and females are asked to estimate their own IQ and that of their father and mother. Their own and parents' actual IQ is also measured. What test is required to test the following:
   (a) Males' estimates of their own IQ are higher than those of females.
   (b) Participants estimate their fathers' IQs to be higher than their mothers' IQs.
   (c) The measured IQs of fathers differ from those of mothers.
   (d) The higher the mothers' IQs, the higher are their sons' IQs.
9. A group of people has been assessed for depression on two separate occasions. Raw scores have been discarded and, for each person, we know only whether they have improved, worsened or stayed exactly the same. What test would tell us whether there is significant improvement?

ANSWERS

See Table 10.1.

KEY TERMS

Distribution-dependent tests   Non-parametric tests
Homogeneity of variance   Parametric tests

Table 10.1 Answers to problems on selecting the appropriate test (bold indicates the preferred test, because that is the more powerful)

Problem	Decision 1 difference/ correlation	Decision 2 level of data	Decision 3 related/unrelated design	Tests possible
1	Difference	Interval (number of words)	Unrelated – different participants for each condition	**Unrelated *t*** Mann-Whitney
2	Correlation	Ordinal – one measure is a human estimate – see p. 108	Related – two scores for each participant All correlations are related	Spearman
3	Difference (between males and females)	Nominal – each measure is either did or did not mention security etc. and male/female	Unrelated – males vs females	Chi-square
4	Correlation	Interval	Related. All correlations are related	**Pearson** Spearman
5	Difference	Interval	Related – each participant does both conditions	**Related *t*** Wilcoxon Sign test
6	Difference – across different car types	Nominal – can only record type of car and whether stopped or not	Unrelated – different types of car	Chi-square
7	Difference	Nominal – walked under or didn't; male/female	Unrelated – males vs females	Chi-square
8a	Difference	Treat as ordinal – human estimates	Unrelated – males vs females	Mann-Whitney
8b	Difference	Treat as ordinal – human estimates	Related – two scores from same person	Wilcoxon
8c	Difference	Interval – measured IQ	Related – parents are matched pairs!	Related *t*
8d	Correlation	Interval – measured IQ	Related – mother and son. All correlations are related	Pearson
9	Difference	Nominal – we have no scores, just categories	Related – originally there were two scores for each person	Sign test

chapter
11

Test of difference

Look back to the beginning of the last chapter and you'll see that we raised the question of whether the difference found between groups in an experiment could be taken as a 'real' difference. We now know that we can take a difference as provisional evidence for an underlying real effect. This happens if the probability of it occurring, *if there wasn't any effect*, is less than 0.05 – that is, more formally, if the probability of it occurring under H_0 is less than 0.05. In these next two chapters we look at the kinds of test you are likely to need in order to work out just what that probability is.

The tests we use are known as statistical **SIGNIFICANCE TESTS** or **INFERENTIAL TESTS**; we use them to infer an effect in the population *from* only the results for the samples that we have drawn. When we conduct an inferential test we go through several stages, as follows:

STEPS IN CONDUCTING A STATISTICAL SIGNIFICANCE TEST:

1. Gather data and decide what test is appropriate (see Chapter 10).
2. Conduct the test.
3. Finish with a value for the **TEST STATISTIC**.
4. Decide whether a one- or two-tailed test is appropriate.
5. Find the probability of obtaining this test statistic under the null hypothesis.
6.

| If the probability is less than or equal to 0.05 reject H_0. Declare a significant difference (or correlation) | If the probability is greater than 0.05 retain H_0. Declare a non-significant difference (or correlation) |

Chapter 10 attempted to provide the information required to select an appropriate test. However, the examples given here with each test should also help you decide whether it is the right test for your data. For each test we will look at the steps in conducting it without necessarily giving a deep statistical explanation of *why*. It is assumed that, at this stage, you are just being asked to analyse your data rather than understand precisely how each test works and why it does so. The important point after every test, and this will be reinforced in Chapter 14 on writing reports, is to report your test statistic, whether your test was one- or two-tailed, the probability associated with your test statistic and whether or not you decide this gives you the confidence to reject H_0. Chapter 14 will also tell you what *else* is expected in a results section but here we simply tell you how to report the test result.

PARAMETRIC TESTS OF DIFFERENCE

THE RELATED t TEST

Let's start with a test that is one of a set of tests that calculate the statistic known as *t*. This test was introduced by William Gossett. Gossett suffered the inconvenience of working for Guinness who wouldn't permit him to publish the work he did on their time in his own name. Hence the test has become formally know as Student's *t* test after Gossett adopted 'Student' as a *nom de plume*.

When to use the related *t* test		
Type of relationship tested	**Level of data required**	**Design of study**
Difference	Interval	Related: Matched pairs Repeated measures

Assumptions: data drawn from normally distributed population(s).
Advantages: sensitive test – will sometimes give significance when Wilcoxon's *T* test does not; uses more information from the data.
Disadvantages: need to satisfy parametric assumptions; complex to calculate.

There will be a box like this one to introduce each inferential test. In some A Level syllabuses you are asked the reason for selecting a particular test. Your strategy should be to use two or three of the pieces of information here and usually:

- ❑ type of relationship tested (difference or correlation)
- ❑ level of data required (nominal, ordinal, interval)
- ❑ design of study: related or unrelated.

The *t* test is one of a class known as *parametric tests*. These tests rely on the assumption that data were drawn from a normally distributed population. We talked about these in Chapter 10. It is usually enough to inspect the data and check that there is no obvious skew. At more advanced levels you would be asked to check more formally using calculations of skew. To be normally distributed the data need to be gathered at an *interval* level of measurement and this is also one of the requirements for a parametric test.

Data for our test

Imagine that we have given 13 participants a list of 20 words to try to recall under two conditions. In the first condition they are asked to form a mental image of each word, whereas in the second condition they are instructed only to repeat each word before hearing the next. After each list has been presented they are distracted for a few minutes then asked to recall all the words in the list. Conditions are counterbalanced (see p. 42) to counteract order effects. The resulting data appear in Table 11.1.

Table 11.1   Number of words correctly recalled under imagery and rehearsal conditions

Imagery condition	Rehearsal condition	Difference (d)	d^2
6	6	0	0
15	10	5	25
13	7	6	36
14	8	6	36
12	8	4	16
16	12	4	16
14	10	4	16
15	10	5	25
18	11	7	49
17	9	8	64
12	8	4	16
7	8	−1	1
15	8	7	49
		$\bar{d} = 4.54$	
		$s_d = 2.6$	
		$\sum d = 59$	$\sum d^2 = 349$

A little explanation

In the experiment described the expectation is that people will do better in the imagery condition. That is, we would expect them to *improve* in this condition compared with the rehearsal condition.

How do we measure improvement? Well, we simply take their score in the rehearsal condition *from* their score for imagery. The difference is a measure of their improvement. These differences are shown in column 3 of Table 11.1. If there is no advantage at all with imagery (the null hypothesis) then all these differences should be close to zero. Some will be a little above and some a little below, with only *sampling errors* responsible for any variations. Try to imagine taking a handful of these differences at random and finding their average each time. If we did this over and over again we would end up with a distribution looking like that in Figure 11.1. We want *our* obtained average of differences to be a value that is much higher than zero, giving us confidence in claiming that it didn't occur just by chance. Statistic *t* will tell us just how unlikely it is that our average difference would occur under the null hypothesis. Let's get on with the calculation.

Figure 11.2 Taking the mean of 13 differences many times, under H_0

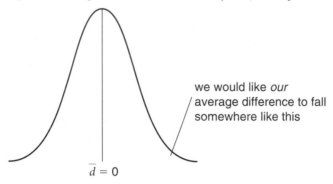

we would like *our* average difference to fall somewhere like this

$\bar{d} = 0$

TIP: When you arrange your data in a table like this it makes sense to put the column that is expected to hold the higher values (imagery in this case) to the left of the other group of scores. Then you take the right-hand figure from the left-hand and should end up with mainly positive values if your hypothesis is correct. Remember, you must **always** subtract in the same direction for every pair of scores. If you end up with a lot of negative differences then your result is in the opposite direction from what you expected and your value for *t* will be negative. This has no effect on checking for significance – see below – but you could claim a significant difference only if you conducted a two-tailed test – see p. 147.

Formula for related t

$$t = \frac{\bar{d}}{s/\sqrt{N}}$$

What the formula above asks us to do is to find the mean of the differences, that's $\bar{d}$, and then divide by the standard deviation (*s*), itself divided by the square root of the number of people in the sample $\sqrt{N}$.

Procedure for calculation of related *t*	Calculation on our data
1. Find the mean of the differences	$\bar{d} = 4.54$ – see Table 11.1
2. Find the standard deviation of the differences = *s* (for calculation procedure see p. 119 or see below)	$s = 2.6$ – see Table 11.1
3. Find $\sqrt{N}$	$N = 13$ so $\sqrt{N} = 3.61$

4. Divide s by $\sqrt{N}$

$$\frac{s}{\sqrt{N}} = \frac{2.6}{3.61} = 0.72$$

5. Divide $\bar{d}$ by result of step 4 to get t

$$t = \frac{\bar{d}}{0.72} = 6.31$$

6. Find degrees of freedom $(df)^{a}$.
   For a related design this is $N - 1$
   $df = 13 - 1 = 12$.

7. Use Table 3, Appendix 2 to find the critical value for t (see p. 141). Use the line for the value of df you have just found. Use two-tailed values (see p. 147) and check under the '0.05' column.

You should find that the appropriate value is 2.179. Our **OBTAINED VALUE**[b] of t easily exceeds this so we have a significant result and may reject H_0. In fact, our value also beats the critical value for $p \leq 0.01$, which is 3.055. Some researchers would claim a 'highly significant difference' on this basis.

---

[a]**What are degrees of freedom?** This is a complicated question to answer. However, using them is easy and they are required whenever you look up probability for a parametric test and for a test called chi-square, which we will encounter later in this chapter.
[b]Also know as a 'calculated value'.

Finding the standard deviation of the differences

Using the procedure on p. 119 to find the standard deviation of the d values in Table 11.1 can be a little fiddly. Instead you can use this formula and proceed as outlined below:

$$s = \sqrt{\frac{\sum d^2 - (\sum d)^2/N}{N-1}}$$

Be very careful here to distinguish between $\sum d^2$ and $(\sum d)^2$ see p. 133.

1. Find $\sum d^2$ as shown in Table 11.1 = 349.
2. Find $\sum d$ and square it = 59^2 = 3481.
3. Divide result of step 2 by $N = \dfrac{3481}{13} = 267.77$.
4. Take result of step 3 from result of step 1 = 349 − 267.77 = 81.33.
5. Divide result of step 4 by $N - 1 = \dfrac{81.33}{12} = 6.78$.
6. Take square root of result of step 5 = $\sqrt{6.78} = 2.60$.

When you have to conduct and report a significance test

Conducting and reporting significance tests are very tricky operations for the student new to psychology and often cause the greatest fear and confusion. Hence I am providing in Table 11.2 a 'cookbook' procedure for conducting *any* significance test but using the t test we have just conducted as an example. If you have to write a research report then you will need to be very careful in reporting your results. Chapter 14 will help you with this and guide you past several common pitfalls. In one way or another *all* the steps taken in Table 11.2 will need to be mentioned in your results section. I strongly suggest that you turn to Table 11.2 each time you have to deal with significance tests. The way to report just the *result* of your t test is given in Box 11.1.

Table 11.2 Procedure for selecting, conducting and reporting a test of significance

Choose an appropriate inferential statistical test	Chapter 10 will help you with this. In a report you usually need to justify your choice; to do this use the information given when each test is introduced in this book.
Calculate the test statistic	In the example we have just covered the test was t and our result was $t = 6.31$. All statistical tests calculate a test statistic with a letter to identify it.
Compare test statistic with critical value from tables. Take account of:	Tables are provided in the appendices. In this example we took the following points into account:
1. df or N – for each test you will be given the information on this	1. We used df, which were $N - 1$ for a related test and therefore 12
2. One- or two-tailed test	2. We used a two-tailed test (see p. 147)
3. Appropriate level of significance required	3. Usually this is $p \leq 0.05$ and this is what we used above
Decide which side of the critical value your own result is on. The table will tell you whether your test statistic needs to be *higher* or *lower* than the critical value	When we checked for t we found it was well above the critical level required for significance at 0.05 and at 0.01. The table tells us that t needs to be *higher* than the critical value in order for the difference to be regarded as significant.
Report your decision	Since our t is higher than the critical value we reject the null hypothesis with confidence (because we reached $p \leq 0.01$). Box 11.1 shows you an accepted way to report the results of a t test.

Box 11.1 Reporting the result of a t test analysis

As predicted, the mean number of words recalled in the imagery condition (M = 13.38, SD = 3.52) was higher than the mean for the rehearsal condition (M = 8.85, SD = 1.68). The difference between means was significant, $t\,(12) = 6.31$, $p \leq 0.01$, two-tailed.

If this result was not significant do NOT say it was 'insignificant'. Write:

… This difference was not significant, $t\,(12) = 2.15$, $p > 0.05$.

THE UNRELATED t TEST

When to use the unrelated _t_ test		
Type of relationship tested	**Level of data required**	**Design of study**
Difference	Interval	Unrelated: Independent samples/ groups/measures

Assumptions: data drawn from normally distributed population(s)
homogeneity of variance (explained on p. 154)

> **Advantages:** more sensitive test – will sometimes give significance when Mann-Whitney U test does not; uses more information from the data than non-parametric tests.
> **Disadvantages:** need to satisfy parametric assumptions; complex to calculate.

Data for our test

Researchers asked a sample of participants to keep a sleep diary for one month. They identified two groups of participants, those who recorded high levels of disturbed sleep and those who recorded low levels. The two samples were then tested for anxiety and the responses they gave are shown in Table 11.3.

Table 11.3 Anxiety scores for high and low sleep-disturbed participants

High sleep-disturbed participants		Low sleep-disturbed participants	
x_h	x_h^2	x_l	x_l^2
14	196	8	64
11	121	10	100
11	121	9	81
12	144	7	49
13	169	9	81
9	81	8	64
12	144	12	144
11	121	11	121
13	169	13	169
9	81		
Mean = 11.5		9.67	
$\sum x_h = 115$	$\sum x_h^2 = 1347$	$\sum x_l = 87$	$\sum x_l^2 = 873$

Subscript $_h$ stands for 'high' and $_l$ for 'low'.

A little explanation

This is the test that would be appropriate when testing the two samples of screws discussed in Chapter 9. Look back at that chapter for a fuller explanation. For now all we need to re-emphasize is that we are testing the difference between the means of two samples that it is assumed have been drawn from the same (or identical) populations. The null hypothesis is that the anxiety mean for the high sleep-disturbed population is equal to the mean for the low sleep-disturbed population. We will test this hypothesis by finding the probability that our difference could have occurred if it is true. Now take a deep breath and look at the formula for unrelated t.

Formula for unrelated t

$$t = \frac{|\bar{x}_a - \bar{x}_b|}{\sqrt{\left[\frac{\left(\sum x_a^2 - \frac{(\sum x_a)^2}{N_a} \right) + \left(\sum x_b^2 - \frac{(\sum x_b)^2}{N_b} \right)}{(N_a + N_b - 2)} \right] \times \left[\frac{N_a + N_b}{N_a N_b} \right]}}$$

OK, this looks a bit scary! However, it only contains a lot of simple operations, which you will be taken through below. There is a sneaky alternative, however, if you really don't feel up to the calculations, and that is to conduct a Mann-Whitney test instead – see p. 167.

Procedure for calculation of unrelated t	Calculation on our data
1. Add all the scores in the high group	$\sum x_h = 115$ (see Table 11.3)
2. Add all the squares of the high group scores	$\sum x_h^2 = 1347$ (see Table 11.3)
3. Square the result of step 1 (**be careful** to distinguish $\sum x_h^2$ from $(\sum x_h)^2$	$(\sum x_h)^2 = 115^2 = 13225$
4. Divide the result of step 3 by N_h – the number of scores in the high group	$\dfrac{(\sum x_h)^2}{N_h} = \dfrac{13225}{10} = 1322.5$
5. Subtract result of step 4 from result of step 2	$\sum (x_h)^2 - \dfrac{(\sum x_h)^2}{N_h} = 1347 - 1322.5 = 24.5$
6–10. Repeat steps 1–5 on the low scores	$\sum x_l = 87$ (see Table 11.3)
7.	$\sum x_l^2 = 873$ (see Table 11.3)
8.	$(\sum x_l)^2 = 7569$
9.	$\dfrac{(\sum x_l)^2}{N_l} = \dfrac{7569}{9} = 841$
10.	$\sum x_l^2 - \dfrac{(\sum x_l)^2}{N_l} = 873 - 841 = 32$
11. Add the results of steps 5 and 10	$24.5 + 32 = 56.5$
12. Divide the result of step 11 by $N_h + N_l - 2$	$\dfrac{56.5}{17} = 3.324$
13. Multiply the result of step 12 by $(N_a + N_b)/N_a N_b$	$3.324 \times \dfrac{10 + 9}{10 \times 9} = 0.702$
14. Find the square root of the result of step 13	$\sqrt{0.702} = 0.838$
15. Find the difference between the two means	$\bar{x}_h - \bar{x}_l = 11.5 - 9.67 = 1.83$
16. Divide the result of step 15 by the result of step 14 to give t	$t = \dfrac{1.83}{0.838} = 2.183$!!!
17. Calculate df. For an unrelated t test these are $N_a + N_b - 2$ (note we calculated this in step 12)	$df = 10 + 9 - 2 = 17$
18. Consult Table 3 in Appendix 2 and enter it with $df = 17$, two-tailed test, $p \leqslant 0.05$	Critical value given is 2.11 so we just squeaked past this and may report our difference as significant.

Report the result of this test as for the result of a related t test given earlier.

NON-PARAMETRIC TESTS OF DIFFERENCE

The next two tests are known as *non-parametric tests* since they do not make the assumptions about the underlying data that parametric tests do. We do *not* need normally distributed data nor do we need the data to be gathered on a truly interval scale. Both these tests are appropriate when we do not feel that the data we are testing can be trusted as true interval data – see p. 108. You can also see these two tests as equivalent to the related and unrelated t tests, producing almost the same results (but see p. 168) yet being much easier to calculate.

THE WILCOXON MATCHED-PAIRS SIGNED RANKS TEST

When to use the Wilcoxon T test

Type of relationship tested	Level of data required	Design of study
Difference	Ordinal (or above)	Related: Repeated measures Matched pairs

Assumptions: none, apart from the above. Don't confuse this test with the t tests; its statistic is T (always capital).
Advantages: no need to satisfy parametric assumptions. Easier to calculate.
Disadvantages: less sensitive to data than related t and therefore may not always give significance when a t test does.

Data for our test

Suppose some lecturers at a college are keen to make changes to a module that they hope eventually to deliver entirely through computer-based learning. There will be no traditional lectures or classroom sessions and all content will be delivered via a computer network. In order to test the scheme for feasibility they pilot the module in two halves, first with the conventional approach for one term and then with the computer-based approach for a second term. They ask 15 students to rate each half on an attitude scale that can score from 10 to 50. The data appear in Table 11.4.

Table 11.4   Attitude scores produced through student assessment of conventional and computer-based module delivery methods

Conventional delivery (A)	Computer-based delivery (B)	Difference (B − A)	Rank of difference	Ranks of positive differences	Ranks of negative differences
23	33	10	12	12	
14	22	8	9.5	9.5	
35	38	3	3	3	
26	30	4	5	5	
28	31	3	3	3	
19	17	2	1		1
42	42	0	−		
30	25	−5	6		6
26	34	8	9.5	9.5	
31	24	−7	8		8
18	21	3	3	3	
25	46	21	14	14	
23	29	6	7	7	
31	40	9	11	11	
30	41	11	13	13	
		Sum of ranks:		Pos: **90**	Neg: **15**

A little explanation

The Wilcoxon works on *pairs* of scores. That is, either two scores from the same person under two different conditions or scores from matched pairs of participants. We want to see whether, in each pair, the score for one of the conditions tends to be higher than the other. In our example, if the computer-based course is intended to be more useful to students, we would expect the computer course score *in each pair* to be the higher score. If we look at the difference in each pair, always taking the traditional score from the computer-based score, we can say, roughly speaking, that we want the differences to be positive and that the negative differences are 'unwanted' – they tend to lower the case for our hypothesis that the computer-based approach is better. Since this is an ordinal data test we change the differences to ranks – we rank the differences according to size, *ignoring the sign (or direction) of the difference.* We then add up the two sets of ranks, one for negative differences and the other for positive differences. The negative differences are the ones we don't want, so the ranks for these, we hope, will be small. We expect the positive rank sum to be higher than the negative rank sum; we want as few negative ranks knocking around as possible.

Procedure for calculation of Wilcoxon's T	Calculation on our data
1. Find the difference between each pair of scores. Take the one expected to be smaller from that expected to be larger for all cases	See Table 11.4
2. Rank all the differences, ignoring the sign of the difference. Ignore any zeros. These are excluded from the overall analysis	See Table 11.4
3. Find the sum of ranks of positive and negative differences separately. **The smaller of these is T**	Rank sum of positive differences $= 90$ Rank sum of negative differences $= 15$ $T = 15$
4. Enter Table 4, Appendix 2, using N (which does not include cases with zero difference) and appropriate tails. **In this test your T must be *lower* than the critical value found in tables**	$N = 14$; use two-tailed test (they may have preferred the lecture method more); use $p \leq 0.05$. Relevant critical value is 21 and our value for T is lower. Hence the difference is significant. We could claim that our difference was significant with $p \leq 0.02$ since we also equalled the critical value for this level

Box 11.2   Reporting the result of a Wilcoxon analysis

One student's result showed no preference for either method and was discarded from the analysis and N was therefore 14. Rank totals were found to be 90 in favour of the computer-based method and 15 in favour of the conventional method. A Wilcoxon analysis showed that $T = 15$, $p \leq 0.05$, two-tailed.

The Mann-Whitney U test

Data for our test

We are going to look again at the data in Table 11.3 and this time perform a Mann-Whitney *U* test. The reasoning here is pretty much the same as when you look at how two teams perform when each person on one team plays each person in the other. If all five members of the Duck and Feathers darts team beat every member of the White Horse team there would be few who would dare to suggest that it was 'all luck'. There are 25 matches altogether, since five people in one team each play all five in the other team. Of the 25 matches, if the Duck and Feathers win 13 and the White Horse 12, we are not at all certain that luck did not play a large part in the result.

The data are displayed again in Table 11.5. Go through the table awarding points for each value in it. The rules for calculating the points shown in columns 2 and 4 are as follows:

❏ award one point each time a score in one group is beaten by a score in the other group
❏ award half a point each time a score in one group ties with a score in the other group.

For example, taking the second high sleep-disturbed score of 11, this is beaten by the scores of 12 and 13 in the other group (giving 2 points) and is equal to the 11 in that group too (giving a half point). Hence total points here are 2.5. The odd thing about this scoring system is that the worse you are, the more points you gather; so, rather like golf, the aim is to achieve *low* points in the group that you predicted to have *higher* scores overall. The lower of the two totals of points is taken as Mann-Whitney's *U*. There were 90 'contests' here (10×9) so the points must total to 90, and they do. You can always check a Mann-Whitney calculation by finding the number of 'contests' ($= N_1 \times N_2$) and ensuring that U_1 and U_2 add up to this. So:

$$N_1 \times N_2 = U_1 + U_2$$

Table 11.5   Anxiety scores for high and low sleep-disturbed participants (Mann-Whitney test)

High sleep-disturbed participants		Low sleep-disturbed participants	
x	Points	x	Points
14	0	8	10
11	2.5	10	8
11	2.5	9	9
12	1.5	7	10
13	0.5	9	9
9	5	8	10
12	1.5	12	4
11	2.5	11	6.5
13	0.5	13	2
9	5		
	$\Sigma = 21.5$		$\Sigma = 68.5$

To check the significance of U enter Table 5, Appendix 2, with the value of U, numbers in each group, number of tails and an appropriate level for p. If we say this test is two-tailed, and we want $p \leq 0.05$ then we choose Table 5c on p. 261 because it covers $p \leq 0.05$ two-tailed. The critical value given there for $N_1 = 10$ and $N_2 = 9$ is 20. Note that it doesn't matter which participant total you call N_1 and which N_2. Our value for U is 21.5 so we have narrowly *failed* to show significance.

Box 11.3   Reporting the result of a Mann-Whitney analysis

> The anxiety scores in each group were allocated points when they were exceeded by or equalled scores in the other group. The lower points total was taken as a Mann-Whitney U value for $N = 10$ and $N = 9$. Lower anxiety scores were found in the low sleep-disturbed group but the difference was not significant with $U = 21.5$, $p > 0.05$, two-tailed. Points for the low sleep-disturbed group were 68.5 and for the high sleep-disturbed group were 21.5.

COMPARING PARAMETRIC AND NON-PARAMETRIC TESTS

The result leads to a point of interest because for the same data using an unrelated t test we achieved significance. This shows the slightly more sensitive nature of the parametric t test compared with the non-parametric U test on this occasion. On about 96% of occasions the t and U or T tests will produce the same results. The parametric tests have greater power because they use more of the available data, as explained on p. 154.

EXERCISES

1. Find out whether the test statistics in examples a, b, c and d in the table below are significant and give the lowest value for p that can be assumed from tables, for the one- or two-tailed tests indicated. You are given the numbers in groups and the appropriate test. You can put the lowest probability value (p) in the blank columns under 'significant'.

Number in each group		Mann-Whitney	Significant				Wilcoxon	Significant	
N_a	N_b	U	1-tailed	2-tailed	N	T		1-tailed	2-tailed
a 15	14	49			c 18	35			
b 8	12	5			d 30	48			

2. Use tables to check the significance or otherwise of the following t values. You can complete the last two columns of the table.

t	N	Design of study	One- or two-tailed	$p \le$	Reject null hypothesis?
a 1.75	16	Related	1		
b 2.88	20	Unrelated	2		
c 1.7	26	Unrelated	1		
d 5.1	10	Unrelated	1		
e 2.09	16	Related	2		
f 3.7	30	Related	2		

3. Carry out the appropriate test (Mann-Whitney or Wilcoxon) on the data in Table 11.1 and check the result for significance using a two-tailed test.
4. Have a look at the data in Tables a and b below. In each case decide whether it is wise to proceed with a t test. Check the assumptions for the test.

a.	17	23		b.	17	23
	18	9			18	11
	18	31			18	24 (related data)
	16				16	29
	18	(unrelated data)			12	19
	17				15	16
	6					

Also: select the appropriate non-parametric test for each set of data. Calculate the t value for each set of data and the non-parametric equivalent.
5. A report claims that a t value of 2.85 is significant ($p < 0.01$) when the number of people in a repeated measures design was 11. Could the hypothesis tested have been two-tailed?

ANSWERS

1. a. 0.01 (one-tail), 0.02 (two-tail); b. 0.005 (one-tail), 0.01 (two-tail); c. 0.025 (one-tail), 0.05 (two-tail); d. 0.001 (one-tail), 0.002 (two-tail).

2. a. NS, retain H_0; b. 0.01, reject H_0; c. NS, retain H_0; d. 0.005, reject H_0; e. NS, retain H_0; f. 0.01, reject H_0.
3. Wilcoxon's $T = 1$; $p < 0.002$.
4. a. Variances not at all similar, unrelated design and very different sample numbers. Hence, unwise. Non-parametric equivalent: Mann-Whitney. b. Lack of homogeneity of variance but related design. Therefore, safe to carry on with t. Non-parametric equivalent: Wilcoxon Signed Ranks. a. t (unrelated) 1.14; b. t (related) 1.57. a. $U = 6$; b. $T = 4.5$.
5. No. $df = 10$. Critical value (two-tailed) at $p \leq 0.01 = 3.169$.

KEY TERMS

Critical value	Significance test
Inferential test	t test; related; unrelated
Mann-Whitney test	Test statistic
Obtained value	Wilcoxon Matched Pairs test

TESTS FOR CATEGORICAL DATA

THE CHI-SQUARE TEST (WRITTEN AS χ^2, PRONOUNCED 'KY SQUARE')

When to use chi-square

Type of relationship tested	Level of data required	Design of study
Association or difference	Nominal	Unrelated

Assumptions: (for detail see the end of this section)
Cases (usually people) may appear in one only of the cells of the cross-tabs data table.
Low expected frequencies are a problem.
Advantages: this is the only well-recognized test at this level for categorical unrelated data.
Disadvantages: see the assumptions and details below concerning low expected frequencies and types of data that can be used.

DATA FOR OUR TEST

The chi-square test is used when you have data gathered as *frequencies*. Very often they are arranged as in Table 11.6. Typically you have categories of people (or cars, as in the example given) on one variable and you want to see if these categories differ on another variable which is *also* categorical – i.e. data are frequencies in categories. Because each object observed can be a thing (e.g. car) as well as a person, we often refer to the items observed as *cases*. In practical work at this level it is very popular to observe differences between sexes. Typical practicals involve an observation of whether males differ from females in the way they carry books (under arm or held to chest), take a parking space (forwards or reverse), turn when passing someone in a narrow place (towards or away), advertise in personal ads and so on. Each time the first category variable is gender and the second is the observed behaviour. To use chi-square the observed behaviour must be *categorized* and not scored. You can, however, start with scores – e.g. participants rate a person from 1 to 10 on attractiveness – and then *reduce* these data to nominal by dividing the scores into, for instance, 'high', 'middle' and 'low'.

Table 11.6   Frequencies of old and new cars stopping or not stopping at an amber light

Behaviour at amber light	Age category of car		
	New	Old	Total
Stopped	90$_a$	88$_b$	178
Did not stop	56$_c$	89$_d$	145
Total	146	177	323

An arrangement of frequency data as in Table 11.6 is known as a **CROSS-TABS** table. There is no limit on the number of rows and columns you can have when performing a chi-square analysis, apart from limits you might set yourself in terms of simplicity and lack of confusion. For instance, the data in Table 11.6 might have been arranged as in Table 11.7 if we had observed more detail about the cars and their drivers' behaviour at the traffic light.

Table 11.7   More detailed version of data in Table 11.6

Behaviour at amber light	Age of car		
	New (less than 2 years)	Recent (2–5 years old)	Old (more than 5 years old)
Stopped	65$_a$	68$_b$	45$_c$
Slowed down	35$_d$	18$_e$	20$_f$
Kept same speed	15$_g$	26$_h$	31$_i$

On some occasions we can perform a chi-square analysis on data arranged in just one column, as in Table 8.1, so long as we can compare these data with how they *should* be arranged if the null hypothesis is true. Also see Table 11.8 and p. 175 for a fuller explanation.

Some explanation

Suppose you read somewhere that extroverts are the sort of people who are not bothered by social conventions, who do not mind being 'on show'. If this is true, then it might be expected that extroverts would not mind being naked on a beach; in fact they might quite enjoy nude bathing. What a brilliant idea for a practical, you think! You pop off to a sunny Greek island beach known for its tolerance of nudism and give everyone on the beach an extroversion/introversion test. I am really not recommending this practical by the way – check the ethics (see Chapter 13) with your tutor before proceeding!

Suppose you decide to define an 'extrovert' as someone who scores above the mean on your test and an 'introvert' as someone falling below the mean. The data you gather might appear as in the row labelled **OBSERVED FREQUENCIES** in Table 11.8. Here we see that there were 40 naked extroverts and 10 naked introverts. The null hypothesis that we test here is that there is no difference between extrovert and introvert on nakedness. If this were true then the population of introverts should contain as many people likely to take their clothes off as the population of extroverts. On this occasion then, assuming this null hypothesis is true, we would expect to find that half our sample are introvert and half are extrovert. That is, of 50 naked people 25 should have been extrovert and 25 introvert. This is what we *expect* and therefore we produce what are called the **EXPECTED FREQUENCIES** – see Table 11.9. The expected frequencies are what we would expect to find among our *sample if the null hypothesis is true*. Chi-square looks at the size of the difference between what we observed and what we expected under the null hypothesis.

Table 11.8   Frequencies of naked extroverts and introverts

	Extroverts	Introverts	Total
Observed frequencies	40_a	10_b	50

Table 11.9   Expected frequencies of naked extroverts and introverts related to Table 11.8

	Extroverts	Introverts	Total
Expected frequencies	25_a	25_b	50

Calculating chi-square

To conduct a chi-square analysis, first identify each cell of the observed frequencies with a letter. A *cell* is one 'box' of original data in the table (but *not* a 'total' cell). In Table 11.8 we have just two cells, so label these a and b. The expected frequencies need identical letters for the corresponding cells.

Formula for chi-square

$$\chi^2 = \sum \frac{(O - E)^2}{E}$$

O is each observed cell frequency and *E* is each corresponding expected cell frequency. The formula asks us to do a calculation on each pair of *O* and *E* values and then to add up the results as follows.

	O − E	$(O - E)^2$	$\dfrac{(O - E)^2}{E}$	Result
Extroverts	$40 - 25 = 15$	225	$\dfrac{225}{25}$	9
Introverts	$10 - 25 = -15$	225	$\dfrac{225}{25}$	9
			$\chi^2 =$	18

For each observed cell, first we subtract the expected frequency (*E*) from the observed frequency (*O*). We then square the result. We then divide this result by the expected cell frequency. We do this for each cell in turn, then finally add up the results as shown in the column on the right of the calculation table above.

CHECKING THE RESULT IN TABLES: before we check the significance of our χ^2 result we need to find degrees of freedom. In this special version of chi-square *df* is just the number of observed cells minus 1, so we get $2 - 1 = 1$. On this special occasion of a two-cell data table we can use a one-tailed test. **IN ALL OTHER CASES OF CHI-SQUARE TWO-TAILED VALUES *must* BE USED.** Consulting Table 6, Appendix 2, we find that for $p \leq 0.05$ we need a chi-square value *greater than* 2.71. In fact, our value beats all other levels in the table for $df = 1$ so the result is highly significant. We can assume strong support for the hypothesis that extroverts are more likely to go naked on a beach.

Or can we ...

What we did above was to make a very poor test of the hypothesis that extroverts are more likely than introverts to take off their clothes on a beach. We used only the sample of naked people on a beach. We ignored other people. What if introverts just don't like going to beaches? Suppose there were 50 dressed people on the beach and, of these, again we find that 10 are introverts and 40 are extroverts. Now we know that the proportion of introverts who were naked was the same as the overall proportion of introverts on the beach and so we do not have good support for the hypothesis that introverts are less likely to go naked. What we *should* do is to find the proportions of naked and dressed extroverts and introverts *on the beach* to make a fair comparison. We have two variables now, both categorical. One is the variable of personality with two levels, extrovert and introvert. The other is the variable of dress state – naked or dressed. If we found our data were organized as shown in Table 11.10 then we could make a much fairer claim that introverts like to stay dressed.

Table 11.10   Observed frequencies of naked and dressed extroverts and introverts on beach

Personality type	Dress state		Total
	Naked	Dressed	
Extrovert	40_a	10_b	50
Introvert	10_c	40_d	50
Total	50	50	100

Here we find (conveniently for the purposes of explanation!) that although there were as many introverts as extroverts on the beach, only ten of the introverts were naked compared with the 40 out of 50 extroverts who stripped off.

Calculating expected frequencies in a cross-tabs table

Earlier we said that in a chi-square analysis the difference is tested between observed frequencies and those frequencies expected under the null hypothesis. The null hypothesis here says that (at least for people on beaches) introverts do not differ from extroverts in frequency of nakedness. If that is so, then what would we *expect* in the cells of Table 11.10? I hope you'll agree that if half the people were introverted and if half the people were naked then, *if there is no difference between extrovert and introvert,* we would expect half the introverts to be naked. In fact we would expect the frequencies shown in Table 11.11.

Table 11.11   Expected frequencies of naked and dressed extroverts and introverts on a beach

Personality type	Dress state	
	Naked	Dressed
Extrovert	25_a	25_b
Introvert	25_c	25_d

If you agreed that 25 of the 50 introverts should be naked then somehow or other you used, in your head, a version of the following formula:

$$\text{Expected frequency (for each cell)} = \frac{RC}{T} \text{ where } R \text{ is the total of the row the}$$

cell is in, C is the total of the column the cell is in and T is the total of all the

cells. In this case for each of cells a, b, c and d we would get $\dfrac{50 \times 50}{100} = 25$.

Calculating chi-square for a 2 × 2 cross-tabs table

We will calculate our chi-square on the data in Table 11.6 so that the task is not too easy and is more likely to resemble the sort of data you will be working with.

Procedure	Calculation on our data
1. Give each observed data cell a letter	See Table 11.6
2. Calculate expected frequencies according to the formula just provided	Cell a: $E = \dfrac{146 \times 178}{323} = \mathbf{80.46}$
	Cell b: $E = \dfrac{177 \times 178}{323} = \mathbf{97.54}$
	Cell c: $E = \dfrac{146 \times 145}{323} = \mathbf{65.54}$
	Cell d: $E = \dfrac{177 \times 145}{323} = \mathbf{79.46}$

3. Calculate χ^2 according to the formula given on p. 172, as follows:

	$O - E$	$(O - E)^2$	$\dfrac{(O - E)^2}{E}$	Result
Cell a:	$90 - 80.46 = 9.54$	$9.54^2 = 91.01$	$\dfrac{91.01}{80.46} =$	**1.13**
Cell b:	$88 - 97.54 = -9.54$	$-9.54^2 = 91.01$	$\dfrac{91.01}{97.54} =$	**0.93**
Cell c:	$56 - 65.54 = -9.54$	$-9.54^2 = 91.01$	$\dfrac{91.01}{65.54} =$	**1.39**
Cell d:	$89 - 79.46 = 9.54$	$9.54^2 = 91.01$	$\dfrac{91.01}{79.46} =$	**1.15**

$$\chi^2 = \text{(total of results)} = \mathbf{4.6}$$

4. Calculate degrees of freedom (df) according to the formula $(R - 1)(C - 1)$ where R is the number of rows and C is the number of columns　$df = (2 - 1) \times (2 - 1) = 1$
5. Check the significance of χ^2 in Table 6, Appendix 2, using two-tailed values and the appropriate df. **Remember** that all χ^2 tests **must be** two-tailed apart from the special one-row, two-cell version covered earlier.
   We have 1 df. The table gives a critical value of 3.84, which our value for χ^2 must exceed. 4.6 is greater than 3.84 so we have a significant difference with $p \leq 0.05$
   It appears that more old than new cars fail to stop at an amber traffic light.

Box 11.4　Reporting the results of a chi-square test

89 of 177 drivers in old cars did not stop at the amber light whereas only 56 out of 146 drivers of new cars did not stop. A χ^2 analysis of the frequencies of stopping and not stopping for old and new cars was significant, χ^2 (1, $N = 323$) = 4.6, $p < 0.05$.

Quick 2 × 2 formula

This can be used only where there are two columns and two rows, as in the example above. It saves the labour of calculating expected frequencies and, if you're handy with a calculator, you'll find this can be done in one move from the cell totals:

$$\chi^2 = \frac{N(ad - bc)^2}{(a + b)(c + d)(a + c)(b + d)}$$

where N is the total sample size and a, b, c and d are the appropriate cell values.

More complex cross-tabs tables

The calculation procedure detailed above (*not* the quick formula) can be extended to more complex tables such as Table 11.7. Here the df would be $(R - 1)(C - 1) = (3 - 1) \times (3 - 1) = 4$. You can work out the χ^2 value as an exercise if you wish and I'll give the result here, which is 15.99 and this exceeds the critical value of 9.49 that would be required for significance with $p \le 0.05$, 4 df, two-tailed.

The 'goodness of fit' χ^2 test – data in one row from a single variable

The chi-square test can be used when you have data in several categories on just one variable – as when we started on our example of number of naked extroverts on a beach. We had one variable – personality type: extrovert or introvert – and so we had just two cells for this variable. Suppose you had data on the number of withdrawals from Maths classes during the winter term in four different Maths classes run by four different tutors. Each tutor started with 30 students and each student can be in only one class. Have a look at the data in Table 11.12. Here we might suspect that there is a problem with Ricky's class. If you do have data of this kind you must be able to assume an underlying null hypothesis. Here we would assume that there is no problem with any tutor's class and therefore that all frequencies should be equal. On some occasions you might be able to make a different proposal for the expected frequencies – for instance that all withdrawals should be proportional to the number of students in each class originally where these, unlike in this example, were all different.

Table 11.12   Number of withdrawals in the winter term from four different Maths classes at Everlearn College

	Name of Maths tutor				Total
	Phil	Shirley	Ricky	Mick	
Number of winter-term withdrawals	5	2	9	4	20

The χ^2 calculation for this table is performed in exactly the same way as that shown at the beginning of this section for the one-row two-category test (p. 172) on naked introverts and extroverts, except that here we must calculate for cells a, b, c and d (not just cells a and b). The expected frequencies, as before, follow H_0 that withdrawals are spread randomly across the number of cells. We have 20 withdrawals and four cells. So, 20/4 gives 5 as the expected frequency for each cell. df are again (and for all one-row tests) one less than the number of categories, giving us a value of 3. You might like to calculate χ^2 and interpret the result from tables. If so, here is what you should find: χ^2 (3, $N = 20$) = 5.2, NS. 'NS' means 'not significant'. The critical value with 3 df at $p \le 0.05$ is 7.82 and our obtained value does not reach this.

Limitations on the use of chi-square

1. **Cases must appear in one cell only**. If a student had enrolled in more than one class and then withdrawn they might appear in *two* of the cells in Table 11.12. This would invalidate the analysis. A similar example would occur where you ask people what sport they participate in and count frequencies for each sport. If you recorded someone as participating in both swimming and cycling they would appear in more than one cell and chi-square cannot then be performed on the data.

2. **Only frequencies can appear in cells**. Chi-square cannot be performed if the cells of the cross-tabs table contain percentages, means, ratios or anything but a count of single occurrences.

3. **Low expected frequencies are a problem**. Your result for chi-square is untrustworthy if more than 20% of the expected frequency cells fall below 5. Hence, in a 2 × 2 analysis this would mean a problem if *any* of the expected cells were under 5 since each cell is 25% of all the cells. This rule of thumb is seen as a little restrictive by some statisticians and more detail is provided in Coolican (2004). It is commonly thought that it is fine to proceed if only one or two of the expected frequencies are under 5 *and the sample is larger than 20*. However, the best thing to do is to design your study and collect sufficient data not to be in this predicament.

Typical designs where too little data will appear in one cell are those investigating a relatively rare type of person such as left-handers, those with dyslexia, those following an unusual religion (for this country), those in favour of flogging or simply children under 4 years old who can conserve liquid volume. Avoid designs where it is hard to find people in one category and always allow yourself time and resources to collect data on plenty of people.

THE BINOMIAL SIGN TEST

When to use the Sign test		
Type of relationship tested	**Level of data required**	**Design of study**
Difference	Nominal	Related

Assumptions: none, providing data are in pairs.
Note: use when, for each pair of scores, you can only safely say that the participant 'improved' (or went in one direction), 'worsened' (went in the other direction) or stayed the same.
Advantages: this is the only well-recognized test at this level for categorical related data.
Disadvantages: uses little of the raw data available. Insensitive. Will often not give significance where a more sensitive test would.

Sometimes we have data where all we can say about each person is that they went one way, went the other or stayed the same. We *can* say this with the data in Table 11.1. We *can* perform a Sign test on these data by only noting for each participant whether they improved in the second condition (they have a '+'), worsened (they have a '−') or stayed the same (in which case they are not counted in the analysis). However, this is mostly not advisable. We lose too much of the original information in treating the results like this and, although the Sign test is then very easy to perform, we would often find no significance when it is certainly there. We would make too many Type II errors.

Data for our test

However, take a situation where children have been asked to perform a Piagetian conservation task. The only information we record is whether they did or did not 'conserve'. We test them first in the conventional manner by asking the child whether two glasses of orange juice have the same amount. When they agree that they do, we then pour the contents of one of the glasses into a different-shaped glass. We then ask them whether one glass has more, less or is the same in quantity. If the child conserves, they say 'the same'. In the second test we omit the first stage of asking whether the two identical glasses have the same amount of juice. This is in order to avoid giving the child the clue that 'something must be different' if two questions have been asked. Of course, there is a problem with practice in giving these two different trials but let's assume that is accounted for in the design and see what we would expect from our children if the second method (the 'one question' method) is a fairer way of asking and will be more likely to show that children can conserve liquid volume.

The data for this imaginary study are presented in Table 11.13, where most children have not conserved on the traditional trial but conserved on the one-question trial, indicated with a '+'. Where the child conserved first, then didn't (the child 'worsened'), we use a '−'. Where the child performed in the same way on both trials we indicate this with a '0' and exclude that result from the final analysis.

A little explanation

The Sign test simply assumes that, if the null hypothesis is true, there should be an equal number of + and − signs. This is exactly the reasoning and procedure we used for the data from the baby-gender guesser in Chapter 8. We expect there to be few negative signs. We calculate the probability of getting the number of negative signs we *did* get if the null hypothesis is true (that negatives and positives are equally likely). If this probability is less than 0.05 we have support for the proposition that the one-question method prompts conservation (or rather, that the two question version inhibits it).

Table 11.13   Children's conservation performance in two versions of the liquid volume test

Child	Conventional method	One question method	Sign
A	N	C	+
B	C	N	−
C	N	C	+
D	C	C	0
E	N	C	+
F	N	C	+
G	C	N	−
H	N	C	+
I	N	C	+
J	N	C	+

C = conserved; N = did not conserve; + = conserved 2nd time only; − = conserved first then failed; 0 = same performance both times.

Calculation of S in the binomial sign test

1. Give each pair of scores a '+' for one direction (usually 'improved'), a '−' for the opposite direction (usually 'worsened') or a 0 if they stayed the same.
2. Exclude from the analysis any case with a 0.
3. Count the number of the least-occurring sign and call this value S. In our example above, negative signs are less frequent and there are two of these, so $S = 2$.
4. Check against the critical values in Table 7, Appendix 2. The obtained S must be less than the critical value. For our example using a two-tailed test, with $p \leq 0.05$ and $N = 9$ (note we excluded child D), the critical value is 1. Unfortunately our value of 2 is not less than this so the result is not significant and we cannot assume that the one-question method makes a difference in this study. We narrowly avoided significance so it would be wise to repeat this study with more participants.

Box 11.5　Reporting the result of a Sign test

For each child, conservation on the second trial but not the first was counted as positive. Initial conservation and then non-conservation were counted as negative. One child conserved on both trials and this result was excluded. The remaining nine results were analysed using the sign test and it was found that the difference between positive and negative performance was not significant, $S = 2$, $p > 0.05$, NS.

PROGRESS REVIEW 11.2

EXERCISES

1. In a survey, 17 *Guardian* readers were pro- fox-hunting and 48 were against, whereas among *Daily Express* readers 33 were pro-hunting and 16 opposed it. Carry out a chi-square analysis on these data and interpret the result.
2. Should a chi-square test be carried out on the following data?

	Conserved	Did not conserve
4-year-olds	1	7
6-year-olds	7	1

3. In another survey, 40 people agreed with a complete ban on the sale of cigarettes whereas 60 disagreed.
   (a) What version of chi-square is required to analyse these data to see whether there is a significant majority in favour of retaining cigarette sales?
   (b) Calculate the chi-square and interpret the result.
   (c) Could this test be one-tailed?
   (d) If another survey showed that 74% were against a ban and 26% for it, could chi-square be used on these data?
4. Nine people were sent on an interpersonal-skills training course. They were asked their opinion on the need for this kind of course in their company both before and after attending. Having attended, seven people thought the need for the course was lower than they had thought before the course started. One person rated the need higher than they had done previously and one person rated the need at the same level both times.
   (a) What test will tell us whether this apparent negative effect of the course is significant?
   (b) Calculate the test statistic and interpret the result.

ANSWERS

1. $\chi^2 (1, N = 114) = 19.25$, $p < 0.001$.
2. No. All expected frequencies are under five and there are less than 20 participants.
3. (a) The one-row two-cell chi-square
   (b) $\chi^2(1, N = 100) = 4$, $p < 0.05$ (just!). Reject H_0
   (c) Yes – this is the only version that can be
   (d) No, these are percentages. Only frequencies can be used with chi-square.
4. (a) The sign test
   (b) $S = 1$, $N = 8$ (because the non-changer is eliminated) so critical value is 0 but we have 1, so the difference between pre- and post-course ratings is not significant.

KEY TERMS

Chi-square test
Cross-tabs table
Expected frequencies

Goodness of fit test
Observed frequencies
(binomial) Sign test

chapter
12

Correlation – things that go together

What's in this chapter?

This chapter focuses on the concepts and procedures involved with *correlation*.
- ❑ We learn that correlation is the measurement of the extent to which pairs of related values on two variables tend to change together. If one variable tends to increase with the other, the correlation is *positive*. If the relationship is *inverse*, it is a *negative correlation*.
- ❑ We see that *strength* is a measure of the correlation and is signified by a value from -1 (strong negative), through 0 (no correlation) to $+1$ (strong positive).
- ❑ We learn that *significance* assesses how unlikely such a correlation was to occur under the null hypothesis (usually that the population correlation is zero).
- ❑ We look at how correlations can be depicted on a *scattergraph*.
- ❑ Two major calculations for correlation are introduced:
    - *Pearson's (r) product-moment correlation* – for interval-level data.
    - *Spearman's rho (r_s) rank correlation* – a Pearson calculation on the ranks of the values in the dataset. Used with ordinal-level data.
- ❑ We note that Important points about correlations are:
    - *cause* cannot be inferred from the existence of a strong correlation between variables
    - variables to be correlated cannot be categorical.

You are already quite familiar with the concept of correlation in day-to-day life. You know that the harder you work on an assignment, the higher the mark you are likely to get. In childhood you know that the older you get, the taller you become. **CORRELATION** is *the relationship between two variables*. Imagine you run a stall selling cold drinks. You know that *the hotter the temperature the more sales you would make*. Here we have a relationship between the two variables of drink sales and temperature. When thinking about correlations it is often tempting to concentrate only on one direction of the relationship – hotter and more sales. But on your cold drinks stall it would *also* be true that *the cooler the temperature, the fewer sales you would make*. Your proposed correlation is between the two *operationalized* variables of temperature and sales. Here are some more proposed correlations with the two variables stated in possible measurable terms. These are the two variables you would measure in a study to test the proposed relationship.

Table 12.1 Possible correlations and appropriate variables

Proposed relationship	Variables
1. The more you give kids, the more they expect	Resources, expectation (e.g. Christmas present estimates)
2. Taller people are more successful in their careers	Height, success (e.g. level reached, salary)
3. The older we get, the less we remember	Age, recall score
4. The hotter it gets, the more aggressive people become – see Figure 12.1	Temperature, aggression (e.g. assaults, bad language)
5. The more you practise guitar, the fewer mistakes you make	Time in practice, errors
6. Intelligence runs in families	Parent IQ, child IQ

Figure 12.1 The higher the temperature, the more aggressive people are

POSITIVE AND NEGATIVE CORRELATIONS

In a **POSITIVE CORRELATION** if a person scores high on one variable they tend also to score high on the other variable. Likewise, a low score on one tends to be related to a low score on the other. An example might be:

The more papers you have to deliver, the longer it takes you.

In a psychological context we might expect self-esteem to be positively correlated with confidence. People scoring high on self-esteem would also tend to score high on confidence. Those low on self-esteem would be low on confidence.

Where a value is high on one variable but *low* on the other variable, we call this a **NEGATIVE CORRELATION**. For instance:

The more papers you have to carry, the slower you walk.

A psychological example might be that self-esteem would be negatively correlated with anxiety. Those with high self-esteem would have low anxiety scores and *vice versa*. The correlation between the distances d1 and d2 in Figure 12.2 would be perfectly negative; when one is high the other is low and *vice versa*.

Figure 12.2   A perfect negative correlation between up and down

MEASURING THE STRENGTH OF CORRELATION

To measure correlation we must have *pairs of measures* – a measure on each of the two variables to be correlated. The data in Table 12.2 are typical, where, for each participant, there is a score on self-esteem and a score on confidence. We will look at two ways of calculating a correlation but in each case we end up with a value called a **CORRELATION COEFFICIENT**. This will always be a value between −1 and +1, as indicated in Figure 12.3. Note that you might be asked in an examination to describe the level of correlation given to a value – for instance 'strong', 'moderate' or 'weak'.

Figure 12.3   Measuring correlation from completely negative to completely positive

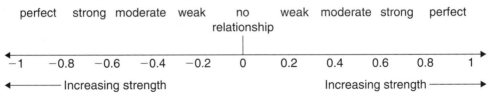

It might seem odd to call a *negative* value such as −0.9 'strong'. What is meant here is that the correlation is *negative*, as explained above, but as we move from −0.1 to −0.9 so the extent to which positive scores on one variable are related to negative scores on the other increases.

It is not possible to get a correlation greater than +1 or less than −1. If you do find such a result for your correlation coefficient you'll need to check your calculations because you will have made a mistake somewhere or other (or you may have incorrectly told your computer or calculator what to do). A correlation value of zero tells us that there is absolutely no relationship between the two variables. For example, we might expect no relationship between the time of day a person was born and the number of chicken nuggets they eat at their 16th birthday party. When we test a correlation coefficient for significance (p. 186), we assume, as a null hypothesis, that there is no correlation at all in the population.

TIP FOR EXAMS: It is very easy to assume that '*negative correlation*' means '*no correlation*'. You need to remember that 'no correlation' means there is no relationship at all but that negative correlation means there *is* a correlation but one where high scores on one variable are related to low scores on the other and *vice versa*.

SCATTERGRAPHS – PICTURES OF CORRELATIONS

A valuable way to visualize correlations is to draw a **SCATTERGRAPH** (otherwise known as 'scattergram', 'scatterplot') – something you will have almost certainly done at some time in school, perhaps showing the relationship between shoe size and height, which is a teachers' favourite. Looking at Figure 12.4 it is important to recognize that each dot represents a *pair* of scores from one person (or 'case'). Imagine here that six people have taken a driving test, one has had only one practice trial, one has had two practice trials and so on. The person who had four trials has scored 105 points and this is represented on the scattergraph by a point that is vertically above 4 on the 'trials' axis and horizontally opposite 105 on the 'points' axis. Note that the horizontal axis is commonly known as 'X' and the vertical axis as 'Y'.

Figure 12.4 then shows a very strong *positive* correlation. Figure 12.5, however, shows a very strong *negative* correlation – the more practice acquired, the less time taken on the task. Note the shapes of these two relationships, because they often occur in exams. In Figure 12.6 the points appear all over the place, in no obvious line shape either way. This is what we expect when there is no correlation between two variables. Here the value of the correlation coefficient would be near zero. There are rare occasions when a coefficient can be zero but there *is* a clear relationship between two variables. Take a look at Figure 12.7 which shows a **CURVILINEAR RELATIONSHIP**. This could occur for so-called 'arousal' and performance: when we are bored (understimulated) we perform at a low level, when we are stimulated we perform well, but when we are overstimulated we might perform worse because of anxiety and general overload.

Figure 12.4   Highly positive correlation – number of practice trials by driving test score

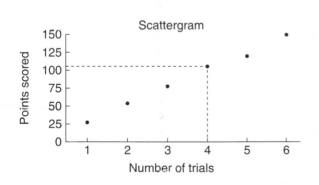

Data		
Number of trials		Points scored
1		27
2		54
3		78
4		105
5		120
6		149

Figure 12.5   Highly negative correlation – number of practice trials by time taken on task

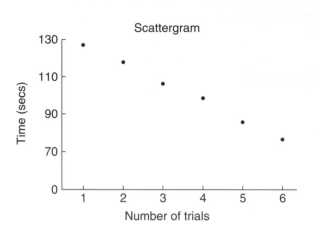

| Data | |
Number of trials	Time to complete route (secs)
1	127
2	118
3	106
4	98
5	85
6	76

Figure 12.6   Zero correlation – number of practice trials by words spoken during task

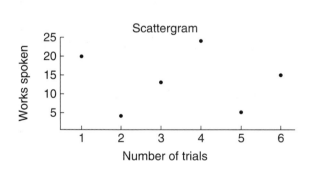

| Data | |
Number of trials	Number of words spoken
1	20
2	4
3	13
4	24
5	5
6	15

Figure 12.7   A curvilinear relationship between two variables

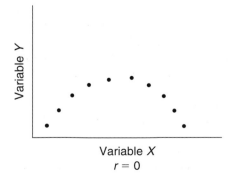

Figure 12.8   Consumption of red wine across various residential areas by consumption of mystery product (Y axis) – data from Argyle (1994) *Psychology of Social Class*, London: Routledge. See Progress review 12.1, question 5

Consumption of red wine correlates negatively with what?

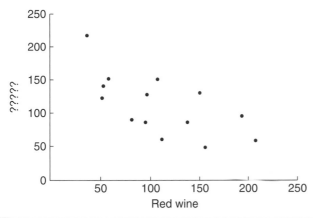

Red wine

EXERCISES

1. Decide which of the correlations suggested in Table 12.1 are positive and which are negative.
2. Try drawing the scattergraph for the data in Table 12.2.
3. Design studies that would test the proposals that:
   (a) practice makes perfect
   (b) eating fish makes people intelligent
   (c) power corrupts.
4. A student colleague tells you that she has obtained a correlation coefficient of 2.68. What might you tell her?
5. Just for fun, take a look at Figure 12.8 and try to guess the mystery variable on the Y axis. Each dot is a residential area (e.g. 'affluent suburban', 'poorest council estate' and so on). In each area the average amount of red wine consumed was recorded, as was consumption of the mystery product. So some areas consume a lot of red wine but little of the mystery product, while others take little red wine but a lot of the mystery product. What is it? These were data in a genuine study indicated in the figure title.
6. How would you describe the strength of the correlation shown in Figure 12.9, p. 186?

ANSWERS

1. 1, positive; 2, positive; 3, negative (more years/less recalled); 4, positive; 5, negative; 6, positive.
3. (a) An example is the study described above where participants are given more or fewer practice trials and their performance is recorded in measurable units; (b) we need a measure of how much fish people eat, e.g. weight per month, and some measure of intelligence such as IQ; (c) take each person's hierarchical level in their organization (e.g. manager, senior manager, executive) and use some scale or set of scenarios for them to respond to, such as what they consider to be an excessive amount for an expenses claim.
4. She needs to re-do her calculations. The highest possible value for a correlation coefficient is $+1$.
5. Brown sauce!
6. Moderate and negative.

PROGRESS REVIEW 12.1

KEY TERMS

Correlation   Negative correlation
Correlation coefficient   Positive correlation
Curvilinear relationship   Scattergraph

Figure 12.9   Scattergraph for question 6 in Progress review 12.1

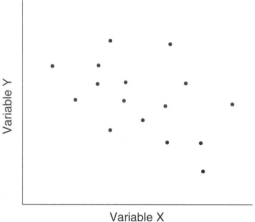

Variable Y

Variable X

THE SIGNIFICANCE AND STRENGTH OF CORRELATIONS

It is very important to remember that there is a big difference between saying that a correlation is *strong* and saying it is *significant*.

Suppose I have three green raffle tickets numbered one to three, and three red tickets also numbered one to three. Suppose I give one red and one green ticket at random to each of three friends. What would be the probability that each friend would end up with the same two numbers – that is, of getting a perfect correlation? If we kept doing this boring task we would expect the 'perfect correlation' to occur one time in six. There are only six possible events here so the probability of the perfect match occurring is 1/6 or 0.17.

We have just found the probability of our result occurring by chance if the null hypothesis is true. But we know that this probability must be under 0.05 for significance. Hence, with only three participants in a correlation it is impossible to get a significant result. As the number of participants increases, so the probability of getting a significant correlation at random gets less and less.

In the example just given we had a very strong correlation that was not significant. We can also have a significant correlation that is not very strong. Table 8, Appendix 2, will show us, when we come to use it, that with 60 participants a correlation as low as 0.25 is significant. Scientists often report such correlations as a 'weak but significant trend'. So it is important to remember that:

A strong correlation need not be significant.
A significant correlation need not be strong.

And it all depends on *N*. When *N* is high then a quite weak correlation can be significant. When *N* is low then even very strong correlations may not be significant. The message, once again, is to make sure that you include a sensibly large number of people in your sample when you conduct a research project so that, if there *is* a relationship there, you will have enough people or cases to show it.

Now we turn to the question of how to calculate the strength of a correlation and how to check this correlation for significance.

PEARSON'S ('PRODUCT-MOMENT') CORRELATION COEFFICIENT – *r*

When to use the Pearson's *r*		
Type of relationship tested	Level of data	Design
Correlation	Interval or ratio	Related – pairs of data

Conditions: parametric assumptions – data need to be at interval level or above and should conform to having been drawn from a normal distribution – see p. 154.
Advantages: more sensitive test – will sometimes give significance when Spearman doesn't.
Disadvantages: need to satisfy parametric assumptions; complex to calculate.

The imposing title, including 'product-moment', is not usually used and this test is normally known simply as Pearson's *r*. However, the complex title is matched by rather complex calculations. You will get much the same results with a Spearman's rho test (described after this test) as you do with Pearson but the latter is a more sensitive test. This mirrors the relationship between the *t* test and Wilcoxon in the last chapter. Occasionally, you will get significance with Pearson but not Spearman, as happens with our calculations below. You pays yer money and you takes yer choice.

We shall conduct our Pearson calculations on the data in Table 12.2. Here the data gathered are the bold numbers in the columns headed 'self-esteem' and 'confidence'. Imagine we have administered scales for these two variables to ten participants; the self-esteem scale has a top score of 20 whereas the top score on confidence is a possible 30. Note that each of the two variables to be correlated can be measured on any kind of interval- or ratio-level scale; they do not have to have similar number ranges. We can, if we like, correlate degrees centigrade with salary earned per year. The formula we have to work with is, I'm afraid:

$$r = \frac{N\sum(xy) - \sum x \sum y}{\sqrt{[N\sum x^2 - (\sum x)^2][N\sum y^2 - (\sum y)^2]}}$$

This looks rather nasty. There are several versions of this equation so don't worry if it looks different from one you have been given elsewhere. This one has the advantage that you do not have to calculate means or standard deviations but can work from just the values given in the last two lines of Table 12.2, which can be found using a simple calculator.

Table 12.2 Self-esteem and confidence scores for ten people

Parti-cipant	Self esteem x	Confi-dence y	x^2	y^2	$x \times y$
A	17	25	289	625	425
B	8	12	64	144	96
C	3	8	9	64	24
D	12	8	144	64	96
E	11	10	121	100	110
F	18	22	324	484	396
G	6	19	36	361	114
H	10	14	100	196	140
I	11	16	121	256	176
J	14	23	196	529	322
	$\sum x = 110$	$\sum y = 157$	$\sum x^2 = 1404$	$\sum y^2 = 2823$	$\sum(x \times y) = 1899$
	$(\sum x)^2 = 12{,}100$	$(\sum y)^2 = 24{,}649$			

A little explanation

The Pearson correlation looks at *deviations* of scores from the mean – see p. 118 for a reminder. The idea is that if x and y are strongly correlated then the tendency is that if a person is high above the mean on one variable they will also be high above the mean on the other, and *vice versa*. Hence their deviations will both be high. In the Pearson calculation, deviations are *multiplied together* (though the version of the equation above does not show this directly). We obtain the maximum values we can when both deviations are equally high or low. For instance, if I am 5 above the mean on x and 5 above on y we get 25, whereas if I am only 2 above on y we only get 10. There is a fuller explanation of the Pearson calculation in Coolican (2004).

Calculation of Pearson's r

Procedure	Calculation/result of steps
1. Find $\sum x$	See column 2, Table 12.2 = 110
2. Find $(\sum x)^2$ (this is $\sum x$ times itself)	See column 2, Table 12.2 = 12,100
3. Add all x^2 to get $\sum x^2$. Be careful to distinguish this from $(\sum x)^2$	See column 4, Table 12.2 = 1404
4. Multiply result of step 3 by N	$1404 \times 10 = 14{,}040$
5. Subtract result of step 2 from result of step 4	$14{,}040 - 12{,}100 = 1940$
6–10. Repeat steps 1 to 5 on the y data	From Table 12.2
	$\sum y$ = 157
	$(\sum y)^2$ = 24,649
	$\sum y^2$ = 2823
	$N\sum y^2$ = 28,230
	$N\sum y^2 - (\sum y)^2 = 28{,}230 - 24{,}649 = 3581$
11. Multiply result of step 5 by result of step 10	$1940 \times 3581 = 6{,}947{,}140$
12. Find square root of step 11 result	$\sqrt{6{,}947{,}140} = 2635.74$
13. Multiply $\sum x$ by $\sum y$	$110 \times 157 = 17{,}270$
14. Find $\sum xy$	From column 6, Table 12.2, $\sum xy = 1899$
15. Multiply result of step 14 by N	$10 \times 1899 = 18{,}990$
16. Subtract result of step 13 from result of step 15	$18{,}990 - 17{,}270 = 1720$
16. Divide result of step 16 by result of step 12	$r = \dfrac{1720}{2635.74} = \mathbf{0.653}$

To find whether this result for r is significant see Table 8 in Appendix 2 using $df = N - 2$. If either positive or negative direction is predicted then a one-tailed test is possible but, as explained on p. 147, this would mean that a result in the opposite direction would logically have to be of no interest to psychology whatsoever. This is unlikely, so two-tailed tests are almost always used. $df = 8$; critical value for $p \leq 0.05$ is 0.632 (two-tailed) and our obtained value is just larger than this and hence significant.

If N is > 100 then r can be converted to a t value and checked in t tables – see p. 191.

Writing up the result of a correlation

The Pearson correlation between scores on the self-esteem scale and on the confidence scale was found to be significant with $r(8) = 0.653$, $p < 0.05$, two-tailed.

Negative correlations

If your value for r comes out negative this is OK, so long as that is what you were predicting – see the explanation of negative correlation at the start of the chapter. For significance checking just use the value of r as if it did not have a negative sign.

SPEARMAN'S RHO (ρ) CORRELATION COEFFICIENT

When to use Spearman's ρ

Type of relationship tested	Level of data	Design
Correlation	Ordinal	Related – pairs of data

Advantages: no need to satisfy parametric assumptions. Easier to calculate.
Disadvantages: less sensitive to data than Pearson and therefore may not always give significance when Pearson does.

For this correlation calculation we can use the same data as for the last and make a comparison of the results. The formula for Spearman is:

$$\rho = 1 - \frac{6\sum d^2}{N(N^2 - 1)}$$

where N is the number of pairs of data and d is the difference between the ranks of each pair of scores, as explained below.

A little explanation

As with the Wilcoxon test we look at the difference between paired ranks. However, here, if there is to be a strong *positive* correlation, we would expect all differences between ranks to be small. Each person should get much the same rank on one variable as they did on the other. If we want a strong *negative* correlation then people should get a high rank on one variable paired with a low rank on the other *and vice versa*. In the formula for Spearman, if the differences are low then $6 \times \sum d^2$ will be low and the big fraction will be small. Therefore there will be only a little to take from 1 and the resulting value for ρ will be close to 1. A Spearman correlation is actually a Pearson correlation but carried out on the ranks of each score instead of the scores themselves – i.e. a Pearson on columns 4 and 5 (from the left) of Table 12.3.

Table 12.3 Self-esteem and confidence scores prepared for Spearman's rho calculation

Participant	Self-esteem	Confidence	Self-esteem rank	Confidence rank	Difference between ranks (d)	d^2
	x	y				
A	17	25	9	10	−1	1
B	8	12	3	4	−1	1
C	3	8	1	1.5	−0.5	0.25
D	12	8	7	1.5	5.5	30.25
E	11	10	5.5	3	2.5	6.25
F	18	22	10	8	2	4
G	6	19	2	7	−5	25
H	10	14	4	5	−1	1
I	11	16	5.5	6	−0.5	0.25
J	14	23	8	9	−1	1
						$\sum d^2 = 70$

Calculation of Spearman's ρ

Procedure	Calculation/result of steps
1. Give ranks to x scores	See column 4 of Table 12.3
2. Give ranks to y scores	See column 5 of Table 12.3
3. Subtract each rank on y from each rank on x	See column 6 of Table 12.3
4. Square results of step 3	See column 7 of Table 12.3
5. Add the results of step 4	= 70 (see bottom of column 7 of Table 12.3)
6. Insert the results found into the formula for Spearman given above	$\rho = 1 - \dfrac{6 \times 70}{10(10^2 - 1)} = 1 - \dfrac{420}{990} = \mathbf{0.576}$
7. Check result against the critical value found in Table 9, Appendix 2	$N = 10$. Using two-tailed values ρ must be greater than 0.648 for significance. In this case we do not get a significant correlation and must retain the null hypothesis of no correlation.

Notice here that Pearson gave us significance but Spearman does not. This is the difference in power between parametric and non-parametric tests at work.

IF N IS LARGE, i.e. >30

You might have spotted that the Spearman tables only go up to $N = 30$. Pearson's go up to 100 but quite often there are more people than this in a survey. What to do? The answer is to convert your r value to a t value and then check the significance of t as we did in the last chapter. The formula for the conversion is:

$$t = r\sqrt{\frac{N-2}{1-r^2}}$$

which works for either Pearson or Spearman.

SOME GENERAL POINTS ABOUT CORRELATION

CORRELATION DOES NOT IMPLY CAUSE

Think back to the cold drinks example on p. 180. We had a correlation between sales of drinks and temperature. You would think me pretty odd if I said 'Well, that's evidence that selling drinks makes the temperature go up'. You know that sales cannot affect temperature and that it is highly likely that rising temperatures are a direct cause of higher drinks sales. This is because you know from life's experiences, in clear cases such as this, what causes what. However, in psychology nothing is that certain. Consider the following correlation claim:

   The more physical punishment children receive, the more aggressive they become.

   This correlation between physical punishment and later aggression has been demonstrated in many studies. However, the statement above is poorly worded. From the statement it is very tempting to assume that hitting children *causes* them to become aggressive. However, from the *correlation* evidence we can say *only* that there is a relationship. Perhaps children who are naturally aggressive cause their parents to hit them more! Personally, I doubt this interpretation but in doing science we must keep an open mind until there is further direct evidence. In this case there *is* more direct evidence from a natural experiment. In 1979 Sweden made the hitting of children by anyone, even parents, illegal. Contrary to predictions of undisciplined and violent children roaming the streets creating havoc, Durrant (2000) found that rates of youth involvement in crime, alcohol and drug use, rape and suicide had *declined* over the period more than could be predicted from other factors affecting other similar societies.

INTERPRETATIONS OF CORRELATIONS

When we know that there is a correlation between A and B there are then several possible interpretations, including the following most obvious ones:

❑ Variable A has a direct effect on variable B.
❑ Variable B has a direct effect on variable A.
❑ Variables A and B are both affected by variable C or a set of other variables.
❑ The correlation is a Type I error – it was just a fluke.

The third alternative above says that variable A *and* variable B may be affected by another variable. For instance, aggression might not be caused by physical punishment, nor might physical punishment be brought about by children being aggressive. It could be that *both* these variables, punishment and aggression, are associated with certain types of home environment. Perhaps parents who physically punish do other things that encourage aggression, such as being aggressive themselves or failing to curb aggressive behaviour. These possible interpretations are depicted in Figure 12.10.

Figure 12.10 Possible interpretations of a correlation between physical punishment and aggression

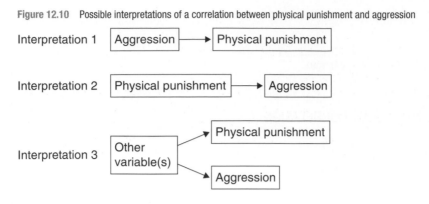

Comparison of correlation and experimental studies

As we have just seen, a *weakness* of studies using correlation is that the correlation *alone* cannot tell us which variable has an effect on which. Because well-controlled experiments manipulate an independent variable (IV) and *then* observe the effect on the dependent variable (DV), we can more confidently claim that the IV causes the DV to change. With correlation we can only use the existence of a relationship between two variables as more indirect evidence that one variable has an effect on the other.

The *advantage* of correlation studies is that they can often be carried out when no comparable experiment is possible. We cannot ask people to smoke so many cigarettes and then see how ill they get. However, we can ask how many they smoke and correlate this variable with other variables, such as days off sick, visits to the doctor, number of smoking-related illnesses suffered and so on.

MAKE SURE BOTH YOUR VARIABLES ARE MEASURED

In a correlation both variables *must* be at least at ordinal level. They will almost always be 'scores', looking like interval level, which may or may not be converted to ordinal when a Spearman calculation is chosen. You *cannot* correlate when you have a score and a category for each person. For instance, you cannot correlate a person's gender with, say, extroversion scores. Gender is a *categorical variable* (see p. 105) and the sensible thing to do here would be to conduct a *difference* test, where the 'independent variable' is gender with two levels, male and female. We would look for the difference between males and females on extroversion. Actually, having said you can't correlate gender there are special procedures where you *may* correlate a category variable providing it has only two all-inclusive values such as male/female or car-owner/non-car-owner. These procedures are, however, probably too advanced for your syllabus but you can find them if you wish in Coolican (2004). Here are some typical category variables that students often try to correlate, with disastrous results:

❏ Marital status (if you call '1' single and '2' married, how can married be twice single?)
❏ Area (e.g. North/South)
❏ Religion
❏ Type of car owned
❏ Left-handed/right-handed
❏ Conserved/didn't conserve
❏ Music preference.

EXERCISES

1. From an article in the *Times Educational Supplement*, 3 June 1988:

    > ... teaching the sound and shape of letters can give pre-school children a head start ... children who performed best at the age of seven tended to be those who had the most knowledge and understanding of the three Rs at the age of four.
    >
    > In the case of reading, the strongest predictor of ability among seven-year-olds was 'the number of letters the child could identify at the age of four-and-three-quarters' ... Tizard concludes that nursery teachers should give more emphasis to literacy and numeracy skills.

    (a) What conclusion, other than the researcher's, could be drawn from the last paragraph of the passage?

    (b) Briefly describe a study that could help us decide between these alternative interpretations.

    (c) What sort of correlation would the researchers have found between number of letters identified at four years and number of reading errors at seven – positive or negative?

    (d) Suppose the correlation between adding ability at five years and mathematical ability at seven years was 0.83. How would you describe the strength of this coefficient verbally?

    (e) What level of significance would the (Pearson) correlation of 0.83 have reached (two-tailed) if the sample of children had numbered 33?

2. Spearman's correlation may always be used instead of Pearson's. Is the reverse of this true? Please give a reason.

3. A researcher correlates participants' scores on a questionnaire concerning 'ego strength' with measures of their anxiety level obtained by rating their verbal responses to several pictures. Which measure of correlation should be employed?

4. A student friend has carried out a practical project in which she asked people whether they went to state school, private school, public school or some other type of school. She also asked them to fill out her *attitude to study* questionnaire. She now wishes to correlate *type of education* with *attitude to study*. What would you advise her to do?

ANSWERS

1. (a) Early letter-recognition at four years old correlated with reading ability at seven years but may not have *caused* the superior reading. It may be general home environment that affects both early letter-recognition and seven-year-old reading ability. Encouraging the recognition of letters may not automatically lead to an increase in reading ability at seven years.

    (b) You could take an experimental group at age four, matched with a control group, and train the experimental group children for letter recognition. Then follow through to seven years and compare groups on reading. You could also attempt to balance out all conceivable third factors (thought possibly to cause both improved letter recognition at four years and better reading at seven years), then follow groups from four to seven years on reading.

    (c) Negative; note that better skill should accompany fewer errors.

    (d) Strong/very strong.

    (e) $\rho \leq 0.001$

2. No. For Pearson, data must meet parametric requirements.
3. Spearman. Data should be treated as ordinal since human judgement ratings are used and the measures are not described as standardized tests.
4. Her type of education variable is categorical, so a correlation cannot be conducted. She can:
   (a) collapse her attitude data into two groups (e.g. above and below median) and her school categories into two groups (e.g. state/private) and calculate chi-square
   (b) just collapse the school categories as in (a) and run an unrelated t test of difference.

KEY TERMS

Pearson's product-moment correlation
Spearman's rho (ρ) correlation

chapter
13

Ethical issues in psychological research

What's in this chapter?

- ❑ Psychologists have to behave ethically in several areas, including work with clients, publishing their work and academic research with human participants. This chapter looks at the first two of these areas very briefly, then concentrates on the third.
- ❑ We look at the British Psychological Society's ethical principles for research with humans.
- ❑ The issues of *confidentiality* and *anonymity* are discussed, the two concepts often being confused. Additionally, the issue of *privacy* is reviewed.
- ❑ The arguments for and against *deception* are reviewed, along with possible alternatives.
- ❑ The consequent need for *debriefing* is described and the question raised as to whether or not it is effective.
- ❑ Protection of participants both *mentally* and *physically* is of paramount importance and various issues surrounding this are discussed, including that of *psychological stress*.
- ❑ Participants need to have given their *informed consent* to the investigation's procedures before participation. However, if deception is involved this consent cannot always be said to be *fully* informed. Implications of this are discussed, along with the *special power of the investigator*.
- ❑ Observation of people at a distance can mean that those observed are participants without being asked to give consent. The issue of *involuntary participation* is therefore involved. We look at serious and less serious instances.
- ❑ Finally, we look at some of the ethical issues involved when psychologists carry out *intervention studies*. These have an intended impact on the lives of participants. However, this impact cannot be realistically extended to all who might benefit from the psychological effects that have been demonstrated, such as improvements in reading or cognitive ability.

Psychologists, as professionals who deal with the general public, must work ethically. Because they have a certain amount of power and influence over the people they work with in their daily lives as researchers or practitioners (see below), there must be assurances and safeguards for the public to be able to trust the psychologists they encounter and to feel that they are not being exploited or harmed.

Indeed, surely we all agree, psychologists should not harm or exploit people at all, knowingly or unwittingly. There are three major areas in which ethical issues are important:

1. Where psychologists work in an applied field, as professionals helping members of the general public.
2. Where psychologists publish the findings of psychological research that may be picked up by the media and broadcast to the general public.
3. Where psychologists work with members of the general public acting as research participants.

PSYCHOLOGISTS AS PRACTITIONERS

Many psychologists work as *practitioners*. That is, they use their psychological knowledge and expertise to try to help people in their everyday lives. They might be educational psychologists, sports psychologists, therapists or counsellors, among several other things. These psychologists work with *clients*, and it is to these clients that psychologists then have professional responsibilities.

In the USA such clients, for some time, have been able to bring complaints to the ethics committee of the American Psychological Association (APA), who then adjudicate. The Standards of the APA are enforceable. The psychologist concerned can be reprimanded, dismissed from the Association or required to alter their behaviour or attend relevant training. This breadth of principles and disciplinary power reflects the far wider application of psychology to the general public as consumers in the USA.

Since 1987, the Royal Charter of the British Psychological Society (BPS) has been amended, taking us some way towards the American model described above. The Society now maintains a 'Register' of 'Chartered Psychologists'. These are people who practise psychology either in an applied or in a research capacity. Members of the register use the formal letters 'C. Psychol', they can be struck off for unprofessional behaviour and, it is hoped, they will become recognized as *bona fide* 'trademarked' practitioners whom the general public can recognize and trust.

The BPS published a Code of Conduct in 1993 that it expects all psychologists registered with the Society to follow (see British Psychological Society, 2000). As this book is going to press, this Code is under review and a revised Code should be adopted in 2006. However, as we are discussing research methods rather than applied practice here, we will not spend time on the Code of Practice but, for those interested, it can be found at:

http://www.bps.org.uk/the-society/ethics-rules-charter-code-of-conduct/code-of-conduct/a-code-of-conduct-for-psychologists.cfm

PUBLISHING THE FINDINGS OF PSYCHOLOGICAL RESEARCH

As part of a research community, psychologists have responsibilities to publish only well-founded results with conventional support. These findings, and the methods used to produce them, must also be made available to any interested researcher who wishes to analyse, verify and/or replicate them in some way. Researchers must pay attention to possible social effects of research results and assess these in the prevailing social, moral and political climate. The research area where this has probably mattered most over the last century has been that of the highly-controversial subject of supposed 'race' differences in intelligence. Here the poorly-supported notion that one 'race' has apparently higher general levels of IQ than another has sparked campus riots. Depressingly, it has also been used by extreme political groups to argue for different patterns of education for different ethnic groups and for the removal of support for education and welfare programmes. Proponents of 'race differences' argue that such programmes would have no effect if so-called 'racial' levels of intelligence are largely genetic in origin. The evidence for such differences is extremely weak and the case is usually poorly argued. Again, the issue is too detailed and complex for the purposes of this book but further coverage is provided in Coolican, 2004: chapter 20 or in specialist texts such as Richards (1997). The point here, however, is simply to state that psychologists who publish research have a public duty to consider the possible impact and repercussion of their often-tentative findings on a public that is usually unaware of the provisional and limited implications of psychological research.

WHAT THE BRITISH PSYCHOLOGICAL SOCIETY SAYS ABOUT HUMAN RESEARCH ETHICS

The BPS publishes a booklet (2000) covering a wide range of ethical topics including the Code of Conduct mentioned earlier and its *Ethical Principles for Conducting Research with Human Participants*, which were adopted by the Society in 1992. The Principles are available at:

http://www.bps.org.uk/the-society/ethics-rules-charter-code-of-conduct/code-of-conduct/ethical-principles-for-conducting-research-with-human-participants.cfm

As a student conducting a small research project you would be well-advised to consult these principles before beginning. You should treat them as a *minimum* set of guidelines to follow. You should also take your tutor's advice on what is possible for you or what is an ethical hazard in the project that you propose to conduct. The BPS advises members as follows:

Members should also draw the principles to the attention of research colleagues who are not members of the Society. Members should encourage colleagues to adopt them and ensure that they are followed by all researchers whom they supervise (e.g. research assistants, postgraduate, undergraduate, A-Level and GCSE students). (Section 1.3)

The principles begin with a general section that emphasizes the welfare and feelings of participants and the need for the researcher to check on the context of the research *from the point of view of the participant population*. It cannot be assumed that the researcher knows best about what may or may not be acceptable behaviour towards research participants.

In all circumstances, investigators must consider the ethical implications and psychological consequences for the participants in their research. The essential principle is that the investigation should be considered from the standpoint of all participants; foreseeable threats to their psychological well-being, health, values or dignity should be eliminated. Investigators should recognise that, in our multi-cultural and multi-ethnic society and where investigations involve individuals of different ages, gender and social background, the investigators may not have sufficient knowledge of the implications of any investigation for the participants. It should be borne in mind that the best judge of whether an investigation will cause offence may be members of the population from which the participants in the research are to be drawn. (Section 2.1)

The main headings of the BPS's ethical research principles are listed in Box 13.1. We shall refer to these whilst discussing the various ethical implications of research with human participants. It should be noted that in UK universities today there is almost always an ethics committee that reviews research proposals (of staff and students) for unacceptable procedures in any of the areas that we are about to consider.

Box 13.1 The main headings of the British Psychological Society's Ethical Principles for Conducting Research with Human Participants

1. Consent (including the general issue of the power of the investigator over participants).
2. Deception (which can also lower the public's trust in psychological research).
3. Debriefing (informing participants fully about the research after it has been carried out and returning them to their pre-test state).
4. Withdrawal from the investigation.
5. Confidentiality (of results and those who produced them; this includes the less-limited concept of anonymity).
6. Protection of participants (from mental and physical harm).
7. Observational research (including the issue of observation in public places).
8. Giving advice to participants.
9. Colleagues (ensuring colleagues also behave ethically).

THE CONDUCT OF RESEARCH WITH HUMAN PARTICIPANTS

CONFIDENTIALITY, ANONYMITY AND PRIVACY

Aside from any ethical considerations, there is a purely pragmatic argument for guaranteeing anonymity for participants at all times. If psychologists published identities along with results, the general public would soon cease to volunteer or agree to participate in research.

An investigator can guarantee **ANONYMITY** by guaranteeing that a participant's identity will never be revealed when data are published. This has to be carefully thought through if details of the person, even though they are not named, make it obvious who they are (e.g. in an applied project in a small company). Investigators can also request permission to identify individuals. Such identification may occur through the use of video recordings, as in Milgram's recordings of his obedience experiments (1974). Research participants who have been seriously deceived may exercise the general right of *all* participants to witness destruction of any records they do not wish to be kept. If records *are* kept, participants have the right to assume these will be safeguarded and used as anonymous data only by thoroughly-briefed research staff.

We need to distinguish here between *anonymity* and **CONFIDENTIALITY**. If results (e.g. of interviews) are published then they are *not* confidential but they can certainly remain anonymous. In fact, keeping data confidential would not be much use to the cause of research where data need to be accessible to other researchers. Confidentiality, then, is more a feature of psychological *practice* (keeping clients' data confidential) than it is a feature of research and publication.

There are very special circumstances where an investigator might contravene the anonymity rule and these are where there are clear dangers to human life. An investigator conducting participant observation into gang life would have a clear obligation to break confidence where a serious crime was about to be committed. A psychiatric patient's plan to kill either himself or a roommate would be reported. The ethical principles involved here are broader than those involved in conducting scientific research.

The participant obviously has the right to *privacy*, and procedures should not be planned that directly invade this without warning. Where a procedure is potentially intimate, embarrassing or sensitive, the participant should be clearly reminded of the right to withhold information or participation. Particular care would be required, for instance, where participants are being asked about sexual attitudes or behaviour.

This principle is difficult to follow in the case of covert participant *observation*, and serious criticism has been levelled at users of this approach on these grounds – see the example of Humphreys (1970) below. In such cases it is also difficult to check out, with participants, the final version of reports in order to verify that an accurate account of their statements has been made.

MILGRAM – THE CLASSIC EXPERIMENT FOR ETHICAL DEBATE

Any discussion of ethical principles in psychological research inevitably throws up fairly early on in the proceedings Milgram's famous demonstrations of obedience. Several ethical issues are involved in this study, so let me describe it briefly and then ask you to think about what these issues are.

Box 13.2   A brief description of the Milgram obedience paradigm

Volunteers were introduced to another 'participant' who was actually an experimental confederate. The volunteer became a 'teacher' who was asked to administer electric shocks, increasing by 15 volts for each mistake made by the confederate. 375 volts was described as 'Danger: severe shock'. A tape-recording of screams and refusals deceived the teacher-participant into believing the confederate was experiencing great pain and wished to end the session. The teacher-participant was pressured into continuing by 'prods' from the experimenter, such as 'The experiment requires that you continue' and 'You have no choice but to go on'. To Milgram's surprise, 65% of participants delivered shocks to the end of the scale (450 volts), even though the confederate had ceased responding at 315 volts. Milgram had consulted 'experienced and disinterested colleagues' who predicted that no more than 0.1% of participants would obey to the end. The teacher-participant often displayed extreme anxiety. One even suffered a mild seizure. An observer wrote:

I observed a mature and initially poised businessman enter the laboratory smiling and confident. Within 20 minutes he was reduced to a twitching, stuttering wreck, who was rapidly approaching a point of nervous collapse. He constantly pulled at his ear lobe and twisted his hands. At one point he pushed his fist into his forehead and muttered, 'Oh God, let's stop it'.

(Milgram, 1974)

The results of this demonstration were used to argue that, under pressure, many ordinary people are capable of behaving in a manner that, retrospectively, is considered cruel. Atrocities are not necessarily carried out by purely evil persons or 'cultures'.

List the aspects of this investigation that you consider to be unethical. Should the investigation have been carried out at all? Do the ends (scientific and surprising knowledge) justify the means?

DECEPTION

Milgram's participants were grossly deceived. Not only did they believe they were shocking an innocent victim and that the victim suffered terribly, but also the whole purpose of the research was completely distorted, being presented to participants as an experiment on the effects of punishment on learning.

DECEPTION, or at least the withholding of information, is exceedingly common in psychology experiments. In a survey of articles in the prestigious research journal *Journal of Personality and Social Psychology*, it was shown that the rate of deception in studies was much the same in the 1990s as it had been in the 1970s, at around 47% (Sieber, Iannuzzo and Rodriguez, 1995). This figure is argued by some to be lower and the difference in percentages might occur because of varying definitions of 'deception'. The figure of 47% includes studies in which participants are not told the true purpose of the experiment, whereas this figure would drop if a stricter definition of deception were used, specifically 'telling the participant things which are not true' (Ortmann and Hertwig, 1998). Some (e.g. Ortmann and Hertwig, 1997) have argued that, given the ethical principles of the APA, professional psychologists should support a complete ban on the use of deception in investigations. Others argue that such a ban might stultify psychological research (e.g. Kimmel,1998).

Some deception seems fairly innocuous. Some participants are told a baby is male, others that it is female, and their descriptions of it are compared. Participants performing a sensorimotor task, where the true aim is to record the effect of an observer on performance, are told that the observer is present in order to note details of the skilled behaviour involved. Children are told not to play with a toy because it belongs to another child who is next door. Students are told their experimental rats are 'bright'. Even the use of placebos can be a deception, though participants are often informed that a placebo might possibly be used.

Some deception is more serious. Participants have been told that test results demonstrate they are poorly adjusted. Female participants have been given feedback that they are considered attractive or unattractive by the men who will later interview them. Bramel (1962) gave male participants false feedback about their emotional reaction to photographs of men, such that their responses seemed homosexually related. Participants in Latané and Darley's (1976) experiments thought they were overhearing an authentic epileptic seizure. The dependent variable was the speed or occurrence of reporting the seizure.

So what can the investigator do if deception is to be used? First, the 1992 BPS Principles recommend that, wherever possible, consultation should be conducted with individuals who share the social and cultural background of the participants. Second, *debriefing* should be very carefully attended to – see below. Third, in some cases it is possible to obtain permission to deceive. Volunteers can be asked to select what sort of research they would be prepared to participate in, from, for instance:

❏ research on recognition of commercial products
❏ research on safety of products
❏ research in which you will be misled about the purpose until afterwards
❏ research involving questions on attitudes.

DEBRIEFING

Before participants actually perform in an experiment they are **briefed** – that is, they are told about the research study as a whole (without 'giving the game away' if deception is used) and they are given instructions on what is required of them. Don't get this *pre*briefing mixed up with *de*briefing. In all research studies, the investigator has a responsibility to **DEBRIEF** each participant. *After* participation is complete, the true purpose and aims of the study are revealed and every attempt is made to ensure that participants feel the same about themselves when they leave as they did when they arrived. As an example, Johnston and Davey (1997) ran an experiment in which one of the conditions was to listen to a news tape that contained only very negative items. Because this might be emotionally disturbing, the researchers asked participants in that condition to listen to two minutes of a relaxation tape on a personal stereo before telling them all about the study and paying them their fee.

If a study involves serious deception, the responsibility for debriefing includes a substantial effort in reassurance and explanation. The debriefing itself may have to involve a little more deception, as when children are told they 'did very well indeed' whatever the actual standard of their performance. In Milgram's experiments, participants who went to the end of the scale were told that some people did this 'quite gleefully'. The idea was to help the obedient participants compare their own unwillingness to proceed, and their experienced anxiety, fairly favourably with the fictitious happily-obedient participants. (Milgram never reported that any participant did proceed happily.) Even with this comparison, at least 26 out of 40 participants knew, when they left, that they were capable, under pressure, of inflicting extreme pain, if not death, on an innocent human being. It hardly seems possible that these people left the laboratory feeling the same about themselves as they did before they entered.

Does debriefing work?

Milgram sent a questionnaire to his participants after the study. 84% said they were glad to have participated, whereas only 1% regretted being involved, the remainder reporting neutral feelings. 80% believed more research like Milgram's should be carried out. 75% found the experience meaningful and self-enlightening. Some writers discounted this broad range of appreciative and illuminating comments as an attempt by Milgram to justify an ethically unacceptable study. Ring, Wallston and Corey (1970) decided to evaluate the consequences to the participant in a study that, even though the investigators were critical of Milgram, not only included the deceptions of the original study but also used a dishonest primary debriefing before an honest second one. They showed that an initial, superficial debriefing dramatically reduced the tendency of participants to evaluate the research negatively. However, they also found that one-third of participants reported residual anger and disappointment with themselves even after the second, complete, debriefing. The fact that even a few participants felt quite negative about themselves well after the experiment, and that many participants felt extremely upset during it, has led many researchers to the position that such extreme deception and stress are ethically unacceptable.

Aside from the question of ethics, it is unwise of investigators to indulge in a great deal of deception. Students very often suspect that the manifest structure and explanation of a study in which they participate is false. Ring *et al.* (1970) found that 50% of their participants claimed they would be more wary and suspicious of psychology experiments in the future. Many researchers have shown that participants say they do not mind being deceived. However, Taylor and Shepperd (1996) showed that even where this is true, participants' *behaviour* is affected by knowledge of deception. They arranged for participants to know they had been deceived during the course of an experiment. These participants continued to act as though nothing had happened and would not disclose the fact that they knew about the deception, even when asked several times by the experimenter whether they had noticed anything odd or suspicious in the procedures. So deception does seem to run the risk of creating less cooperative participants (as Ortmann and Hertwig, 1998, argued) and, as Reason and Rowan (1981) put it, 'Good research means never having to say you are sorry'.

STRESS AND DISCOMFORT – PROTECTION OF PARTICIPANTS

There is no argument with the principle that psychological investigators should guarantee the safety of their participants and that everything possible should be done to protect them from harm or discomfort. The difficulty comes in trying to decide what kind of stress or discomfort, physical or mental, is unacceptable. Humanists and others might argue that any traditional experimental research on 'subjects' is an affront to human dignity. At a lesser extreme, those who see value in the human experimental procedure have nevertheless criticized some investigators for going too far.

Mental stress

Examples of studies involving a possibly substantial degree of mental stress were given above. These involved deterioration of a person's self-image or the strain of feeling responsible for action, as in the Latané and Darley (1976) study.

Not all mental stress emanates from deception. Participants may be exposed to pornographic or violent film sequences. Extreme psychological discomfort, in the form of delusions and hallucinations, was experienced by participants undergoing 'sensory deprivation' (deprived of sound, touch and sight), such that they often terminated the experience after three days (Jolyon, 1962). Zimbardo's (1972) simulation of authority and obedience had to be stopped after six of the 14 days for which it was supposed to run. Students played the part of prison guards far too well, becoming aggressive, sadistic and brutal. Their 'prisoners' (other students) became extremely passive and dependent. Within two days, and on the following few, participants had to be released, because they were exhibiting signs of severe emotional and psychological disorder (uncontrollable crying and screaming) and one even developed a nervous rash.

There is an obligation for investigators not only to debrief but also to attempt to remove even long-term negative effects of psychological research procedures. One year after the experiment, 40 of Milgram's participants were examined by a psychiatrist who reported that no participant had been harmed psychologically by their experience. The 1992 BPS Principles urge investigators to inform participants of procedures by which they can contact the investigators should stress or other harm occur after participation.

Physical discomfort

Many psychological experiments have manipulated the variables of, for instance, electric shock, extreme noise level, food and sleep deprivation, anxiety- or nausea-producing drugs and so on.

As is well known, Watson and Rayner (1920) caused 'Little Albert', a young infant, to exhibit anxiety towards a white rat he had previously fondled quite happily, by producing a loud, disturbing noise whenever he did so. Apparently Albert even became wary of other furry white objects. Before Albert could be deconditioned, his family moved away and so Albert was removed from the project. This procedure developed into that known as 'aversive conditioning', which is intended to rid willing clients of unwanted or destructive behaviour.

The term 'willing' creates difficulties. In the sensitive cases of gay men submitting themselves to aversive therapy (which have occurred), it has been argued that treatment is unethical because the men are succumbing to a conventional-norm structure that treats their sexual preference as undesirable or 'sick'. In general research work, a 'willing' participant may act under social pressure. They may feel they are ruining the experiment or letting down the experimenter (the special power of the investigator is discussed below). For these reasons, the investigator has a set of obligations to participants to ensure they do not suffer unduly or unnecessarily. These are outlined in the following section. In any research where discomfort might be expected the investigator is obliged to seek opinion and advice from 'disinterested' professional colleagues before going ahead.

CONSENT AND THE RIGHT TO NON-PARTICIPATION

In all research that involves individual participation, the investigator is obliged to:

1. Give the participant full information as to the likely level of discomfort and to emphasize the voluntary nature of the exercise and the **RIGHT TO WITHDRAW** at any time.
2. In the light of this information, to obtain from the participants their **INFORMED CONSENT** to undergoing the experimental procedures. Although it might not be possible *fully* to inform participants, because they could then direct their behaviour towards the hypothesis, they can be given *enough* information to make a decision, e.g. 'Your drink *may* contain a high level of caffeine'.
3. Remind the participant of this right to withdraw at any point in the procedure where discomfort appears to be higher than anticipated.
4. Terminate the procedure where discomfort levels are substantially higher than anticipated and/or the participant is obviously disturbed to an unacceptable level.

Now we can see one of the most controversial aspects of Milgram's study. He was actually testing the power of the experimenter over the participant. His experimenter flagrantly contravened all these principles. The duty to respect the participant's right to withdraw and to remind the participant of this right are both now stressed by the APA and BPS. Contrary to this, in Milgram's study, and in a perhaps less humanistic era, each participant wishing to stop was commanded to continue in the interests of the research programme. Continuing was 'absolutely essential' and the participant had 'no choice but to go on' – phrases used by the experimenter when participants attempted to stop responding. The APA and BPS now also stress special vigilance when the investigator is in a position of power over the participant. This was, of course, the very position forcefully exploited and examined in the Milgram study.

As we shall see below, it is not always a simple matter to obtain informed consent before research is conducted. Consent, though not necessarily fully-informed consent, can however always be obtained for laboratory experiments. In research with children, the informed consent of parents must first be obtained. For obvious reasons, children cannot be subject to great stress, even in the unlikely instance that parents agree (though little Albert's mother did). Two factors working against informed consent are the investigator's need to deceive on some occasions, as already discussed, and the significant power attaching to the investigator role.

THE SPECIAL POWER OF THE INVESTIGATOR

In general, then, the investigator is obliged to give the participant every chance not to participate, both before and during the experimental procedure. Working against this, as we have just said, is the position of influence, prestige and power of the investigator. Torbert (1981) says:

> ... the unilaterally controlled research context is itself only one particular kind of social context and a politically authoritarian context at that. It should not be surprising that some of its most spectacularly well-conceived findings concern persons' responses to authoritarianism. *(p. 144)*

An additional dimension to this power emerges when we consider the common position of psychology undergraduates in the USA, who often face obligatory participation in a research project, though they may choose which one. Usually an exemption is offered but it costs one additional term paper, making the choice more apparent than real. This system is now beginning to appear in several UK universities.

INVOLUNTARY PARTICIPATION – THE SPECIAL NATURE OF SOME OBSERVATION STUDIES

In participant-observation studies, and in naturalistic (covert) observation, the persons observed are quite often unaware of their participation. This seems fairly unobjectionable where completely unobtrusive observation is made and each person observed is just one in a frequency count: for instance, when drivers are observed in order to determine whether more males or more females stop at a 'Stop' road sign. The general rule is that if anyone could have observed the behaviour anyway, because the context was public, it is unproblematic to record it.

In participant-observation studies, people's private space may be invaded. Humphreys (1970) investigated the behaviour of consenting homosexuals by acting as a public washroom 'lookout'. Persons observed were completely unaware of the study and of the fact that their car-registration numbers were recorded in order to obtain more background information through interviews later on.

Some field studies carried out in the public arena involve manipulations that interfere with people's lives. A street survey obviously delays each respondent but here consent is always sought first. In Piliavin, Rodin and Piliavin's (1969) studies on bystander intervention, a person, appearing to be either lame or drunk, 'collapsed' in a subway train. In one version the actor bit into a capsule that produced a blood-like trickle on his chin. Predictably, the 'lame' person got more help than the drunk. The 'blood' condition also had a lowering effect on helping. Piliavin *et al.*'s study, in fact, contravenes the principles of openness (no deception), stress avoidance and informed consent before participation. 'Participants' could not decide not to participate.

Doob and Gross (1968) delayed drivers at a traffic light with either a very smart, new car or an older, lower-status one. Effects were predictable in that it took drivers longer to hoot at the smarter car! If these results are fairly unsurprising, couldn't willing participants simply be asked to imagine the situation and consider their likely response? Would simulation work here? Doob and Gross also used a questionnaire, and found no difference between the times predicted by independent samples of students for hooting at either car. An odd finding occurred only among those who said they would not hoot at all at one of the cars. Of these, all six who would not hoot at the low-status car were male, and all five of those not hooting at the high-status car were female. The 'as if' findings were so different from actual behaviour that the defenders of field research seemed vindicated in their claim to more realistic data. However, by 1991, a computer simulation had been devised, and this produced results confirming the original findings (Bradley, 1991).

INTERVENTION

Some aspects of brief **INTERVENTION** with naïve participants have been dealt with above. Several studies have involved intervention on a substantial scale but with willing participation. For instance, psychologists have worked with parents and children in the home in an effort to demonstrate the beneficial effects of parental stimulation on the child's learning and cognitive performance (e.g. Klein, 1991). In such studies a *control group* is often necessary for baseline comparison. In hospital experiments with new drugs, trials are halted if success is apparent, on the grounds that it would be unethical to withhold the new treatment drug from those in the placebo and control groups. Unfortunately, in *psychological* intervention research, even if success is apparent, there would not usually be the political power and resources to implement the 'treatment' across all disadvantaged families. Ethical issues arise, therefore, in selecting one group for special treatment.

Where intervention occurs for research purposes only, and involves the production of behaviour usually considered socially unacceptable, ethical principles need very careful consideration. Leyens *et al.* (1975), for instance, raised levels of aggression in boys who were shown a series of violent films. These boys were observed to be more aggressive in daily activities compared with a control group who were shown non-violent films. It is quite difficult to see how debriefing alone could put the boys back to where they were before the study began.

THE USE OF ANIMALS IN PSYCHOLOGICAL RESEARCH

Animal lovers will be pleased to hear that in psychology pure research using animals has greatly decreased. One argument for their use would be that they can be used where humans can't, though this rather begs the whole question. It is also argued that some basic aspects of behaviour are common to human and non-human, that greater control can be exerted over variables in laboratory learning experiments and that comparisons with animal behaviour might lead to fresh insights into human behaviour (as occurred with the theory of attachment, for instance).

Arguments against using animals can be purely ethical: for instance, that experimenting with animals is an attack on a natural universe that we should strive to respect and protect. They can also be practical, focusing mainly on the lack of value of knowledge gained from animals when they are so different from humans in terms of, for instance, number of instinctive responses, lack of language, and their readiness for certain types of behaviour and not others.

Research on animals in Britain, where it exists, is carried out under guidelines issued by the BPS (2000). In these the following points are made:

❑ Knowledge to be gained must justify procedure; trivial research is not encouraged; alternative methods are.
❑ The smallest possible number of animals should be used.
❑ No members of endangered species should ever be used.
❑ Caging, food deprivation, procedures causing discomfort or pain should all be assessed relative to the particular species studied. A procedure relatively mild to one can be damaging to another.
❑ Naturalistic studies are preferred to laboratory ones, but animals should be disturbed as little as possible in the wild.
❑ Experimenters must be familiar with the technical aspects of anaesthesia, pharmacological compounds and so on; regular post-operative medical checks must be made.

CONCLUSION

All in all, it appears to be difficult to conduct much research at all without running into ethical arguments. Certainly it seems impossible to proceed with anything before considering possible ethical objections, but this is as it should be. Other sciences also have associations and committees for considering social responsibility in scientific research. They argue about the use to which findings might be put or the organizations from whom it would not be prudent to accept sponsorship. They consider the likely impact of their work on society as a whole.

Psychology has to make similar considerations. However, since humans, as individuals in society, are also the focal point of research, it is hardly surprising that psychology, as a research community, has to be very much on its toes in spotting malpractice, abuse, thoughtlessness and lack of professionalism. If psychologists prefer not to have people take one step backwards at parties and say things such as 'I bet you're testing me' or 'Is this part of an experiment?', they need to reassure the public constantly that some excesses of the past cannot now happen and that deception really is only used when necessary.

The humanists and qualitative researchers appear to have gained the moral high ground on these ethical issues, not just because they put dignity, honesty and humanity first, but because they see their participative or non-directive methods as the only route to genuine, uncoerced information. According to Reason and Rowan (1981), Maslow has said, '… if you prod at people like things, they won't let you know them' (p. xviii).

Well, what do you think?

You'll probably discuss quite heatedly, with fellow students or colleagues, the rights and wrongs of conducting some experiments. I can't help feeling that the information from Milgram's work is extremely valuable. It certainly undermined stereotypes I had, a long time ago, about whole cultures tending to be more obedient or capable of harming others. But I also can't help thinking immediately about those participants who went all the way. Can we be so sure we'd be in the 35% who stopped? Not even all these stopped as soon as the victim was clearly in trouble. How would we feel for the rest of our lives? Should we inflict such a loss of dignity on others? I haven't made any final decision about this issue, as about many other psychological debates and philosophical dilemmas. Fortunately, I'm not in a position where I have to vote on it. But what do you think?

Further reading

Oliver (2003) *The Student's Guide to Research Ethics*.

PROGRESS REVIEW 13.1

EXERCISES

What major ethical issues are involved in the following fictitious proposed research projects?

1. Researchers arrange for an actor to fall down in the street, appearing to be ill. They are interested in whether passers-by will stop less often in this condition than in one where the actor has red liquid oozing from his mouth.
2. For her third-year project a student decides to conduct a longitudinal case study in which she covertly records the behaviour and speech of a class colleague who she believes to be in the developmental stages of anorexia.
3. A researcher believes that greater use of the Internet is associated with greater depression. She asks students to complete a questionnaire on Internet use and to complete a scale that measures clinical depression.
4. Participants in an experiment are asked to complete a task involving the solving of logical puzzles. Half the group are then informed that they have done well whereas the other half are informed that they have done rather poorly. Participants are then assessed on the extent to which they make internal or external attributions for their performance in the task.
5. What is the difference between confidentiality and anonymity?
6. Does 'informed consent' mean that the participant is fully informed before participation?

ANSWERS

1. Involuntary participation; informed consent; deception; psychological stress.
2. Lack of informed consent; involuntary participation; lack of professional expertise in the area; general lack of respect.

3. Problem of what to do should a participant turn out to score very highly on depression; researcher may not be qualified to counsel or offer any kind of professional support; hence there is a serious debriefing problem.
4. Deception; mental stress; careful debriefing needed for the 'poor' group.
5. Confidentiality means that the psychologist promises that any information given by the client or participant will not be seen by anyone else. Anonymity means that such information may well be published but that the client's or participant's identity will not be revealed to anyone.
6. No. The participant is given sufficient information on what the study is *about*, so that they can decide whether or not to participate, but some information may need to be withheld so that the participant's behaviour is not affected by *expectancy*.

KEY TERMS

Anonymity	Informed consent
Confidentiality	Intervention
Debriefing	Involuntary participation
Deception	Right to withdraw

chapter
14

Planning practicals and writing reports

What's in this chapter?

This chapter is all about designing, carrying out and writing up a small piece of practical research.

❑ First there is advice on finding a suitable and workable topic and then on formulating a testable hypothesis.

❑ We go on to give advice on the specific design features of your study, how to obtain and deal with participants, how to organize materials and procedures and, most important of all, ethical considerations. You should not do anything that is not easily within the ethical guidelines of the British Psychological Society.

❑ Next we look at writing up your report. We note that the write-up is a story and hence is always written in the past tense. All sections are written in prose and there should be no lists or sections where only numerical data are presented.

❑ Advice is given on plagiarism, a growing problem for which penalties can be fairly severe.

❑ Traditional sections of a report are presented and then described in some detail.

❑ Finally, an average student report is presented with a marking commentary. This is followed by a 'good' report of the same research.

PLANNING YOUR PRACTICAL PROJECT

Your course in psychology will probably include assessment of some practical work. Here you will design and conduct an empirical investigation, very often collecting quantitative data and applying descriptive or inferential statistics. At the time of writing this was true of all A Level boards and the International Baccalaureate, but each of these syllabuses has features and requirements that are too lengthy to advise you on in specific detail here. However, what follows are some general features, some advice and some help in understanding why certain requirements are made.

Remember that the 'practical' doesn't start when you actually begin running your trials or questioning your participants. That is a tiny part of the whole process. There is a large portion of time to spend planning and another large portion to spend analysing and (dare I say it?) writing up your report!

THE TOPIC OF YOUR PRACTICAL INVESTIGATION

The good thing about doing a practical investigation is that this is your one chance actually to *do* psychology. You can take an idea and test it out, analyse results and see if the effect on people you were looking for does really occur – within ethical boundaries, of course. Here are two different approaches made to a tutor by a student trying to select a topic for a practical project:

a. 'I'd like to do something to do with telepathy.'
b. 'I liked Beloff's research showing that people generally rate their fathers higher on IQ than their mothers. I wondered if this would happen for older and younger children when they're grown up. Do older brothers think their younger brothers are less intelligent, I wonder?'

Which of these students has an idea with clear aims and predictions so that they can go away, with minimal advice from their tutor, and start working on the details of their design? Which has an idea to test that is relatively simple to turn into an operationalized hypothesis? Which of these students is covering an area of psychology that is almost certainly on their syllabus (i.e. social perception, stereotypes, gender)?

You will usually be asked to tackle a topic which is part of the theory syllabus for your course. Hence don't be disgruntled if your tutor frowns on your wizzo idea for a practical. You certainly must run your ideas past your tutor and you would be really well advised to take their advice since they've been doing this longer than you have!

On this point, some syllabuses deduct a few points where the tutor has suggested the aims and details of the design to the student. At present, and as an example, on the A2 AQA Specification A marking scheme for 2007 onwards, the amount lost by having your tutor provide the hypothesis and design is just three marks out of 60, or 5%. If you think that's a lot, remember this is only one of six modules on the course. The module contributes just 15% to the A Level mark as a whole. Hence, not designing your own practical loses you just 5% of 15%, that is, a mere three-quarters of a mark. What you need to weigh up is the cost of three-quarters of a mark overall with what you might lose if you decide to invent your own idea and design completely on your own. Not many students can see all the pitfalls, anticipate all the design problems and create satisfactory measures that will unambiguously test the hypothesis proposed. It may therefore be worth accepting full guidance from your tutor, along with the loss of just three-quarters of a mark, rather than losing far more marks with an inadequate hypothesis and design.

Most syllabuses also permit you to work with a 'small group of students' on the design of your investigation. Again a few marks may be lost. However a LOT of marks will be lost if you do not eventually write up the investigation *in your own words*. We will talk about plagiarism later (see p. 216). Plagiarism is presenting as your *own* work what is in fact, at least in part, the work of someone else. This *includes* the work of other students. Think about this if you work with others (an admirable approach in principle – most science is collaborative discovery) and make sure you have enough information at the end to go away and write up your *own* report.

If you do want to (or have to) find your own topic

Keep a special notepad with you throughout all lectures and, whenever an interesting but simple study crops up, make a note of it. Alternatively, flip through your textbook and look for a simple and interesting study. Think how you might replicate at least part of it or, better still, adapt it or a part of it, for instance by using different materials, a different population (e.g. not students, not in the USA, not conducted in 1956). Perhaps you can think of a more radical adaptation. For instance, you might decide to test the self-serving bias in attribution theory by asking football fans to give reasons for their team's performance after both a win and a loss. According to the theory, they should attribute wins *internally*, by referring to the team's skills, and losses *externally*, by referring to some kind of bad luck, bad refereeing etc. The study must be feasible for you: for example, not a cross-cultural study of attachment behaviour in Japan and Korea.

You can look for ideas in publications such as *Psychology Review*, *The Psychologist*, *New Scientist*. You can read the *abstract* (see p. 218) of many current articles by going onto the Internet and typing 'psychology journals' into the search engine. The *Journal of Applied Psychology*, for instance, provides an abstract of each article in its current table of contents and also supplies full versions of a few selected articles. You could also use *Psychinfo* if your tutors can get you access to a local University. You can also try just about any other human-interest media for ideas, but you *absolutely must* remember that your idea has to be backed up by some *relevant* prior research or theory – see p. 218. Your tutor may be able to help you see what might be relevant. Whatever happens, **never** claim that your idea is completely original ('So far, no one has tested this prediction'). How could you possibly know this? It almost certainly will have been covered somewhere, sometime.

FORMULATING YOUR HYPOTHESIS

There is a simple golden rule here – ignore it at your peril!

BEFORE STARTING TO GATHER DATA YOU MUST KNOW YOUR RESEARCH PREDICTION AND HOW EXACTLY YOU ARE GOING TO ANALYSE YOUR RESULTS.

Think about what you are predicting will happen and how you will show that it has. If you're not sure how your results will be analysed then don't start; see your tutor and get advice. I wish I had a pound for each time I have seen a distraught student with loads of data but no sensible way to analyse them. This is not a pretty sight and you should absolutely avoid this situation.

We saw on p. 137 that a hypothesis is a claim about a population. Although your syllabus might talk about your hypothesis at this point, what we are really talking about is your **research prediction**. You might predict, for instance, that 'Males will estimate their IQ higher than females will'. It is this prediction that must be set in specifically-measurable terms and it is these measures that you will use in your data-gathering procedure. You might be making a prediction about differences in 'caring attitude', 'empathy' or 'self-esteem'. How will you measure these variables? Many tests are accessible from textbooks or the Internet (e.g. the General Health Questionnaire, Goldberg, 1978; or Rotter's (1966) Locus of Control scale) but you may have to invent your own as a part of the project.

You might want to alter the slant of your aims/hypotheses somewhat, depending upon what measures are available. You must certainly make sure that there is enough **research literature** that you can include in the introduction to your report to justify the prediction you are making. Research predictions will gain few marks if based mainly on 'common sense'.

THE DESIGN OF YOUR INVESTIGATION

Many of my students start their very first session on planning their practical stating 'I want to use a questionnaire' to which my response is always 'Why?' and they look bemused. The point is that you can't *know* you need to use a questionnaire until you have considered what it is exactly that you want to find out, what your overall design will be and what measures you will need to use and/or develop.

Your design is your overall approach to structuring your study in order to test your research prediction. If, for instance, you have argued that anxiety should be negatively related to self-esteem, then this pretty well demands a correlational approach and you need to find measures for the two variables anxiety and self-esteem. You may have chosen an experimental approach, in which case do make sure it really is an experiment. For instance, showing that young children tend to say the amount of orange juice has changed in the standard Piaget conservation routine is not an experiment; there is no independent variable; this is a *demonstration*. You can introduce an independent variable if you compare older with younger children but this is not an *experimental* variable; this is a group-difference study – see Chapter 4.

Don't get carried away with independent variables

Are you dealing with too many variables? Say you wanted to see whether introverts improve on a task when alone as compared with in front of an audience, whereas extroverts deteriorate. You'd like to see whether this is more true for males than for females and perhaps whether age also has an effect. Admirable thinking on interacting variables, but the statistical analysis will be very complex. The syllabuses at this level all direct you to inferential statistics appropriate for ONE independent variable with TWO levels only (unless you perform a chi-square – see p. 170).

Repeated measures?

Can you use repeated measures? If so, then all the better, because you will require fewer participants for testing overall as well as not having to worry about whether your samples were equivalent – see p. 40. However, sometimes participants *must* be naïve for their condition of the study. If you are using a *vignette study* (see Box 14.1) it makes no sense to use repeated measures since seeing both the scenarios gives the game away completely to your participants. You need to use an independent-samples (or 'independent-measures') design so that each participant takes part in only one of the conditions.

Box 14.1   Using a vignette design

Very often we would like to vary just one piece of information as our independent variable. For instance, we might like to know whether people blame a car driver more if the accident he causes has more severe consequences. Obviously we can't set this up as a realistic experiment and it would be difficult and costly to produce a short film for the purpose. What we can do here is to use vignettes – these are short descriptions of a scenario that the participant reads and then has to make some kind of judgement about – for instance, a numerical rating of the degree of responsibility they feel applies to the car driver.

Walster (1966) showed that participants did indeed ascribe more responsibility the greater the damage. Later, McKillip and Posavac (1975) showed that similarity of the participant to the victim also has an effect on judgements of severity and responsibility. Participants who were regular marijuana users found the marijuana-using (but fictitious) driver in a serious accident less responsible, gave lower fines and saw the accident as more externally caused than did participants who were non-users. This supported the theory that perceived similarity helps to lower ascriptions of responsibility.

Obviously you can't ask your participants about drug taking but you certainly can test the similarity hypothesis by, for instance, making the driver a student, a female, a jogger and so on, and testing the appropriate member and non-member groups.

You could also use the vignette-type approach to test:

1. Whether an article written by a male is judged differently from the same article written by a female (see Goldberg, 1968),
2. Whether people told to read a story about a house and its contents from the perspective of a burglar recall more valuable items (e.g. paintings) and fewer 'household' items (e.g. leaky roof) than do participants told to read from the perspective of a prospective buyer (Pichert and Anderson, 1977).
3. Whether a fictitious person who is described as being a *Sun* reader gets a longer sentence for accidental death than one who reads the *Guardian* (or vice versa).
   ... and so on.

Camouflaging the independent variable

In a vignette study or similar, if you want to make sure that the participant has noted that the author is female or that the driver was a student (etc.), you can ask some pre-reading questions such as how old was the author, where did they live (having already provided the information to them on the stimulus materials). You can then slip in a crucial question such as 'what sex was the author?' without arousing suspicion that this is the experimental variable.

Think about your variables

Although we will discuss measures under 'The materials' it is wise to think here about the level of measurement (see p. 105) of your variables. If you need to *correlate*, then it is no good selecting categorical variables – see p. 105. If you want to 'correlate' gender with anxiety – think again. What you must sensibly do is to test the *difference* between gender samples on anxiety. So, if you require a variable to be at interval level make sure that you use an appropriate scale. Instead of recording whether a driver stopped or not perhaps you can record their speed (time between two points on the road).

Observation studies

If you want to conduct an observation study be very careful that it does not end up as what coursework moderators like to call a 'day at the zoo study' or 'my cute baby cousin'. You must develop adequate observation schedules or coding systems and/or plan exactly what it is that your observation will focus upon. Almost certainly you will need to run a pilot observation to see how hard it is to gather useful information that you can write up into a report. The closer your report comes to what a journalist or animal lover might write, the further you are away from an adequate psychology practical report.

Interviews

If you intend to use an interview but you want quantitative data you need to think about how you will code the qualitative content, unless you intend only to administer a fixed-choice questionnaire (i.e. with closed questions). If you want the interview content to be rated, think about acquiring someone to rate it independently to avoid your own personal bias; you would need to create a strict coding system and train your colleague in its use.

Interviews also take a lot of time and you may need equipment, so make sure you can use it! Consider whether this is all feasible in the time available.

Obtaining and dealing with participants

❑ Will you be able to get enough people for your chosen design? Will you be able to match pairs appropriately? You may not be able to obtain the information you need for this (e.g. level of education).

❑ If you are going to use repeated measures, with tests on two different occasions, will everyone be available second time around?

❑ Avoid designs that require hard-to-find participants (left-handers, fifth-borns etc).

❑ If you want to carry out a study of group difference(s), e.g. a gender-difference study, you need to ensure that the two groups are very carefully matched on all the possibly relevant variables you can manage.

❑ If you need a control group try to have them experience everything the experimental participants do except the crucial level of the independent variable. For instance, if you are looking at difference in recall performance when rehearsing or making images of word-list items, you will give your experimental participants more time and make their task more interesting since you have to give examples of what you want them to do. Try to spend as much time and energy with the control participants too, so that this lack of input cannot be responsible for any difference found.

❑ Are your participants going to be the familiar 'friends and acquaintances' or students in the canteen? If so, might they give your game away to others?

❑ You cannot select a random sample from the population (don't ever say you did) but you can try to match groups for certain important variables such as age, sex, qualifications etc. You *can* randomly allocate your participants to conditions – see p. 40.

❑ If you suspect some participants of 'mucking around' or of already knowing the aim and perhaps trying to 'look good', you'll have to decide, having asked them afterwards, whether it is legitimate to drop their results. You can discuss this with tutors or colleagues.

❑ Make sure samples are of an adequate size for the job – as a rough rule, for experiments, you should have at least 10 if repeated measures, 20 if independent samples and at least 30–40 if you are conducting some form of survey. Some students once presented, quite seriously, the results of a project that they claimed supported their hypothesis that northerners (in the UK) were less racist than southerners, having used one or two questions about tolerance for racist jokes. Trouble was, they had tested just eight northerners and five southerners!

The materials

❑ Are materials equivalent for both conditions? It is no use testing to see whether concrete words are easier to recall than abstract words if the abstract words are generally *longer* than the concrete words. Try to make sure there are no possibly confounding differences between materials apart from the difference of the independent variable.

❑ Can two memory word-lists be equivalent? Can you say that the words in each are equally frequent in normal language use, or that two sets of anagrams are equally hard to solve? You can use pre-testing of the materials to show there is no real difference or you can get hold of word frequency lists; here is a useful Internet source for these: http://www.itri.brighton.ac.uk/~Adam.Kilgarriff/bnc-readme.html

❑ Are instructions to participants intelligible? If you're unsure of the wording in a questionnaire, do get the help of someone who's good with language. Respondents will not respect or take seriously a badly-written questionnaire with several spelling mistakes.

❑ If you want to construct a questionnaire (see Chapter 6) remember, a test for an attitude is often made not with questions but with *statements* with which people agree/disagree or say how far it represents their view. Don't say 'Do you believe in abortion/nuclear power/strikes?'. These things exist! We want to know what people *think* about them. You should set several questions with the same answering format then add up the points that each person scored on the scale as a whole – do not analyse individual items.

❑ The Internet is a source for psychological scales but **beware** – many are put together by charlatans or amateurs and in all cases remember that you need the *scoring system*. If you are really keen you could look at this site managed by the American Psychological Association: http://www.apa.org/science/findingtests.pdf

❑ If you are focusing on a specific group of people, such as a minority ethnic group or people with a disability, then please check carefully, consult with members of the group concerned or other experts about your choice of language. It is easy not just to cause offence but also to show ignorance by using unacceptable, derogatory or patronising terms. This applies wherever a specific group is the focus, whether members of that group will themselves be questioned or not.

❑ In all cases, pilot! Try out materials on friends and relatives.

The procedure

❑ If you are gathering data as part of a small group of students don't be shy to ask your colleagues to do a final check before they rush off after a lot of hurried changes. Don't feel stupid if you don't feel confident about exactly what you have to do. Ask your colleagues or the tutor where appropriate. You do not want your group to end up with unusable results that just can't be put together because some of you have misunderstood the procedure you were supposed to follow. Also, it is extremely important to remember your colleagues when data are being collected. If you don't turn up, the entire project may be put on hold, making everybody late, or worse, with their report of the work.

❑ Record all the information on the spot. If you decide to wait till later to record age or occupation of your interviewee, you may well forget. Then the result may be wasted. Remember to note which group a participant was in or what gender they were, if relevant. If you forget, your efforts are wasted!

❑ Be prepared to put participants at their ease and give an encouraging introduction. Work out the exact instructions to participants. Have a simulated run-through with a colleague. What have you failed to explain? What else might people need/want to know?

❑ Decide how you will answer questions your participants might ask. Will you have stock answers or will you ask participants to wait until after the testing?

❑ If the study is an observation:
 – Will the observations really be unobtrusive? Check out the recording position beforehand.
 – Will recording be easy? Does talking into a tape recorder attract too much attention, for instance? Does the coding system work? Is there time and ample space to make written notes?
 – Will more than one person make records simultaneously in the interests of reliability?

Ethics

As a student you will not have been trained sufficiently to be able to conduct satisfactory debriefing sessions. These days, professional research psychologists themselves often argue about the adequacy of debriefing in returning people to their starting point and 'undoing' any psychological harm done. Therefore it is extremely important that your proposed research project will *not* involve any of the following:

- ❑ Invasion of privacy
- ❑ Causing participants to lose dignity
- ❑ Causing participants to think less of themselves
- ❑ Deception that causes resentment or hostility
- ❑ Unnecessary withholding of information
- ❑ Pain or discomfort
- ❑ Breaking of local prohibitions (for instance, drinking alcohol)
- ❑ Anything at all about which participants feel uncomfortable.

Assure participants that anonymity will be maintained, and maintain it! It is discourteous and bad practice to talk with close colleagues in the project, or very best friends, in a derogatory manner about participants, even if anonymous. It develops an elitist, manipulative approach to people who have tried to help you in your work.

Also, assure participants that they will not feel or look stupid, or reveal anything they don't wish to reveal about themselves – and make sure this, too, is true! Assure them that they can have destroyed any record of behaviour, in particular any they feel very uncomfortable about. Remind them they can stop any procedure if they wish to.

WRITING YOUR PRACTICAL REPORT

Now we come to the part that every student just adores — writing up a report of your practical work. My first piece of advice is **don't put it off**! You'll find it much harder to do when any initial enthusiasm you had for the project has worn off, and you won't be able to understand why certain precautions were taken or just what certain conditions were all about. You'll find essential details of data and analysis are missing and you may need the help of your class colleagues who've now lost their raw data or are too busy to help.

If it's any consolation, as you slog away through the small hours finishing your work, consider the general skills you are acquiring that will help you through your working life. Students often report that what they found most useful during their degree course at University was learning to write a report. It is the one thing you are very likely to do, in some form or another, in a professional career, in further study or even as a member of a local community or interest group. Reports are all about clear communication to others.

WHAT IS THE PURPOSE OF A REPORT? – IT'S YOUR STORY

There are two main purposes, neither of which is to do with keeping your tutor happy. First, you are telling your reader just what you did, why you did it and what you think it adds to the stockpile of knowledge and theory development. Second, you are recording your procedures in enough detail for some of those readers, who are so inclined, to replicate your work. We have seen elsewhere why this is so important to scientific method. Golden rule number one for report writing, then, is:

MAKE SURE YOU WRITE WITH ENOUGH DEPTH AND CLARITY FOR A COMPLETE STRANGER OF AVERAGE INTELLIGENCE TO REPEAT EXACTLY WHAT YOU DID IN EVERY DETAIL.

The practical report is a **story**. It is your account to other people of what you thought you might test and why, what you did, how you did it, what happened and what you concluded as a result. Several things follow from this, the most important being:

❏ Always use the past tense.

Do **NOT** write: 'This experiment will try to show …', 'Participants will be tested …' etc.

❏ Make sure your readers know what you're talking about. They weren't there so they don't know what you did and they don't have telepathy.

For instance, early on, when you talk about '*the* questionnaire' or '*the* vignette story', stop briefly and ask yourself, 'From the reader's point of view, would I know what that is? Have I introduced this yet?'. Speaking as someone who is a marker, one of the most frustrating things is knowing that the student is not talking to a reader but is just getting things down on paper because they have to!

HOW DO I KNOW WHAT TO DO?

There are generally-accepted conventions on how to present an academic report but they vary greatly in their details. A Level boards issue details of what they would like to see and so should the organizers of any other course you might be on (if not, ask them!). Most of the requirements are there to help you organize your presentations clearly and fairly. Have a look at articles on the Internet – make sure they are in good academic journals – and/or ask your tutor if they can let you look at one or at some old student work that got decent marks. I have included an average-level report at the end of this chapter with a marking commentary. Look at the resource materials provided by your examination board. An extremely useful, if not rather dauntingly pedantic, book that would certainly help you in all aspects of writing in psychology is *The Principles of Writing in Psychology* by T.R. Smyth (2004).

PLAGIARISM

PLAGIARISM is presenting another's work as if it is your own. This includes taking other people's data, and it includes not just exactly-copied work but also *closely-paraphrased work*. If the author says 'The experiment showed that significantly more words were recalled under hot rather than cold conditions' and you write 'The experiment demonstrated that significantly more words were remembered under hot rather than cold conditions', you are plagiarising. The penalties for plagiarism are severe, and so they should be, since it is technically theft. Plagiarism is exactly the same as cheating in an exam and many students have lost their degree or their A Level because of it. The main point is that coursework marked as individual must be your own work. Don't attempt the 'I copied notes from an article, then didn't realize when I copied from the notes' gambit. Plagiarism is plagiarism, intentional or not. Copying notes directly from texts is, in any case, quite pointless. Educationally we learn very little from copying, as you'll know from your psychological studies of memory and learning processes. Ethically, copying is stealing. Just don't *ever* copy from texts. Copying from Internet authors is just plain daft. They don't know exactly what question was set nor the specific guidelines set for this particular assignment. Of course, you can't invent your ideas. Learning *is* about appreciating what has gone before, then, hopefully, adding to it. However, the whole point of coursework is to show that *you* can handle the required concepts yourself *in your own words*. The best procedure is to read, make your own notes, close any books, ask yourself questions to see how far you've understood, then attempt to write out the ideas as you now see them. If you use a direct quotation you must make this clear and you *must* give the source **and page number** of the quotation. This is just as important in the introduction and discussion sections of practical reports as in any essay. In either case you should not rely too much on quotations and certainly you should not use them in order to avoid defining some complex or tricky point *in your own words* to show that you understand it.

THE SECTIONS OF A STANDARD REPORT

Box 14.2 shows the standard headings of research reports. These must not be considered as written in stone. You could pick up any journal article and find it varies from this pattern. It all depends on the particular journal and its historical origins in, for instance, 'hard science' (e.g. cognitive neuropsychology) or elsewhere (e.g. social psychology, health psychology). However, if you are writing up a conventional quantitative report for your coursework, use Box 14.2 in lieu of any specific instructions you are provided with.

Box 14.2   Main sections of a research report

Heading in report	Conventional report sections What goes under each heading
Title	Informs reader of exact area and focus of study
Abstract	Summary
Introduction	General background to topic area
	Relevant research
	Argument/rationale
	Overall aims
	Research prediction ('hypothesis')
Method	Exactly what you did
Design	The type of study used, IV, levels and DV
Participants	Exactly who took part
Materials/apparatus	Equipment etc.
Procedure	What actually happened; instructions to participants
Results	What you found
Descriptive statistics	Means, standard deviations etc., including tables and charts
Inferential analysis	Justification and use of inferential test with precise result and significance level reached. Conclusion
Discussion	Discuss results; place in context of research in introduction; critique the study; conclude
References	All works referred to in body appear here in detail
Appendices	Extra materials not essential to reader

THE TITLE

This should be as concise as possible. You don't need 'An investigation to see whether ...'. You just need the main variables. Very often, in an experiment, you can use the IV and DV. For instance, 'The effect of an imagery method on recall of verbal material' will adequately describe a (probably familiar) study. For a field investigation using correlation, 'The relationship between age and attitude to environmental issues' says enough. Avoid questions and comic titles such as 'Do boys exaggerate their IQ?' or 'Watching the detectives'. If you really can't resist such a pre-title then make sure you add a fully-informative second half such as, '... gender differences in self-estimation of IQ' or '... content analysis of stereotype assumptions in television police-based drama series'.

ABSTRACT

Your abstract should stand out from the rest of the report by being in a different font and/or indented. It is a skeleton summary of the main features of the work, 'abstracted' from it, in around 200 words at most. You do not need any detail of methods, just theory on which your research is based, main design, significant effects and any major emergent critical points or conclusions. Have a look at the 'good report' example.

Why on earth do we have a summary at the beginning? Well, suppose you were interested in whether anyone had done work on your proposed topic: anxiety and jogging behaviour in red-bearded vegetarian East Londoners. As you flip through dozens of articles looking for related work, how much easier it is to see the summary of findings right at the beginning of the article, without having to wade through to the end.

INTRODUCTION

I like to think of this as a funnel:

Start with the work in the psychological topic area. Discuss theory
and research work which is relevant to the research topic,
especially your rationale. Move from the research
findings to an argument for conducting *your*
research study. Generally introduce
it and, using earlier findings, relate
your study to the hypothesis
under test by making
a specific
RESEARCH PREDICTION.

Your research prediction must follow from an argument (known as a '*rationale*') that depends on the results of prior research or existing theory reported in the earlier part of your introduction. You will lose a lot of marks if there is no obvious link between the prior research you describe, your rationale and your research prediction. Your sources are likely to be textbooks, research articles, electronic databases and the Internet. Be sure to make a note of every reference you wish to use. It is sometimes painful to try to track them down a long time after you read them.

As an example of the funnelling argument required, let's run through the introduction to an experiment to test the hypothesis that using imagery improves recall of a learned word-list. The introduction to a study testing this hypothesis should *not* contain a five-page essay on the psychology of memory, including Ebbinghaus's work and the performance of eye-witnesses in court. The hypothesis test belongs within a specialized area of memory research, the argument over whether rehearsal is the central and necessary mechanism for transferring items from short- to long-term memory stores. We can move our reader through the introduction in the following steps:

1. The concepts of short- and long-term memory stores.
2. Outline of the two-process memory model.
3. Phenomena the model explains, such as primacy and recency in free-recall tasks.
4. Focus in on the model's emphasis on rehearsal as the process by which material is transferred to the long-term store.

5. Introduce the 'cognitive' objection that humans always attempt to construct meaning out of incoming sensory data; give an example of what this means.
6. From this theory it follows that an attempt to give an unconnected word-list some 'life', by visualizing the items and connecting them, should be more successful for memory than the rehearsal that we assume occurs when participants just read for learning.
7. Additional support could be given here, referring to previous similar studies and the work on imagery in the literature.

We have argued through to, and are now ready for, our specific prediction. Note that the 'average' report starting on p. 228 is rather rambling in its introduction, whereas the better one is more tightly arranged around relevant literature.

What you must avoid is what I call the *falling-off-a-cliff-edge* syndrome. This is where the writer goes on and on about the general topic area, that is, writes an essay on memory, then suddenly and from nowhere introduces the hypothesis tested in the study – no explanation, no rationale. This will lose a bucketful of marks.

THE HYPOTHESIS

It only remains now to state our prediction (or hypothesis) in the clearest terms so there can be no doubt about what is the expected outcome. Although conventional quantitative studies do test hypotheses, what is usually given at the end of a report's introduction is a *research prediction*. What we are testing in the imagery experiment, for instance, is the general hypothesis that imagery improves recall. However, in order to be specific as to how that hypothesis is to be tested, we set up a design and then *predict*, or at least outline, what should happen if the hypothesis is to be *supported*. On some courses you may be asked to write out specifically what the 'hypothesis' is, but most research articles include *research predictions* in the final paragraph of the introduction as part of the normal prose progression of the article. There should *not* be a separate heading for '*The hypothesis*'. For instance, in our report for the memory practical, our last paragraph might run:

> Rehearsal of word-list items does not necessarily involve semantic treatment of them. However, using imagery demands a deeper involvement with the verbal material. Hence, if it is true that greater involvement and semantic processing are factors likely to increase recall then we would expect to find that the **groups asked to use imagery have a higher mean recall score than those asked simply to rehearse the words**.

If you are asked to write out your hypothesis separately then the sentence given in bold will do, though in reality it is a research prediction.

There is a tradition, which you might encounter, of attempting to write out the **null hypothesis** at this point. This is an odd requirement and shows misunderstanding by those examining your course. No researcher writes a null hypothesis at this point and rarely is one given at all. As I explained in Chapter 9, the null hypothesis is purely statistical and is used as a baseline of no effect to calculate the probability of an event occurring if it is true. Statistical tests incorporate the null hypothesis into their calculations. If you are asked to give a null hypothesis use the following example and adapt it:

> Under the null hypothesis we would expect no difference between sample means for recall of words after imagery and recall after rehearsal.

This statement is true but it is *not* the null hypothesis. It is what is expected *if* it is true. However, examiners will recognize the wording they are looking for and full marks will be awarded. (You might ask your tutor, though, to write to the board and ask them to change the syllabus!)

What is *essential* here is that your prediction is made absolutely clear *in operationalized terms*. Remember, your inferential results analysis must relate back directly to the exact predictions made here. It will be uninformative to say 'people will remember better after caffeine'. You must state how 'remembering better' is *defined*: for instance, increased number of words correctly recalled. The hypothesis or prediction should also not contain the underlying rationale. For example, we do not say 'There is a correlation between self-esteem and academic achievement because people feel better when they are successful' – this is part of the *argument* for the hypothesis. We simply predict a correlation between self-esteem scores and a precise measure of academic achievement – say, number of GCSE and A Level passes.

Table 14.1 contains loosely- and tightly-worded research predictions appropriate to some of the exercises on p. 155. The exercise numbers are given to the left. You might like to try writing out column two whilst looking only at column one.

Table 14.1 Making tight predictions

Exercise no.	Loosely worded prediction	Research prediction
1	Imagery makes recall of words easier	The mean recall score in the imagery condition will be higher than the mean recall score in the rehearsal condition
2	Extroverts will have higher confidence scores	There will be a positive correlation between extroversion scores and confidence ratings
5	People will perform worse on a sorting task in front of an audience	Mean sorting times will be longer in the audience condition than the working-alone condition
6	More expensive cars are more likely to stop at traffic lights	The ratio of stopping to not stopping will increase across the categories of cheap, mid-range and expensive cars

The inseparability of 'more' and 'than'

There is a very common tendency to assume that your reader will know what you mean by 'more' when in fact they can't. Remind yourself of suggestion number 2 for a practical at the bottom of Box 14.1. Now read this example of a prediction:

> It was expected that those in the burglar condition would recall more valuable items.

Obvious what the writer means, isn't it? Really?? Being picky, aren't I?

Well, is it being predicted that the burglar participants will recall more valuable items than household items **OR** is the prediction that they will recall more valuable items than the buyer participants? We really can't tell and a prediction like this is ambiguous. ALWAYS, if you use the word 'more' or 'less' remember to put in the 'than' and finish off the sentence – even if you *do* think it's obvious. Usually you just can't use 'more' without 'than'. While we're on tips, use 'less' if you can't count what you're referring to; use 'fewer' if you *can* – less porridge, fewer crisps.

THE METHOD

Design

This describes the 'skeleton' outline of the study – its basic framework. For instance, is it an experiment or not? If it is, what design is used (repeated measures etc.)? What conditions are there, and how many groups are used? What is the purpose of each group (control, placebo etc.)? How many participants are in each group? (though this information can go in the 'participants' section below). In many cases, describing the groups will be a way of describing the IV. In any case and where appropriate, the IV, its levels and the DV should be specified *precisely* here. In addition, it might be relevant to identify any further controls such as counterbalancing, though this can otherwise be dealt with in the procedure section. In our experiment on imagery, we could say:

> We used a repeated-measures design with one group of 15 participants who were presented with a 20-item word list. In one condition participants were instructed to use image-linking and in the other they were told only to repeat each word. Order of taking conditions was reversed for half the participants. The dependent variable was the number of correct items produced under free-recall conditions.

… and that's enough. You don't need to give any details of procedure or materials used, and you certainly should not give details here that are repeated further on.

If the study is non-experimental, its overall approach (e.g. observational) can be stated, along with design structures such as longitudinal, cross-sectional etc. There may be independent and dependent variables that are uncontrolled, such as number of pedestrians waiting at a crossing and whether a driver stops or not. Controls, such as measures of interobserver reliability, may have been incorporated. Don't mention details here, just that the control was employed.

Participants

Give numbers, including how many in each group, and other details relevant to the study. If someone wishes to replicate your findings about 'adolescents' and their self-concepts, it is important for them to know exactly what ages and sex your participants were and where they were from. These variables are less important in technical laboratory tasks, though general age range is usually useful and handedness may be relevant. Other variables, such as social class or occupation, might be highly relevant for some research topics. Certainly important is how naïve participants were to psychology. Otherwise, keep details to a minimum. How were participants obtained? How were they allocated to the various experimental groups?

Never be tempted to say that you drew a 'random sample'. If, however, it was *haphazardly* drawn, say so. The description 'opportunity sample' is useless; it gives no information about selection *at all* other than that participants were conveniently available. Give *some* information about how participants were obtained, even if it was just by grabbing who was around at the time plus your parents and boy/girlfriend. Do not say 'Participants were from an opportunity sample'; say 'Participants *were* an opportunity sample'.

Figure 14.1   The materials and procedure sections are like a recipe for a cake

Materials/apparatus

At various workshops for teachers I have observed Cara Flanagan liken the process of writing the method section to writing the recipe for a cake; the materials and procedure sections, in particular, can be seen as the ingredients and the instructions – what you used and how you used them. A golden rule here is: *give enough detail for a full replication to be possible.* This means giving specifications of constructed equipment (finger-maze, illusion box) and source (manufacturer, make, model) of commercial items (maze, computer). You can give essential details here and give exact details in an appendix, e.g. word lists, questionnaires, lists, pictures, vignettes and so on. You do **NOT** need to give details of blank paper or pencils!

Do not simply write out a list of materials. The materials section should be just like any other, written in normal English prose. It may also be useful to include a diagram or photo of an experimental set-up or seating arrangement, but don't go overboard; only do this *if necessary*. There are no Brownie points available for artistic merit!

In our memory study we would need two lists of words because we can't have people learning the same list twice without a mammoth confounding variable. We would state in this section how we justify the equivalence of our two lists, e.g. selected from word-frequency lists. The words would be best placed in an appendix but you must then tell your reader where they are! If you have consulted a source for equivalent words, such as the Internet site given earlier, then you must include the full reference to this source.

A reference must also be provided for any published psychological measures that you have used; the full reference should appear in your references section. If questionnaires are 'home-grown' then there should be a description of how the measure was developed.

Procedure

The rule here is simple. Describe exactly what happened *from start to finish* of the testing; think of the cake-making recipe. The account must be good enough for exact replication. Any standardized instructions should be included here or in an appendix. The exact wording used in training participants to use imagery in our memory experiment should be included, together with instructions for the rehearsal condition and any practice trials.

It might be tempting to skim the rather dry and descriptive Methods section. However, marks are available here for what is an essential piece of communication, so don't rush this bit. Have a good look afterwards to make sure that a psychologically naïve friend of yours could do exactly what you did. If they can't, you haven't finished yet!

RESULTS

Description

It is very important to realize that one's description of results at this point continues the prose style of the previous sections of the report. You tell your reader, *in words*, what you found. Tables and charts are *supplementary* aids to communication. You cannot simply present a table of data as 'The results'. Raw data (e.g. participants' actual scores) go in an appendix. Do *not* present each participant's individual score. A *summary* table of these (only) is presented; for instance, means and standard deviations or frequencies. You should not include every measure of central tendency and dispersion you can think of. Marks are awarded for *appropriate* selection of statistical summaries, not for a shotgun approach. The mean *or* the median *or* the mode will be appropriate, *not* all three.

Any tables (appearing here or in the appendix) should be fully headed and labelled. For instance, a summary of our experimental results presented as in Table 14.2 is inadequate. What do the numbers measure? We need a heading, such as 'Number of words correctly recalled in imagery and control conditions'. If results are times, state 'seconds' or 'minutes'; if they are distance measurements, state the units. The title of the table *must* tell the reader what the numbers are measures *of*.

Table 14.2   Inadequate results table – no heading or information about measures

	Imagery	Control
Mean	12.4	8.3
SD	1.5	1.1

You probably have to present a chart of your data, such as a bar chart or scattergram. Make sure these are clearly headed too, and that the vertical and horizontal axes have titles. If colours or shading are used for different sets of data your chart will also require a 'legend'. Don't label bars in a bar chart as 'Group 1' and 'Group 2' – use the description of the conditions, e.g. 'Imagery group' and 'Rehearsal group'.

Tables and charts should occur in the text of the report where they are relevant, *not* in an appendix. They will also need to be numbered (for reference purposes) and to have informative headings. The number is placed with the title. Note that charts are 'figures'; *tables* of data (like the inadequate Table 14.2) are not 'figures'.

Again, don't go overboard; don't litter your work with charts looking at the data from various angles. Usually only one chart is useful in a simple experiment, one that demonstrates the main effect found. Why should the reader be interested in a chart showing a column for each individual's score (see p. 124)? Why would they want to see a pie chart, bar chart *and* line chart of the *same* data? Why would they want to see the distribution of all scores unless this is referred to in parametric screening? Ask yourself, 'What does my reader *need*?', not 'How can I make the report look as stunning or pretty as possible?'. You will not be given extra marks for superfluous charts.

Don't trust computers to draw your charts for you. Without an understanding of what the chart should be representing you are very likely to produce a naff graph. Computer-drawn charts still require full labelling and heading. Charts with 'Variable 0001' on one axis are not terribly useful.

Analysis or 'treatment' of results

It is best to tell your reader when you've finished describing your data and are about to analyse them by using an inferential statistical test. State which statistical test is being applied, to which data, and justify the application using the type of decision procedure outlined in Chapter 10 (this might include giving details of why a non-parametric test is used in preference to a parametric one). ***Never*** say 'The results were tested ...'. State exactly *which* results: for example, 'The difference between the means for imagery and rehearsal scores'. The simplest table of data can be tested in several ways.

State the result of the test clearly and compare this with the appropriate critical value, if not using a statistical analysis program. Justify the choice of this critical value, including N or degrees of freedom, number of tails and the corresponding level of probability under H_0 (e.g. '$p < 0.05$'). Some computer programs tell you that '$p = 0.000$' – this is actually impossible; probability cannot be zero for *possible* events. The computer has to round to only three places of decimals and your result is far lower than that. Such a result should be reported as $p < 0.01$ or possibly $p < 0.001$. Box 14.3 is a quick exercise in noting what can be missing from statements of significance. Note that for each test presented in this book there is an accompanying demonstration of the accepted way of reporting such a result.

Box 14.3   Incomplete significance statements

Significance statements	What's missing
'The *t* test showed that differences were significant.'	Only *one* difference at a time can be tested with a *t* test. *Which* difference? Significant at what level? How many degrees of freedom? Tails? One- or two-tailed test?
'There was a strong correlation between the two variables.'	*Which two?* Positive or negative? What value? Was it significant? If so, at what level? One- or two-tailed?
'There was a significant difference between the two conditions at the 1% level.'	*Which* conditions? One- or two-tailed?

State whether the null hypothesis is being rejected or retained. State the conclusion: for example, 'The suggestion that imagery produces better recall performance than mere rehearsal was supported'.

Calculations of your tests, if you wish to include them, should appear *only* in an appendix. Many calculations these days will be performed by computer or dedicated calculator. The software used, and intermediary results, can be mentioned in an appendix but are not really relevant, except for specialist data treatments.

DISCUSSION

Do not be tempted to give brief attention to your findings here, then revert back to another essay on your topic. In general, very little, if any, new research or background theory should be introduced into your discussion. You should rely on what you wrote in your introduction. Here you discuss your findings in the light of the argument in the introduction. On occasion, because of what has shown up in your study, or as an overall comment, you might include a new reference, but these should be absolutely minimal.

Summarizing the findings

The first step here is to relate the result back in a little more detail to the hypothesis and theory you set out to test, and to the original aims of the research. These, in turn, are then related to the background theory, showing support or a need to modify theory in the light of contradictory or ambiguous findings. Unexpected findings or 'quirks' in the results, such as extreme 'rogue' scores or unexpected effects, can also be discussed as a secondary issue. From time to time, such 'oddities' lead in novel research directions. You can try to offer some explanations of these if you have good reasons.

Evaluating the method

The conscientious researcher always evaluates the design and method, picking out flaws and areas of weakness. This isn't just to nitpick. A reader of the report might well come back and accuse the researcher of not considering such weaknesses. The researcher can forestall such criticism by presenting a good argument as to why the weakness should not have serious effect. The emphasis of the evaluation depends partly on the outcome:

a. If we got the result we expected, we should look carefully at the design for possible confounding variables producing a Type I error. If we were expecting to find no difference (e.g. to reject an earlier finding of difference), we should look for ways in which the design and procedures may have hidden differences or relationships.
b. If we failed to get a predicted difference, we should look for sources of random error (though research with a successful outcome may also have been affected by these). What aspects of the design, procedures and materials used did we find unsatisfactory? We should also look for any *confounding* variable that might have acted in a direction which obscures our predicted effect.

Not everything in an experiment or investigation can be perfect. There is no need to talk about not controlling temperature or background noise unless there is good reason to suppose that variation in these could have seriously affected results. Usually this is quite unlikely.

Suggest modifications and extensions

Most research leads on to more research. From the considerations made so far you should be able to suggest modifications of this design, *first* in order to check the critical points made, and *second*, to follow up speculations and suggestions for new directions with the research topic.

If you find yourself stuck for something to say, do avoid the knee-jerk reaction of 'We should have tested more participants'. This is often said under a misapprehension of the purpose and nature of experiments and sampling. Chapter 2 explains why, to some extent, larger samples aren't always better. If you tested 30 participants in two conditions of a tightly-controlled experiment then you shouldn't require more, especially if you did get a significant effect. If you do say you needed more participants then you should explain exactly *why* you think so. The same goes for the suggestion that a gender difference for the effect should now be investigated or that 'people from different cultures' should now be tested. This latter statement begs the question of *which* culture the author is assuming he/she *and* the reader are both from; the most important point in this context, though, is the question *why*? Why are you suggesting an improvement that you do suggest? Unless you can think of a good *reason* to extend the study in this way it is better not to appear to be padding out your discussion because you can't think of anything else!

Conclusion

Your report should end with a final comment; however, a heading for this last paragraph is not usually required. Avoid repeating the summary or abstract at this point. That is not necessary. What you can do is to make some summarizing comment in terms of overall findings, their relationship to the relevant model or theory and implications for the future. Try not to overblow your findings by claiming, for instance, that 'A new effect has been found' or 'This result should be useful to all clinical psychologists...'.

REFERENCES

Make a note that you will need either a primary or secondary reference for *every* item of published evidence that you refer to in your introduction and elsewhere in your report. Completing your list can be fiddly, especially if you've referred to a lot of different research studies in your work. It is also the section that will infuriate tired marking tutors if omitted or poorly done. There is often a lot of confusion over exactly what counts as a reference. Exactly what should be included? The golden rule is:

> **If you referred to it directly somewhere in your text, include it. If you didn't refer to it, don't include it!**

If you wrote '… Arnold (2003) argues that ...', this is a *primary* reference. The date tells us the year of publication of Arnold's original research article or book and you are claiming to have got your information *directly* from Arnold (2003). If, however, as happens in many early-stage reports, you obtained the information about Arnold (2003) from Smith (2004) then *Smith* is the source for you and this must be made clear. You might write 'Arnold (2003, in Smith, 2004) argues that …'. The reference you are making here is *secondary* and *only* Smith (2004) need appear in your reference list at the end of your report, though some systems require both (e.g. the standard Harvard system). Psychologists generally use the APA system described below.

You should *not* cite in your reference list the textbooks that you might have consulted (but not cited) whilst preparing your report. If you used Gross (2001) to look up some information but you did not refer directly to Gross anywhere in your report then Gross is *not* a reference. Strictly speaking, if you checked what Bower (1977) said, then your reference should be 'Bower (1977, in Gross, 2001) and you proceed as above for a secondary reference. Additional reading *can* be cited in a 'Bibliography' but this is unusual in psychological research articles. Beware also the fact that sociologists use the term 'Bibliography' in the way that psychologists use the term 'References'!

INTERNET references are tricky. An author should always be included if possible and, if not possible, then be very careful with the information; without a name it is highly suspect. Give the author, web address, date of your access to the address and any page numbers.

REFERENCE SYSTEM. Most psychologists write references in the way they appear at the back of this book – a version of the Harvard system recommended by the American Psychological Association. The format is:

For a **BOOK**: Author's name, initials, (year), *title*. Place of publication: publisher.
For an **ARTICLE**: Author's name, initials, (year), title. *Journal, volume number*, part, page numbers.

Notice that journal articles have the journal title in italics (you can use underline) with a capital letter for each substantive word, whereas for books the title is in italics but only the first word gets a capital. There can be a few awkward ones, which were articles in someone else's collection of articles, government reports, MSc theses and so on. In all cases the important criterion is simply that your reader can easily locate the specific work.

APPENDICES

These might contain: calculations, details of instructions given to participants, memory-list items, questionnaires and so on. These continue your normal page numbering. Separate topics go in separate, numbered appendices ('Appendix 1', 'Appendix 2' etc.).

GENERAL PRESENTATION

You should have page numbering throughout your report. You might find it convenient to refer to pages in your text. A title page sets the whole project off well and a contents page helps the reader go to specific sections, though some tutors discourage this.

KEY TERMS

Abstract	Rationale
Harvard system	Secondary reference
Plagiarism	Vignette
Primary reference	

COMMENTS ON A STUDENT PRACTICAL REPORT

What you see below are two fictitious student reports. The first is not a good report, so please use it carefully as a model, taking into account all the comments I've made beside it. My reasoning was this. If I comment on a perfect report the recent newcomer to psychology and its practical writing conventions would have little clue as to what typically goes wrong in report writing. To include all possible mistakes would be to produce an unreadable piece of work serving little purpose. You should also note that I have avoided spelling and grammatical errors but that student reports usually do have a few of these, if not many. Where there *are* many errors it is perfectly correct for your tutors to advise use of a spell-checker or dictionary. Demanding good spelling is *not* being fussy. It is difficult to read poorly-spelled work and it really is worth practising good spelling while you are a student (and can sort of get away with it) so that your job applications do not let you down and you are not embarrassed or penalized in employment when other people have to read your work. Whatever you do, don't try using text-messaging format; you have absolutely no need to save character spaces!

I have also, because of strong demand, included a 'good' version of the report and this follows the 'average' version. I resisted this for a while because I would be concerned that the 'good' version might be seen as *the* model, with tutors having constantly to explain that, although a student's report follows all the points in the 'good' version, it still has faults in the context of the particular assignment that has been set. So please see this as a fair example for specific circumstances and not a gold-standard model that can serve all purposes.

The 'average' report is probably mid-range but, because of differing criteria from different boards, I've refrained from assessing it formally. It contains quite a lot of omissions and ambiguities, but few outright mistakes. Too many of these might be misleading. I have coded comments as follows:

✓ A good point

✗ An error, omission, ambiguity; in general, a point that would count cumulatively to lower the overall mark for the report

? An ambiguity or odd point that would not lower the mark on its own but could contribute to an overall lower mark if it were repeated. This is also used for grammatical and conventional style points that, again, are not terribly bad on their own but that may accumulate into a feeling of 'not quite so good' (but this does depend on your level of study).

Assume that materials mentioned as being in appendices were included. For ease of reference, the comments are laid out progressively, side by side with the report.

AN EXPERIMENT TO SHOW WHETHER PEOPLE ARE[1] AFFECTED BY KNOWING A WRITER'S SEX WHEN THEY JUDGE A PIECE OF WRITING

ABSTRACT

We[2] set out to see whether people make sexist assumptions about an author when they read their writing. We asked 39 participants to read an article and told half of them (19) that the author was a man and the others that it was a woman. We did this by making the writer's name 'John Kelly' for one version of the article and 'Jean Kelly' for the other.[3] Because of stereotyping we expected the 'Jean Kelly' group to think worse of the article's quality.[4] Results were not significant[5] and the null hypothesis was kept. It was thought that the article was too neutral and women might have been voted lower on a technical article and men lower on a child-care article. If results were valid this could be interpreted as a change in attitude since Goldberg's (1968) work.[6]

INTRODUCTION

People use stereotypes when they look at other people. When we perceive people it's like looking at things in the world. We look through a framework of what we've learnt and we don't see the real thing but our impressions of it are coloured by what we expect and our biases. Bruner (1957) said we 'go beyond the information given';[7] we use what's there as 'cues' to what we interpret is really there. For example, when we see a car on the road and a mountain behind it, the mountain might look only twice as high as the car but because we know how far away the mountain is we can estimate what size it really is. When we take a picture of a pretty sight we often get telephone wires in the way because we've learnt not to see what isn't important. Also, we take a shot of Uncle Arthur on the beach and he comes out really small because we thought he looked much bigger in the viewfinder because he's important to us. Bruner and his friends started the 'new look' in perception where they experimented with perception to show that we're affected by our emotions, motivation and 'set'. In one experiment they showed sweet jars to children that were either filled with sand or sweets.[8] The children saw the jars with sweets as larger, so we are affected by our past experience and what we want. (Dukes and Bevan, 1951.)[9]

To show that a small bit of information affects our judgement of persons, Asch (1946, in Brewer and Crano, 1994)[10] gave some people some words to describe a person. The words were the same except that 'warm' and 'cold' were different. This even works when the person is real because Kelley (1950) introduced students to a 'warm' or 'cold' person and they liked the 'warm' one more. The 'warm' person was seen quite differently from the 'cold' one.

Sex differences are a myth.[11] Condry and Condry (1976) showed people a film of a nine-month-old child reacting to a jack-in-the-box. If they were told he was a boy the reaction was thought of as 'anger' but for a 'girl' it was thought of as 'fear'. Deux (1977) reviewed several studies and found females often explain their performance as luck, even if they do well, but men say their ability helped them. This was where the task they did was unfamiliar. This means that men and women accept their stereotype and go along with it in their lives.[12] Maccoby and Jacklin's experiment[13] in 1974 showed that males describe themselves with independent terms (e.g. intelligent, ambitious) but females use more social terms (e.g. co-operative, honest).

A psychologist called[14] Goldberg (1968) got female students to read articles written by a man or a woman (they thought). The articles written by a man were rated as better. This is the experiment we're doing here.[15] If gender stereotypes affect our judgments we would expect that participants told an author is male will think some articles are better written than participants told the author is female.[16]

1. **?**   Don't need 'An experiment to show …'; title could be shorter: 'The effect of author's sex on evaluation of an article'.

2. **?**   Conventional reports are written in *passive* not personal mode; e.g. 'The theory was tested that author's sex affects judgement of writing'. '39 participants were asked …'.

3. **✓**   IV is clearly described.

4. **✗**   DV is not defined. How was 'thinking worse of' measured? (It was rated, we find out later on.)

5. **✗**   Result very poorly reported. What data were tested and how?

6. **✓**   Some brief statement of conclusions included.

7. **✓**   Quoted phrase is in quote marks and attributed to an author, with date – this must be referenced at the end of the report. It's a small quotation but technically the page number should be provided.

8. **?**   (Poor children! – you wouldn't think they'd let psychologists do that sort of thing!)

9. **? ✗**   Does not stay close to the topic. Factors affecting perceptual judgement are kind of relevant but the report could stay *much* closer to *social* perception or stereotyping.

10. **✓**   An appropriate secondary reference. The writer obtained the information from Brewer and Crano and doesn't have access to the original.

11. **✗ !!!** A gigantic and unjustified assumption made here; there are *some* differences (e.g. reading development rate); the claim needs qualifying with the use of 'some', 'many' or examples and trends.

12. **✗**   Another grand assumption here, following a very specific result; needs qualification.

13. **✗**   It wasn't an experiment; it was a review of mostly *post-facto* studies.

14. **?**   Don't need 'A psychologist called …'; simply delete these words here.

15. **✗**   The leap into the hypothesis is far too sudden here; we lurch from fair background description straight into the hypothesis without some introduction to the current study and a *rationale* for it.

16. **✗**   Hypothesis is vague. The research prediction states the IV but should also specify the *operationalized* DVs of 'quality' and 'interest'. Hence there are *two* predictions – one for quality and one for interest.

METHOD[17]

Design

The experiment used an independent-samples design.[18] There were two groups. The independent variable was the sex of the author and the dependent variable was the way they judged the article.[19]

Participants

We used a random sample[20] of 39 participants from the college canteen. Originally there were 20 in the male-author condition and 20 in the female-author condition but the results for one in the male-author condition went missing. The participants were all students except for one who was a friend of one of the students.

Materials

We used an article from the *Guardian Weekend* magazine about travelling in Tuscany. This is in Appendix 1. It was 908 words long and was printed on two sheets of A4 paper. We also used a rating sheet (in Appendix 2) where participants recorded their rating of the article for quality and interest on a 10-point scale.[21, 22] This also had some questions on it to make sure the participants had noticed the name of the author.[23]

Procedure

We sat each participant down and made them feel at ease. We told them there would be no serious deception and that they would not be 'tested' or made to feel stupid in any way. We said we just wanted their opinion of something and that their opinion would be combined with others and their results would be anonymous.[24] We then gave them the instructions shown below. All this was done in a standardized way.[25]

> We would like you to read the article we are about to give you. Please read it once quickly, then again slowly. When you have done that, please answer the questions on the sheet which is attached to the article. Try to answer as best you can but please be sure to answer all questions in the order given.[26]

If the participant's number was odd they received the female author where the article was written by 'Jean Kelly'. The other participants were given 'John Kelly' sheets. In one case this order was reversed by mistake.[27]

Participants were then left to read the article and no questions were answered by the experimenters unless the question did not concern the reading at all: for instance, if they wanted the light turned on or heater turned off. Questions about the reading were answered: 'Please answer as best you can and we can talk about ('that problem') after you've finished. That way, all our participants do exactly the same thing. Thank you for your co-operation.' The experimenters kept a watchful eye to ensure that instructions were followed in the correct order.

RESULTS

The results from the two groups were collected and organized into the table of raw data shown in Appendix 3. The averages and standard deviations were calculated and these are shown in Table 1.[28]

17. ✓   Good that all sections of the method are present and correctly titled.

18. ✓   Correct design and this *is* an experiment.

19. ✗   Again, DV not specified; there is no need for a complete description here but there should be an operational definition of the measure – 'quality was measured by scores given on a 10-point scale' or similar. Other controls have not been specified.

20. ✗   Almost certainly not a 'random' selection from the canteen. If it *was* random, explain how achieved; no mention of participant gender and this *is* relevant given the topic and aims of this study; what kind of students and where from?

21. ✓   Materials well described.

22. ✗   Notice that tucked away here is the first mention of the precise DVs. We still don't know which way the scale runs – is 10 high or low?

23. ✗   The technique of asking questions, including dummy ones, in order to ensure participants noticed the sex of the author, deserves clearer explanation. We need to know the order of events – see p. 212 on camouflaging the IV.

24. ✓   Ethical considerations well implemented.

25. ?   Ambiguity; was the initial rapport session standardized, or just the instruction-giving?

26. ✓   Exact instructions used are included here.

27. ?   This system of allocation of participants might have been mentioned in the 'design' or 'participants' sections; ✓ good that the mistake was reported, however.

Table 1

| | Sex of author | |
	Female	Male
Quality		
Mean	6.7	6.3
SD	1.5	2.3
Interest		
Mean	4.3	5.2
Sd	1.1	1.3

You can see from this Table[29] that the male got a lower rating on quality but a higher rating on interest. This may be because people think men can write more interestingly, in general, but women are more likely to be accurate and are generally better with language and the rules of grammar.[30]

Analysis[31]

We decided to use an unrelated *t* test on this data to test for difference between the male and female quality and interest means. *t* tests are parametric and it must be possible to assume that the sample is drawn from a normal distribution. Also, there should be homogeneity of variance and the level of measurement should be interval. [32, 33, 34]

Our *t* was 0.97 for quality and 1.43 for interest. Neither of these is significant and in both cases we retained the null hypothesis.[35]

Figure 1[36]

DISCUSSION

As we see above, there were small differences between the male- and female-author groups but the tests showed there was no significance. It could be that there is a difference but our design has failed to show this.[37] Or else[38] there really is no difference in the way people judge this article according to the sex of the author. If this is true then we have contradicted Goldberg's results but these were done in 1968. Perhaps things have changed since then and people no longer judge according to sex on writing. First we will look at the things that could be wrong with our design.[39]

We asked participants to answer some 'dummy' questions so that we could be sure they'd noticed the sex of the author *before* they rated the article.[40] When we thought about it afterwards, we decided perhaps we should have got them to do the questions (or some of them) before they read the article so that they would be aware of the author's sex while they were reading it. This might have made a

28. ✗ Table has no title; it does not state what the values '6.7' etc. *are*; it should refer to these as 'Mean and standard deviation of quality and interest ratings'.

29. ? Should describe and summarize for the reader, not refer to them in this personal style.

30. ✗ This kind of interpretation or speculation belongs in the 'Discussion' section; here, just the factual results should be reported.

31.   Note that not all reports require this heading.

32.   You would not always be required to justify the use of your test on all these criteria.
33. ✓ Good that test data and *t* test criteria are recognized and described fairly well.
34. ✗ The use of the *t* test here has not been *justified* – there should be an answer to the criteria given here, showing that these data *are* therefore suitable for a *t* test.
35. ✗ *t* not reported in conventional form; no *df*, no value for *p*; was the test two-tailed?

36. ✗ Chart has no title; 'M' and 'F' have no key (yes, it's obvious what they mean but clarity is the keyword here); the vertical scale has no values; the chart is correctly drawn as a clustered bar chart (not histogram). However it is not referred to anywhere in the text of the report.

37. ✓ Recognition that a Type II error could have occurred and that the outcome, if genuine, needs interpretation in the light of its contradiction of other work.
38. ? Grammar! Can't start a sentence this way.

39. ✓ Deals with Type II error possibility first, i.e. looks critically at the method to see what might have prevented the demonstration of an effect.
40. ? Again, role of dummy questions should have been made clear earlier but we have already taken this weakness into account in our assessment – not a double penalty.

difference and we could do another study like this sometime.[41] We didn't take any notice of the sex of our participants but obviously this might make a difference. Perhaps males would downrate[42] female authors and maybe *vice versa*. In a future study we could take groups of men and women separately.[43] Another problem was that not everybody would use our scale in the same way. 'Good' might be 7 to one person and 9 to another. We could perhaps have standardized by getting them to rate something else first and then discussing the points on the scale with them.[44] Also, we should have used more participants[45] and participants may have guessed what was going on and there may have been demand characteristics.[46]

We felt that the article used was on a very neutral subject. Goldberg used a selection of articles. Some were on traditionally male subjects and some of the subjects would be more associated with females. We could do the study again using, perhaps, an article on car maintenance and one on child care to see whether this made a difference, like Mischel did.[47,48]

Perhaps participants would expect a travel writer to be male. Eysenck (2004) says 'seeing or hearing stereotypical information increases the tendency to think and behave in stereotype-consistent ways' (p. 774).[49] The stereotype of travel writers being male could have helped participants to rate the male article as better but this didn't happen. Stangor *et al*.[50] (1992), though, found that, among individuals having weak or moderate stereotypes, information *incongruent* with the stereotype was generally remembered better than congruent information. However, congruent information was better remembered than incongruent information for individuals having strong stereotypes. Thus memory processes serve to maintain stereotypes only for those who already possess strong stereotypes.[51] Our participants were students and could therefore have weaker stereotypes. Perhaps this meant that some of them therefore rated the female higher (incongruent information) while others did the opposite and hence we got no difference.[52]

REFERENCES[53]

Asch, S.E. (1946) Forming impressions of personality. *Journal of Abnormal and Social Psychology*, 4, 258–90.

Brewer, M.B. and Crano, W.D. *Social psychology*. St Paul, MN: West Publishing Company.

Bruner, J.S. (1957) Going beyond the information given. In *Contemporary Approaches to Cognition: a symposium held at the University of Colorado*. Cambridge, MA: Harvard University Press.

Condry, J. and Condry, S. (1976) Sex differences: a study in the eye of the beholder. *Child Development*, 47, 812–19.

Deux, K. (1977) *The social psychology of sex roles*. In Wrightsman, L., *Social Psychology*. Monterey, CA: Brooks/Cole.

Dukes, W.F. and Bevan, W. (1951) Accentuation and response variability in the perception of personally relevant objects. *Journal of Personality*, 20, 457–65.

Eysenck, M.W. (2004) *Psychology: an international perspective*. Hove: Psychology Press.

Goldberg, P. (1968) Are women prejudiced against women? *Transaction*, April, 1968.

Kelley, H.H. (1950) The warm–cold variable in first impressions of people. *Journal of Personality*, 18, 431–39.

Maccoby, E.E. and Jacklin, C.N. (1974) *The psychology of sex differences*.[54]

Stangor, C. and McMillan, D. (1992) Memory for expectancy-congruent and expectancy-incongruent information; A review of the social and social-developmental literatures. *Psychological Bulletin*, 111, 42–61.

Rogers, W.S. (2003) *Social psychology: experimental and critical approaches*. Maidenhead: Oxford University Press.[55]

41. ✓ Suggests modifications based on an analysis of the present study's outcomes and weaknesses.
42. ? Is there such a word – use the dictionary!

43. ✓ Good! This point from our earlier debits has now been picked up so we can balance this in our assessment.
44. ✓ This point has also been picked up but it's a pity the relevance to the *t* test justification is not spotted; should the data have been accepted as interval-level, then? Really, this is a partial ✗.
45. ✗ WHY?!! Should avoid this knee-jerk point, unless there is a good reason to include it; there were a fair number of participants and with no reason given this is rather an empty point, 'thrown in'.
46. ✗ ? A difficult one; is the point that people may have guessed *and* there could have been 'demand characteristics'? If so, there should be an explanation of why the effect of demand characteristics is suspected; in what way? If people's guessing was meant as a demand characteristic, is this feasible? It must always be remembered in independent-samples designs of this kind that *you* know what the IV is but how can the participants know? Why should they suspect that another author will be a different sex? One needs to see the participant's perspective here.
47. ✓ Good extension of study proposed, though this would involve more complex statistics.
48. ✗ 'Mischel' has no date and does not appear in the reference list.
49. ✓ Has quoted and acknowledged, with page number.
50. ✗ This may sound petty but the convention is that you do not use '*et al.*' on the first mention of a publication unless it has more than five names. *After* that you may use '*et al.*' (but this one actually only has two so both should always be used and '*et al.*' is inappropriate).
51. ✗ !!! Alarm bells ring for markers when they encounter a sudden change of style like this, sounding more academic compared with most of the rest of the report. Most markers, after only a little experience, can spot this kind of change and will reach for the most likely textbooks to check for plagiarism. It is, in fact, cribbed straight from Eysenck (2004: 774). There is a little clue just above! This really would be a shame in an otherwise fair report. The reference should therefore be secondary and Eysenck should be included as primary.
52. ✗ Not too well explained, final point is ambiguous and there should really be an overall, general conclusion, not this abrupt ending.
53. ✓ Good references, put in conventional style and most in alphabetical order. ✓ However, Mischel (****) should appear here too.

54. ✗ No place of publication or publisher.

55. ✗ 'Allo, 'allo! What's this one doing here? It's not in alphabetical order and it wasn't referred to in the text of the report at any time. It's probably been read to do the report but it isn't a reference. It could be included as 'background reading' but isn't necessary at all unless it was the source of evidence for some of the apparently 'primary' references.

A BETTER REPORT OF THE SAME PRACTICAL NOW FOLLOWS.

EFFECT OF AUTHOR'S APPARENT SEX ON ASSESSMENT OF A WRITTEN ARTICLE

ABSTRACT

In an attempt to assess current effects of sex-role stereotyping on judgement of writing skill, Goldberg's (1968) study was partially replicated. 25 participants were asked to read an article. Twelve participants were told the author was male whilst 13 were told the author was female. Whilst the 'female' author was rated higher on quality and lower on interest than was the 'male' author, neither difference was significant. The neutrality of the assessed article is discussed and the suggestion made that judgements might vary according to author's sex if the supposed authored articles had themselves been sex-typed (e.g. technical or child-care related). The result is only tentatively accepted as evidence of a change in social attitude since Goldberg's work.

INTRODUCTION

Just as our perception of the physical world is affected by the subjective, interpretive and constructive nature of perception, so is our perception of people. In Bruner's words (1957) we 'go beyond the information given' in constructing our perceptual world of objects.

Expectancies about sex-associated behaviour and traits seem to affect strongly our perception of people. Condry and Condry (1976) showed people a film of a 9-month-old child reacting to a jack-in-the-box. If they were told the child was a boy the reaction was more likely to be reported as 'anger' whereas for a 'girl' the more common description was that of 'fear'. This study suggests that people's assessments of others are perhaps unknowingly affected by knowledge of a person's gender. Being students whose performance is often assessed, we were interested in whether knowledge of a person's gender might influence judgements of their written work. This is obviously an important question since, in a climate of equal opportunity, a person's gender or sex ought not to be relevant to the assessment of their ability.

The effects of gender bias can work at an apparently subtle level. In a classic study, Goldberg (1968) showed that female students rated several articles more highly when the article indicated a male author than when the apparent author was female. Mischel (1974) found that participants of both sexes rated a male author more highly on a male-dominated topic and a female author more highly on a female-dominated topic. This raises the issue of whether these participants *consciously* used the gender of author information when making their assessments. This is unlikely since they would not have known that sex of author was the independent variable for the experiment.

It has been suggested that stereotypical knowledge might affect judgements more when these judgements are made under pressure and/or with minimal information available. Fiske and Taylor (1991) argued for a *continuum model* of impression formation. They suggest that initially, on encountering someone or hearing about them, we make a simple initial categorization. If we are not going to interact further then there is no more analysis. However, if we have to interact with or make some judgement about them then we seek further information. If there is a popular, well-permeated stereotype for this category then the characteristics of this stereotype might pervade until we find contradictory information that might force us to re-categorize (e.g. a 'hard' businessman who nevertheless sets up childcare facilities for his staff); alternatively we might simply find our stereotype information reinforced (we meet a politician who *is* boring and spin-oriented). Evidence for this position is plentiful, including the finding that judgements of people are more stereotype-based when made in a hurry rather than when relaxed (Pratto and Bargh, 1991). Nelson, Acker and Manis (1996) showed that participants lowered their stereotypical judgements if they knew they had to justify them later or were discouraged from taking gender into account.

The continuum model predicts that participants in Goldberg's study *would* be affected by the gender information since they have minimal information about the person (just their name and the article they have written) but yet they are asked to make a judgement about that person's ability, or at least the work they have produced. To discover whether this effect might still occur, 30 years on, we attempted a partial replication of this study using just one 'gender-neutral' article, where Goldberg had used several, some more male-oriented and some more female-oriented. His participants were all female whereas we involved both male and female students. We asked participants to rate the article on both 'quality' and on 'interest'. If popular gender stereotypes are still available to students, and are more powerful when judgements have to be made swiftly and with minimal information, then we would expect participants told the author was male to give higher mean ratings for interest and quality of the article than would participants told the author was female.

METHOD

Design

We used an independent-samples experimental design with two groups. The independent variable, being apparent sex of the author, was manipulated so that one group was informed that the author was male while the other group was informed that the author was female. Dummy questions were used to ensure that the participant was made aware of the sex of the author (via their name). The dependent variables were ratings of quality and interest of the article, both assessed on a 10-point scale.

Participants

We asked a sample of 39 participants from the students' union to participate, selected as haphazardly as possible. There were 12 males and 8 females in the male-author condition and 9 males and 10 females in the female-author condition. Participants were allocated to conditions on an alternate basis, as selected, and were all students except for one who was a friend of one of the students. Numbers in each condition were originally equal but one participant's results were subsequently mislaid.

Materials

We used an article from the *Guardian Weekend* magazine about travelling in Tuscany. This is provided in Appendix 1. It was 908 words long and was printed on two sheets of A4 paper. One version gave the author's name as 'John Kelly' while the other version used 'Jean Kelly'. We also used a rating sheet (in Appendix 2) where participants recorded their rating of the article for quality and interest on a 10-point scale where 10 signified a high value. We also used a sheet with dummy questions (such as the title of the article, the number of pages and so on) in order to make sure that participants were aware of the name, and therefore the sex, of the author, when they were making their assessments. Since the question asking for the author's name was among eight others, it was assumed that participants would not be able to guess the purpose of the experiment from this aspect of the procedure. The request to rate the article on quality and interest followed these questions.

Procedure

Each participant was asked to sit down and an attempt was made to make them feel at ease. They were told that there would be no deception and that they would not be 'tested' or made to feel stupid in any way. They were assured that the researchers simply wanted their opinion of something and that their opinion would be combined with others and their results would be anonymous. The instructions (given below) were then administered. The instructions and all statements used in the preliminary briefing were standardized.

Instructions used

We would like you to read the article we are about to give you. Please read it once quickly, then again slowly. When you have done that, please answer the questions on the sheet which is attached to the article. Try to answer as best you can but please be sure to answer all questions in the order given.

If the participant's number was odd they received the female-author version where the article was written by 'Jean Kelly'. The other participants were given 'John Kelly' sheets. In one case this order was reversed by mistake.

Participants were then left to read the article and answer the questions. No question was answered by the experimenters unless it did not concern the reading at all: for instance, if they wanted the light turned on or heater turned off. Questions about the reading were answered: 'Please answer as best you can and we can talk about that (problem) after you've finished. That way, all participants do exactly the same thing. Thank you for your co-operation.' The experimenters monitored participants and checked that instructions were followed in the correct order.

RESULTS

The results from the two groups were collected and organized into the table of raw data shown in Appendix 3. Summary statistics are given in Table 1. The male author received a lower mean rating (6.3) than the female author (6.7) on quality, but a higher mean rating on interest (female mean = 4.3; male mean = 5.2). Dispersion among ratings was higher for the male author on both dependent variables, but particularly so for the quality rating (male sd = 2.3; female sd = 1.5). The mean values are also displayed in Figure 1.

Table 1   Mean (and sd) of quality and interest ratings for female- and male-author conditions

| | Apparent sex of author | |
	Female	Male
Quality		
Mean	6.7 (1.5)	6.3 (2.3)
Interest		
Mean	4.3 (1.1)	5.2 (1.3)

Analysis

Since the 10-point rating scale was unstandardized it was felt that data were not gathered on a truly interval scale. To test for differences between the male-author and female-author conditions on quality and interest we therefore used a non-parametric Mann-Whitney analysis on the unrelated data reduced to ranks. Median values for quality were female author 6.2, male author 6.1, and for interest, female author 4.5, male author 4.9.

For quality of the article, $U(N_a = 20, N_b = 19) = 183$, $p > 0.05$. For interest of the article, $U(N_a = 20, N_b = 19) = 164$, $p > 0.05$. (For $N_a = 20$ and $N_b = 19$, critical value of $U = 119$). Neither null hypothesis could therefore be rejected.

Figure 1   Mean ratings on quality and interest for female- and male-author conditions

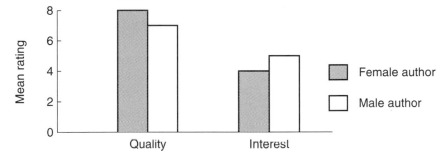

DISCUSSION

Although there were small differences between the male- and female-author groups on quality and interest, inferential analysis showed that these were not significant. In fact, although the mean interest rating for the male author was higher, the rating for quality was higher for the female author. However, for the inferential test used, the median ratings are more relevant and these showed even smaller differences. The only conclusion possible from the present study is one of no effect of author's sex on article rating. This failure to support Goldberg's work may be related to real changes in the effects of sex-role stereotyping since the time of his study. It could be that the effects reported by Pratto and Bargh (1991) and Nelson et al. (1996) are gross in comparison to the original Goldberg effect, which is now too subtle to show given heightened public sensitivity to gender stereotypes over three decades of feminist publication and an equal-opportunity climate. On the other hand, it may well be that our design has failed to identify an existing difference and we should look now at several weaknesses that could possibly have contributed to this outcome.

We asked participants to answer some 'dummy' questions so that we could be sure they had noticed the sex of the author before they rated the article. In fact, this does not ensure that participants' stereotype schemas are operating as they read and interpret the article, only when they are asked to assess it. A solution would be to present some of the dummy questions, including the crucial author-name item, before participants read the article so that they would be aware of the sex during the reading.

Goldberg's participants were all female college students. It could be that females will tend to rate male authors higher and vice versa. However, in our study, with participant sex not separated, any male-author bias by female participants could be counteracted, within the results, by female-author bias from male participants. We could re-analyse the results separately but then there would be rather a small number of results in each category (male ratings of female author etc.). There could also be an interaction here with the masculinity or femininity of the article's content, as shown by Mischel (1974). We could repeat the study using unambiguously male- and female oriented articles, such as one on car maintenance and one on childcare (though even these topics are challenged these days as being typically 'male' or 'female'). We had no measure of the 'femininity' or 'masculinity' of the content of our article. We could have partially achieved this either by asking other participants to rate it on this dimension, or by investigating any difference in ratings between male and female participants in a control group not given any author name.

Since our scale was invented for the study we have no evidence of it being used in a standard way by all participants. 'Good' might be 7 to one person and 9 to another. We could perhaps have standardized the scale by getting other participants to rate the same article and then discussing the points on the scale with them.

It is difficult to see how demand characteristics could have operated here to produce a result of no difference. It is unlikely that naïve participants would have guessed the purpose of this experiment or the nature of the hypothesis, given they served in only one condition. However, some students may have served in similar designs elsewhere and many are suspicious of psychology experiments in general. They may just have suspected an independent variable of author sex but they might just as well have suspected a hypothesis based on ethnicity or nationality, given the 'author's' surname. A solution would be to test a non-student sample and/or to include questions about these suspicions in the debriefing session.

Bem (1975) saw sex stereotypes as a 'straitjacket' (Gross, 1996: 696), and argued that society would improve with a shift towards 'androgyny'. Perhaps, from our results, we might tentatively speculate that such a shift may now have occurred, or at least that people are less likely today to take sex into account when judging the quality of writing. There may have been no shift but simply a weakening of the strength of sex-stereotyped assumptions in snap judgements.

REFERENCES

Assume these were perfect!

appendix
1

Exam-type questions

Below are some questions of the type you might encounter in an A Level Psychology examination or similar. It is difficult to give *exactly* the kind of question you will encounter because there are several boards, and syllabuses are changing all the time. However, you should look at the content of your own syllabus (if it is A Level, the glossary in this book will tell you which concepts are currently examined) and try to get hold of old examination papers. Some, but not all, of the boards publish papers and marking schemes on their web sites, available for free. At the time of writing, the AQA board makes available several past papers whereas the OCR and Edexcel boards make specimen papers available but past papers must be purchased. This, of course, might change in the future.

Questions 1 to 5 are generic – that is, the questions in them would be asked by any of the boards, though some of the terminology might vary slightly. Some boards test a few topics that others don't and these are mainly: *significance, selecting appropriate significance tests, justifying choice of significance test, levels of measurement of data, the null hypothesis, one- and two-tailed tests, Type I and Type II error, ecological validity* (see p. 48 for misunderstanding of this term), *counterbalancing, case studies, content analysis, quota, systematic and stratified samples.* Questions 6 and 7 include most of these concepts.

The answers given would, I believe, gain full marks in each case. I have indicated in italic after an answer where special attention should be paid or where there is an oddity.

HOW TO GET GOOD MARKS IN EXAMINATIONS!

So how do you get good marks on these types of questions? There are one or two points that students consistently slip up on and I have highlighted these here and sometimes after the specific answers as examples.

Look at the marks for each question and be complete!

Some questions ask you only to *state* a point (e.g. state one ethical principle …). These usually gain only 1 mark. However, where you are asked to *describe* a concept (e.g. *describe* one ethical principle) you must do more than simply give a term. You *must* describe it in a little detail to get the 2 marks that are usually on offer.

Don't write brief notes in case they are just too brief, e.g. single terms. Just use a few more words to be absolutely sure that your answer is complete and unambiguous. For instance, in question 4, h, ii, you are asked to *describe* an alternative method. Just writing 'questionnaire' will not do and would gain one mark at most.

Remember the point about 'more than' on p. 220 and this applies to 'different from' as well. **Always finish off the use of 'more' with an ending that begins 'than …'.** For example, for question 2, c, i, '**Children shown violent films produce more aggressive responses**' is *incomplete* and should end '**… than children shown nature films**'.

Putting the answer in context

If a question makes it clear that you are expected to answer *in the context of the research setting described* then you will get no mark for a general answer. For instance, if you are asked '**What was the independent variable in this investigation?**', then saying: '**The independent variable is the variable manipulated by the experimenter**' will gain no mark because it is a *definition* that could be remembered before the exam is sat. The examiners want you to *apply* your existing knowledge to the research setting that they have described in the preamble to the questions.

Shotgun answers

If you are asked to give (or describe) ONE advantage of using an interview in research you might answer like this: '**Interviews are complex, time-consuming and expensive**'. If you do, I'm afraid the examiner will take *only* the first 'advantage', which is 'complex'. You have given *several* advantages where only one was asked for. Unfortunately, that interviews are complex is debateable, without further explanation, and you might get no mark at all even though 'time-consuming' is a good point.

Linked questions

This is a particular problem if questions are *linked*. For instance, in question 1, h, i, if you gave two answers (for example '**Informed consent and anonymity**') and then proceeded in 1, h, ii, to explain why anonymity is important, then you would receive no mark for the second answer, since 1, h, i would have been marked on informed consent only.

Findings and conclusions

Make sure to distinguish between these two ideas. Findings are *what actually happened* in the study: the results. For instance, the means and standard deviations and the result of the significance test are findings. Conclusions are the *interpretation* you make of the results: for instance, that physical punishment does produce greater aggression in children, or at least that we have evidence to support this proposition. If asked what the researcher might *conclude* from a finding that more concrete than abstract words were recalled in an experiment on memory, you would get no marks for '**The mean for recall of concrete words was higher than the mean for abstract words**'. This is a *finding*, not a *conclusion*.

THE QUESTIONS

1. A psychologist wanted to investigate the theory that hitting children as punishment is a source of aggression in the child because they can copy the behaviour of an older aggressive person who is

their parent. She therefore looked for a relationship between amount of physical punishment used by the parent and the degree of aggression shown by the child. A questionnaire was administered to 26 mothers at a primary school, who volunteered. With the permission of the parents but unknown to the individual children, the researchers used naturalistic observation to record the aggressive actions of each child for a week during school playtimes. The correlation between aggression in the child and amount of physical punishment received was 0.42 and this was significant with $p < 0.05$.

    (a) Describe **one** advantage and **one** disadvantage of using questionnaires in psychological research. [2+2]

    (b) Explain why it was important that the children were not aware that they were being observed. [2]

    (c) Explain what is meant by *naturalistic observation* as a method. [2]

    (d) Explain how the researcher could check that observations being made were reliable. [2]

    (e) (i) Was the correlation between aggression and punishment received positive or negative? [1]

        (ii) Explain what is meant by a *positive correlation* using the variables in this investigation. [2]

        (iii) How would you describe the strength of the correlation found? [1]

    (f) Explain what is meant by claiming that the correlation was *significant*. [3]

    (g) The mothers participating were volunteers:

        (i) Explain why this might be a 'threat to the validity' of the study. [2]

        (ii) State what other sampling method might have been used and explain how it might have been applied in this study. [1+2]

    (h) (i) State **one** ethical principle that would have been important in this investigation. [1]

        (ii) Explain why you think this principle was important. [2]

2. In order to support the theory that children model adult aggressive behaviour, 20 children took part in an experiment at their nursery. They were shown a film in which several adults acted quite aggressively. The children were then allowed to play on a bouncy castle. They were observed and the number of aggressive responses each child produced was counted, using a pre-constructed checksheet that had earlier been piloted. A second group of 20 children at the nursery were shown a non-violent nature film. They also then played on the bouncy castle and were observed for aggressive responses. The children were allocated to the different film conditions on a random basis. The means and standard deviations of number of aggressive responses in each condition are shown in Table A1.

Table A1 Mean and standard deviation of number of aggressive responses in violent-film and non-violent-film conditions

	Violent film condition	Non-violent film condition
Mean	8.7	3.2
Standard deviation	1.31	0.64

    (a) Identify the independent and dependent variables in this study. [2]

    (b) (i) What was the experimental design of this study? [1]

        (ii) Describe one advantage of this design. [2]

        (iii) Explain why the study is a *field experiment*. [2]

    (c) (i) Write a suitable directional hypothesis for this study. [2]

        (ii) Explain why the hypothesis should be directional in this case. [2]

(d) In the experiment a control group of children were shown a non-violent film.
　　(i)　Explain the purpose of a control group in an experiment. [2]
　　(ii) State the method that should have been used to allocate children to groups. [1]
(e) Explain how the dependent variable in this experiment has been operationalized. [2]
(f) Explain why the observation checklist had been piloted. [2]
(g) The mean of the observation scores was used.
　　(i)　State one other measure of central tendency that could have been used. [1]
　　(ii) Explain why the mean might have been preferred to this other measure of central tendency. [2]
　　(iii) Describe one other finding that the researchers made. [2]
(h) If the difference between means had been significant what conclusion might the researchers have drawn from the study? [2]

3. Thirty participants took part in both conditions of an experiment. In one condition, participants were asked to learn a list of 20 words with a picture accompanying each word. In the other condition, the participants were asked to learn a different set of 20 words but without the pictures. Half the words in each list were concrete words and the other half were abstract words. Both groups were tested by the investigator for recall 30 minutes after learning the words. The number of words recalled correctly was taken as the participant's score in each condition. The results are depicted in Figure A1.

Figure A1　Mean recall of concrete and abstract words with and without pictures

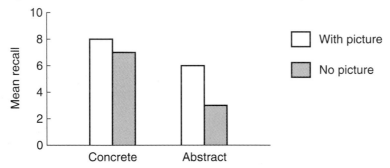

The researcher predicted that pictures would help in the recall of abstract words but not concrete words.
　　(a) Describe the aims of this study. [3]
　　(b) (i)　State the experimental design of the study. [1]
　　　　(ii) Describe one advantage and one disadvantage of this type of design. [2+2]
　　(c) Referring to Figure A1:
　　　　(i)　State the name of the type of chart shown. [1]
　　　　(ii) Explain how the researchers' predictions have been supported. [3]
　　(d) (i)　Describe the concept of *demand characteristics*. [2]
　　　　(ii) Explain how demand characteristics might have occurred in this study. [2]
　　(e) (i)　What is an *extraneous variable*? [2]
　　　　(ii) Explain how the recall of abstract words could have been worse in the no-picture condition because of an extraneous variable *and not* because of the lack of pictures. [2]
　　(f) (i)　Explain what is meant by an *investigator effect*. [2]
　　　　(ii) Identify a way in which investigator effects could have affected the results found in this study. [2]
　　(g) The researchers summarized results using the mean. What is the mean a measure of? [1]

4. Two schools were identified that were equivalent in the type of area served and the social and educational levels of the students at each school. One of the schools was just starting an anti-bullying programme whereas the other school was not. After the programme had been running for nine months psychologists interviewed a random sample of 30 pupils from each school, excluding those who had recently been found guilty of bullying. The interview contents were scored by independent raters who did not know the school from which each interview transcript had come. The raters had been previously trained to score for perceived safety in the school from bullies as expressed by the interviewee. Those in the anti-bullying school perceived significantly greater safety than those in the other school.

    (a) Explain why this design would be called a natural experiment.   [2]
    (b) State an appropriate hypothesis for this study.   [2]
    (c) State the independent and dependent variables used in this design.   [2]
    (d) Explain why it was important to use an equivalent control group.   [2]
    (e) (i) Explain how you would take a random sample of 30 children from a population of 400.   [2]
          (ii) Name one other sampling method that could have been used to select the children.   [1]
    (f) Explain why the raters were kept in ignorance of the school from which each interview transcript was taken.   [2]
    (g) (i) Explain what is meant by the *external validity* of a psychological effect.   [2]
          (ii) Describe one reason why the external validity of this experimental finding might be limited.   [2]
    (h) (i) Describe one advantage and one disadvantage of using interviews to gather psychological data.   [2+2]
          (ii) Describe one other way in which data could have been gathered in this study on the effects of the anti-bullying programme.   [2]
    (i) What conclusion might the researchers draw from the results of this study?   [2]

5. A psychologist wanted to test the theory that anxiety is related to low self-esteem. She used two psychological questionnaires to measure both these variables. She asked all the students in one of her classes to complete both the questionnaires. The summary of results she found are shown in Table A2 and pairs of scores are plotted in Figure A2.

Table A2   Means and standard deviations of self-esteem and anxiety scores

	Self-esteem	Anxiety
Mean	11.9	13.6
Standard deviation	5.26	6.13

Figure A2 Correlation between self-esteem and anxiety scores

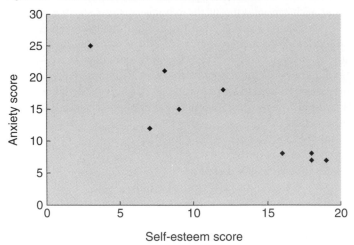

Self-esteem score

(a) Describe one advantage and one disadvantage of using psychological questionnaires as measures of psychological variables. [2+2]

(b) Describe the way in which the self-esteem questionnaire could have been shown to be reliable. [2]

(c) How would you describe the design of this study? [2]

(d) Describe one ethical issue that the researcher should have taken into account when conducting this study. [2]

(e) What is the standard deviation a measure of? [2]

(f) (i) What kind of correlation is shown in Figure A2 – positive or negative? [1]

(ii) Give a reason for your answer to question f, i. [1]

(iii) What can be concluded from your answer to question f, i about the nature of the relationship between anxiety and self-esteem? [2]

(g) A local newspaper picks up the research and publishes a story which tells readers that improving their self-esteem will reduce their anxiety. Explain why this conclusion is not necessarily true and not definitely shown in the findings. [3]

(h) The researcher also interviewed each participant, producing qualitative data.

(i) What is meant by *qualitative data*? [1]

(ii) Describe one advantage and one disadvantage of using qualitative data compared with quantitative data. [2+2]

(i) The researcher later tests 100 more participants and wishes to use a chart to show the distribution of all the self-esteem scores. What kind of chart should she use? [1]

6. A researcher investigated Freud's theory of the anal personality. According to this theory people who have particularly problematic experiences at the stage of potty training, especially anything that inhibits a smooth operation, can end up as 'anal personalities', being excessively tidy and organized. The researcher interviewed parents of now grown-up children. She identified pairs of children, close to each other in age, where one child had been problematic at the potty stage and the other had had no difficulty at all. When the interviews with parents took place the children were all over the age of 18 years. She administered to the children (now grown-up) a standardized psychological scale that measured, via questionnaire, a person's degree of anal personality. She tested the difference between the mean for the problematic group and the mean for the normal group. The difference was significant with $p < 0.05$.

(a) (i) Describe briefly the ethical principle of '*informed consent*'.   [2]
    (ii) In what way would this ethical principle be important in the study described?   [2]
(b) A researcher who is critical of the study suggests that it might have been wiser to conduct a few case studies on people who are excessively neat and organized.
    (i) Explain what is meant by a *case study*.   [2]
    (ii) Describe one advantage and one disadvantage of conducting a case study to gather data.   [2+2]
(c) Explain why the researcher used carefully matched pairs in this study.   [2]
(d) Identify the level of measurement for the anal personality data.   [1]
(e) The researcher made a directional hypothesis when setting up the study.
    (i) Explain what is meant by a directional hypothesis.   [2]
    (ii) Suggest a suitable directional hypothesis for the study.   [2]
(f) Explain what is meant by the phrase 'The difference was significant with $p < 0.05$'.   [3]
(g) (i) Identify a suitable statistical test for assessing the significance of the difference between the two anal personality score means.   [1]
    (ii) State two factors that justify your choice of test in question g, i.   [2]
    (iii) Explain why the researcher used a one-tailed test.   [2]

7. A team of researchers tested the hypothesis that the content of television news can affect our mood. They expected that participants shown a 'negative' news bulletin would be more depressed and worried after viewing the bulletin than they would after viewing a 'positive' bulletin. Participants were selected at random from among the student population at the university where the research was carried out. News bulletins were piloted and were found to be no different in dramatic effect but one was rated positive (it contained items on lower unemployment, children found alive etc.) while the other was rated negative (and contained stories of children missing, terrorist attacks etc.). Each bulletin lasted the same length of time and each item was roughly of the same length.

Students were asked to watch one of the bulletins and then complete a measure of worried thinking known as a 'worry scale'. Two weeks later the same participants were asked back to the research laboratory to watch the news bulletin that they had not watched on the first occasion. The participants were again tested on the worry measure after the viewing. For half the participants the first bulletin was positive and the second was negative, while for the other half the order was reversed. The worry scores for the negative news condition were higher than for the positive condition.

(a) Describe the aim of this study.   [2]
(b) (i) What kind of experimental design is used in this study?   [1]
    (ii) Give one advantage of using this method compared with another design.   [2]
    (iii) The conditions are *counterbalanced*. Explain why this procedure is used.   [2]
(c) Suggest a suitable alternative hypothesis for the data collected.   [2]
(d) (i) Explain why debriefing must be used in any study.   [2]
    (ii) What is a particular issue in the debriefing for *this* study, given that the procedures affect people's positive or negative moods?   [2]
(e) The worry scores are measured on a standardized psychological scale.
    (i) What measure of central tendency would be appropriate to use on the data?   [1]
    (ii) What would be a suitable significance test to use on the difference between worry scores for positive- and negative-mood conditions?   [1]
    (iii) Give two reasons that support your choice of test in question e, ii.   [2]
(f) (i) Explain what is meant by a *confounding variable*.   [2]
    (ii) Although several variables were controlled in this study suggest a variable that could have had a confounding effect on the result and give a reason for your answer.   [1+2]

(iii) If the nature of the news does *not* affect mood but the difference was significant because of some quirks in the data, would a Type I or a Type II error have been made? Explain your answer.   [1+2]

ANSWERS

1. (a) An advantage is that data can be collected relatively quickly compared with an experiment. A disadvantage is that it is quite easy for respondents to 'look good' and not answer honestly.
    (b) If people know they are being observed they can act artificially and the children might have done this; for example, in order to be noticed *(makes it contextual at the end)*.
    (c) Naturalistic observation is where people are observed in their natural habitat and there is no intervention.
    (d) The recordings by one observer and by those of another for the same children could be correlated and the value should be relatively high (close to 1).
    (e) (i) Positive. (ii) The more punishment the child received, the more aggressive they would be and *vice versa*. The two variables increase or decrease together. (iii) 0.42 is moderate.
    (f) The probability of getting a correlation this high is very low (under 0.05) under the null hypothesis.
    (g) (i) Volunteers can be a different kind of person from average. They may have certain qualities more or less than others. This is a threat to population validity because the results may only apply to people like volunteers. (ii) Random sampling: select mothers lottery-style so that each has an equal chance of being selected (but some mothers might refuse to take part).
    (h) (i) Informed parental consent (but any to do with human participation could be made relevant). (ii) It is important that any participant is fully informed before participation (British Psychological Society) so that they can withdraw if they wish to; but here it is the parent or guardian of the children who must be consulted and give consent. *Note a link problem here. If you gave two answers to h,i then your h,ii answer MUST be relevant to the first and not the second since examiners only take your first answer where ONE answer is required – see the introduction above.*

2. (a) The independent variable is the film type and the dependent variable is number of aggressive responses (note: 'aggression' might not gain a mark because not operationalized).
    (b) (i) Independent samples/groups/measures. (ii) There can be no order effects. *Saying 'order effects' would earn one mark or none.* (iii) The data gathering is carried out in the normal environment of their nursery and not in a laboratory.
    (c) (i) Children produce more aggressive responses after viewing an aggressive adult model than after viewing a neutral stimulus. (ii) The researcher's theory is that viewing aggression causes aggression, hence their prediction should be in that direction only.
    (d) (i) A control group gives a baseline measure of what would happen in the experimental situation if the independent variable were not applied. (ii) Random allocation.
    (e) The dependent variable is aggression and it has been operationalized by using a pre-constructed and tested checksheet that tells observers how to count aggressive responses.
    (f) The checklist was piloted so that the researcher could be sure that it was effective for observers in recording aggressive responses and that it produced the right kind of results.
    (g) (i) Median. *Mode would need to be justified since it deals with categorical variables only and here we have scores – see p. 105.* (ii) The mean is more sensitive than the median

and will use more of the information available about the scores. (iii) They found that the standard deviation was higher in the aggressive-film condition than in the nature-film condition.

(h) They would have concluded that they had support for the hypothesis that children learn aggression at least partly through viewing aggressive models.

3. (a) The researchers wanted to see if pictures would aid the recall of words that participants had to learn and recall. They also wanted to see whether this happened for abstract words but not concrete words.

(b) (i) Repeated measures. (ii) An advantage is that there can be no difference because of participant variables, that is, uncontrolled differences between two experimental groups. A disadvantage is that there can be order effects because participants can learn from one condition to the next.

(c) (i) This is a bar chart. (ii) The results shown in the chart appear to support the researcher because the means for concrete words are both higher than the mean for abstract words, but in the abstract-word condition a lot more words have been recalled with than without pictures.

(d) (i) Demand characteristics are where cues in the experimental situation are used by participants to guess what is expected of them. (ii) The participants took part in both conditions, so they might guess that better recall was expected when pictures accompanied the words.

(e) (i) An extraneous variable is any variable not part of the experimental design that might affect the results of the experiment. (ii) The abstract words might also have been less commonly seen in written material, less frequently used generally or even just longer than the concrete words.

(f) (i) Any effect on the experimental result caused by the presence or actions of the investigator. (ii) The investigator might have selected more difficult words for the abstract words or could have made one set of pictures more interesting to look at. *This is a 'shotgun' approach (see above) – only the first idea would be marked.*

(g) Central tendency of the data.

4. (a) The researcher took advantage of a situation that could be treated as an experiment but that was happening in the real world outside the researcher's control.

(b) Anti-bullying programmes increase pupils' perceived level of safety at school.

(c) The independent variable was the bullying programme (present or not) and the dependent variable was the rating of perceived safety.

(d) Because if the schools had differed in one important feature, this feature, and not the anti-bullying programme, might have been responsible for any differences in perceived safety that were reported.

(e) (i) Give all 400 a number from 1 to 400 and then select 30 numbers at random using random-number tables. (ii) Opportunity sampling (*or systematic, quota, stratified*).

(f) If the raters knew the school and also knew the hypothesis they might be biased in how they made the judgements whether towards or away from the hypothesis.

(g) (i) To what extent results can be generalized from the specific study setting. (ii) The results might not generalize to schools in areas that are very different from these two.

(h) (i) Interviews are better at getting valid data from participants because the interviewer can check out discrepancies and misunderstandings with the participant (compared with questionnaires). A disadvantage is that they can be time-consuming. (ii) They could have distributed questionnaires anonymously to pupils to assess perceived safety. *'Questionnaire' only one mark.*

(i) That anti-bullying programmes, at least in this kind of school, do play a part in reducing the level of perceived bullying.

5. (a) See answer 1, a.

(b) It could be tested on one set of people then tested on them again sometime later, say two months, to see if the scores correlated strongly.

(c) A correlational design; not an experiment.

(d) *Most will do but some would have to be made obviously relevant.*

(e) It is a measure of dispersion of scores around the mean. *Dispersion 1 mark only.*

(f) (i) Negative. (ii) Because higher scores on self-esteem are paired with lower scores on anxiety, and *vice versa*. (iii) There is a negative correlation between anxiety and self-esteem.

(g) The research only demonstrates a correlation, not which variable causes which. It has not been shown that improved self-esteem will result in lowered anxiety though this *may* be the case and the idea is *supported* by the result.

(h) (i) Data that are not numerical but are usually verbal, such as the contents of a speech. (ii) An advantage is that people's talk is not reduced to mere numbers and the original meaning is maintained. A disadvantage is that it is difficult to compare results across different studies.

(i) A histogram.

6. (a) (i) When people are asked to participate in a psychological investigation they should have enough information about the study to be able to decide whether they wish to participate or not. (ii) The investigation covers what could be a sensitive or embarrassing area. People may well be offended or disturbed, so they should be informed before they start.

(b) (i) A case study is an investigation in depth on one individual or group, often gathering a variety of types of data. (ii) An advantage is that a lot of information about the individual is gathered and a holistic picture can be built of their experiences. A disadvantage is that it can be difficult to compare one case with another because much of the information will be unique.

(c) Because if not, any differences found could be to do with extraneous variables that the pairs of people do not hold in common.

(d) Interval. *Because scale is 'standardized'.*

(e) (i) A directional hypothesis makes a claim about which way results will go: for example, which group's mean will be higher. (ii) When grown up, children having problems at the toilet-training stage have more anal personalities than people who do not have problems.

(f) The probability of this difference occurring under the null hypothesis is less than 0.05.

(g) (i) Unrelated *t* test. *Without 'unrelated' no mark might be awarded.* (ii) The data level is interval (standardized measure) and the design is matched pairs. *Mann-Whitney could be chosen and this answer would need to follow it; i.e. data level is ordinal – needs justification since test is standardized.* (iii) There was a directional hypothesis and a result in the opposite direction (potty-problem group with *lower* anal scores) would be of no scientific interest.

7. (a) The researchers wanted to show that mood is affected by news content by showing that people would be more worried after negative news than after positive news.

(b) (i) Repeated measures. (ii) There can be no effect from differences between participants in two groups as would happen with independent samples. (iii) Because there could be order effects. Counterbalancing reduces these by having some in one order and the rest in the other order, in this way learning effects cancel out.

(c) Means for worry scores after negative news are higher than the means after positive news.

(d) (i) So that participants are fully informed and can be assumed to be the same after the study as when they arrived. (ii) The participants may be unnecessarily unhappy or worried after the negative news, so the researchers should make especially sure that they feel better and feel the same as when they arrived, perhaps by counselling them.

(e) (i) The mean. (ii) Related *t* test. *See answers to question 6, g, i and ii.* (iii) Interval-level data (test is standardized) and related design (repeated measures).

(f) (i) A variable that has not been properly controlled and that may be the actual variable responsible for differences rather than the independent variable. (ii) Something appearing in the negative film, a person or a location, might be associated with worry, e.g. a recent terrorist incident, even though that incident is not a part of the bulletin. (iii) Type I because this is what happens when the null hypothesis is rejected but the result was actually due only to random variation.

appendix
2

Statistical Tables

Table 1   Random numbers

```
03 47 43 73 86    39 96 47 36 61    46 98 63 71 62    33 26 16 80 45    60 11 14 10 95
97 74 24 67 62    42 81 14 57 20    42 53 32 37 32    27 07 36 07 51    24 51 79 89 73
16 76 62 27 66    56 50 26 71 07    32 90 79 78 53    13 55 38 58 59    88 97 54 14 10
12 56 85 99 26    96 96 68 27 31    05 03 72 93 15    57 12 10 14 21    88 26 49 81 76
55 59 56 35 64    38 54 82 46 22    31 62 43 09 90    06 18 44 32 53    23 83 01 30 30

16 22 77 94 39    49 54 43 54 82    17 37 93 23 78    87 35 20 96 43    84 26 34 91 64
84 42 17 53 31    57 24 55 06 88    77 04 74 47 67    21 76 33 50 25    83 92 12 06 76
63 01 63 78 59    16 95 55 67 19    98 10 50 71 75    12 86 73 58 07    44 39 52 38 79
33 21 12 34 29    78 64 56 07 82    52 42 07 44 38    15 51 00 13 42    99 66 02 79 54
57 60 86 32 44    09 47 27 96 54    49 17 46 09 62    90 52 84 77 27    08 02 73 43 28

18 18 07 92 46    44 17 16 58 09    79 83 86 16 62    06 76 50 03 10    55 23 64 05 05
26 62 38 97 75    84 16 07 44 99    83 11 46 32 24    20 14 85 88 45    10 93 72 88 71
23 42 40 64 74    82 97 77 77 81    07 45 32 14 08    32 98 94 07 72    93 85 79 10 75
52 36 28 19 95    50 92 26 11 97    00 56 76 31 38    80 22 02 53 53    86 60 42 04 53
37 85 94 35 12    83 39 50 08 30    42 34 07 96 88    54 42 06 87 98    35 85 29 48 38

70 29 17 12 13    40 33 20 38 26    13 89 51 03 74    17 76 37 13 04    07 74 21 19 30
56 62 18 37 35    96 83 50 87 75    97 12 25 93 47    70 33 24 03 54    97 77 46 44 80
99 49 57 22 77    88 42 95 45 72    16 64 36 16 00    04 43 18 66 79    94 77 24 21 90
16 08 15 04 72    33 27 14 34 90    45 59 34 68 49    12 72 07 34 45    99 27 72 95 14
31 16 93 32 43    50 27 89 87 19    20 15 37 00 49    52 85 66 60 44    38 68 88 11 80

68 34 30 13 70    55 74 30 77 40    44 22 78 84 26    04 33 46 09 52    68 07 97 06 57
74 57 25 65 76    59 29 97 68 60    71 91 38 67 54    13 58 18 24 76    15 54 55 95 52
27 42 37 86 53    48 55 90 65 72    96 57 69 36 10    96 46 92 42 45    97 60 49 04 91
00 39 68 29 61    66 37 32 20 30    77 84 57 03 29    10 45 65 04 26    11 04 96 67 24
29 94 98 94 24    68 49 69 10 82    53 75 91 93 30    34 25 20 57 27    40 48 73 51 92

16 90 82 66 59    83 62 64 11 12    67 19 00 71 74    60 47 21 29 68    02 02 37 03 31
11 27 94 75 06    06 09 19 74 66    02 94 37 34 02    76 70 90 30 86    38 45 94 30 38
35 24 10 16 20    33 32 51 26 38    79 78 45 04 91    16 92 53 56 16    02 75 50 95 98
38 23 16 86 38    42 38 97 01 50    87 75 66 81 41    40 01 74 91 62    48 51 84 08 32
31 96 25 91 47    96 44 33 49 13    34 86 82 53 91    00 52 43 48 85    27 55 26 89 62

66 67 40 67 14    64 05 71 95 86    11 05 65 09 68    76 83 20 37 90    57 16 00 11 66
14 90 84 45 11    75 73 88 05 90    52 27 41 14 86    22 98 12 22 08    07 52 74 95 80
68 05 51 18 00    33 96 02 75 19    07 60 62 93 55    59 33 82 43 90    49 37 38 44 59
20 46 78 73 90    97 51 40 14 02    04 02 33 31 08    39 54 16 49 36    47 95 93 13 30
64 19 58 97 79    15 06 15 93 20    01 90 10 75 06    40 78 78 89 62    02 67 74 17 33

05 26 93 70 60    22 35 85 15 13    92 03 51 59 77    59 56 78 06 83    52 91 05 70 74
07 97 10 88 23    09 98 42 99 64    61 71 62 99 15    06 51 29 16 93    58 05 77 09 51
68 71 86 85 85    54 87 66 47 54    73 32 08 11 12    44 95 92 63 16    29 56 24 29 48
26 99 61 65 53    58 37 78 80 70    42 10 50 67 42    32 17 55 85 74    94 44 67 16 94
14 65 52 68 75    87 59 36 22 41    26 78 63 06 55    13 08 27 01 50    15 29 39 39 43
```

Abridged from R. A. Fisher and F. Yates (1974) *Statistical Tables for Biological, Agricultural and Medical Research*, 6th ed. Pearson Education Ltd.

Table 2 Areas under the normal distribution

z	0 z	0 z	z	0 z	0 z	z	0 z	0 z
0.00	0.0000	0.5000	0.40	0.1554	0.3446	0.80	0.2881	0.2119
0.01	0.0040	0.4960	0.41	0.1591	0.3409	0.81	0.2910	0.2090
0.02	0.0080	0.4920	0.42	0.1628	0.3372	0.82	0.2939	0.2061
0.03	0.0120	0.4880	0.43	0.1664	0.3336	0.83	0.2967	0.2033
0.04	0.0160	0.4840	0.44	0.1700	0.3300	0.84	0.2995	0.2005
0.05	0.0199	0.4801	0.45	0.1736	0.3264	0.85	0.3023	0.1977
0.06	0.0239	0.4761	0.46	0.1772	0.3228	0.86	0.3051	0.1949
0.07	0.0279	0.4721	0.47	0.1808	0.3192	0.87	0.3078	0.1922
0.08	0.0319	0.4761	0.48	0.1844	0.3156	0.88	0.3106	0.1894
0.09	0.0359	0.4761	0.49	0.1879	0.3121	0.89	0.3133	0.1867
0.10	0.0398	0.4602	0.50	0.1915	0.3085	0.90	0.3159	0.1841
0.11	0.0438	0.4562	0.51	0.1950	0.3050	0.91	0.3186	0.1814
0.12	0.0478	0.4522	0.52	0.1985	0.3015	0.92	0.3212	0.1788
0.13	0.0517	0.4483	0.53	0.2019	0.2981	0.93	0.3238	0.1762
0.14	0.0557	0.4443	0.54	0.2054	0.2946	0.94	0.3264	0.1736
0.15	0.0596	0.4404	0.55	0.2088	0.2912	0.95	0.3289	0.1711
0.16	0.0636	0.4364	0.56	0.2123	0.2877	0.96	0.3315	0.1685
0.17	0.0675	0.4325	0.57	0.2157	0.2843	0.97	0.3340	0.1660
0.18	0.0714	0.4286	0.58	0.2190	0.2810	0.98	0.3365	0.1635
0.19	0.0753	0.4247	0.59	0.2224	0.2776	0.99	0.3389	0.1611
0.20	0.0793	0.4207	0.60	0.2257	0.2743	1.00	0.3413	0.1587
0.21	0.0832	0.4168	0.61	0.2291	0.2709	1.01	0.3438	0.1562
0.22	0.0871	0.4129	0.62	0.2324	0.2676	1.02	0.3461	0.1539
0.23	0.0910	0.4090	0.63	0.2357	0.2643	1.03	0.3485	0.1515
0.24	0.0948	0.4052	0.64	0.2389	0.2611	1.04	0.3508	0.1492
0.25	0.0987	0.4013	0.65	0.2422	0.2578	1.05	0.3531	0.1469
0.26	0.1026	0.3974	0.66	0.2454	0.2546	1.06	0.3554	0.1446
0.27	0.1064	0.3969	0.67	0.2486	0.2514	1.07	0.3577	0.1423
0.28	0.1103	0.3897	0.68	0.2517	0.2483	1.08	0.3599	0.1401
0.29	0.1141	0.3859	0.69	0.2549	0.2451	1.09	0.3621	0.1379
0.30	0.1179	0.3821	0.70	0.2580	0.2420	1.10	0.3643	0.1357
0.31	0.1217	0.3783	0.71	0.2611	0.2389	1.11	0.3665	0.1335
0.32	0.1255	0.3745	0.72	0.2642	0.2358	1.12	0.3686	0.1314
0.33	0.1293	0.3707	0.73	0.2673	0.2327	1.13	0.3708	0.1292
0.34	0.1331	0.3669	0.74	0.2704	0.2296	1.14	0.3729	0.1271
0.35	0.1368	0.3632	0.75	0.2734	0.2266	1.15	0.3749	0.1251
0.36	0.1406	0.3594	0.76	0.2764	0.2236	1.16	0.3770	0.1230
0.37	0.1443	0.3557	0.77	0.2794	0.2206	1.17	0.3790	0.1210
0.38	0.1480	0.3520	0.78	0.2823	0.2177	1.18	0.3810	0.1190
0.39	0.1517	0.3483	0.79	0.2852	0.2148	1.19	0.3830	0.1170

Table 2   *Continued*

z	0 z	0 z	z	0 z	0 z	z	0 z	0 z
1.20	0.3849	0.1151	1.60	0.4452	0.0548	2.00	0.4772	0.0228
1.21	0.3869	0.1131	1.61	0.4463	0.0537	2.01	0.4778	0.0222
1.22	0.3888	0.1112	1.62	0.4474	0.0526	2.02	0.4783	0.0217
1.23	0.3907	0.1093	1.63	0.4484	0.0516	2.03	0.4788	0.0212
1.24	0.3925	0.1075	1.64	0.4495	0.0505	2.04	0.4793	0.0207
1.25	0.3944	0.1056	1.65	0.4505	0.0495	2.05	0.4798	0.0202
1.26	0.3962	0.1038	1.66	0.4515	0.0485	2.06	0.4803	0.0197
1.27	0.3980	0.1020	1.67	0.4525	0.0475	2.07	0.4808	0.0192
1.28	0.3997	0.1003	1.68	0.4535	0.0465	2.08	0.4812	0.0188
1.29	0.4015	0.0985	1.69	0.4545	0.0455	2.09	0.4817	0.0183
1.30	0.4032	0.0968	1.70	0.4554	0.0446	2.10	0.4821	0.0179
1.31	0.4049	0.0951	1.71	0.4564	0.0436	2.11	0.4826	0.0174
1.32	0.4066	0.0934	1.72	0.4573	0.0427	2.12	0.4830	0.0170
1.33	0.4082	0.0918	1.73	0.4582	0.0418	2.13	0.4834	0.0166
1.34	0.4099	0.0901	1.74	0.4591	0.0409	2.14	0.4838	0.0162
1.35	0.4115	0.0885	1.75	0.4599	0.0401	2.15	0.4842	0.0158
1.36	0.4131	0.0869	1.76	0.4608	0.0392	2.16	0.4846	0.0154
1.37	0.4147	0.0853	1.77	0.4616	0.0384	2.17	0.4850	0.0150
1.38	0.4162	0.0838	1.78	0.4625	0.0375	2.18	0.4854	0.0146
1.39	0.4177	0.0823	1.79	0.4633	0.0367	2.19	0.4857	0.0143
1.40	0.4192	0.0808	1.80	0.4641	0.0359	2.20	0.4861	0.0139
1.41	0.4207	0.0793	1.81	0.4649	0.0351	2.21	0.4864	0.0136
1.42	0.4222	0.0778	1.82	0.4656	0.0344	2.22	0.4868	0.0132
1.43	0.4236	0.0764	1.83	0.4664	0.0336	2.23	0.4871	0.0129
1.44	0.4251	0.0749	1.84	0.4671	0.0329	2.24	0.4875	0.0125
1.45	0.4265	0.0735	1.85	0.4678	0.0322	2.25	0.4878	0.0122
1.46	0.4279	0.0721	1.86	0.4686	0.0314	2.26	0.4881	0.0119
1.47	0.4292	0.0708	1.87	0.4693	0.0307	2.27	0.4884	0.0116
1.48	0.4306	0.0694	1.88	0.4699	0.0301	2.28	0.4887	0.0113
1.49	0.4319	0.0681	1.89	0.4706	0.0294	2.29	0.4890	0.0110
1.50	0.4332	0.0668	1.90	0.4713	0.0359	2.30	0.4893	0.0107
1.51	0.4345	0.0655	1.91	0.4719	0.0351	2.31	0.4896	0.0104
1.52	0.4357	0.0643	1.92	0.4726	0.0344	2.32	0.4898	0.0102
1.53	0.4370	0.0630	1.93	0.4732	0.0336	2.33	0.4901	0.0099
1.54	0.4382	0.0618	1.94	0.4738	0.0329	2.34	0.4904	0.0096
1.55	0.4394	0.0606	1.95	0.4744	0.0256	2.35	0.4906	0.0094
1.56	0.4406	0.0594	1.96	0.4750	0.0250	2.36	0.4909	0.0091
1.57	0.4418	0.0582	1.97	0.4756	0.0244	2.37	0.4911	0.0089
1.58	0.4429	0.0571	1.98	0.4761	0.0239	2.38	0.4913	0.0087
1.59	0.4441	0.0559	1.99	0.4767	0.0233	2.39	0.4916	0.0084

Table 2 *Continued*

z	0 z	0 z	z	0 z	0 z	z	0 z	0 z
2.40	0.4918	0.0082	2.72	0.4967	0.0033	3.04	0.4988	0.0012
2.41	0.4920	0.0080	2.73	0.4968	0.0032	3.05	0.4989	0.0011
2.42	0.4922	0.0078	2.74	0.4969	0.0031	3.06	0.4989	0.0011
2.43	0.4925	0.0075	2.75	0.4970	0.0030	3.07	0.4989	0.0011
2.44	0.4927	0.0073	2.76	0.4971	0.0029	3.08	0.4990	0.0010
2.45	0.4929	0.0017	2.77	0.4972	0.0028	3.09	0.4990	0.0010
2.46	0.4931	0.0069	2.78	0.4973	0.0027	3.10	0.4990	0.0010
2.47	0.4932	0.0068	2.79	0.4974	0.0026	3.11	0.4991	0.0009
2.48	0.4934	0.0066	2.80	0.4974	0.0026	3.12	0.4991	0.0009
2.49	0.4936	0.0064	2.81	0.4975	0.0025	3.13	0.4991	0.0009
2.50	0.4938	0.0062	2.82	0.4976	0.0024	3.14	0.4992	0.0008
2.51	0.4940	0.0060	2.83	0.4977	0.0023	3.15	0.4992	0.0008
2.52	0.4941	0.0059	2.84	0.4977	0.0023	3.16	0.4992	0.0008
2.53	0.4943	0.0057	2.85	0.4978	0.0022	3.17	0.4992	0.0008
2.54	0.4945	0.0055	2.86	0.4979	0.0021	3.18	0.4993	0.0007
2.55	0.4946	0.0054	2.87	0.4979	0.0021	3.19	0.4993	0.0007
2.56	0.4948	0.0052	2.88	0.4980	0.0020	3.20	0.4993	0.0007
2.57	0.4949	0.0051	2.89	0.4981	0.0019	3.21	0.4993	0.0007
2.58	0.4951	0.0049	2.90	0.4981	0.0019	3.22	0.4994	0.0006
2.59	0.4952	0.0048	2.91	0.4982	0.0018	3.23	0.4994	0.0006
2.60	0.4953	0.0047	2.92	0.4982	0.0018	3.24	0.4994	0.0006
2.61	0.4955	0.0045	2.93	0.4983	0.0017	3.25	0.4994	0.0006
2.62	0.4956	0.0044	2.94	0.4984	0.0016	3.26	0.4995	0.0005
2.63	0.4957	0.0043	2.95	0.4984	0.0016	3.27	0.4996	0.0004
2.64	0.4959	0.0041	2.96	0.4985	0.0015	3.28	0.4997	0.0003
2.65	0.4960	0.0040	2.97	0.4985	0.0015	3.45	0.4997	0.0003
2.66	0.4961	0.0039	2.98	0.4986	0.0014	3.50	0.4998	0.0002
2.67	0.4962	0.0038	2.99	0.4986	0.0014	3.60	0.4998	0.0002
2.68	0.4963	0.0037	3.00	0.4987	0.0013	3.70	0.4999	0.0001
2.69	0.4964	0.0036	3.01	0.4987	0.0013	3.80	0.4999	0.0001
2.70	0.4965	0.0035	3.02	0.4987	0.0013	3.90	0.49995	0.00005
2.71	0.4966	0.0034	3.03	0.4988	0.0012	4.00	0.49997	0.00003

The left-hand column in each set of three shows the particular z-value. The centre column shows the area contained between the mean and this z-value. The right-hand column shows the area left in the whole distribution to the right of this z-value. The whole area is one unit and values shown are decimal portions of it. These are also the probabilities of finding a value within the area concerned. For percentages, multiply all area values by 100. For areas between −z and +z, double the values shown.

SOURCE: R. P. Runyon and A. Haber, *Fundamentals of Behavioral Statistics* (1976) 3rd edition. Reading, Mass.: McGraw-Hill, Inc. Used with permission. Artwork from *Fundamental Statistics for Psychology*, (2nd edition) by R. B. McCall © (1975). Reprinted with permission of Brooks/Cole, a division of Thomson Learning: www.thomsonrights.com. Fax 800 730-2215.

Table 3   Critical values of t

Degrees of freedom	Level of significance for a one-tailed test			
	0.05	0.025	0.01	0.005
	Level of significance for a two-tailed test			
	0.10	0.05	0.02	0.01
1	6.314	12.706	31.821	63.657
2	2.920	4.303	6.965	9.925
3	2.353	3.182	4.541	5.841
4	2.132	2.776	3.747	4.604
5	2.015	2.571	3.365	4.032
6	1.943	2.447	3.143	3.707
7	1.895	2.365	2.998	3.499
8	1.860	2.306	2.896	3.355
9	1.833	2.262	2.821	3.250
10	1.812	2.228	2.764	3.169
11	1.796	2.201	2.718	3.106
12	1.782	2.179	2.681	3.055
13	1.771	2.160	2.650	3.012
14	1.761	2.145	2.624	2.977
15	1.753	2.131	2.602	2.947
16	1.746	2.120	2.583	2.921
17	1.740	2.110	2.567	2.898
18	1.734	2.101	2.552	2.878
19	1.729	2.093	2.539	2.861
20	1.725	2.086	2.528	2.845
21	1.721	2.080	2.518	2.831
22	1.717	2.074	2.508	2.819
23	1.714	2.069	2.500	2.807
24	1.711	2.064	2.492	2.797
25	1.708	2.060	2.485	2.787
26	1.706	2.056	2.479	2.779
27	1.703	2.052	2.473	2.771
28	1.701	2.048	2.467	2.763
29	1.699	2.045	2.462	2.756
30	1.697	2.042	2.457	2.750
40	1.684	2.021	2.423	2.704
60	1.671	2.000	2.390	2.660
120	1.658	1.980	2.358	2.617
∞	1.645	1.960	2.326	2.576

Calculated t must EQUAL or EXCEED the table (critical) value for significance at the level shown.

SOURCE: Abridged from R. A. Fisher and F. Yates (1974) *Statistical Tables for Biological, Agricultural and Medical Research*, 6th ed. Pearson Education Ltd.

Table 4   Critical values of *T* in the Wilcoxon Signed Ranks test

	Levels of significance			
	One-tailed test			
	0.05	0.025	0.01	0.001
	Two-tailed test			
Sample size	0.1	0.05	0.02	0.002
N = 5	*T* ≤ 0			
6	2	0		
7	3	2	0	
8	5	3	1	
9	8	5	3	
10	11	8	5	0
11	13	10	7	1
12	17	13	9	2
13	21	17	12	4
14	25	21	15	6
15	30	25	19	8
16	35	29	23	11
17	41	34	27	14
18	47	40	32	18
19	53	46	37	21
20	60	52	43	26
21	67	58	49	30
22	75	65	55	35
23	83	73	62	40
24	91	81	69	45
25	100	89	76	51
26	110	98	84	58
27	119	107	92	64
28	130	116	101	71
29	141	125	111	78
30	151	137	120	86
31	163	147	130	94
32	175	159	140	103
33	187	170	151	112

Calculated *T* must be EQUAL TO or LESS THAN the table (critical) value for significance at the level shown.

SOURCE: Adapted from R. Meddis (1975) *Statistical Handbook for Non-Statisticians*, McGraw-Hill, London, with the kind permission of the author and publishers.

Table 5a Critical values of U for a one-tailed test at 0.005; two-tailed test at 0.01* (Mann–Whitney)

n_1

n_2	1	2	3	4	5	6	7	8	9	10	11	12	13	14	15	16	17	18	19	20
1	—	—	—	—	—	—	—	—	—	—	—	—	—	—	—	—	—	—	—	—
2	—	—	—	—	—	—	—	—	—	—	—	—	—	—	—	—	—	—	0	0
3	—	—	—	—	—	—	—	—	0	0	0	1	1	1	2	2	2	2	3	3
4	—	—	—	—	—	0	0	1	1	2	2	3	3	4	5	5	6	6	7	8
5	—	—	—	0	0	1	1	2	3	4	5	6	7	7	8	9	10	11	12	13
6	—	—	—	0	1	2	3	4	5	6	7	9	10	11	12	13	15	16	17	18
7	—	—	0	1	3	4	6	7	9	10	12	13	15	16	18	19	21	22	24
8	—	—	—	1	2	4	6	7	9	11	13	15	17	18	20	22	24	26	28	30
9	—	—	0	1	3	5	7	9	11	13	16	18	20	22	24	27	29	31	33	36
10	—	—	0	2	4	6	9	11	13	16	18	21	24	26	29	31	34	37	39	42
11	—	—	0	2	5	7	10	13	16	18	21	24	27	30	33	36	39	42	45	48
12	—	—	1	3	6	9	12	15	18	21	24	27	31	34	37	41	44	47	51	54
13	—	—	1	3	7	10	13	17	20	24	27	31	34	38	42	45	49	53	56	60
14	—	—	1	4	7	11	15	18	22	26	30	34	38	42	46	50	54	58	63	67
15	—	—	2	5	8	12	16	20	24	29	33	37	42	46	51	55	60	64	69	73
16	—	—	2	5	9	13	18	22	27	31	36	41	45	50	55	60	65	70	74	79
17	—	—	2	6	10	15	19	24	29	34	39	44	49	54	60	65	70	75	81	86
18	—	—	2	6	11	16	21	26	31	37	42	47	53	58	64	70	75	81	87	92
19	—	0	3	7	12	17	22	28	33	39	45	51	56	63	69	74	81	87	93	99
20	—	0	3	8	13	18	24	30	36	42	48	54	60	67	73	79	86	92	99	105

* Dashes in the body of the table indicate that no decision is possible at the stated level of significance.

For any n_1 and n_2 the observed value of U is significant at a given level of significance if it is *equal* to or *less* than the critical values shown.

SOURCE: R. P. Runyon and A. Haber (1976) *Fundamentals of Behavioral Statistics*, 3rd edition. Reading, Mass.: McGraw-Hill, Inc. with kind permission of the publisher.

Table 5b   Critical values of U for a one-tailed test at 0.01; two-tailed test at 0.02* (Mann-Whitney)

n_2										n_1										
	1	2	3	4	5	6	7	8	9	10	11	12	13	14	15	16	17	18	19	20
1	—	—	—	—	—	—	—	—	—	—	—	—	—	—	—	—	—	—	—	—
2	—	—	—	—	—	—	—	—	—	—	—	—	0	0	0	0	0	0	1	1
3	—	—	—	—	—	—	0	0	1	1	1	2	2	2	3	3	4	4	4	5
4	—	—	—	—	0	1	1	2	3	3	4	5	5	6	7	7	8	9	9	10
5	—	—	—	0	1	2	3	4	5	6	7	8	9	10	11	12	13	14	15	16
6	—	—	—	1	2	3	4	6	7	8	9	11	12	13	15	16	18	19	20	22
7	—	—	0	1	3	4	6	7	9	11	12	14	16	17	19	21	23	24	26	28
8	—	—	0	2	4	6	7	9	11	13	15	17	20	22	24	26	28	30	32	34
9	—	—	1	3	5	7	9	11	14	16	18	21	23	26	28	31	33	36	38	40
10	—	—	1	3	6	8	11	13	16	19	22	24	27	30	33	36	38	41	44	47
11	—	—	1	4	7	9	12	15	18	22	25	28	31	34	37	41	44	47	50	53
12	—	—	2	5	8	11	14	17	21	24	28	31	35	38	42	46	49	53	56	60
13	—	0	2	5	9	12	16	20	23	27	31	35	39	43	47	51	55	59	63	67
14	—	0	2	6	10	13	17	22	26	30	34	38	43	47	51	56	60	65	69	73
15	—	0	3	7	11	15	19	24	28	33	37	42	47	51	56	61	66	70	75	80
16	—	0	3	7	12	16	21	26	31	36	41	46	51	56	61	66	71	76	82	87
17	—	0	4	8	13	18	23	28	33	38	44	49	55	60	66	71	77	82	88	93
18	—	0	4	9	14	19	24	30	36	41	47	53	59	65	70	76	82	88	94	100
19	—	1	4	9	15	20	26	32	38	44	50	56	63	69	75	82	88	94	101	107
20	—	1	5	10	16	22	28	34	40	47	53	60	67	73	80	87	93	100	107	114

* Dashes in the body of the table indicate that no decision is possible at the stated level of significance.

For any n_1 and n_2 the observed value of U is significant at a given level of significance if it is *equal* to or *less* than the critical values shown.

SOURCE: R. P. Runyon and A. Haber (1976) *Fundamentals of Behavioral Statistics*, 3rd edition. Reading, Mass.: McGraw-Hill, Inc. with kind permission of the publisher.

Table 5c   Critical values of U for a one-tailed test at 0.025; two-tailed test at 0.05* (Mann–Whitney)

n_1

n_2	1	2	3	4	5	6	7	8	9	10	11	12	13	14	15	16	17	18	19	20
1	—	—	—	—	—	—	—	—	—	—	—	—	—	—	—	—	—	—	—	—
2	—	—	—	—	—	—	—	0	0	0	0	1	1	1	1	1	2	2	2	2
3	—	—	—	—	0	1	1	2	2	3	3	4	4	5	5	6	6	7	7	8
4	—	—	—	0	1	2	3	4	4	5	6	7	8	9	10	11	11	12	13	13
5	—	—	0	1	2	3	5	6	7	8	9	11	12	13	14	15	17	18	19	20
6	—	—	1	2	3	5	6	8	10	11	13	14	16	17	19	21	22	24	25	27
7	—	—	1	3	5	6	8	10	12	14	16	18	20	22	24	26	28	30	32	34
8	—	0	2	4	6	8	10	13	15	17	19	22	24	26	29	31	34	36	38	41
9	—	0	2	4	7	10	12	15	17	20	23	26	28	31	34	37	39	42	45	48
10	—	0	3	5	8	11	14	17	20	23	26	29	33	36	39	42	45	48	52	55
11	—	0	3	6	9	13	16	19	23	26	30	33	37	40	44	47	51	55	58	62
12	—	1	4	7	11	14	18	22	26	29	33	37	41	45	49	53	57	61	65	69
13	—	1	4	8	12	16	20	24	28	33	37	41	45	50	54	59	63	67	72	76
14	—	1	5	9	13	17	22	26	31	36	40	45	50	55	59	64	67	74	78	83
15	—	1	5	10	14	19	24	29	34	39	44	49	54	59	64	70	75	80	85	90
16	—	1	6	11	15	21	26	31	37	42	47	53	59	64	70	75	81	86	92	98
17	—	2	6	11	17	22	28	34	39	45	51	57	63	67	75	81	87	93	99	105
18	—	2	7	12	18	24	30	36	42	48	55	61	67	74	80	86	93	99	106	112
19	—	2	7	13	19	25	32	38	45	52	58	65	72	78	85	92	99	106	113	119
20	—	2	8	13	20	27	34	41	48	55	62	69	76	83	90	98	105	112	119	127

* Dashes in the body of the table indicate that no decision is possible at the stated level of significance.

For any n_1 and n_2 the observed value of U is significant at a given level of significance if it is *equal* to or *less* than the critical values shown.

SOURCE: R. P. Runyon and A. Haber (1976) *Fundamentals of Behavioral Statistics*, 3rd edition. Reading, Mass.: McGraw-Hill, Inc. with kind permission of the publisher.

Table 5d   Critical values of U for a one-tailed test at 0.05; two-tailed test at 0.10* (Mann-Whitney)

n_2 \ n_1	1	2	3	4	5	6	7	8	9	10	11	12	13	14	15	16	17	18	19	20
1	—	—	—	—	—	—	—	—	—	—	—	—	—	—	—	—	—	—	0	0
2	—	—	—	—	0	0	0	1	1	1	1	2	2	2	3	3	3	4	4	4
3	—	—	0	0	1	2	2	3	3	4	5	5	6	7	7	8	9	9	10	11
4	—	—	0	1	2	3	4	5	6	7	8	9	10	11	12	14	15	16	17	18
5	—	0	1	2	4	5	6	8	9	11	12	13	15	16	18	19	20	22	23	25
6	—	0	2	3	5	7	8	10	12	14	16	17	19	21	23	25	26	28	30	32
7	—	0	2	4	6	8	11	13	15	17	19	21	24	26	28	30	33	35	37	39
8	—	1	3	5	8	10	13	15	18	20	23	26	28	31	33	36	39	41	44	47
9	—	1	3	6	9	12	15	18	21	24	27	30	33	36	39	42	45	48	51	54
10	—	1	4	7	11	14	17	20	24	27	31	34	37	41	44	48	51	55	58	62
11	—	1	5	8	12	16	19	23	27	31	34	38	42	46	50	54	57	61	65	69
12	—	2	5	9	13	17	21	26	30	34	38	42	47	51	55	60	64	68	72	77
13	—	2	6	10	15	19	24	28	33	37	42	47	51	56	61	65	70	75	80	84
14	—	2	7	11	16	21	26	31	36	41	46	51	56	61	66	71	77	82	87	92
15	—	3	7	12	18	23	28	33	39	44	50	55	61	66	72	77	83	88	94	100
16	—	3	8	14	19	25	30	36	42	48	54	60	65	71	77	83	89	95	101	107
17	—	3	9	15	20	26	33	39	45	51	57	64	70	77	83	89	96	102	109	115
18	—	4	9	16	22	28	35	41	48	55	61	68	75	82	88	95	102	109	116	123
19	0	4	10	17	23	30	37	44	51	58	65	72	80	87	94	101	109	116	123	130
20	0	4	11	18	25	32	39	47	54	62	69	77	84	92	100	107	115	123	130	138

* Dashes in the body of the table indicate that no decision is possible at the stated level of significance.

For any n_1 and n_2 the observed value of U is significant at a given level of significance if it is *equal* to or *less* than the critical values shown.

SOURCE: R. P. Runyon and A. Haber (1976) *Fundamentals of Behavioral Statistics*, 3rd edition. Reading, Mass.: McGraw-Hill, Inc. with kind permission of the publisher.

Table 6   Critical values of χ^2

	Level of significance for one-tailed test					
	0.10	0.05	0.025	0.01	0.005	0.0005
	Level of significance for two-tailed test					
df	0.20	0.10	0.05	0.02	0.01	0.001
1	1.64	2.71	3.84	5.41	6.64	10.83
2	3.22	4.60	5.99	7.82	9.21	13.82
3	4.64	6.25	7.82	9.84	11.34	16.27
4	5.99	7.78	9.49	11.67	13.28	18.46
5	7.29	9.24	11.07	13.39	15.09	20.52
6	8.56	10.64	12.59	15.03	16.81	22.46
7	9.80	12.02	14.07	16.62	18.48	24.32
8	11.03	13.36	15.51	18.17	20.09	26.12
9	12.24	14.68	16.92	19.68	21.67	27.88
10	13.44	15.99	18.31	21.16	23.21	29.59
11	14.63	17.28	19.68	22.62	24.72	31.26
12	15.81	18.55	21.03	24.05	26.22	32.91
13	16.98	19.81	22.36	25.47	27.69	34.53
14	18.15	21.06	23.68	26.87	29.14	36.12
15	19.31	22.31	25.00	28.26	30.58	37.70
16	20.46	23.54	26.30	29.63	32.00	39.29
17	21.62	24.77	27.59	31.00	33.41	40.75
18	22.76	25.99	28.87	32.35	34.80	42.31
19	23.90	27.20	30.14	33.69	36.19	43.82
20	25.04	28.41	31.41	35.02	37.57	45.32
21	26.17	29.62	32.67	36.34	38.93	46.80
22	27.30	30.81	33.92	37.66	40.29	48.27
23	28.43	32.1	35.17	38.97	41.64	49.73
24	29.55	33.20	36.42	40.27	42.98	51.18
25	30.68	34.38	37.65	41.57	44.31	52.62
26	31.80	35.56	38.88	42.86	45.64	54.05
27	32.91	36.74	40.11	44.14	46.96	55.48
28	34.03	37.92	41.34	45.42	48.28	56.89
29	35.14	39.09	42.69	49.69	49.59	58.30
30	36.25	40.26	43.77	47.96	50.89	59.70
32	38.47	42.59	46.19	50.49	53.49	62.49
34	40.68	44.90	48.60	53.00	56.06	65.25
36	42.88	47.21	51.00	55.49	58.62	67.99
38	45.08	49.51	53.38	57.97	61.16	70.70
40	47.27	51.81	55.76	60.44	63.69	73.40
44	51.64	56.37	60.48	65.34	68.71	78.75
48	55.99	60.91	65.17	70.20	73.68	84.04
52	60.33	65.42	69.83	75.02	78.62	89.27
56	64.66	69.92	74.47	79.82	83.51	94.46
60	68.97	74.40	79.08	84.58	88.38	99.61

Calculated value of χ^2 must be EQUAL TO or EXCEED the table (critical) values for significance at the level shown.

Abridged from R. A. Fisher and F. Yates (1974) *Statistical Tables for Biological, Agricultural and Medical Research*, 6th edition. Pearson Education Ltd.

Table 7   Critical values in the Binomial Sign Test

N	Level of significance for one-tailed test				
	0.05	0.025	0.01	0.005	0.0005
	Level of significance for two-tailed test				
	0.10	0.05	0.02	0.01	0.001
5	0	—	—	—	—
6	0	0	—	—	—
7	0	0	0	—	—
8	1	0	0	0	—
9	1	1	0	0	—
10	1	1	0	0	—
11	2	1	1	0	0
12	2	2	1	1	0
13	3	2	1	1	0
14	3	2	2	1	0
15	3	3	2	2	1
16	4	3	2	2	1
17	4	4	3	2	1
18	5	4	3	3	1
19	5	4	4	3	2
20	5	5	4	3	2
25	7	7	6	5	4
30	10	9	8	7	5
35	12	11	10	9	7

Calculated S must be EQUAL TO or LESS THAN the table (critical) value for significance at the level shown.

SOURCE: F. Clegg, *Simple Statistics*, Cambridge University Press (1982). With the kind permission of the author and publishers.

Table 8   Critical values of Pearson's *r*

df (N − 2)	Level of significance for a one-tailed test			
	0.05	0.025	0.005	0.0005
	Level of significance for a two-tailed test			
	0.10	0.05	0.01	0.001
2	0.9000	0.9500	0.9900	0.9999
3	0.805	0.878	0.9587	0.9911
4	0.729	0.811	0.9172	0.9741
5	0.669	0.754	0.875	0.9509
6	0.621	0.707	0.834	0.9241
7	0.582	0.666	0.798	0.898
8	0.549	0.632	0.765	0.872
9	0.521	0.602	0.735	0.847
10	0.497	0.576	0.708	0.823
11	0.476	0.553	0.684	0.801
12	0.575	0.532	0.661	0.780
13	0.441	0.514	0.641	0.760
14	0.426	0.497	0.623	0.742
15	0.412	0.482	0.606	0.725
16	0.400	0.468	0.590	0.708
17	0.389	0.456	0.575	0.693
18	0.378	0.444	0.561	0.679
19	0.369	0.433	0.549	0.665
20	0.360	0.423	0.537	0.652
25	0.323	0.381	0.487	0.597
30	0.296	0.349	0.449	0.554
35	0.275	0.325	0.418	0.519
40	0.257	0.304	0.393	0.490
45	0.243	0.288	0.372	0.465
50	0.231	0.273	0.354	0.443
60	0.211	0.250	0.325	0.408
70	0.195	0.232	0.302	0.380
80	0.183	0.217	0.283	0.357
90	0.173	0.205	0.267	0.338
100	0.164	0.195	0.254	0.321

Calculated *r* must EQUAL or EXCEED the table (critical) value for significance at the level shown.

SOURCE: F. C. Powell, *Cambridge Mathematical and Statistical Tables* (1976) Cambridge University Press. With kind permission of the author and publishers.

Table 9 Critical values of Spearman's ρ

	Level of significance for a one-tailed test			
	0.05	0.025	0.01	0.005
	Level of significance for a two-tailed test			
	0.10	0.05	0.02	0.01
$n = 4$	1.000			
5	0.900	1.000	1.000	
6	0.829	0.886	0.943	1.000
7	0.714	0.786	0.893	0.929
8	0.643	0.738	0.833	0.881
9	0.600	0.700	0.783	0.833
10	0.564	0.648	0.745	0.794
11	0.536	0.618	0.709	0.755
12	0.503	0.587	0.671	0.727
13	0.484	0.560	0.648	0.703
14	0.464	0.538	0.622	0.675
15	0.443	0.521	0.604	0.654
16	0.429	0.503	0.582	0.635
17	0.414	0.485	0.566	0.615
18	0.401	0.472	0.550	0.600
19	0.391	0.460	0.535	0.584
20	0.380	0.447	0.520	0.570
21	0.370	0.435	0.508	0.556
22	0.361	0.425	0.496	0.544
23	0.353	0.415	0.486	0.532
24	0.344	0.406	0.476	0.521
25	0.337	0.398	0.466	0.511
26	0.331	0.390	0.457	0.501
27	0.324	0.382	0.448	0.491
28	0.317	0.375	0.440	0.483
29	0.312	0.368	0.433	0.475
30	0.306	0.362	0.425	0.467

For $n > 30$, the significance of ρ can be tested by using the formula:

$$t = \rho\sqrt{\frac{n-2}{1-\rho^2}} \qquad df = n - 2$$

and checking the value of t in Table 3.

Calculated ρ, must EQUAL or EXCEED the table (critical) value for significance at the level shown.

SOURCE: J. H. Zhar, Significance testing of the Spearman Rank Correlation Coefficient, *Journal of the American Statistical Association*, 67, 578–80. Reprinted with permission from the *Journal of the American Statistical Association*. All rights reserved.

Glossary

NOTES

The letters in the right-hand column refer to A Level boards, as follows:

a – AQA Specification A
b – AQA Specification B
e – Edexcel
o – OCR

The terms marked with these letters are either specifically examined or required to be addressed as part of coursework by the boards identified. Some of the OCR terms are embedded into other sections of the syllabuses (e.g. Core Studies). For the other boards the terms identified here appear in research methods assessments. If they appear elsewhere on the syllabus they have not been included (e.g. AQA Specification A examines deception as part of social psychology).

Some terms in the glossary are not specifically mentioned on syllabuses but are implied by broader concepts. For instance, in order to select appropriate statistical tests you must know about levels of measurement, but these are not specified on any syllabus since they are not specifically examined.

GLOSSARY		
Abstract	Summary of hypothesis, design, method, findings and conclusions appearing at the beginning of a practical report or research article	abo
Alternative hypothesis (H_1)	Assumption that an effect exists (e.g. that populations differ)	abe
Anonymity	Keeping participant's or client's identity away from publication or any possible inadvertent disclosure	
Bar chart	Chart in which (usually) the horizontal axis represents a categorical variable and the Y axis can represent frequency, average, percentage etc.	abe

GLOSSARY

Between groups	See 'independent groups'	
Biased sample	Sample in which members of a sub-group of the target population are over- or under-represented	
Calculated value	See 'test statistic'	e
Case study	Study gathering data on one individual or group in depth	beo
Census	Survey of whole population	
Central tendency	Formal term for any measure of the typical/middle value in a dataset	abeo
Chi-square test	Test of association between two categorical variables using unrelated data at a nominal level	beo*
Class interval	Division of a scale on a histogram; category or interval for which frequencies are counted and displayed	
Closed questions/items	Items in a psychological scale that can be responded to only from a fixed set, e.g. 'yes'/'no'	b
Coding system	System for quantifying observations by giving a number to similar observed instances of behaviour	o
Coding (unit)	Item categories identified in qualitative data using content analysis	o
Cohort	Large sample of people, often children of the same age, identified for longitudinal or cross-sectional study	
Conclusion	Inference made from *findings* in a study as to what can be tentatively assumed about the effects they appear to demonstrate	
Concurrent validity	Extent to which test results conform with those on some other valid measure, taken at the same time	
Confidentiality	Keeping data concerning participants or clients away from publication	e
Confounding variable	Variable that is uncontrolled and obscures any effect sought, usually in a systematic manner. Often, a variable responsible for changes in the DV that is not the intended IV	abo
Construct validity	Extent to which test results support a network of research hypotheses based on the assumed characteristics of a theoretical psychological variable	
Content analysis	Search of qualitative materials (especially text) to find 'coding units' (usually words, phrases or themes). Analysis often concentrates on quantitative treatment of frequencies but can be a purely qualitative approach	eo
Content validity	Extent to which test covers the whole of the relevant topic area, as assessed by experts	

GLOSSARY

Control condition/ group	Group or condition used as baseline measure against which performance of experimental group is assessed	
Convenience sample	Sample selected because they are easily available for testing	
Correlation	A measure of the relationship between two variables	abe
Correlation coefficient	Number signifying strength of correlation between two variables	a
Correlational study/ design	Study of the extent to which one variable is related to another, often referring to non-manipulated variables measured outside the laboratory	abe
Counterbalancing	Half of the participants do conditions in a particular order and the other half in the opposite order – this is done to balance possible order effects in a repeated measures design	be
Criterion validity	Extent to which test scores can be used to make a specific prediction on some other variable	
Critical value	Value that a test statistic must reach in order for the null hypothesis to be rejected (e.g. t must be ≥ 2.086, $df - 20$, $p \leq 0.05$, two tailed)	e
Cross-cultural study	Comparative study of two or more different societies or social/ethnic sub-groups	
Cross-sectional study	Comparative study of several sub-groups captured for measurement at a single time	
Cross tabs table	Term for table of frequencies on levels of a variable by levels of a second variable	
Cumulative frequency	Distribution (table or chart) that shows the number of cases that have occurred up to and including the current category	
Curvilinear relationship	Correlation between two variables with low r value because the relationship does not fit a straight line but a good curve	
Dataset	A collection of values that have been gathered in an investigation	
Debriefing	Informing participants of the full nature of the study, after participation, and attempting to reverse any negative influence	e
Deception	Leading participant to believe that something other than the true independent variable is involved or withholding information such that the reality of the investigative situation is masked or distorted	e
Demand characteristics	Cues in a study that help the participant to work out what is expected of him/her	a
Dependent variable	Variable that is assumed to be directly affected by changes in the independent variable in an experiment	abe
Descriptive statistics	Methods for numerical summary of dataset	ae

GLOSSARY

Deviation score	Distance of a value from the mean of the set	
Directional hypothesis	Hypothesis that makes a claim about the *direction* of difference in the population	ae
Discourse analysis	Qualitative analysis of interactive speech that assumes people use language to construct the world as they see it, and according to context and interests. Talk is not evidence of internal psychological processes	
Discrete data	Data that can only come in separate units (e.g. number of children)	
Dispersion	Measure of degree to which values in a set spread out around the average value	abo
Distribution-dependent tests	More formally correct term for '*parametric tests*' – see entry	
Double blind	Experimental procedure where neither participants nor data gatherers know which treatment participants have received	
Ecological validity	Extent to which research effect can be generalized to other places and conditions, in particular from the artificial and/or controlled (e.g. laboratory) to the natural environment	o
Empirical	Based on observation of data or 'facts' in the real world	
Enlightenment	Growing awareness of psychology students that research studies often involve deception and other researcher 'tricks'	
Ethics	Principles of courtesy and professional responsibility towards research participants, publication and clients in applied psychology	abeo
Evaluation apprehension	Participants' concern about being tested, which may affect results	
Event sampling	Making observations of specific events as they occur, defined for the particular study	
Expected frequencies	Frequencies expected in table if no association exists between variables – i.e. if null hypothesis is true	
Experiment	Study in which an independent variable is manipulated, a dependent variable is measured and other variables are held constant	abeo
Experimental condition/ group	Group or condition which receives one of the 'treatments' that are levels of the independent variable; not the control group or condition	
Experimental hypothesis	See 'alternative hypothesis'	abe
Experimental realism	Effect of attention-grabbing, interesting experiment in compensating for artificiality or 'demand characteristics'	
Experimenter	Person who administers experimental procedures to participants and who collects data	

GLOSSARY

Experimenter expectancy	Tendency for experimenter's knowledge of what is being tested to influence the outcome of research	
Experimenter reliability	The extent to which the results produced by two or more experimenters are related	
External reliability	Stability of a test; its tendency to produce the same results when repeated on the same people	
External validity	Extent to which results of research can be generalized across people, places and times	a
Extraneous variable	Anything other than the IV that could affect the dependent variable; it may or may not have been allowed for and/or controlled	ab
Face validity	Extent to which the validity of a test is self-evident	
Field study/experiment	Research study/experiment where data are gathered outside the research centre where participants would normally be	abe
Findings	The summary and analysis of data gathered in a study *without* further speculation as to what can be *concluded* from them	abeo
Fit	Coherent route back from interpretations to original qualitative data	
5% level ($p \leq 0.05$)	Conventional significance level	b
Focus groups	Group asked to convene and discuss specific issue or topic	
Frequency	Count of occurences of a phenomenon or event	
Frequency distribution	Distribution of frequencies in categories	
Generalizability	Aim of being able to generalize findings from samples to entire populations from which samples were drawn	eo
Goodness-of-fit test	Test of whether a distribution of frequencies differs significantly from a theoretical pattern	
Grounded theory	Theory driving the analysis of qualitative data in which patterns emerge from the data and are not imposed on them before they are gathered	
Group-difference study	A *post-facto* study that compares the measurement of an existing variable in two contrasting groups: for example, introvert/extrovert	
Harvard system	A common system of academic referencing	
Hawthorne effect	Effect on human performance caused solely by the knowledge that one is being observed	
Histogram	Chart containing whole of continuous dataset divided into proportional class intervals	ab
Historical validity	Extent to which research effect can be generalized across different periods of time	

GLOSSARY

Homogeneity of variance	Situation where sample variances are similar. A required assumption about data for using a parametric test	
Hypothesis	Precise statement of assumed relationship between variables that is developed from a theory so that the relationship can be specifically tested	abeo
Hypothetico-deductive method	Method of recording observations, developing explanatory theories and testing hypotheses from those theories	
Independent groups/ samples/measures	Experimental design in which each condition of the independent variable is experienced by only one group of participants	abe
Independent variable	Variable that experimenter manipulates in an experiment and that is assumed to have a direct effect on the dependent variable	abe
Inferential statistics	Procedures (significance tests) for making inferences about whole populations from which samples investigated have been drawn	ab
Inferential test	Statistical test that helps us infer the existence of an effect in the population from the statistics of just our sample	ab
Informed consent	Agreement to participate in research in the full knowledge of the research context (but not all detail) and participant rights	e
Internal reliability	A measure of scale reliability using the variance of respondents' scores on each item in relation to overall variance on the scale	
Internal validity	Extent to which effect found in a study can be taken to be real and caused by manipulation of the identified independent variable	a
Inter-observer reliability	See inter-rater reliability	
Interpretive phenomenological analysis	Approach that attempts to describe an individual's experiences from their own perspective as closely as possible but recognizes the interpretive influence of the researcher on the research product	
Inter-rater reliability	Extent to which observers agree in their rating or coding	
Interval level	Level at which each unit on a scale represents an equal change in the variable measured	e
Intervention	Research that makes some alteration to people's lives beyond the specific research setting, usually to create human benefit	
Interview method	Use of interviews, usually one-to-one, to gather data	abe
Investigator	Person with overall responsibility for a research project	
Investigator effect	Any undesired effect on results emanating from the investigator (behaviour or expectancy)	a
Involuntary participation	Taking part in research without agreement or with no knowledge of the study	
Item analysis	Method for assessing consistency of a test within itself	

GLOSSARY

Journal	Regular publication that carries articles that report new findings in research. The basis of almost all advances in a scientific discipline including psychology	
Laboratory study/ experiment	Study/experiment carried out in the researcher's own specialist premises	abo
Level of measurement	Levels at which data are categorized or measured	b
Level (of the IV)	One of the conditions or groups that, along with other conditions or groups, make up the independent variable	
Likert scale	Scale using responses to statements on a scale, often from 'strongly disagree' to 'strongly agree'	
Longitudinal study	Comparative study of one individual or group over a relatively long period (possibly including a control group)	o
Mann-Whitney *U* test	Ordinal-level difference test for two sets of unrelated data	beo˙
Matched pairs	Experimental design in which each participant in one group/ condition is paired on specific variable(s) with a participant in another group/condition	abe
Mean	Measure of central tendency found by adding all scores and dividing by the number of scores there are in the set	abe
Mean deviation	Measure of dispersion – mean of all absolute deviations	
Median	Central value in a dataset	abe
Mode	Most common value in a dataset	abe
Mundane realism	Feature of design where experiment resembles everyday life but is not necessarily engaging	
Natural experiment	Experiment that exploits the occurrence of a naturally occurring independent variable	ae
Naturalistic observation	Observational design conducted on naturally occurring behaviour in the natural habitat for those observed	a
Negative-case analysis	Process of seeking contradictions to emergent categories or theory in order to adjust category system to incorporate more of the data; method used in grounded theory	
Negative correlation	Correlation where, as values of one variable increase, related values of another variable tend to decrease	ab
Negative skew	Description of distribution that contains a longer tail of lower values	
Nominal level	Level of measurement where data are frequencies of occurrences in categories. Numbers, if used, are only labels for categories	e
Non-directional hypothesis	Hypothesis that makes no claim about the *direction* of difference in the population	a

GLOSSARY

Non-equivalent groups	Problem found in independent-samples design that participants in each condition may not be equivalent and this could confound results. The problem of participant variables	
Non-parametric test	Significance test that does not make estimations of parameters in an underlying distribution	b
Normal distribution	Continuous distribution, bell-shaped, symmetrical about its mid-point	eo
Null hypothesis (H_0)	Assumption of no effect in the populations from which samples are drawn (e.g. no mean population difference)	abeo
Observational design	Research design where observation is the data-gathering technique and behaviour observed is relatively unconstrained	beo
Observational study	Research that gathers data by watching and recording behaviour	beo
Observational technique	Use of observation and coding (often in constrained, structured setting)	e
Observed frequencies	Frequencies obtained in a research study using categorical variables	
Observer bias	Threat to validity of observational recordings caused solely by characteristics of the observer	
Obtained (or 'calculated') value	See *test statistic*	e
One-tailed test	Test that can be used if alternative hypothesis is directional (but only when a result in the opposite direction would be ignored even if found significant)	be
Open questions/items	Items in a psychological scale that can be responded to with free and unconstrained human speech	b
Operational definition	Definition of variable in terms of the exact steps taken in measurement of the variable	abeo
Opportunity sample	Sample selected because they are easily available for testing	abe
Order effect	A confounding effect (such as practice, learning or fatigue) caused by experiencing one condition, then another	a
Ordinal level	Level at which data (scores) are arranged in rank positions	e
Panel	Stratified group who are consulted in order that opinion can be assessed	
Parameter	Statistical measure of a population (e.g. mean)	
Parametric test	Relatively powerful significance test that makes estimations of population parameters; the data tested should therefore satisfy certain assumptions; also known as '*distribution-dependent tests*'	b
Participant	Person who participates in a research investigation	abeo

GLOSSARY

Participant expectancy	Effect on study of participants' expectancy about what they think is supposed to happen	
Participant observation	Observation in which observer takes part or plays a role in the group observed	b
Participant variable	Person variables differing in proportion across different experimental groups and possibly confounding results	e
Participant verification	Agreement of participants with qualitative researcher's final interpretations	
Pearson product-moment correlation	Parametric measure of correlation	be
Pilot study/Pilot trials/ Piloting	Preliminary study or trials often carried out to predict snags and assess features of a main study to follow. Piloting is trying out the scale or research design on a small sample	ab
Placebo	Treatment given to participant that appears authentic but lacks vital aspect, e.g., de-caffeinated drink instead of caffeine; used to detect psychological effects of IV treatment alone	
Plagiarism	Presenting work as one's own which in fact is that of someone else	
Pleasing the experimenter	Tendency of participants to act in accordance with what they think the experimenter would like	
Point sampling	Making observations at set time points: for example, at end of each 30-second interval	
Population	All possible members of the group from which a sample is drawn	bo
Population validity	Extent to which research effect can be generalized to rest of population or other populations	
Positive correlation	Correlation where, as values of one variable increase, related values of another variable also tend to increase	ab
Positive skew	Description of distribution that contains a longer tail of higher values	
Positivism	Methodological belief that phenomena are reducible to observable facts and can be measured. If measurement is impossible then the concept cannot be part of science	
Post-facto study	Research where pre-existing variables among people are measured for difference or correlation	
Predictive validity	Extent to which test scores can predict scores on future behaviour or attitude	
Pre-testing	Measure of participants before an experiment in order to balance or compare groups	
Probability	A numerical measure of pure 'chance' (randomly-based) occurrence of events	bo

GLOSSARY

Primary reference	Source that the author has actually read – see 'secondary reference'	
Projective tests	Tests based on psychoanalytic theory that attempt to obtain responses guided by unconscious desires and conflicts	
Psychological construct	Phenomenon assumed to exist, and which can explain observed behaviour	
Psychological scale	Paper-and-pencil instrument designed to measure one or more psychological constructs	
Psychometric test	Test that attempts to quantify psychological variables: skills, abilities, character etc.	o
Psychometrics	The construction of *psychometric tests*	
Qualitative data	Data left in original form of meaning (e.g. speech, text) and not *quantified*	abeo
Qualitative research	Research approach gathering mainly qualitative data	
Quantify	To make a numerical measurement of a phenomenon	
Quantitative data	Data in numerical form, the results of measurement	beo
Quasi-experiment	Experiment in which experimenter does not have complete control over all central variables	
Quasi-interval scale	Scale that appears to be interval but where equal intervals do not necessarily measure equal amounts of the construct	
Questionnaire	Questioning instrument using questions. In fact, most psychological scale measures do not ask questions but present statements to be agreed with or not to a certain degree	abe
Quota sample	Sample where specified groups will appear in numbers proportional to their size in the target population but not randomly selected	e
Random allocation	To put people into different conditions of an experiment on a random basis	
(simple) Random sample	Sample selected in which every member of the target population has an equal chance of being selected and all possible combinations can be drawn	abe
Randomization	To put various trials of an experiment, or stimuli, into an unbiased sequence, where prediction is impossible	
Range	Measure of dispersion – top to bottom value	abe
Rater	Someone who assesses interview or other content according to a standardised scale	
Ratio level	Interval-level scale where proportions on the scale are meaningful because an absolute zero exists	e

GLOSSARY

Rationale	Argument in the introduction to a practical report that justifies why the research is being carried out, based on the preceding review of previous research	
Raw data	Unprocessed data as gathered in a study: for example, the original participants' scores	
Reactivity	Participants' awareness of being studied, which might cause them to alter behaviour accordingly	
Reflexivity	Researcher's recognition that their own knowledge, experience and attitudes will affect how they analyse, construct and present findings. Feature of qualitative research	
Related design	Designs in which individual scores in one condition can be paired with individual scores in other conditions, e.g. repeated measures and matched pairs	
Related t test	Parametric difference test for related data at interval level	be
Reliability	Consistency of a measure or an effect	abeo
Repeated measures	Each participant takes part in all levels of the independent variable	abe
Replication	Repeating a completed study	abe
Research design	Data-gathering structure and strategy of a piece of research	abeo
Research prediction	Prediction in precise terms about how variables will be related in the analysis of data in an investigation	
Research question	The question that a researcher is trying to answer in an investigation	
Respondent	Person who responds to a psychological scale, questionnaire or survey	
Response set	Tendency for people to agree with test items as a habitual response	
Right to withdraw	Participants' right to withdraw themselves, and data gathered on them, from an experiment	
Sample	Group selected from population for an investigation	abeo
Sampling bias	Systematic tendency towards over- or under-representation of some categories in a sample	
Sampling error	Error made in assuming that population parameters are the same as sample statistics	
Saturation	Point (especially in grounded theory) where additional data make only trivial contributions and cannot alter the emerged framework of categories and themes	
Scattergraph/ scattergram	Diagram showing placement of paired values on a two-dimensional chart	abe

GLOSSARY

Scientific method	General method of investigation of the empirical world using induction and deduction	
Secondary reference	Work to which writer referred but did not read. Instead they read about it in another publication. For example, the writer refers to Smith (1999), which they read about in Bolton (2001). Bolton is the primary reference and Smith is the secondary	
Selection bias	See 'sampling bias'	
Self-selecting sample	Sampling selected for study on the basis of members' own action in arriving at the sampling point	
Semantic differential	Scale measuring meaning of an object for the respondent by having them place it between the extremes of several bi-polar adjectives	
Semi-structured interview	Interview with pre-set list of topics but in which 'natural' conversation is attempted and the interviewer 'plays it by ear' as to whether sufficient information has been provided by the interviewee	
(binomial) Sign test	Test of related differences at a categorical/nominal level of data	be
Significance	Decision as to whether the null hypothesis should be retained or rejected based on calculation of probability of occurrence under H_0	abeo
Significance level	Level of probability at which it is agreed to reject H_0. If the probability of obtained results under H_0 is less than the set level, H_0 is rejected	abe
Significance test	See *inferential test*	ae
Significant difference	Difference that is unlikely to occur if the null hypothesis is true	e
Single blind	Procedure in an experiment where participants do not know which treatment they received (i.e. which condition they were in)	
Skewed distribution	Distribution in which a lot more values lie towards one end than the other	
Snowball sample	Sample obtained by using information from key figures who participate earlier in the study	
Social desirability	Tendency of research participants to want to 'look good' and provide socially acceptable answers	
Spearman's rho (ρ) correlation	Non-parametric measure of correlation	beo*
Split-half	Correlation between scores on two equal parts of a test	
Standard deviation	Measure of dispersion – the square root of the sum of all squared deviations divided by $N-1$	abe
Standard score (z score)	Number of standard deviations a particular score is from its sample mean	

GLOSSARY

Standardization	Setting up of measurement norms for the population for whom a psychometric test is intended	
Standardized instructions/procedures	Testing or measuring behaviour with exactly the same formalized routine and instructions for all participants	o
Statistic	Statistical measure of a sample (e.g. mean)	abeo
Stratified sample	Sample selected so that specified groups will appear in numbers proportional to their size in the target population; within each sub-group cases are randomly selected	b
Structured interview	Interview in which there is little variation possible in order or content of questions posed	b
Structured/systematic observation	Observation that uses an explicitly-defined coding system for data recording	
Survey	Relatively structured questioning of large sample	o
Systematic sample	Sample selected by taking every nth case from a list of the target population; 'random' if starting point for n is selected at random	be
Test statistic	The value found for the statistic in an inferential test (e.g. $t = 6.54$)	
Thematic analysis	Use of qualitative data to test hypotheses; in this approach, theory still drives analysis but examples of meaning rather than quantitative data are used as support	
Theory	General model of how events are related to one another in the real world. A speculation about what causes what	
Threats to validity	Any aspect of the design or method of a study that weakens the likelihood that a real effect has been demonstrated or that might obscure the existence of a real effect	
Time sampling	Making observations for set lengths of time at set intervals	
Treatment	The levels of the IV that are expected to affect behaviour beyond what is caused by the control condition. The variables we are investigating to see if they have any effect on behaviour	
Triangulation	Comparison of at least two views/explanations of the same thing(s) – events, behaviour, actions etc.	
Two-tailed test	Test that must be used if alternative hypothesis is non-directional	be
Type I error	Mistake made in rejecting the null hypothesis when it is true	b
Type II error	Mistake made in retaining the null hypothesis when it is false	b
Unrelated design	Design in which individual scores in one condition cannot be paired (or linked) in any way with individual scores in any other condition	
Unrelated t test	Parametric difference test for unrelated data at interval level	be

GLOSSARY

Validity	Extent to which a test measures what was intended	abeo
Variable	Phenomenon that varies and can be given specific quantitative or categorical values	abeo
Variance	Measure of dispersion – square of standard deviation	e
Vignette	Text given to participant in research study that describes a scenario. Very often just one feature of the vignette is varied and this serves as the independent variable	
Visual analogue scale	Scale where respondents mark their position graphically along a dimension from one extreme to the other	
Volunteer sample	Sample comprising volunteers for the investigation	ae
Wilcoxon Matched Pairs test	Ordinal-level difference test for two related sets of data	beo*
Withdraw (right to)	Participant's right to withdraw from any psychological study at any time	e
Within groups	See 'repeated measures'	
3 Score	See 'standard score'	

*The AQA Specification A and OCR do not require that all these tests are available to be examined but do require that at least one inferential test is used as part of coursework and these are the recommended tests to select from. AQA-A requires one test and OCR requires two.

References

The numbers in **bold** denote the text pages on which an article or book is cited.

Abrahamsson, K.H., Berggren U., Hallberg-Lillemor, R.M. & Carlsson, S.G. (2002) Ambivalence in coping with dental fear and avoidance: a qualitative study. *Journal of Health Psychology*, 7, 6, 653–64. **95**

Ainsworth, M.D.S., Bell, S.M. & Stayton, D.J. (1971) Individual differences in strange situation behaviour of one-year-olds. In H.R. Schaffer (ed.) (1971) *The Origins of Human Social Relations*. London: Academic Press. **96**

Anderson, C. (1987) Temperature and aggression: effects on quarterly, yearly, and city rates of violent and non-violent crime. *Journal of Personality and Social Psychology*, 52, 6, 1161–73. **35**

Archer, J. (2000) Sex differences in aggression between heterosexual partners: a meta-analytic review. *Psychological Bulletin*, 126, 651–80. **11**

Argyle, M. (1994) *The Psychology of Social Class*. London: Routledge. **185**

Asch, S.E. (1956) Studies of independences and submission to group pressure. 1. A minority of one against a unanimous majority. *Psychological Monographs*, 70(9) (Whole No. 416). **96**

Awosunle, S. & Doyle, C. (2001) Same-race bias in the selection interview. *Selection Development Review*, 17, 3, 3–6. **86**

Baker, L., Wagner, T.H. & Singer, S. (2003) Use of the Internet and e-mail for health care information: results from a national survey. *Journal of the American Medical Association*, 289, 18, 2400–406. **89**

Bandura, A. (1965) Influence of models' reinforcement contingencies on the acquisition of imitative responses. *Journal of Personality and Social Psychology*, 1, 589–95. **46, 62**

Banyard, P. & Hunt, N. (2000) Reporting research: something missing? *The Psychologist*, 13, 2, 68–71. **6, 26**

Barber, T.X. (1976) *Pitfalls in Human Research*. Oxford: Pergamon. **51**

Benedict, R. (1934) *Patterns of Culture*. Boston: Houghton Mifflin. **59**

Berry, J.W., Poortinga, Y.H., Segall, M.H. & Dasen, P.R. (2002) *Cross-Cultural Psychology: Research and Applications* (2nd edition). Cambridge: Cambridge University Press. **60**

Bradley, D.R. (1991) Anatomy of a DATASIM simulation: the Doob and Gross horn-honking study. *Behavior Research Methods, Instruments and Computers*, 23, 2, 190–207. **204**

Bramel, D.A. (1962) A dissonance theory approach to defensive projection. *Journal of Abnormal and Social Psychology*, 64, 121–9. **200**

British Psychology Society (2000) *Code of conduct, ethical principles and guidelines.* Leicester: British Psychology Society. **196, 197–198, 202, 203, 205**

Brody, G.H., Stoneman, Z. & Wheatley, P. (1984) Peer interaction in the presence and absence of observers. *Child Development*, 55, 1425–28. **66**

Brown, R. (1988) *Group Processes: Dynamics Within and Between Groups.* Oxford: Blackwell. **46**

Carlsmith, J., Elsworth, P. & Aronson, E. (1976) *Methods of Research in Social Psychology.* Reading, Mass.: Addison-Wesley. **48, 50**

Charlesworth, R. & Hartup, W.W. (1967) Positive social reinforcement in the nursery school peer group. *Child Development*, 38, 993–1002. **66, 67**

Cialdini, R.B., Reno, R.R. & Kallgren, C.A. (1990) A focus theory of normative conduct: recycling the concept of norms to reduce litter in public places. *Journal of Personality and Social Psychology*, 58, 1015–20. **54**

Cook, T.D. & Campbell, T.T. (1979) *Quasi-experimentation: Design and Analysis Issues for Field Settings.* Chicago: Rand McNally. **47, 55**

Coolican, H. (2004) *Research Methods and Statistics in Psychology, 4th edition.* London: Hodder Arnold. **55, 87, 95, 119, 147, 176, 188, 197**

Cumberbatch, G. (1990) *Television Advertising and Sex Role Stereotyping: A Content Analysis* (working paper IV for the Broadcasting Standards Council). Communications Research Group, Aston University. **99**

Darley, J.M. & Latané, B. (1968) Bystander intervention in emergencies: diffusion of responsibility. *Journal of Personality and Social Psychology*, 8, 377–83. **10, 16**

David, S.S.J., Chapman, A.J., Foot, H.C. & Sheehy, N.P. (1986) Peripheral vision and child pedestrian accidents. *British Journal of Psychology*, vol. 77, 4. **125**

Doob, A.N. & Gross, A.E. (1968) Status of frustration as an inhibitor of horn-honking responses. *Journal of Social Psychology*, 76, 213–8. **204**

Durrant, J.E. (2000) Trends in youth crime and well-being since the abolition of corporal punishment in Sweden. *Youth and Society*, 31, 4, 437–55. **191**

Earley, P.C. (1989) Social loafing and collectivism: a comparison of the United States and the People's Republic of China. *Administrative Science Quarterly*, 34, 565–81. **46**

Edwards, D. & Potter, J. (1992) *Discursive psychology.* London: Sage. **97**

Ekéus, C., Christensson, K. & Hjern, A. (2004) Unintentional and violent injuries among pre-school children of teenage mothers in Sweden: a national cohort study. *Journal of Epidemiology and Community Health*, 58, 8, 680–85. **58**

Elliott, R., Fischer, C. & Rennie, D. (1999) Evolving guidelines for publication of qualitative research studies in psychology and related fields. *British Journal of Clinical Psychology*, 38, 215–29. **95**

Eron, L.D., Huesmann, L.R. & Lefkowitz, M.M. & Walder, L.D. (1972) Does television violence cause aggression? *American Psychologist*, 27, 4, 253–63. **58**

Felmet, M.B. (1998) The effects of karate training on the levels of attention and impulsivity of children with attention deficit/hyperactivity disorder. *Dissertation Abstracts International Section A: Humanities and Social Sciences*, 59, (4-A), 1077. **42**

Gittelsohn, J., Shankar, A.V., West, K.P., Ram, R.M. & Gnywali, T. (1997) Estimating reactivity in direct observation studies of health behaviours. *Human Organization*, 56, 2, 182–89. **66**

Giles, D. (2002) *Advanced Research Methods in Psychology.* Hove: Routledge. **95**

Glaser, B.G. (1992) *Emergence vs Forcing: Basics of Grounded Theory Analysis.* Mill Valley CA: Sociology Press. **97**

Glaser, B.G. & Strauss, A.L. (1967) *The Discovery of Grounded Theory: Strategies for Qualitative Research.* Chicago IL: Aldine. **96**

Goldberg, D. (1978) *The General Health Questionnaire.* Windsor: NFER-NELSON. **210, 212**

Goldberg, P. (1968) Are women prejudiced against women? *Transaction,* April 1968. **228**

Gregory, R.L. & Wallace, J.G. (1963) *Recovery from Early Blindness.* Cambridge: Heffer. **100**

Harré, R. (1981) The positivist–empiricist approach and its alternative. In R. Reason & J. Rowan (1981) *Human Enquiry: A Sourcebook of New Paradigm Research.* Chichester: Wiley. **93**

Hayes, N. (1997) *Doing Qualitative Analysis in Psychology.* Hove: Psychology Press. **95, 98**

Henwood, K.I. & Pidgeon, N.F. (1992) Qualitative research and psychological theorizing. *British Journal of Psychology,* 83, 97–111. **95**

Hofling, C.K., Brotzman, E., Dalrymple, S., Graves, N. & Pierce, C.M. (1966) An experimental study in nurse–physician relationships. *Journal of Nervous and Mental Disease,* 143, 171–80.

Humphreys, L. (1970) *Tearoom Trade.* Chicago: Aldine. **48**

Jansen, V.A.A., Stollenwerk, N., Jensen, H.J., Ramsay, M.E., Edmunds, W.J. & Rhodes, C.J. (2003) Measles outbreaks in a population with declining vaccine uptake. *Science,* 8, 301, 804. **11**

Johnston, W.M. & Davey, G.C.L. (1997) The psychological impact of negative TV news bulletins: the catastrophizing of personal worries. *British Journal of Psychology,* 88, 85–91. **201**

Jolyon, L. (1962) *Hallucinations.* Oxford: Grune and Stratton. **202**

Jones, F. & Fletcher, C.B. (1992) *Transmission of Occupational Stress: a Study of Daily Fluctuations in Work Stressors and Strains and their Impact on Marital Partners.* VIth European Health Psychology Society Conference (presented as poster), University of Leipzig (August). **94**

Kagan, J., Kearsley, R.G. & Zelazo, P.R. (1980) *Infancy – Its Place in Human Development.* Cambridge, Mass.: Harvard University Press. **58**

Kenrick, D.T. & MacFarlane, S.W. (1986) Ambient temperature and horn honking: a field study of the heat/aggression relationship. *Environment and Behavior,* 18, 2, 179–91. **40**

Kimmel, A.J. (1998) In defence of deception. *American Psychologist,* 53, 7, 803–805. **200**

Kinsey, A.C., Pomeroy, W.B., Martin, C.E. & Gebhard, P.H. (1953) *Sexual Behaviour in the Human Female.* Philadelphia: Saunders. **89**

Klein, P.S. (1991) Improving the quality of parental interaction with very low birth weight children: a longitudinal study using a mediated learning experience model. *Infant Mental Health Journal,* 12, 4, 321–37. **204**

Kvavilashvili, L. & Ellis, J. (2004) Ecological validity and real-life/laboratory controversy in memory research: a critical and historical review. *History of Philosophy and Psychology,* 6, 59–80. **48**

Latané, B. & Darley, J.M. (1976) *Help in a Crisis: Bystander Response to an Emergency.* Morristown, NJ: General Learning Press. **200, 202**

Lawn, S.J. (2004) Systemic barriers to quitting smoking among institutionalised public mental health service populations: a comparison of two Australian sites. *International Journal of Social Psychiatry,* 50, 3, 204–15. **67, 95**

Leyens, J., Camino, L., Parke, R.D. & Berkowitz, L. (1975) Effects of movie violence on aggression in a field setting as a function of group dominance and cohesion. *Journal of Personality and Social Psychology,* 32, 346–60. **204**

Likert, R.A. (1932) A technique for the measurement of attitudes. *Archives of Psychology,* 140, 55. **76–77, 273**

Luria, A.R. (1969) *The Mind of a Mnemonist.* London: Jonathan Cape. **100**

Maguire, E.A., Spiers, H.J. & Good, C.D. (2003) Navigation expertise and the human hippocampus: a structural brain imaging analysis. *Hippocampus,* 13, 2, 250–59. **3**

McKillip, J. & Posavac, E.J. (1975) Judgments of responsibility for an accident. *Journal of Personality,* 43, 2, 248–65. **211**

Mead, G.H. (1934) *Mind, Self, and Society.* Chicago IL: University of Chicago Press. **93**

Milgram, S. (1963) Behavioural study of obedience. *Journal of Abnormal and Social Psychology*, 63, 371–8. **198–203**

Milgram, S. (1974) *Obedience to Authority*. New York: Harper and Row. **48, 96**

Neisser, U. (1978) Memory: what are the important questions? In M.M. Gruneberg, P.E. Morris & R.N. Sykes (eds.) (1988) *Practical Aspects of Memory*. London: Academic Press. **46**

Oliver, P. (2003) *The Student's Guide to Research Ethics*. Maidenhead: Open University. **206**

Ora, J.P. (1965) Characteristics of the volunteer for psychological investigations. Office of Naval Research Contract 2149(03), Technical Report 27. **31**

Orne, M.T. (1962) On the social psychology of the psychological experiment: with particular reference to demand characteristics and their implications. *American Psychologist*, 17, 776–83. **50**

Ortmann, A. & Hertwig, R. (1997) Is deception acceptable? *American Psychologist*, 52, 7, 746–47. **200**

Ortmann, A. & Hertwig, R. (1998) The question remains: is deception acceptable? *American Psychologist*, 53, 7, 806–807. **201**

Osgood, C.E., Suci, G.J. & Tannenbaum, P.H. (1957) *The Measurement of Meaning*. Urbana: University of Illinois. **77**

Penfield, W. & Rasmussen, T. (1950) *The Cerebral Cortex of Man: a Clinical Study of Localization of Function*. New York: Hafner. **92**

Perner, J., Leekam, S.R. & Wimmer, H. (1987) Three-year-olds' difficulty with false belief: the case for a conceptual deficit. *British Journal of Developmental Psychology*, 5, 2, 125–37. **58**

Piaget, J. (1936) *The Origins of Intelligence in the Child*. London: Routledge. **87**

Pichert, J.W. & Anderson, R.C. (1977) Taking different perspectives on a story. *Journal of Educational Psychology*, 69, 4, 309–15. **212**

Piliavin, I.M., Rodin, J. & Piliavin, J.A. (1969) Good Samaritanism: an underground phenomenon? *Journal of Personality and Social Psychology*, 13, 289–99. **204**

Pulkki-Raback, L., Elovainio, M., Kivimaki, M., Raitakari, O. & Keltikangas-Jarvinen, L. (2005) Temperament in childhood predicts body mass in adulthood: the cardiovascular risk in young Finns study. *Health Psychology*, 24, 3, 307–15. **88**

Rank, S. & Jacobson, C. (1977) Hospital nurses' compliance with medication overdose orders: a failure to replicate. *Journal of Health and Social Behaviour*, 18, 188–93. **48**

Reason, P. & Rowan, J. (1981) (eds.) *Human Enquiry: A Sourcebook in New Paradigm Research*. Chichester: Wiley. **201, 206**

Reyner, L.A. & Horne, J.A (2002) Efficacy of a 'functional energy drink' in counteracting driver sleepiness. *Physiology and Behavior*, 75, 3, 331–35. **15**

Richards, G. (1997) *'Race', Racism and Psychology*. London: Routledge.

Ring, K., Wallston, K. & Corey, M. (1970) Mode of debriefing as a factor affecting subjective reaction to a Milgram-type obedience experiment: an ethical inquiry. Representative Research in Social Psychology, 1, 67–88. **201**

Ritov, I. & Baron, J. (1990) Reluctance to vaccinate: omission, bias and ambiguity. *Journal of Behavioral Decision Making*, 3, 263–77. **11**

Robson, C. (2002) *Real World Research*. Oxford: Blackwell. **95**

Roethlisberger, F.J. & Dickson, W.J. (1939) *Management and the Worker*. Oxford: Harvard University Press. **50**

Rogers, C.R. (1961) *On Becoming a Person: a Therapist's View of Psychotherapy*. London: Constable. **97**

Rorschach, H. (1921) *Psychodiagnostics: a Diagnostic Test Based on Perception*. Oxford: Grune and Stratton. **83**

Rosenhan, D.L. (1973) On being sane in insane places. *Science*, 179, 250–8. **67, 92**

Rosenthal, R. (1966) *Experimenter Effects in Behavioural Research.* New York: Appleton-Century-Crofts. **50**

Rosenthal, R. & Jacobson, L. (1968) *Psychology in the classroom.* New York: Holt. **51**

Rosnow, R.L. & Rosenthal, R. (1997) *People studying people: artifacts and ethics in behavioral research.* New York: W.H. Freeman. **31, 86**

Ross, H.L., Campbell, D.T. & Glass, G.V. (1970) Determining the social effects of a legal reform: the British 'breathalyser' crackdown of 1967. *American Behavioral Scientist*, 13, 493–509. **54**

Rotter, J.B. (1966) Generalized expectancies for internal versus external control of reinforcement. *Psychological Monographs, 30*, 1, 1–26. **84, 85, 210**

Rule, B.G., Taylor, B.R. & Dobbs, R.A. (1987) Priming effects of heat on aggressive thoughts. *Social Cognition*, 5, 2, 131–43. **38, 39–40, 41, 46, 53**

Russell, B. (1976) *The Impact of Science on Society.* London: Unwin Paperbacks. **8**

Sears, D. (1986) College sophomores in the laboratory: influences of a narrow database on social psychology's view of human nature. *Journal of Personality and Social Psychology*, 51, 515–30. **27**

Shimizu, R. & Rutter, M. (2005) No effect of MMR withdrawal on the incidence of autism: a total population study. *Journal of Child Psychology and Psychiatry*, 46, 6, 572–79. **11**

Shirav, E. & Levy, D. (2004) *Cross-cultural Psychology: Critical Thinking and Contemporary Applications.* Boston MA: Allyn and Bacon. **60**

Shriberg, L. (1972) Intercorrelations among repression-sensitization, extroversion, neuroticism, social desirability, and locus of control. *Psychological Reports*, 31, 3, 925–26. **84**

Sieber, J.E., Iannuzzo, R. & Rodriguez, B. (1995) Deception methods in psychology: have they changed in 23 years? *Ethics and Behavior*, 5, 1, 67–85. **200**

Smith, J.A. (2003) *Qualitative Psychology: a Practical Guide to Research Methods.* London: Sage. **95, 96, 97**

Smith, P.B. & Bond, M.H. (2005) *Understanding Social Psychology Across Cultures: Living and Working in a Changing World.* London: Sage. **60**

Smith, P.B., Trompenaars, F. & Dugan, S. (1995) The Rotter locus of control scale in 43 countries: a test of cultural relativity. *International Journal of Psychology*, 30, 377–400. **85**

Smyth, T.R. (2004) *The Principles of Writing in Psychology.* Palgrave Macmillan. **216**

Stipek, D. (1998) Differences between American and Chinese in the circumstances evoking pride, shame and guilt. *Journal of Cross-Cultural Psychology*, 29, 5, 616–29. **60**

Strauss, A.L. & Corbin, J.A. (1990) *Basics of qualitative research; grounded theory procedures and techniques.* Newbury Park CA: Sage. **97**

Taylor, K.M. & Shepperd, J.A. (1996) Probing suspicion among participants in deception research. *American Psychologist*, 51, 8, 886–87. **201**

Thigpen, C.H. & Cleckley, H. (1954) A case of multiple personality. *Journal of Abnormal and Social Psychology*, 49, 175–81. **100**

Torbert, W.R. (1981) Why educational research has been so uneducational: the case for a new model of social science based on collaborative enquiry. In P. Reason & J. Rowan (eds.) (1981) *Human Enquiry: A Sourcebook in New Paradigm Research.* Chichester: Wiley. **203**

Triplett, N. (1898) The dynamogenic factors in pacemaking and competition. *American Journal of Psychology*, 9, 505–23. **135**

Walster, E. (1966) Assignment of responsibility for an accident. *Journal of Personality and Social Psychology*, 3, 1, 73–79. **211**

Wardle, J. & Watters, R. (2004) Sociocultural influences on attitudes to weight and eating: results of a natural experiment. *International Journal of Eating Disorders*, 35, 4, 589–96. **54–55**

Watson, J.B. & Rayner, R. (1920) Conditioned emotional reactions. *Journal of Experimental Psychology*, 3, 1–14. **92, 202**

White, W.F. (1943) *Street Corner Society: the Social Structure of an Italian Slum*. Chicago: The University of Chicago Press. **67**

Wigal, J.K., Stout, C. & Kotses, H. (1997) Experimenter expectancy in resistance to respiratory air flow. *Psychosomatic Medicine*, 59, 3, 318–22. **51**

Willig, C. (2001) *Introducing Qualitative Research in Psychology*. Buckingham: Open University Press. **95**

Wilson, S.R., Brown, N.L., Mejia, C. & Lavori, P. (2002) Effects of interviewer characteristics on reported sexual behavior of California Latino couples. *Hispanic Journal of Behavioral Sciences*, 24, 1, 38–62. **86**

Wimmer, H.G.S. & Perner, J. (1985) Young children's conception of lying: moral intuition and the denotation and connotation of 'to lie'. *Developmental Psychology*, 21, 6, 993–95. **59**

Yardley, L. (2000) Dilemmas in qualitative health research. *Psychology and Health*, 15, 215–28. **95**

Zanna, M.P. & Cooper, J. (1974) Dissonance and the pill: an attribution approach to studying the arousal properties of dissonance. *Journal of Personality and Social Psychology*, 29, 703–709. **86**

Zimbardo, P.G. (1972) Pathology of imprisonment. *Society*, April 1972. **63, 202**

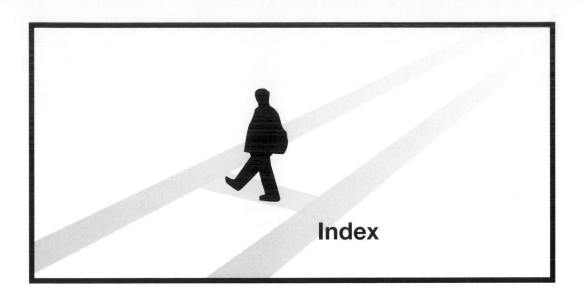

Index

Bold page number denotes glossary entry.